SELECTED MATERIAL FROM

Basic College
MATHEMATICS

Julie Miller
Molly O'Neill
Nancy Hyde

McGraw Hill **Custom Publishing**

Boston   Burr Ridge, IL   Dubuque, IA   New York   San Francisco   St. Louis
Bangkok   Bogotá   Caracas   Lisbon   London   Madrid
Mexico City   Milan   New Delhi   Seoul   Singapore   Sydney   Taipei   Toronto

The McGraw-Hill Companies

SELECTED MATERIAL FROM
Basic College Mathematics

This book is a McGraw-Hill Custom Publishing textbook and contains select material from *Basic College Mathematics* by Julie Miller, Molly O'Neill, and Nancy Hyde. Copyright © 2007 by The McGraw-Hill Companies, Inc. Reprinted with permission of the publisher. Many custom published texts are modified versions or adaptations of our best-selling textbooks. Some adaptations are printed in black and white to keep prices at a minimum, while others are in color.

2 3 4 5 6 7 8 9 0 MER MER 0 9 8 7 6

ISBN-13: 978-0-07-331319-1
ISBN-10: 0-07-331319-X

Editor: James Doepke
Production Editor: Jennifer Pickel
Printer/Binder: Mercury Print Productions, Inc.

MathZone login steps...

I M P O R T A N T : Following are instructions to access online resources to support your McGraw-Hill textbook

www.mathzone.com

Step 1: Use your browser to go to: http://www.mathzone.com

Step 2: Select your textbook from the **please select your text** in the middle of the MathZone home page.

Step 3: Click on **Student Edition** in the MathZone box.

Step 4: Click on **login to your course** and **use your registration code**.

Step 5: Enter your registration code from the box below, and click **continue**.

Step 6: Follow the directions to set up your account.

Step 7: Write your UserID and password down for future reference. Keep it in a safe place.

Step 8: If your instructor has set up a MathZone course and supplied you with a section code, please enter it, and you will be automatically registered in your instructor's course.

Scratch off for registration code

This registration code can be used by one individual and is not transferable.

Higher Education

ISBN-13: 978-0-07-351287-7
ISBN-10: 0-07-351287-7

Contents

Geometry Formulas

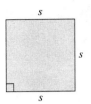

Perimeter of a Square

$P = s + s + s + s$

$P = 4s$

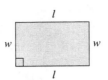

Perimeter of a Rectangle

$P = l + l + w + w$

$P = 2l + 2w$

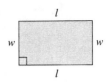

Area of a Rectangle

$A = \text{length} \times \text{width}$

$A = lw$

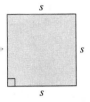

Area of a Square

$A = \text{length} \times \text{width}$

$A = s \cdot s$

$A = s^2$

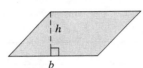

Area of a Parallelogram

$A = \text{base} \times \text{height}$

$A = bh$

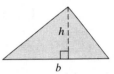

Area of a Triangle

$A = \frac{1}{2} \times \text{base} \times \text{height}$

$A = \frac{1}{2}bh$

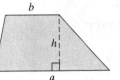

Area of a Trapezoid

$A = \frac{1}{2} \times (\text{sum of the parallel sides}) \times \text{height}$

$A = \frac{1}{2} \cdot (a + b) \cdot h$

Circumference of a Circle

The circumference, C, of a circle is given by: $C = \pi d$ or $C = 2\pi r$

Area of a Circle

The area, A, of a circle is given by: $A = \pi r^2$

Rectangular Solid

$V = lwh$

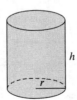

Right Circular Cylinder

$V = \pi r^2 h$

Sphere

$V = \frac{4}{3}\pi r^3$

Conversion of U.S. Customary Units of Length, Time, Weight, Capacity, Energy, and Power

Length	Time
1 foot (ft) = 12 inches (in.) 1 yard (yd) = 3 feet (ft) 1 mile (mi) = 5280 feet (ft) 1 mile (mi) = 1760 yard (yd)	1 year (yr) = 365 days 1 week (wk) = 7 days 1 day = 24 hours (hr) 1 hour (hr) = 60 minutes (min) 1 minute (min) = 60 seconds (sec)
Capacity	**Weight**
3 teaspoons (tsp) = 1 Tablespoon (Tbsp) 1 cup (c) = 8 fluid ounces (fl oz) 1 pint (pt) = 2 cups (c) 1 quart (qt) = 2 pints (pt) 1 gallon (gal) = 4 quarts (qt)	1 pound (lb) = 16 ounces (oz) 1 ton = 2000 pounds (lb)
Energy	**Power**
1 Btu ≈ 778 ft·lb	1 horsepower (hp) = $550 \dfrac{\text{ft} \cdot \text{lb}}{\text{sec}}$

Conversion of the Metric System (Prefix Line)

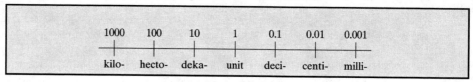

Conversion of U.S. Customary Measurement to Metric

Length	Capacity	Weight/Mass (on the Earth)
1 in. = 2.54 cm	1 qt ≈ 0.95 L	1 lb ≈ 0.45 kg
1 ft ≈ 0.305 m	1 fl oz ≈ 30 mL	1 oz ≈ 28 g
1 yd ≈ 0.914 m	1 mL = 1 cc	
1 mi. ≈ 1.61 km		

Dedication

To Linda, my colleague and friend, for many
years of support

—Julie Miller

To Kevin, Kathleen, Katie, and Kira

—Molly O'Neill

To Harley

—Nancy Hyde

About the Authors

JULIE MILLER

Julie Miller has been on the faculty of the Mathematics Department at Daytona Beach Community College for 16 years, where she has taught developmental and upper-level courses. Prior to her work at DBCC, she worked as a software engineer for General Electric in the area of flight and radar simulation. Julie earned a bachelor of science in applied mathematics from Union College in Schenectady, New York, and a master of science in mathematics from the University of Florida. In addition to this textbook, she has authored several course supplements for college algebra, trigonometry, and precalculus, as well as several short works of fiction and nonfiction for young readers.

"My father is a medical researcher, and I got hooked on math and science when I was young and would visit his laboratory. I can remember using graph paper to plot data points for his experiments and doing simple calculations. He would then tell me what the peaks and features in the graph meant in the context of his experiment. I think that applications and hands-on experience made math come alive for me and I'd like to see math come alive for my students."

—Julie Miller

MOLLY O'NEILL

Molly O'Neill is also from Daytona Beach Community College, where she has taught for 18 years in the Mathematics Department. She has taught a variety of courses from developmental mathematics to calculus. Before she came to Florida, Molly taught as an adjunct instructor at the University of Michigan–Dearborn, Eastern Michigan University, Wayne State University, and Oakland Community College. Molly earned a bachelor of science in mathematics and a master of arts and teaching from Western Michigan University in Kalamazoo, Michigan. Besides this textbook, she has authored several course supplements for college algebra, trigonometry, and precalculus and has reviewed texts for developmental mathematics.

"I differ from many of my colleagues in that math was not always easy for me. But in seventh grade I had a teacher who taught me that if I follow the rules of mathematics, even I could solve math problems. Once I understood this, I enjoyed math to the point of choosing it for my career. I now have the greatest job because I get to do math everyday and I have the opportunity to influence my students just as I was influenced. Authoring these texts has given me another avenue to reach even more students."

—Molly O'Neill

Nancy Hyde has been a full time faculty member of the Mathematics Department at Broward Community College for 24 years. During this time she has taught the full spectrum of courses from developmental math through differential equations. She received a bachelor of science degree in math education from Florida State University and a master's degree in math education from Florida Atlantic University. She has conducted workshops and seminars for both students and teachers on the use of technology in the classroom. In addition to this textbook, she has authored a graphing calculator supplement for College Algebra.

NANCY HYDE

"I grew up in Brevard County, Florida, with my father working at Cape Canaveral. I was always excited by mathematics and physics in relation to the space program. As I studied higher levels of mathematics I became more intrigued by its abstract nature and infinite possibilities. It is enjoyable and rewarding to convey this perspective to students while helping them to understand mathematics."

—Nancy Hyde

Preface

From the Authors

First and foremost, we would like to thank the students and colleagues who have helped us prepare this text. The content and organization are based on a wealth of resources. In addition to an accumulation of our own notes and experiences as teachers, we recognize the influence of colleagues at Daytona Beach Community College and Broward Community College, as well as fellow presenters and attendees of national mathematics conferences and meetings. Perhaps our single greatest source of inspiration has been our students, who ask good, probing questions every day and challenge us to find new and better ways to convey mathematical concepts. We gratefully acknowledge the part that each has played in the writing of this book.

In designing the framework for this text, the time we have spent with our students has proved especially invaluable. Over the years we have observed that students struggle consistently with certain topics. We have also come to know the influence of forces beyond the math, particularly motivational issues. An awareness of the various pitfalls has enabled us to tailor pedagogy and techniques that directly address students' needs and promote their success. Those techniques and pedagogy are outlined here.

Active Classroom

First, we believe students retain more of what they learn when they are actively engaged in the classroom. Consequently, as we wrote each section of text, we also wrote accompanying worksheets called **Classroom Activities** to foster accountability and to encourage classroom participation. Classroom Activities resemble the examples that students encounter in the textbook. The activities can be assigned to individual students or to pairs or groups of students. Most of the activities have been tested in the classroom with our own students. In one class in particular, the introduction of Classroom Activities transformed a group of "clock watchers" into students who literally had to be ushered out of the classroom so that the next class could come in. The activities can be found in the *Instructor's Resource Manual*, which is available through MathZone.

Conceptual Support

While we believe students must practice basic skills to be successful in any mathematics class, we also believe concepts are important. To this end, we have included **Concept Connections** questions and homework exercises that ask students to **"interpret the meaning in the context of the problem."** These questions make students stop and think, so they can process what they learn. In this way, students will learn underlying concepts. They will also form an understanding of what their answers mean in the contexts of the problems they solve.

We have also included special exercises within the section-ending homework exercises called **Number Sense and Estimation** (see page 276, for example). The goal of these exercises is to help students sharpen their reasoning skills. We want to encourage students to get into the habit of asking themselves whether the answers they produce are reasonable. If students can develop this habit, they will become stronger independent thinkers and more confident problem solvers.

Writing Style

Many students believe that reading a mathematics text is an exercise in futility. However, students who take the time to read the text and the features within the margins may cast that notion aside. In particular, the **Tips** and **Avoiding Mistakes** boxes should prove especially enlightening. They offer the types of insights and hints that are usually only revealed during classroom lecture. On the whole, students should be very comfortable with the reading level, as the language and tone are consistent with those used daily within our own developmental mathematics classes.

Real-World Applications

Another critical component of the text is the inclusion of **contemporary real-world examples and applications**. We based examples and applications on information that students encounter daily when they turn on the news, read a magazine, or surf the World Wide Web. We incorporated data for students to answer mathematical questions based on data in tables and graphs. When students encounter facts or information that is meaningful to them, they will relate better to the material and remember more of what they learn.

Study Skills

Many students in this course lack the basic study skills needed to be successful. Therefore, at the beginning of every set of homework exercises, we included a set of **Study Skills Exercises**. The exercises focus on one of nine areas: learning about the course, using the text, taking notes, completing homework assignments, test taking, time management, learning styles, preparing for a final exam, and defining **key terms**. Through completion of these exercises, students will be in a better position to pass the class and adopt techniques that will benefit them throughout their academic careers.

Language of Mathematics

Finally, for students to succeed in mathematics, they must be able to understand its language and notation. We place special emphasis on the skill of translating mathematical notation to English expressions and vice versa through **Translating Expressions Exercises**. These appear intermittently throughout the text. We also include key terms in the homework exercises and ask students to define these terms.

While we have made every effort to fine-tune this textbook to serve the needs of all students, we acknowledge that no textbook can satisfy every student's needs entirely. However, we do trust that the thoughtfully designed pedagogy and contents of this textbook offer any willing student the opportunity to achieve success, opening the door to a wider world of possibilities.

Listening to Students' and Instructors' Concerns

Our editorial staff has amassed the results of reviewer questionnaires, user diaries, focus groups, and symposia. We have consulted with a nine-member panel of basic mathematics instructors and their students on the development of this book. In addition, we have read hundreds of pages of reviews from instructors across the country. At McGraw-Hill symposia, faculty from across the United States gathered to discuss issues and trends in developmental mathematics. These efforts have involved hundreds of faculty and have explored issues such as content, readability, and even the aesthetics of page layout.

What Sets This Book Apart?

While this textbook offers complete coverage of the basic college mathematics curriculum, there are several concepts that receive special emphasis.

Order of Operations

The rules for the order of operations first appear in Section 1.7   Exponents and the Order of Operations. We offer repeated exposure to this topic, including it in the following sections:

Section 2.4   Multiplication of Fractions and Applications
Section 2.5   Division of Fractions and Applications
Section 3.1   Addition and Subtraction of Like Fractions
Section 3.3   Addition and Subtraction of Unlike Fractions
Section 3.5   Order of Operations and Applications of Fractions
Section 4.6   Order of Operations and Applications of Decimals
Section 10.5   Order of Operations and Scientific Notation

By exposing students to the order of operations repeatedly, we hope to reinforce their understanding and boost retention.

Variables

The term *variable* is defined in Chapter 1 (Section 1.5), when the formula for the area of a rectangle is presented. In this context, the student learns to substitute numerical values for variables within a formula and then performs the order of operations. This skill is interspersed throughout the early part of the text, as variables are used in applications. Formulas are then used again in detail in the geometry chapter (Chapter 8) before the formal application of the concept occurs in Chapter 11. By this practice, students may be "eased" into the concept, with early and repeated exposure increasing their familiarity and comfort.

Geometry

An introduction to geometry is covered formally in Chapter 8. However, some geometry topics such as perimeter and area are introduced early as applications of operations on whole numbers, fractions, and decimals. In this way, students have repeated exposure to geometry formulas and will be more likely to remember them in the long term.

Suggestions Welcome!

Many features of this book, and many refinements in writing, illustrations, and content, came about because of suggestions and questions from instructors and their students. We invite your comments with regard to this textbook as we work to further shape and refine its contents.

Julie Miller
millerj@dbcc.edu

Molly O'Neill
oneillm@dbcc.edu

Nancy Hyde
hyde_n@firn.edu

Acknowledgments and Reviewers

The development of this textbook would never have been possible without the creative ideas and constructive feedback offered by many reviewers. We are especially thankful to the following instructors for their valuable feedback and careful review of the manuscript.

Board of Advisers

Allan Brinkman, *Cleveland State University*
Mary Deas, *Johnson County Community College*
Vivian Dennis-Monzingo, *Eastfield College*
Linda Franko, *Cuyahoga Community College*
Shelbra Jones, *Wake Technical Community College*
Chris Kolaczewski-Ferris, *University of Akron*
Joanne Peeples, *El Paso Community College*
Jordan Neus, *Suffolk County Community College–Brentwood*
Susan Santolucito, *Delgado Community College*

Manuscript Reviewers

Rosalie Abraham, *Community College at Jacksonville*
Marwan Abu-Sawwa, *Florida Community College at Jacksonville*
Darla Aguilar, *Pima Community College*
Khadija Ahmed, *Monroe County Community College*
Anthony Aikens, *South Georgia Technical College*
Sheila Anderson, *Housatonic Community College*
Eugene J. D. Bowen, *Brookdale Community College*
Patricia Bower, *Mt. San Antonio College*
Jerome Brown, *Harford Community College*
Connie Buller, *Metropolitan Community College*
Susan Caldiero, *Cosumnes River College*
Carol Caponigro, *Lake Michigan College*
Judy Connell, *Lanier Technical College*
June Decker, *Three Rivers Community College*
Sue Duff, *Guilford Technical Community College*
Jay Faircloth, *Moultrie Technical College*
Thomas Geil, *Milwaukee Area Technical College*
Naomi Gibbs, *Pitt Community College*
David Gillette, *Chemeketa Community College*
Tania Giordani, *Columbia College*
Cynthia B. Gubitose, *Southern Connecticut State University*
Joseph Guiciardi, *CCAC–Boyce*
Richard Hobbs, *Mission College*
Joe Howe, *St. Charles Community College*
Juan Carlos Jiménez, *Springfield Technical Community College*
Jackie King, *Community College of Denver*
Lynette King, *Gadsden State Community College*

Alan Kunkle, *Ivy Tech State College*

Jeanine M. Lewis, *Aims Community College*

Jacqueline J. Lindquist, *Central Lakes College*

Sharon Louvier, *Lee College*

Diane Martling, *William Rainey Harper College*

Val Mohanakumar, *Hillsborough Community College*

Tammy Payton, *North Idaho College*

Faith Peters, *Miami-Dade College*

Mary Rack, *Johnson County Community College*

Manuel Rodriguez, *DeVry University*

Mohammad Sharifian, *Compton Community College*

Moshen Shirani, *Tennessee State University*

Mark A. Shore, *Allegany College of Maryland*

Cathy Singleton, *Glenville State College*

Dennis Stramiello, *Nassau Community College*

Sharon Testone, *Onondaga Community College*

Alexis Thurman, *County College of Morris*

Stephen Toner, *Victor Valley Community College*

Patrick Wagener, *Los Medanos College*

Claire Wladis, *Borough of Manhattan Community College*

Abbas Zadegan, *Florida Memorial College*

Special thanks go to Carrie Green for preparing the Instructor's Solutions Manual and the Student's Solutions Manual, to Yolanda Davis and Patricia Jayne for their appearance in and work on the video series, and to Lauri Semarne for her work in ensuring accuracy. Further thanks go to Ethel Wheland for preparing the instructors notes.

Finally, we are forever grateful to the many people behind the scenes at McGraw-Hill, our publishing family. To Erin Brown, our lifeline on this project, without you we'd be lost. To Liz Haefele, your passion for excellence has been a constant inspiration. To Michael Lange and David Dietz, thanks for your vision and input and for being there all these years. To Barb Owca and David Millage, we marvel at your creative ideas in a world that's forever changing. To Jeff Huettman and Amber Huebner for your awesome work with the technology and to Jodi Rhomberg for her support and keen attention to detail during production.

Most importantly, we give special thanks to all the students and instructors who use *Basic College Mathematics* in their classes.

Julie Miller   Molly O'Neill   Nancy Hyde

A COMMITMENT TO ACCURACY

You have a right to expect an accurate textbook, and McGraw-Hill invests considerable time and effort to make sure that we deliver one. Listed below are the many steps we take to make sure this happens.

OUR ACCURACY VERIFICATION PROCESS

First Round

Step 1: Numerous **college math instructors** review the manuscript and report on any errors that they may find, and the authors make these corrections in their final manuscript.

Second Round

Step 2: Once the manuscript has been typeset, the **authors** check their manuscript against the first page proofs to ensure that all illustrations, graphs, examples, exercises, solutions, and answers have been correctly laid out on the pages, and that all notation is correctly used.

Step 3: An outside, **professional mathematician** works through every example and exercise in the page proofs to verify the accuracy of the answers.

Step 4: A **proofreader** adds a triple layer of accuracy assurance in the first pages by hunting for errors, then a second, corrected round of page proofs is produced.

Third Round

Step 5: The **author team** reviews the second round of page proofs for two reasons: 1) to make certain that any previous corrections were properly made, and 2) to look for any errors they might have missed on the first round.

Step 6: A **second proofreader** is added to the project to examine the new round of page proofs to double check the author team's work and to lend a fresh, critical eye to the book before the third round of paging.

Fourth Round

Step 7: A **third proofreader** inspects the third round of page proofs to verify that all previous corrections have been properly made and that there are no new or remaining errors.

Step 8: Meanwhile, in partnership with **independent mathematicians,** the text accuracy is verified from a variety of fresh perspectives:
- The **test bank author** checks for consistency and accuracy as they prepare the computerized test item file.
- The **solutions manual author** works every single exercise and verifies their answers, reporting any errors to the publisher.
- A **consulting group of mathematicians,** who write material for the text's MathZone site, notifies the publisher of any errors they encounter in the page proofs.
- A video production company employing **expert math instructors** for the text's videos will alert the publisher of any errors they might find in the page proofs.

Final Round

Step 9: The **project manager,** who has overseen the book from the beginning, performs a **fourth proofread** of the textbook during the printing process, providing a final accuracy review.

⇒   What results is a mathematics textbook that is as accurate and error-free as is humanly possible, and our authors and publishing staff are confident that our many layers of quality assurance have produced textbooks that are the leaders of the industry for their integrity and correctness.

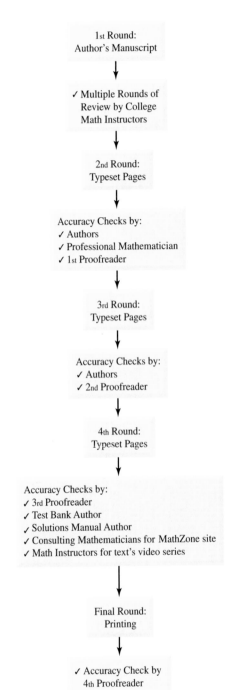

1st Round:
Author's Manuscript

↓

✓ Multiple Rounds of Review by College Math Instructors

↓

2nd Round:
Typeset Pages

↓

Accuracy Checks by:
✓ Authors
✓ Professional Mathematician
✓ 1st Proofreader

↓

3rd Round:
Typeset Pages

↓

Accuracy Checks by:
✓ Authors
✓ 2nd Proofreader

↓

4th Round:
Typeset Pages

↓

Accuracy Checks by:
✓ 3rd Proofreader
✓ Test Bank Author
✓ Solutions Manual Author
✓ Consulting Mathematicians for MathZone site
✓ Math Instructors for text's video series

↓

Final Round:
Printing

↓

✓ Accuracy Check by 4th Proofreader

Guided Tour

Chapter Opener

Each chapter opens with an application relating to an exercise presented in the chapter. Section titles are clearly listed for easy reference.

Decimals

4

4.1 Decimal Notation and Rounding
4.2 Addition and Subtraction of Decimals
4.3 Multiplication of Decimals
4.4 Division of Decimals
4.5 Fractions as Decimals
4.6 Order of Operations and Applications of Decimals

Chapter 4 is devoted to the study of decimal numbers. We begin with a discussion of place values and then perform addition, subtraction, multiplication, and division. The applications of decimal numbers are far-reaching. For example, in 1993, Becky and Keith Dilley were the proud parents of sextuplets (six children from a multiple birth). The children, now in their teen years, weighed just over 2 lb each at birth. See Exercise 56 of Section 4.2 to determine the total birth weight of the Dilley sextuplets.

231

---

 chapter 2 | preview

The exercises in this chapter preview contain concepts that have not yet been presented. These exercises are provided for students who want to compare their levels of understanding before and after studying the chapter. Alternatively, you may prefer to work these exercises when the chapter is completed and before taking the exam.

Section 2.1

1. Identify the fractions as proper or improper.

   a. $\frac{4}{5}$ b. $\frac{16}{8}$ c. $\frac{15}{15}$

2. Write $4\frac{2}{3}$ as an improper fraction.

3. Write $\frac{39}{7}$ as a mixed number.

4. Write a fraction that represents the shaded area.

   a.   b.

5. There are 8 different brands of wine on the wine list at a restaurant. Of these wines, 5 are red wines and the rest are white wines. What fraction represents the white wines?

Section 2.2

6. Is the number 1092 divisible by 2, 3, or 5? Explain your answers.

7. List all the factors of 45.

8. Write the prime factorization of 630.

Section 2.3

9. Which of the following fractions is simplified to lowest terms?

   a. $\frac{16}{25}$ b. $\frac{12}{14}$ c. $\frac{30}{15}$

Section 2.4

For Exercises 10–12, multiply and simplify the answer to lowest terms.

10. $\frac{9}{13} \times \frac{39}{27}$ 11. $\left(\frac{7}{12}\right)\left(\frac{6}{35}\right)$ 12. $12 \cdot \frac{77}{84}$

13. Find the area of the triangle.

Section 2.5

For Exercises 14–16, divide. Simplify the answer to lowest terms.

14. $\frac{64}{21} \div 8$ 15. $\frac{33}{20} \div \frac{44}{15}$ 16. $\frac{3}{0}$

17. George painted $\frac{2}{3}$ of a wall that measures 18 ft by 10 ft. How much area did he paint?

18. If a recipe requires $2\frac{1}{2}$ cups of flour for one batch of cookies, how many batches can be made from 10 cups of flour?

Section 2.6

For Exercises 19–21, multiply or divide the mixed numbers. Write the answer as a mixed number or a whole number.

19. $1\frac{3}{4} \cdot 9\frac{5}{7}$ 20. $8\frac{5}{6} \div 2\frac{1}{2}$ 21. $4\frac{1}{3} \cdot 2\frac{7}{10} \div 1\frac{4}{5}$

Chapter Preview

A Chapter Preview appears at the beginning of each chapter. It contains exercises, grouped by section. The exercises are based on topics not yet presented, offering students an opportunity to compare levels of understanding before and after studying the chapter.

Objectives

A list of important learning objectives is provided at the beginning of each section. Each objective corresponds to a heading within the section, making it easy for students to locate topics as they study or as they work through homework exercises.

---

section 4.1   Decimal Notation and Rounding

1. Decimal Notation

In Chapters 2 and 3, we studied fraction notation to denote equal parts of a whole. In this chapter we introduce decimal notation to denote equal parts of a whole. We first introduce the concept of a decimal fraction. A **decimal fraction** is a fraction whose denominator is a power of 10. The following are examples of decimal fractions.

$\dfrac{3}{10}$ is read as "three-tenths"

$\dfrac{7}{100}$ is read as "seven-hundredths"

$\dfrac{9}{1000}$ is read as "nine-thousandths"

We now want to write these fractions in **decimal notation**. This means that we will write the numbers by using place values, as we did with whole numbers. Therefore, we need to identify place positions for the tenths, hundredths, and thousandths place. The place value chart from Section 1.1 can be extended as shown in Figure 4-1.

Objectives

1. Decimal Notation
2. Writing Decimals as Mixed Numbers or Fractions
3. Ordering Decimal Numbers
4. Rounding Decimals

Tip: Recall from Section 1.7 that powers of 10 are

$10^1 = 10$

$10^2 = 100$

$10^3 = 1000$

and so on.

Concept Connections

Students can test their understanding of what they have read by completing the Concept Connections that appear in the margins. These questions test how well students grasp concepts. Students can check their responses by referring to answers at the bottom of the page.

Skill Practice Exercises

Every worked example is paired with a Skill Practice Exercise. These exercises appear in the margin directly beside the worked examples and offer students an immediate opportunity to work problems that mirror the examples. Students can then check their work by referring to the answers at the bottom of the page.

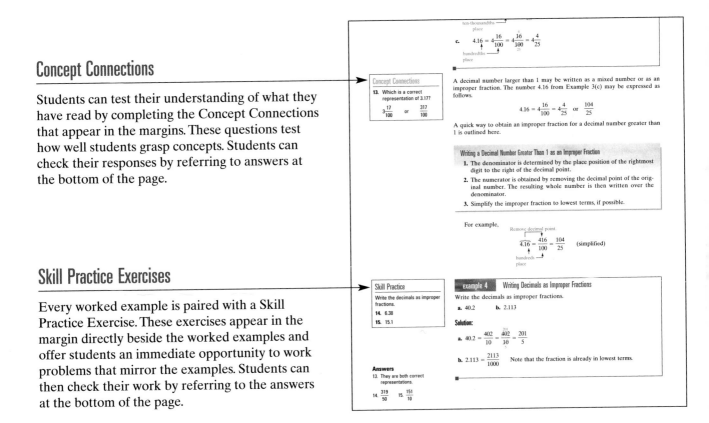

Concept Connections

13. Which is a correct representation of 3.17?

$3\dfrac{17}{100}$ or $\dfrac{317}{100}$

c. $4.16 = 4\dfrac{16}{100} = 4\dfrac{16}{100} = 4\dfrac{4}{25}$

ten-thousandths place

hundredths place

A decimal number larger than 1 may be written as a mixed number or as an improper fraction. The number 4.16 from Example 3(c) may be expressed as follows.

$$4.16 = 4\dfrac{16}{100} = 4\dfrac{4}{25}\quad \text{or}\quad \dfrac{104}{25}$$

A quick way to obtain an improper fraction for a decimal number greater than 1 is outlined here.

Writing a Decimal Number Greater Than 1 as an Improper Fraction

1. The denominator is determined by the place position of the rightmost digit to the right of the decimal point.
2. The numerator is obtained by removing the decimal point of the original number. The resulting whole number is then written over the denominator.
3. Simplify the improper fraction to lowest terms, if possible.

For example,

Remove decimal point.

$$4.16 = \dfrac{416}{100} = \dfrac{104}{25}\quad \text{(simplified)}$$

hundreds place

Skill Practice

Write the decimals as improper fractions.

14. 6.38
15. 15.1

example 4   Writing Decimals as Improper Fractions

Write the decimals as improper fractions.

a. 40.2   **b.** 2.113

Solution:

a. $40.2 = \dfrac{402}{10} = \dfrac{402}{10} = \dfrac{201}{5}$

b. $2.113 = \dfrac{2113}{1000}$ Note that the fraction is already in lowest terms.

Answers

13. They are both correct representations.

14. $\dfrac{319}{50}$ 15. $\dfrac{151}{10}$

Avoiding Mistakes

Through notes labeled Avoiding Mistakes students are alerted to common errors and are shown methods to avoid them.

Tips

Tip boxes appear throughout the text and offer helpful hints and insight.

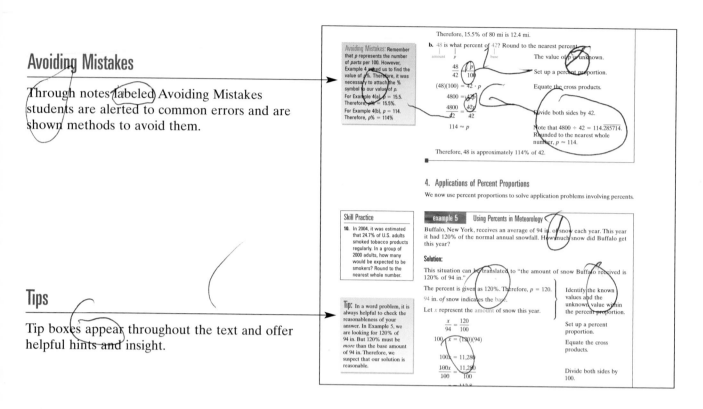

Worked Examples

Examples are set off in boxes and organized so that students can easily follow the solutions. Explanations appear beside each step and color-coding is used, where appropriate. For additional step-by-step instruction, students can run the "e-Professors" in MathZone. The e-Professors are based on worked examples from the text and use the solution methodologies presented in the text.

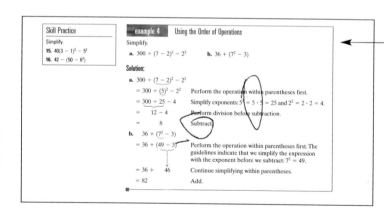

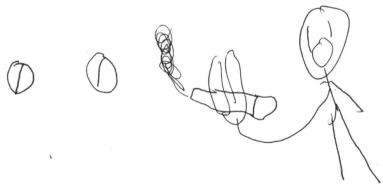

Midchapter Review

Midchapter Reviews are provided to help solidify the foundation of concepts learned in the beginning of a chapter before expanding to new ideas presented later in the chapter.

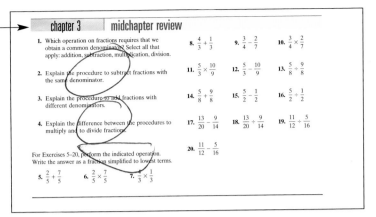

Instructor Note (AIE only)

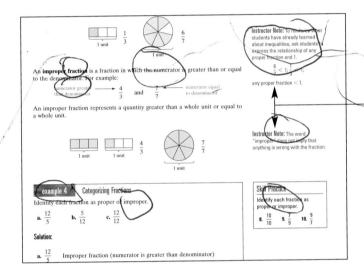

Throughout each section of the Annotated Instructor's Edition (AIE), notes to the Instructor can be found in the margins. The notes may assist with lecture preparation in that they point out items that tend to confuse students, or lead students to err.

References to Classroom Activities (AIE only)

References are made to Classroom Activities at the beginning of each set of Practice Exercises in the AIE. The activities may be found in the *Instructor's Resource Manual*, which is available through MathZone, and can be used during lecture, or assigned for additional practice.

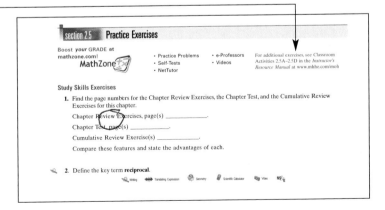

Practice Exercises

A variety of problem types appear in the section-ending Practice Exercises. Problem types are clearly labeled with either a heading or an icon for easy identification. References to MathZone are also found at the beginning of the Practice Exercises to remind students and instructors that additional help and practice problems are available. The core exercises for each section are organized by section objective. General references to examples are provided for blocks of core exercises. **Mixed Exercises** are also provided in some sections where no reference to objectives or examples is offered.

Icon Key

The following key has been prepared for easy identification of "themed" exercises appearing within the Practice Exercises.

Student Edition and AIE

Exercises Keyed to Video

Calculator Exercises

AIE only

Writing

Translating Expressions

Geometry

Number Sense and Estimation

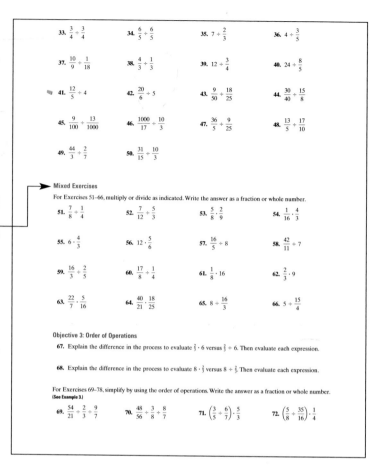

33. $\frac{3}{4} \div \frac{3}{4}$ 34. $\frac{6}{5} \div \frac{6}{5}$ 35. $7 \div \frac{2}{3}$ 36. $4 \div \frac{3}{5}$

37. $\frac{10}{9} \div \frac{1}{18}$ 38. $\frac{4}{3} \div \frac{1}{3}$ 39. $12 \div \frac{3}{4}$ 40. $24 \div \frac{8}{5}$

41. $\frac{12}{5} \div 4$ 42. $\frac{20}{6} \div 5$ 43. $\frac{9}{50} \div \frac{18}{25}$ 44. $\frac{30}{40} \div \frac{15}{8}$

45. $\frac{9}{100} \div \frac{13}{1000}$ 46. $\frac{1000}{17} \div \frac{10}{3}$ 47. $\frac{36}{5} \div \frac{9}{25}$ 48. $\frac{13}{5} \div \frac{17}{10}$

49. $\frac{44}{3} \div \frac{2}{7}$ 50. $\frac{31}{15} \div \frac{10}{3}$

Mixed Exercises

For Exercises 51–66, multiply or divide as indicated. Write the answer as a fraction or whole number.

51. $\frac{7}{8} \div \frac{1}{4}$ 52. $\frac{7}{12} \div \frac{5}{3}$ 53. $\frac{5}{8} \cdot \frac{2}{9}$ 54. $\frac{1}{16} \cdot \frac{4}{3}$

55. $6 \cdot \frac{4}{3}$ 56. $12 \cdot \frac{5}{6}$ 57. $\frac{16}{5} \div 8$ 58. $\frac{42}{11} \div 7$

59. $\frac{16}{3} \div \frac{2}{5}$ 60. $\frac{17}{8} \div \frac{1}{4}$ 61. $\frac{1}{8} \cdot 16$ 62. $\frac{2}{3} \cdot 9$

63. $\frac{22}{7} \cdot \frac{5}{16}$ 64. $\frac{40}{21} \cdot \frac{18}{25}$ 65. $8 \div \frac{16}{3}$ 66. $5 \div \frac{15}{4}$

Objective 3: Order of Operations

67. Explain the difference in the process to evaluate $\frac{2}{3} \cdot 6$ versus $\frac{2}{3} \div 6$. Then evaluate each expression.

68. Explain the difference in the process to evaluate $8 \cdot \frac{2}{3}$ versus $8 \div \frac{2}{3}$. Then evaluate each expression.

For Exercises 69–78, simplify by using the order of operations. Write the answer as a fraction or whole number. **(See Example 3.)**

69. $\frac{54}{21} \div \frac{2}{3} \div \frac{9}{7}$ 70. $\frac{48}{56} \div \frac{3}{8} \div \frac{8}{7}$ 71. $\left(\frac{3}{5} \div \frac{6}{7}\right) \cdot \frac{5}{3}$ 72. $\left(\frac{5}{8} \div \frac{35}{16}\right) \cdot \frac{1}{4}$

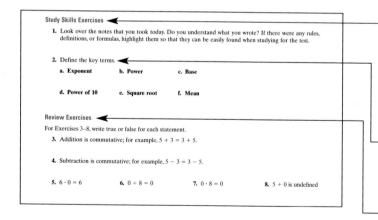

Study Skills Exercises

1. Look over the notes that you took today. Do you understand what you wrote? If there were any rules, definitions, or formulas, highlight them so that they can be easily found when studying for the test.

2. Define the key terms.
   a. Exponent   b. Power   c. Base

   d. Power of 10   e. Square root   f. Mean

Review Exercises

For Exercises 3–8, write true or false for each statement.

3. Addition is commutative; for example, $5 + 3 = 3 + 5$.

4. Subtraction is commutative; for example, $5 - 3 = 3 - 5$.

5. $6 \cdot 0 = 6$ 6. $0 \div 8 = 0$ 7. $0 \cdot 8 = 0$ 8. $5 \div 0$ is undefined

Study Skills Exercises appear at the beginning of the exercise set. They are designed to help students learn techniques to improve their study habits, including exam preparation, note taking, and time management.

In the Practice Exercises, where appropriate, students are asked to define the **Key Terms** that are presented in the section. Assigning these exercises will help students to develop and expand their mathematical vocabulary.

Review Exercises also appear at the start of the Practice Exercises. The purpose of the Review Exercises is to help students retain their knowledge of concepts previously learned.

Writing Exercises ✎ offer students an opportunity to conceptualize and communicate their understanding of arithmetic. These, along with the **Translating Expressions Exercises** ⬌ enable students to strengthen their command of mathematical language and notation and improve their reading and writing skills.

Review Exercises

⬌ For Exercises 2–11, translate the English phrase into a mathematical statement and simplify.

2. 89 decreased by 66   **3.** 71 increased by 14   **4.** 16 more than 42

5. Twice 14   **6.** The difference of 93 and 79   **7.** Subtract 32 from 102

8. Divide 12 into 60   **9.** The product of 10 and 13   **10.** The total of 12, 14, and 15

11. The quotient of 24 and 6

Objective 1: Problem-Solving Strategies

✎ **12.** In your own words, list the guidelines or strategy that you would use to solve an application problem.

✎ For Exercises 13–16, write two or more key words or phrases that represent the given operation. Answers may vary.

13. Addition   **14.** Multiplication   **15.** Subtraction   **16.** Division

Objective 2: Applications Involving One Operation

✎ **17.** A graphing calculator screen consists of an array of rectangular dots called *pixels*. If the screen has 96 rows of pixels and 126 pixels in each row, how many pixels are in the whole screen? **(See Example 3.)**

18. The floor of a rectangular room has 62 rows of tile with 38 tiles in each row. How many total tiles are there?

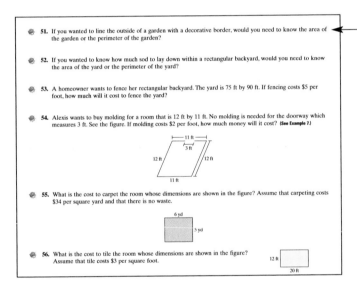

51. If you wanted to line the outside of a garden with a decorative border, would you need to know the area of the garden or the perimeter of the garden?

52. If you wanted to know how much sod to lay down within a rectangular backyard, would you need to know the area of the yard or the perimeter of the yard?

53. A homeowner wants to fence her rectangular backyard. The yard is 75 ft by 90 ft. If fencing costs $5 per foot, how much will it cost to fence the yard?

54. Alexis wants to buy molding for a room that is 12 ft by 11 ft. No molding is needed for the doorway which measures 3 ft. See the figure. If molding costs $2 per foot, how much money will it cost? **(See Example 7.)**

55. What is the cost to carpet the room whose dimensions are shown in the figure? Assume that carpeting costs $34 per square yard and that there is no waste.

56. What is the cost to tile the room whose dimensions are shown in the figure? Assume that tile costs $3 per square foot.

Geometry Exercises ✎ appear throughout the Practice Exercises and encourage students to review and apply geometry concepts.

Calculator Exercises 🖩 signify situations where a calculator would provide assistance for time-consuming calculations. These exercises were carefully designed to demonstrate the types of situations where a calculator is a handy tool rather than a "crutch."

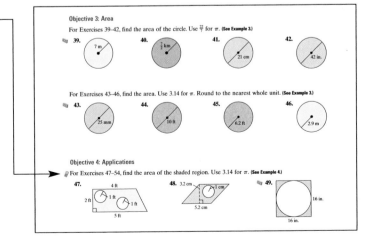

Objective 3: Area

For Exercises 39–42, find the area of the circle. Use $\frac{22}{7}$ for π. **(See Example 3.)**

39. 7 m   **40.** $\frac{2}{5}$ km   **41.** 21 cm   **42.** 42 in.

For Exercises 43–46, find the area. Use 3.14 for π. Round to the nearest whole unit. **(See Example 3.)**

43. 25 mm   **44.** 10 ft   **45.** 6.2 ft   **46.** 2.9 m

Objective 4: Applications

For Exercises 47–54, find the area of the shaded region. Use 3.14 for π. **(See Example 4.)**

47. 4 ft, 2 ft, 1 ft, 1 ft, 5 ft   **48.** 3.2 cm, 1 cm, 5.2 cm   **49.** 16 in., 16 in.

Exercises Keyed to Video 📹 are labeled with an icon to help students and instructors identify those exercises for which accompanying video instruction is available.

57. Ling has three jobs. He works for a lawn maintenance service 4 days a week. He also tutors math and works as a waiter on weekends. His hourly wage and the number of hours for each job are given for a 1-week period. How much money did Ling earn for the week?

	Hourly Wage	Number of Hours
Tutor	$30/hr	4
Waiter	10/hr	16
Lawn maintenance	8/hr	30

58. An electrician, a plumber, a mason, and a carpenter work at a certain construction site. The hourly wage and the number of hours each person worked are summarized in the table. What was the total amount paid for all four workers?

	Hourly Wage	Number of Hours
Electrician	$36/hr	18
Plumber	28/hr	15
Mason	26/hr	24
Carpenter	22/hr	48

Number Sense and Estimation NS&E exercises test students' ability to reason with numbers. The exercises often ask students to determine whether the answers they produce make sense in light of the problems they are asked to solve.

Objective 4: Applications of Decimal Division

NS&E When multiplying or dividing decimals, it is important to place the decimal point correctly. For Exercises 75–78, determine whether you think the number is reasonable or unreasonable. If the number is unreasonable, move the decimal point to a position that makes more sense.

75. Steve computed the gas mileage for his Honda Civic to be 3.2 miles per gallon.

76. The sale price of a new refrigerator is $96.0.

77. Mickey makes $8.50 per hour. He estimates his weekly paycheck to be $3400.

78. Jason works in a legal office. He computes the average annual income for the attorneys in his office to be $1400 per year.

For Exercises 79–84, solve the application. Check to see if your answers are reasonable.

79. A membership at a health club costs $560 per year. The club has a payment plan in which a member can pay $50 down and the rest in 12 equal payments. How much is each payment? **(See Example 9.)**

80. Brooke owes $39,628.68 on the mortgage for her house. If her monthly payment is $695.24, how many months does she still need to pay? How many years is this?

81. It is reported that on average 42,000 tennis balls are used and 650 matches are played at the Wimbledon tennis tournament each year. On average, how many tennis balls are used per match? Round to the nearest whole unit.

82. A package of dental floss contains 100 yd of floss. If Patty uses floss once a day and it lasts for 230 days, approximately how long is each piece that she uses? Round the answer to the nearest tenth of a yard.

83. In baseball the batting average is found by dividing the number of hits by the number of times a batter was at bat. Babe Ruth was at bat 8399 times and had 2873 hits. What was his batting average? Round to the thousandths place. **(See Example 10.)**

84. Ty Cobb was at bat 11,434 times and had 4189 hits, giving him the all time best batting average. Find his average. Round to the thousandths place. (Refer to Exercise 83.)

Applications based on real-world facts and figures motivate students and enable them to hone their problem-solving skills.

Expanding Your Skills, found near the end of most Practice Exercises, challenge students' knowledge of the concepts presented.

Expanding Your Skills

Sometimes an expression will have parentheses within parentheses. This is called *nested parentheses*. Often different shapes such as ( ), [ ], or { } are used to make it easier to match up the pairs of parentheses, for example,

$$\{300 - 4[4 + (5 + 2)^2] + 8\} - 31$$

It is important to note that the symbols ( ), [ ], or { } all represent parentheses and are used for grouping. When nested parentheses occur, simplify the innermost set first. Then work your way out. For example, simplify

$$\{300 - 4[4 + (5 + 2)^2] + 8\} - 31$$

The solution is

$$\{300 - 4[4 + (5 + 2)^2] + 8\} - 31$$

$$= \{300 - 4[4 + (7)^2] + 8\} - 31 \quad \text{Simplify within the innermost parentheses first ( ).}$$

$$= \{300 - 4[4 + 49] + 8\} - 31 \quad \text{Simplify the exponent.}$$

$$= \{300 - 4[53] + 8\} - 31 \quad \text{Simplify within the next innermost parentheses [ ].}$$

$$= \{300 - 212 + 8\} - 31 \quad \text{Multiply before adding.}$$

$$= \{88 + 8\} - 31 \quad \text{Subtract and add in order from left to right within the parentheses { }.}$$

$$= 96 - 31 \quad \text{Simplify within the parentheses { }.}$$

$$= 65 \quad \text{Simplify.}$$

For Exercises 97–100, simplify the expressions with nested parentheses.

97. $3[4 + (6 - 3)^2] - 15$

98. $2[5(4 - 1) + 3] \div 6$

99. $5\{21 - [3^2 - (4 - 2)]\}$

100. $4\{18 - [(10 - 8) + 2^3]\}$

Optional Calculator Connections are located at the end of the Practice Exercises and appear intermittently. They can be implemented at the instructor's discretion depending on the amount of emphasis placed on the calculator in the course. The Calculator Connections display keystrokes and include a set of exercises that provide an opportunity for students to apply the skill introduced.

Calculator Connections

Topic: Evaluating expressions with exponents on a calculator

Many calculators use the $\boxed{x^2}$ key to square a number. To raise a number to a higher power, use the $\boxed{\wedge}$ key (or on some calculators, the $\boxed{x^y}$ key or $\boxed{y^x}$ key).

Expression	Keystrokes	Result
26^2	26 $\boxed{x^2}$ $\boxed{\text{Enter}}$	676
	↑ On some calculators, you do not need to press $\boxed{\text{Enter}}$	
3^7	3 $\boxed{\wedge}$ 7 $\boxed{\text{Enter}}$	2187
or	3 $\boxed{y^x}$ 7 $\boxed{=}$	2187

Calculator Exercises

For Exercises 101–104, use a calculator to perform the indicated operations.

101. 156^2 **102.** 418^2 **103.** 12^5 **104.** 35^4

End-of-Chapter Summary and Exercises

The **Summary**, located at the end of each chapter, outlines key concepts for each section and illustrates those concepts with examples.

Following the Summary is a set of **Review Exercises** that are organized by section. A **Chapter Test** appears after each set of Review Exercises. Chapters 2–11 also include **Cumulative Reviews** that follow the Chapter Tests. These end-of-chapter materials provide students with ample opportunity to prepare for quizzes or exams.

chapter 3   summary

section 3.1   Addition and Subtraction of Like Fractions

Key Concepts

Adding Like Fractions
1. Add the numerators.
2. Write the sum over the common denominator.
3. Simplify the fraction to lowest terms, if possible.

Subtracting Like Fractions
1. Subtract the numerators.
2. Write the difference over the common denominator.
3. Simplify the fraction to lowest terms, if possible.

Examples

Example 1
$$\frac{5}{8} + \frac{7}{8} = \frac{12}{8} = \frac{2 \cdot 2 \cdot 3}{2 \cdot 2 \cdot 2} = \frac{3}{2}$$

Example 2
$$\frac{25}{10} - \frac{7}{10} = \frac{18}{10} = \frac{2 \cdot 3 \cdot 3}{2 \cdot 5} = \frac{9}{5}$$

chapter 3   review exercises

Section 3.1

For Exercises 1–4, add or subtract the like units.

1. 5 books + 3 books   **2.** 12 cm + 6 cm

3. 25 mi – 13 mi   **4.** 13 CDs – 2 CDs

5. Explain what is meant by the term *like fractions*.

For Exercises 7–14, add or subtract the like fractions. Simplify the answer to lowest terms.

7. $\frac{5}{6} + \frac{4}{6}$ **8.** $\frac{4}{15} + \frac{6}{15}$

9. $\frac{5}{12} + \frac{1}{12}$ **10.** $\frac{2}{9} + \frac{7}{9}$

chapter 3   test

For Exercises 1–2, add or subtract the like fractions.

1. $\frac{4}{5} + \frac{3}{5}$ **2.** $\frac{23}{16} - \frac{15}{16}$

3. Explain the difference between evaluating these two expressions:
$$\frac{5}{11} - \frac{3}{11} \quad \text{and} \quad \frac{5}{11} \times \frac{3}{11}$$

4. a. List four multiples of 24.

20. $\left(\frac{2}{5}\right)^2 + \left(1\frac{1}{10} + 2\frac{5}{6}\right)$ **21.** $\left(7\frac{1}{4} - 5\frac{1}{6}\right) \cdot 1\frac{3}{5}$

22. A fudge recipe calls for $1\frac{1}{2}$ lb of chocolate. How many pounds are required for $\frac{2}{3}$ of the recipe?

23. The towing capacity of the 2004 Ford Expedition is $4\frac{13}{40}$ times that of the 2004 Buick Rendezvous. If the Rendezvous can tow 1 ton (2000 lb), what is the towing capacity of the Expedition (in pounds)?

chapters 1–3   cumulative review

1. Write the number in words: 23,400,806

2. Find the sum of 72 and 24.

3. Find the difference of 72 and 24.

4. Find the product of 72 and 24.

5. Find the quotient of 72 and 24.

6. Round the numbers to the ten-thousands place to estimate the product: 54,923 × 28,543.

15. Which of the numbers is divisible by 3 and 5?
   a. 2390   **b.** 1245   **c.** 9321

16. Label the numbers as prime, composite, or neither.
   a. 51   **b.** 52   **c.** 53

17. Find the prime factorization of 360.

18. Simplify the fraction to lowest terms: $\frac{180}{900}$

19. Multiply: $\frac{15}{16} \cdot \frac{2}{5}$

SUPPLEMENTS

For the Instructor

Instructor's Resource Manual

The *Instructor's Resource Manual* (IRM), written by the authors, is a printable electronic supplement available through MathZone. The IRM includes discovery-based classroom activities, worksheets for drill-and-practice, materials for a student portfolio, and some tips for implementing successful cooperative learning. Numerous classroom activities are available for each section of text and can be used as a complement to lecture or can be assigned for work outside of class. The activities are designed for group or individual work and take about 5–10 minutes each. With increasing demands on faculty schedules, these ready-made lessons offer a convenient means for both full-time and adjunct faculty to promote active learning in the classroom.

 www.mathzone.com

McGraw-Hill's **MathZone 2.0** is a complete **web-based tutorial and course management system** for mathematics and statistics, designed for greater ease of use than any other system available. Free upon adoption of a McGraw-Hill textbook, the system enables instructors to **create and share courses and assignments** with colleagues, adjunct faculty members, and teaching assistants with only a few mouse clicks. All **assignments, exercises, "e-Professor" multimedia tutorials, video lectures, and NetTutor® live tutors** follow the textbook's learning objectives and problem-solving style and notation. Using MathZone's **assignment builder**, instructors can **edit questions and algorithms, import their own content**, and **create announcements and due dates** for homework and quizzes. Math-Zone's **automated grading function** reports the results of easy-to-assign algorithmically generated homework, quizzes, and tests. All student activity within MathZone is recorded and available through a **fully integrated gradebook** that can be downloaded to Microsoft Excel®. MathZone also is available on CD-ROM. (See "Supplements for the Student" for descriptions of the elements of MathZone.)

Instructor's Testing and Resource CD

This cross-platform CD-ROM provides a wealth of resources for the instructor. Among the supplements featured on the CD-ROM is a **computerized test bank** utilizing Brownstone Diploma ® algorithm-based testing software to create customized exams quickly. This user-friendly program enables instructors to search for questions by topic, format, or difficulty level; to edit existing questions or to add new ones; and to scramble questions and answer keys for multiple versions of a single test. Hundreds of text-specific open-ended and multiple-choice questions are included in the question bank. Sample chapter tests are also provided.

ALEKS (**A**ssessment and **LE**arning in **K**nowledge **S**paces) is an artificial intelligence-based system for mathematics learning, available over the web 24/7. Using unique adaptive questioning, ALEKS accurately assesses what topics each student knows and then determines exactly what each student is ready to learn next. ALEKS interacts with the students much as a skilled human tutor would, moving between explanation and practice as needed, correcting and analyzing errors, defining terms, changing topics on request, and helping them master the course content more quickly and easily. Moreover, the new ALEKS 3.0 now links to text-specific videos, multimedia tutorials, and textbook pages in PDF format. ALEKS also offers a robust classroom management system that allows instructors to monitor and direct student progress toward mastery of curricular goals. See www.highed.aleks.com.

Miller/O'Neill/Hyde Video Lectures on Digital Video Disk (DVD)

In the videos, qualified instructors work through selected problems from the textbook, following the solution methodology employed in the text. The video series is available on DVD or online as an assignable element of MathZone (see next page). The DVDs are closed-captioned for the hearing impaired, subtitled in Spanish, and meet the Americans with Disabilities Act Standards for Accessible Design. Instructors may use them as resources in a learning center, for online courses, and/or to provide extra help for students who require extra practice.

Annotated Instructor's Edition

In the *Annotated Instructor's Edition* (*AIE*), **answers to all exercises and tests appear adjacent to each exercise**, in a color used *only* for annotations. The *AIE* also contains **Instructor Notes** that appear in the margin. The notes may assist with lecture preparation. Also found in the *AIE* are icons within the Practice Exercises that serve to guide instructors in their preparation of homework assignments and lessons.

Instructor's Solutions Manual

The *Instructor's Solutions Manual* provides comprehensive, worked-out solutions to all exercises in the Chapter Previews; the Practice Exercises; the Midchapter Reviews; the end-of-chapter Review Exercises; the Chapter Tests; and the Cumulative Review Exercises.

For the Student

 **www.mathzone.com**

McGraw-Hill's MathZone is a powerful web-based tutorial for homework, quizzing, testing, and multimedia instruction. Also available in CD-ROM format, MathZone offers:

Practice exercises based on the text and generated in an unlimited quantity for as much practice as needed to master any objective

Video clips of classroom instructors showing how to solve exercises from the text, step-by-step

e-Professor animations that take the student through step-by-step instructions, delivered on-screen and narrated by a teacher on audio, for solving exercises from the textbook; the user controls the pace of the explanations and can review as needed

NetTutor, which offers personalized instruction by live tutors familiar with the textbook's objectives and problem-solving methods

Every assignment, exercise, video lecture, and e-Professor is derived from the textbook.

Student's Solutions Manual

The *Student's Solutions Manual* provides comprehensive, worked-out solutions to the odd-numbered exercises in the Chapter Previews, the Practice Exercise sets; the Midchapter Reviews, the end-of-chapter Review Exercises, the Chapter Tests, and the Cumulative Review Exercises.

Video Lectures on Digital Video Disk (DVD)

The video series is based on exercises from the textbook. Each presenter works through selected problems, following the solution methodology employed in the text. The video series is available on DVD or online as part of MathZone. The DVDs are closed-captioned for the hearing impaired, subtitled in Spanish, and meet the Americans with Disabilities Act Standards for Accessible Design.

NetTutor

Available through MathZone, NetTutor is a revolutionary system that enables students to interact with a live tutor over the Web. NetTutor's Web-based, graphical chat capabilities enable students and tutors to use mathematical notation and even to draw graphs as they work through a problem together. Students can also submit questions and receive answers, browse previously answered questions, and view previous sessions. Tutors are familiar with the textbook's objectives and problem-solving styles.

Whole Numbers

Chapter 1 begins with adding, subtracting, multiplying, and dividing whole numbers. We also include rounding, estimating, and applying whole numbers in a variety of real-world situations. For example, in Exercise 43 in Section 1.4, the total sales for five top-selling candy bars is given. After rounding each value to the nearest million, we find that consumers spent over $150 million on these items.

Brand	Sales ($)
M&Ms	97,404,576
Hershey's Milk Chocolate	81,296,784
Reese's Peanut Butter Cups	54,391,268
Snickers	53,695,428
KitKat	38,168,580

chapter 1 | preview

The exercises in this chapter preview contain concepts that have not yet been presented. These exercises are provided for students who want to compare their levels of understanding before and after studying the chapter. Alternatively, you may prefer to work these exercises when the chapter is completed and before taking the exam.

Section 1.1

1. For the number 6,873,129 identify the place value of the underlined digit.

2. Write the number in standard form: five million, two hundred three thousand, fifty-one

3. Write the following inequality in words: $130 < 244$

Section 1.2

For Exercises 4–5, add.

4. $73 + 41$

5. $71 + 4 + 81 + 106$

Section 1.3

For Exercises 6–7, subtract. Check by using addition.

6. $284 - 171$

7. $\begin{array}{r} 1001 \\ -235 \\ \hline \end{array}$

Section 1.4

8. Approximate the perimeter of the triangle by first rounding the numbers to the hundreds place.

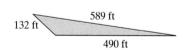

132 ft   589 ft   490 ft

For Exercises 9–10, estimate the sum or difference by first rounding the numbers to the tens place.

9. $682 + 249$

10. $768 - 241$

Sections 1.5 and 1.6

For Exercises 11–16, multiply or divide as indicated.

11. $31 \cdot 8$

12. $12\overline{)1032}$

13. $737 \div 7$

14. $\begin{array}{r} 409 \\ \times 228 \\ \hline \end{array}$

15. $\dfrac{0}{61}$

16. $0\overline{)341}$

17. Find the area of the rectangle.

5 m   28 m

Section 1.7

18. Write the repeated multiplication in exponential notation. Do not evaluate.

a. $7 \cdot 7 \cdot 7 \cdot 7 \cdot 7 \cdot 7$

b. $3 \cdot 3 \cdot 3 \cdot 3 \cdot 10 \cdot 10 \cdot 10$

19. Simplify the expression, using the order of operations: $14 - 2(20 \div 5)$

20. Herman collects snow globes. He purchased 4 in the past year and paid $25, $30, $19, and $22. What is the average price per globe?

Section 1.8

21. When migrating, a hawk travels a distance of 9445 mi while a swallow travels 9258 mi. Determine how much farther the hawk travels.

22. Liz is taking a natural herb in capsule form. She purchased 4 bottles containing 30 capsules each. The directions state that she can take either 2 or 3 capsules per day.

a. How many days will the capsules last if Liz takes 3 per day?

b. How many days will the capsules last if she takes only 2 per day?

c. How many more days can she take the herb if she takes only 2 per day?

section 1.1   Introduction to Whole Numbers

Objectives

1. Place Value
2. Standard Notation and Expanded Notation
3. Writing Numbers in Words
4. The Number Line and Order

1. Place Value

Numbers provide the foundation that is used in mathematics. We begin this chapter by discussing how numbers are represented and named. All numbers in our numbering system are composed from the **digits** 0, 1, 2, 3, 4, 5, 6, 7, 8, and 9. In mathematics, the numbers 0, 1, 2, 3, 4, 5, 6, 7, 8, 9, 10, 11, 12, ... are called the *whole numbers*. (The three dots are called *ellipses* and indicate that the list goes on indefinitely.)

For large numbers, commas are used to separate digits into groups of three called **periods**. For example, the number of live births in the United States in a recent year was 4,058,614 (Source: *The World Almanac*). Numbers written in this way are said to be in **standard form**. The position of each digit within a number determines the place value of the digit. To interpret the number of births in the United States, refer to the place value chart (Figure 1-1).

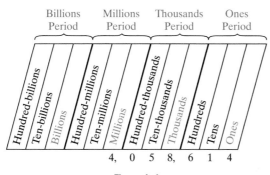

Figure 1-1

Concept Connections

1. Explain the difference between the two 3s in the number 303.

The digit 5 in the number 4,058,614 represents 5 ten-thousands because it is in the ten-thousands place. The digit 4 at the left represents 4 millions, whereas the digit 4 on the right represents 4 ones.

---

example 1   Determining Place Value

Determine the place value of the digit 2 in each number.

a. 417,216,900 **b.** 724 **c.** 502,000,700

Solution:

a. 417,216,900 hundred-thousands

b. 724 tens

c. 502,000,700 millions

Skill Practice

Determine the place value of the digit 4 in each number.

2. 547,098,632
3. 1,659,984,036

---

example 2   Determining Place Value

Mount Everest, the highest mountain on earth, is 29,035 feet (ft) tall. Give the place value for each digit in this number.

Answers

1. First 3 (on the left) represents 3 hundreds, while the second 3 (on the right) represents 3 ones.
2. Ten-millions
3. Thousands

Solution:

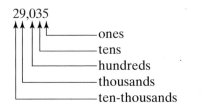

2. Standard Notation and Expanded Notation

A number can also be written in an expanded form by writing each digit with its place value units. For example, the number 287 can be written as

$$287 = 2 \text{ hundreds} + 8 \text{ tens} + 7 \text{ ones}$$

This is called **expanded form**.

example 3   Converting Standard Form to Expanded Form

Convert to expanded form.

a. 4,672

b. 257,016

Solution:

a. 4,672   4 thousands + 6 hundreds + 7 tens + 2 ones

b. 257,016   2 hundred-thousands + 5 ten-thousands +
                7 thousands + 1 ten + 6 ones

example 4   Converting Expanded Form to Standard Form

Convert to standard form.

a. 2 hundreds + 5 tens + 9 ones

b. 1 thousand + 2 tens + 5 ones

Solution:

a. 2 hundreds + 5 tens + 9 ones = 259

b. Each place position from the thousands place to the ones place must contain a digit. In this problem, there is no reference to the hundreds place digit. Therefore, we assume 0 hundreds. Thus,

$$1 \text{ thousand} + 0 \text{ hundreds} + 2 \text{ tens} + 5 \text{ ones} = 1,025$$

3. Writing Numbers in Words

The word names of some two-digit numbers appear with a hyphen while others do not. For example:

Number	Number Name
12	twelve
68	sixty-eight
40	forty
42	forty-two

9. Write the name of a two-digit number that is not hyphenated. Write the name of a two-digit number that is hyphenated.

To write a three-digit or larger number, begin at the leftmost group of digits. The number named in that group is followed by the period name, followed by a comma. Then the next period is named, and so on.

---

example 5   Writing a Number in Words

Write the number 621,417,325 in words.

Solution:

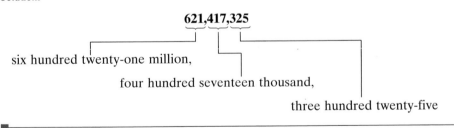

621,417,325

six hundred twenty-one million,

four hundred seventeen thousand,

three hundred twenty-five

Skill Practice

10. Write the number 1,450,327,214 in words.

Notice from Example 5 that when naming numbers, the name of the ones period is not attached to the last group of digits. Also note that for whole numbers, the word *and* should not appear in word names. For example, the number 405 should be written as four hundred five.

---

example 6   Writing a Number in Words

Write the number 1,206,427,200 in words.

Solution:

1,206,427,200

One billion, two hundred six million, four hundred twenty-seven thousand, two hundred

Skill Practice

11. Write the number 401,207 in words.

Answers

9. For example: fourteen
   For example: fifty-six
10. One billion, four hundred fifty million, three hundred twenty-seven thousand, two hundred fourteen
11. Four hundred one thousand, two hundred seven

example 7   Writing a Number in Standard Form

Write the number in standard form.

Six million, forty-six thousand, nine hundred three

Solution:

6,046,903

We have seen several examples of writing a number in standard form, in expanded form, and in words. Standard form is the most concise representation. Also note that when we write a four-digit number in standard form, the comma is often omitted. For example, the number 4,389 is often written as 4389.

4. The Number Line and Order

Whole numbers can be visualized as equally spaced points on a line called a *number line* (Figure 1-2).

Figure 1-2

The whole numbers begin at 0 and are ordered from left to right by increasing value.

    A number is graphed on a number line by placing a dot at the corresponding point. For any two numbers graphed on a number line, the number to the left is less than the number to the right. Similarly, a number to the right is greater than the number to the left. In mathematics, the symbol $<$ is used to denote "is less than," and the symbol $>$ means "is greater than." Therefore,

$3 < 5$ means   3 is less than 5

$5 > 3$ means   5 is greater than 3

example 8   Determining Order Between Two Numbers

Fill in the blank with the symbol $<$ or $>$.

a. $4 \boxed{} 10$ **b.** $7 \boxed{} 0$ **c.** $82 \boxed{} 30$

Solution:

a. $4 \boxed{<} 10$

b. $7 \boxed{>} 0$

c. $82 \boxed{>} 30$

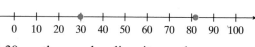

To visualize the numbers 82 and 30 on the number line, it may be necessary to use a different scale. Rather than setting equally spaced marks in units of 1, we can use units of 10. The number 82 must be somewhere between 80 and 90 on the number line.

section 1.1   Practice Exercises

Boost *your* GRADE at
mathzone.com!

MathZone

- Practice Problems
- Self-Tests
- NetTutor
- e-Professors
- Videos

Study Skills Exercises

In this text we provide skills for you to enhance your learning experience. Each set of practice exercises begins with an activity that focuses on one of eight areas: learning about your course, using your text, taking notes, doing homework, taking an exam (test and math anxiety), managing your time, recognizing your learning style, and studying for the final exam.

Each activity requires only a few minutes and will help you to pass this class and become a better math student. Many of these skills can be carried over to other disciplines and help you to become a model college student.

1. To begin, write down the following information.

    a. Instructor's name

    b. Instructor's office number

    c. Instructor's telephone number

    d. Instructor's email address

    e. Instructor's office hours

    f. Days of the week that the class meets

    g. The room number in which the class meets

    h. Is there a lab requirement for this course? If so, how often and what is the location of the lab?

2. Define the key terms.

    a. Digit   **b. Standard form**   **c. Periods**   **d. Expanded form**

Objective 1: Place Value

3. Name the place values for each of the digits in the number 8,213,457. **(See page 3, Figure 1-1.)**

4. Name the place values for each of the digits in the number 103,596.

For Exercises 5–24, determine the place value for each underlined digit. **(See Example 1.)**

5. 3<u>2</u>1

6. 6<u>8</u>9

7. 21<u>4</u>

8. 73<u>8</u>

9. 8,<u>7</u>10

10. 2,<u>2</u>93

11. <u>1</u>,430

12. 3,<u>1</u>01

13. <u>4</u>52,723

14. 6<u>5</u>5,878

15. <u>1</u>,023,676,207

16. <u>3</u>,111,901,211

17. 22,<u>4</u>22

18. <u>5</u>8,106

19. 51,0<u>3</u>3,201

20. 9<u>3</u>,971,224

21. The number of U.S. travelers abroad in a recent year was <u>1</u>0,677,881. **(See Example 2.)**

22. The area of Lake Superior is 31,820 mi^2.

23. For a recent year, the total number of U.S. $1 bills in circulation was 7,653,468,440.

24. For a certain flight, the cruising altitude of a commercial jet is 31,000 ft.

Objective 2: Standard Notation and Expanded Notation

For Exercises 25–34, convert the numbers to expanded form. (See Example 3.)

25. 58   **26.** 71   **27.** 539   **28.** 382

29. 503   **30.** 809   **31.** 10,241   **32.** 20,873

33. 2,006,004   **34.** 5,001,009

For Exercises 35–42, convert the numbers to standard form. (See Example 4.)

35. 5 hundreds + 2 tens + 4 ones   **36.** 3 hundreds + 1 ten + 8 ones

37. 1 hundred + 5 tens   **38.** 6 hundreds + 2 tens

39. 1 thousand + 9 hundreds + 6 ones   **40.** 4 thousands + 2 hundreds + 1 one

41. 8 ten-thousands + 5 thousands + 7 ones   **42.** 2 ten-thousands + 6 thousands + 2 ones

43. Write your favorite three-digit number in both standard form and expanded form.

44. Write your favorite four-digit number in both standard form and expanded form.

45. Name the first four periods of a number (from right to left).

46. Name the first four place values of a number (from right to left).

Objective 3: Writing Numbers in Words

For Exercises 47–56, write the number in words. (See Examples 5 and 6.)

47. 241   **48.** 327   **49.** 603   **50.** 108

51. The Shuowen jiezi dictionary, an ancient Chinese dictionary that dates back to the year 100, contained 9,535 characters. Write the number 9,535 in words.

52. Researchers calculate that about 590,712 stone blocks were used to construct the Great Pyramid. Write the number 590,712 in words.

53. 31,530   **54.** 52,160   **55.** 100,234   **56.** 400,199

57. Mt. McKinley in Alaska is 20,320 ft high. Write the number 20,320 in words.

58. There are 1,800 seats in the Regal Champlain Theater in Plattsburgh, New York. Write the number 1,800 in words.

59. Interstate I-75 is 1,377 miles (mi) long. Write the number 1,377 in words.

60. In the United States, there are approximately 60,000,000 cats living in households. Write the number 60,000,000 in words.

For Exercises 61–66, convert the number to standard form. **(See Example 7.)**

61. Six thousand, five   **62.** Four thousand, four

63. Six hundred seventy-two thousand   **64.** Two hundred forty-eight thousand

65. One million, four hundred eighty-four thousand, two hundred fifty

66. Two million, six hundred forty-seven thousand, five hundred twenty

Objective 4: The Number Line and Order

For Exercises 67–68, graph the numbers on the number line.

67. a. 6   **b.** 13   **c.** 8   **d.** 1

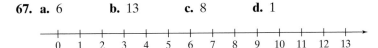

68. a. 5   **b.** 3   **c.** 11   **d.** 9

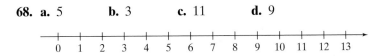

69. On a number line, what number is 4 units to the right of 6?

70. On a number line, what number is 8 units to the left of 11?

71. On a number line, what number is 3 units to the left of 7?

72. On a number line, what number is 5 units to the right of 0?

For Exercises 73–76, translate the inequality to words.

73. $8 > 2$ **74.** $6 < 11$ **75.** $3 < 7$ **76.** $14 > 12$

For Exercises 77–88, insert the appropriate inequality. Choose from $<$ or $>$. **(See Example 8.)**

77. $6 \square 11$ **78.** $14 \square 13$ **79.** $21 \square 18$ **80.** $5 \square 7$

81. $3 \square 7$ **82.** $14 \square 24$ **83.** $95 \square 89$ **84.** $28 \square 30$

85. $0 \square 3$ **86.** $8 \square 0$ **87.** $90 \square 91$ **88.** $48 \square 47$

Expanding Your Skills

89. Answer true or false. The number 12 is a digit.

90. Answer true or false. The number 26 is a digit.

91. What is the greatest two-digit number?

92. What is the greatest three-digit number?

93. What is the greatest whole number?

94. What is the least whole number?

95. How many zeros are there in the number ten million?

96. How many zeros are there in the number one hundred billion?

97. What is the greatest three-digit number that can be formed from the digits 6, 9, and 4? Use each digit only once.

98. What is the greatest three-digit number that can be formed from the digits 0, 4, and 8? Use each digit only once.

section 1.2   Addition of Whole Numbers

1. Addition of Whole Numbers Using the Number Line

We use addition of whole numbers to represent an increase in quantity. For example, suppose Jonas types 5 pages of a report before lunch. Later in the afternoon he types 3 more pages. The total number of pages that he typed is found by adding 5 and 3.

$$5 \text{ pages} + 3 \text{ pages} = 8 \text{ pages}$$

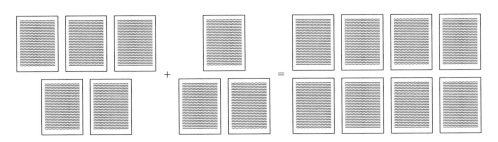

The result of an addition problem is called the **sum**, and the numbers being added are called **addends**. Thus,

$$5 + 3 = 8$$

addends   sum

Concept Connections

1. Identify the addends and the sum.

   $3 + 7 + 12 = 22$

The number line is a useful tool to visualize the operation of addition. To add 5 and 3 on a number line, begin at 0 and move 5 units to the right. Then move an additional 3 units to the right. The final location indicates the sum.

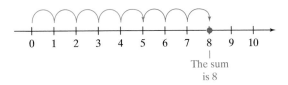

The sum
is 8

You can use a number line to find the sum of any pair of digits. The sums for all possible pairs of one-digit numbers should be memorized (see Exercise 9). Memorizing these basic addition facts will make it easier for you to add larger numbers.

2. Addition of Whole Numbers

To add whole numbers, line up the numbers vertically by place value. Then add the digits in the corresponding place positions.

example 1   Adding Whole Numbers

Add.

$$24 + 61$$

Skill Practice

2. Add. $\begin{array}{r} 47 \\ + 32 \\ \hline \end{array}$

Answers

1. Addends: 3, 7, and 12; sum: 22
2. 79

Solution:

$$24 = 2 \text{ tens} + 4 \text{ ones}$$
$$\underline{+\,61 = 6 \text{ tens} + 1 \text{ one}}$$
$$85 = 8 \text{ tens} + 5 \text{ ones}$$

---

example 2   Adding Whole Numbers

Add.

$$261 + 28$$

Solution:

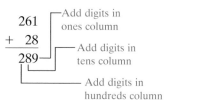

Sometimes when adding numbers, the sum of the digits in a given place position is greater than 9. If this occurs, we must do what is called *carrying* or *regrouping*. Example 3 illustrates this process.

---

example 3   Adding Whole Numbers with Carrying

Add.

$$35 + 48$$

Solution:

$$35 = 3 \text{ tens} + 5 \text{ ones}$$
$$\underline{+\,48 = 4 \text{ tens} + 8 \text{ ones}}$$
$$7 \text{ tens} + 13 \text{ ones} \longleftarrow$$

The sum of the digits in the ones place exceeds 9. But 13 ones is the same as 1 ten and 3 ones. We can *carry* 1 ten to the tens column while leaving the 3 ones in the ones column. Notice that we placed the carried digit above the tens column.

$$\overset{1 \text{ ten}}{35} = 3 \text{ tens} + 5 \text{ ones}$$
$$\underline{+\,48 = 4 \text{ tens} + 8 \text{ ones}}$$
$$83 = 8 \text{ tens} + 3 \text{ ones}$$

The sum is 83.

---

example 4   Adding Whole Numbers With Carrying

Add.

$$458 + 67$$

Solution:

$$\overset{\scriptstyle 1}{458}$$
$$+\ \ 67$$
$$\overline{5}$$

Add the digits in the ones column: $8 + 7 = 15$. Write 5 in the ones column, and carry the 1 to the tens column.

$$\overset{\scriptstyle 1\,1}{458}$$
$$+\ \ 67$$
$$\overline{25}$$

Add the digits in the tens column (including the carry): $1 + 5 + 6 = 12$. Write the 2 in the tens column, and carry the 1 to the hundreds column.

$$\overset{\scriptstyle 1\,1}{458}$$
$$+\ \ 67$$
$$\overline{525}$$

Add the digits in the hundreds column.

The sum is 525.

Addition of numbers may include more than two addends.

---

example 5   Adding Whole Numbers

Add.

$$21{,}076 + 84{,}158 + 2419$$

Solution:

$$\overset{\scriptstyle 1\ \ \ \ 1\,2}{21{,}076}$$
$$84{,}158$$
$$+\ \ 2{,}419$$
$$\overline{107{,}653}$$

In this example, the sum of the digits in the ones column is 23. Therefore, we write the 3 and carry the 2.

---

3. Properties of Addition

We present three properties of addition that you may already have discovered.

Addition Property of 0

The sum of any number and 0 is that number.

Examples:
$$5 + 0 = 5$$
$$0 + 2 = 2$$

Commutative Property of Addition

Changing the order of two addends does not affect the sum.

Example: $5 + 7$ is equivalent to $7 + 5$

In mathematics we use parentheses ( ) as grouping symbols. To add more than two numbers, we can group them and then add. For example:

$(2 + 3) + 8$ Parentheses indicate that $2 + 3$ is added first, and the result is added to 8.

$= 5 + 8$

$= 13$

$2 + (3 + 8)$ Parentheses indicate that $3 + 8$ is added first, and the result is added to 2.

$= 2 + 11$

$= 13$

Concept Connections

9. Explain the difference between the commutative property of addition and the associative property of addition.

Associative Property of Addition

The manner in which addends are grouped does not affect the sum.

Example: $(1 + 7) + 3$ is equivalent to $1 + (7 + 3)$

Skill Practice

10. Rewrite $3 + 5$, using the commutative property of addition.

11. Rewrite $(1 + 7) + 12$, using the associative property of addition.

example 6   Applying the Properties of Addition

a. Rewrite $9 + 6$, using the commutative property of addition.

b. Rewrite $(15 + 9) + 5$, using the associative property of addition.

Solution:

a. $9 + 6 = 6 + 9$ Change the order of the addends.

b. $(15 + 9) + 5 = 15 + (9 + 5)$ Change the grouping of the addends.

4. Translations and Applications Involving Addition

In the English language, there are many different words and phrases that imply addition. A partial list is given in Table 1-1.

table 1-1

Word/Phrase	Example	In Symbols
Sum	The sum of 6 and 2	$6 + 2$
Added to	3 added to 8	$8 + 3$
Increased by	7 increased by 2	$7 + 2$
More than	10 more than 6	$6 + 10$
Plus	8 plus 3	$8 + 3$
Total of	The total of 9 and 6	$9 + 6$

Answers

9. The commutative property involves the *order* in which two addends are added. The associative property involves the manner in which three addends are *grouped* when being added.
10. $3 + 5 = 5 + 3$
11. $(1 + 7) + 12 = 1 + (7 + 12)$

---

example 7   Translating an English Phrase to a Mathematical Statement

Translate each phrase to an equivalent mathematical statement and simplify.

a. 12 added to 109   **b.** The sum of 1386 and 376

Solution:

a. 109 + 12

$$\begin{array}{r} \overset{1}{1}09 \\ +\ 12 \\ \hline 121 \end{array}$$

b. 1386 + 376

$$\begin{array}{r} \overset{11}{1}386 \\ +\ 376 \\ \hline 1762 \end{array}$$

Skill Practice

Translate and simplify.

12. 50 more than 80

13. 12 increased by 14

14. The sum of 10, 20, and 30

Addition of whole numbers is sometimes necessary to solve application problems.

---

example 8   Solving an Application Problem

Carlita works as a waitress at El Pinto restaurant in Albuquerque, New Mexico. Her tips for the last five nights were $30, $18, $66, $102, and $45. Find the total amount she made in tips.

Solution:

To find the total, we add.

$$\begin{array}{r} \overset{12}{\$\ 30} \\ 18 \\ 66 \\ 102 \\ +\ 45 \\ \hline \$261 \end{array}$$

Carlita made $261 in tips.

Skill Practice

15. Talita received test scores of 92, 100, 84, and 96 on her first four math tests. She also earned 8 points of extra credit. How many total points did she earn?

Tables and graphs are often used to summarize information in an organized manner. Examples 9 and 10 demonstrate the interpretation of these tools.

---

example 9   Solving an Application Problem Involving a Table

The following table gives the top five most-visited websites for a recent month.

Website	Number of Visitors
AOL Time Warner Network	97,995
MSN-Microsoft sites	89,819
Yahoo! sites	83,433
Google sites	37,460
Terra Lycos	36,173

Find the total number of visitors to the top five most-visited websites.

Answers

12. 80 + 50; 130
13. 12 + 14; 26
14. 10 + 20 + 30; 60
15. 380

Skill Practice

16. The table gives the number of gold, silver, and bronze medals won in the 2002 Winter Olympics for selected countries. Find the total number of medals won by Canada.

	Gold	Silver	Bronze
Germany	12	16	7
United States	10	13	11
Norway	11	7	6
Canada	6	3	8

Skill Practice

17. Samira's monthly expenses are summarized in the graph. Find the sum of her expenses.

Monthly Budget

Utilities $170
Car $340
Food $300
Other $250
Rent $660

Solution:

$$
\begin{array}{r}
{\scriptstyle 3\ 32\ 22}\\
97,995\\
89,819\\
83,433\\
37,460\\
+\ \ 36,173\\
\hline
344,880
\end{array}
$$

There were 344,880 combined visitors to these websites.

---

example 10   Solving an Application Problem Involving a Graph

The graph in Figure 1-3 gives the number of new AIDS cases in the United States for the years 2000, 2001, and 2002. The red bars in the graph represent the values for the number of women (aged 13 and older). The blue bars in the graph represent the values for the number of men (aged 13 and older). (Source: Centers for Disease Control.)

Find the total number of new AIDS cases for women in the United States in the years 2000–2002.

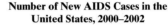

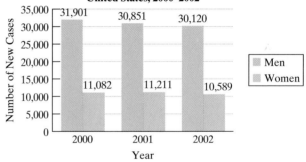

Figure 1-3

Solution:

We need to find the number of new AIDS cases for women only. Therefore, add the values corresponding to the red bars in the graph.

$$
\begin{array}{r}
{\scriptstyle 1\ 1}\\
11,082\\
11,211\\
+\ 10,589\\
\hline
32,882
\end{array}
$$

There were 32,882 new AIDS cases attributed to women in the years 2000–2002.

Answers

16. 17 medals
17. $1720

5. Perimeter

One special application of addition is to find the perimeter of a polygon. A **polygon** is a flat figure formed by line segments connected at their ends.

Familiar figures such as triangles, rectangles, and squares are examples of polygons. See Figure 1-4.

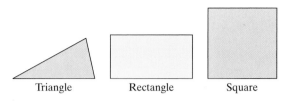

Triangle   Rectangle   Square

Figure 1-4

The **perimeter** of any polygon is the distance around the outside of the figure. To find the perimeter, add the lengths of the sides.

---

example 11   Finding Perimeter

Find the perimeter of the triangle.

Solution:

The perimeter is the sum of the lengths of the sides.

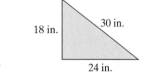

$$\begin{array}{r} \overset{1}{18} \text{ in.} \\ 24 \text{ in.} \\ +\ 30 \text{ in.} \\ \hline 72 \text{ in.} \end{array}$$

The perimeter is 72 inches (in.).

Skill Practice

18. Find the perimeter of the rectangle.

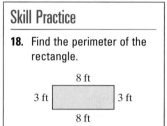

---

example 12   Finding Perimeter

A paving company wants to edge the perimeter of a parking lot with concrete curbing. Find the perimeter of the parking lot.

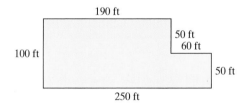

Solution:

The perimeter is the sum of the lengths of the sides.

$$\begin{array}{r} \overset{3}{190} \text{ ft} \\ 50 \text{ ft} \\ 60 \text{ ft} \\ 50 \text{ ft} \\ 250 \text{ ft} \\ +\ 100 \text{ ft} \\ \hline 700 \text{ ft} \end{array}$$

The distance around the parking lot (the perimeter) is 700 ft.

Skill Practice

19. Find the perimeter of the garden.

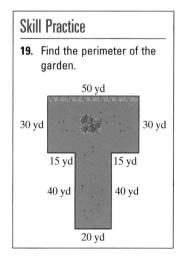

Answers

18. 22 ft
19. 240 yd

section 1.2   Practice Exercises

Study Skills Exercises

1. Taking 12 credit-hours is the equivalent of a full-time job. Often students try to work too many hours while taking classes at school.

   a. Write down how many hours you work per week and the number of credit-hours you are taking this term.

   Number of hours worked per week _____

   Number of credit hours this term _____

   b. The table gives a recommended limit on the number of hours you should work based on the number of credit-hours you are taking at school. (Keep in mind that other responsibilities in your life such as your family might also make it necessary to limit your hours at work even more.) How do your numbers from part (a) compare to those in the table? Are you working too many hours?

Number of Credit-hours	Maximum Number of Hours of Work per Week
3	40
6	30
9	20
12	10
15	0

2. Define the key terms.
   a. Sum   b. Addends   c. Polygon   d. Perimeter

Review Exercises

For Exercises 3–8, write the number in the form indicated.

3. Convert the number 351 to expanded form.

4. Write the number 351 in words.

5. Convert the number 107 to expanded form.

6. Write the given number in standard form: two thousand, four

7. Write the given number in standard form: four thousand, twelve

8. Convert the given number to standard form: 6 thousands + 2 hundreds + 6 ones

Objective 1: Addition of Whole Numbers Using the Number Line

9. Fill out the chart. Use the number line if necessary.

+	0	1	2	3	4	5	6	7	8	9
0										
1										
2										
3										
4										
5										
6										
7										
8										
9										

For Exercises 10–15, identify the addends and the sum.

10. $5 + 9 = 14$

11. $2 + 8 = 10$

12. $12 + 5 = 17$

13. $11 + 10 = 21$

14. $1 + 13 + 4 = 18$

15. $5 + 8 + 2 = 15$

Objective 2: Addition of Whole Numbers

For Exercises 16–31, add. **(See Examples 1 and 2.)**

16.
$$\begin{array}{r} 42 \\ + 33 \\ \hline \end{array}$$

17.
$$\begin{array}{r} 21 \\ + 53 \\ \hline \end{array}$$

18.
$$\begin{array}{r} 39 \\ + 20 \\ \hline \end{array}$$

19.
$$\begin{array}{r} 15 \\ + 43 \\ \hline \end{array}$$

20.
$$\begin{array}{r} 12 \\ 15 \\ + 32 \\ \hline \end{array}$$

21.
$$\begin{array}{r} 10 \\ 8 \\ + 30 \\ \hline \end{array}$$

22.
$$\begin{array}{r} 7 \\ 21 \\ + 10 \\ \hline \end{array}$$

23.
$$\begin{array}{r} 6 \\ 11 \\ + 2 \\ \hline \end{array}$$

24. $341 + 225$

25. $407 + 181$

26. $890 + 107$

27. $444 + 354$

28. $4 + 13 + 102$

29. $11 + 221 + 5$

30. $31 + 7 + 430$

31. $24 + 14 + 160$

For Exercises 32–51, add the whole numbers with carrying. **(See Examples 3–5.)**

32.
$$\begin{array}{r} 76 \\ + 45 \\ \hline \end{array}$$

33.
$$\begin{array}{r} 25 \\ + 59 \\ \hline \end{array}$$

34.
$$\begin{array}{r} 87 \\ + 24 \\ \hline \end{array}$$

35.
$$\begin{array}{r} 38 \\ + 77 \\ \hline \end{array}$$

36.
$$\begin{array}{r} 658 \\ + 231 \\ \hline \end{array}$$

37.
$$\begin{array}{r} 642 \\ + 295 \\ \hline \end{array}$$

38.
$$\begin{array}{r} 152 \\ + 549 \\ \hline \end{array}$$

39.
$$\begin{array}{r} 462 \\ + 388 \\ \hline \end{array}$$

40. $15 + 5 + 9$ **41.** $2 + 31 + 8$ **42.** $14 + 9 + 17$ **43.** $7 + 18 + 4$

44. $79 + 112 + 12$ **45.** $62 + 907 + 34$ **46.** $331 + 422 + 76$ **47.** $87 + 119 + 630$

48. $4980 + 10{,}223$ **49.** $23{,}112 + 892$ **50.** $8721 + 3212$ **51.** $12{,}333 + 788$

Objective 3: Properties of Addition

For Exercises 52–55, rewrite the addition problem, using the commutative property of addition. **(See Example 6.)**

52. $12 + 6 = \square + \square$ **53.** $30 + 21 = \boxed{7} + \boxed{1}$ **54.** $101 + 44 = \square + \square$ **55.** $8 + 13 = \square + \square$

For Exercises 56–59, rewrite the addition problem using the associative property of addition, by inserting a pair of parentheses.

56. $(4 + 8) + 13 = 4 + 8 + 13$ **57.** $(23 + 9) + 10 = 23 + 9 + 10$

58. $7 + (12 + 8) = 7 + 12 + 8$ **59.** $41 + (3 + 22) = 41 + 3 + 22$

60. Explain the difference between the commutative and the associative properties of addition.

61. Explain the addition property of 0. Then simplify the expressions.

     a. $423 + 0$ **b.** $0 + 25$ **c.** $\begin{array}{r} 67 \\ + 0 \\ \hline \end{array}$

Objective 4: Translations and Applications Involving Addition

For Exercises 62–71, translate the English phrase into a mathematical statement and simplify. **(See Example 7.)**

62. The sum of 13 and 7   **63.** The sum of 100 and 42   **64.** 45 added to 7

65. 81 added to 23   **66.** 5 more than 18   **67.** 2 more than 76

68. 1523 increased by 90   **69.** 1320 increased by 448   **70.** The total of 5, 39, and 81

71. The total of 78, 12, and 22

For Exercises 72–77, write an English phrase from the mathematical statement. Answers may vary.

72. $54 + 24$ **73.** $33 + 15$ **74.** $12 + 88$ **75.** $70 + 15$

76. $4 + 23 + 77$ **77.** $11 + 41 + 53$

78. The attendance at a high school play during one weekend was as follows: 103 on Friday, 112 on Saturday, and 61 at the Sunday matinee. What was the total attendance?

79. To schedule enough drivers for an upcoming week, a local pizza shop manager recorded the number of deliveries each day from the previous week: 38, 54, 44, 61, 97, 103, 124. What was the total number of deliveries for the week?
(See Example 8.)

80. Three top television shows entertained the following number of viewers in one week: 27,300,000 for *CSI*, 20,800,000 for *Survivor*, and 19,900,000 for *ER*. Find the sum of the viewers for these shows.

81. To travel from Houston to Corpus Christi, a salesperson must stop in San Antonio. If it is 195 mi from Houston to San Antonio and 228 mi from San Antonio to Corpus Christi, how far will she travel on this trip?

82. Nora earned $43,000 last year. This year her salary was increased by $2500. What is her present salary?

83. The number of participants in the Special Olympics increased by 1,205,655 since it began in 1968 with 1000 athletes. How many athletes are presently participating?

84. The table gives the number of desks and chairs delivered each quarter to an office supply store. What is the total number of desks delivered for the year?

	Chairs	Desks
March	220	115
June	185	104
September	201	93
December	198	111

85. A portion of Jonathan's checking account register is shown. What is the total amount of the four checks written?
(See Example 9.)

Check No.	Description	Credit	Debit	Balance
1871	Electric bill		$60	$180
1872	Groceries		52	128
1873	Department store		75	53
	Payroll	$1256		1309
1874	Restaurant		58	1251
	Transfer from savings	150		1401

86. The graph displays the number of public school teachers in the United States. Find the number of elementary school teachers (include prekindergarten and kindergarten).

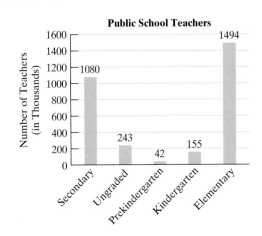

87. The staff for U.S. public schools is categorized in the graph. Determine the number of staff other than teachers.

Number of Public School Staff

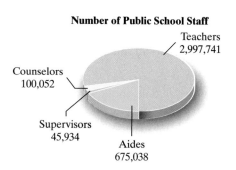

Teachers
2,997,741

Counselors
100,052

Supervisors
45,934

Aides
675,038

88. The pie graph shows the costs incurred in managing Sub-World sandwich shop for one month. From this information, determine the total cost for one month.

Sub-World Monthly Expenses

Food
$7329

Labor
$9560

Nonfood items
$1248

Overhead
$3500

89. The Student Career Experience Program is a program that places students in government jobs. The chart displays the number of participants during 2006 in the top six agencies. Find the total number of participants in the program. **(See Example 10.)**

Student Career Experience Program, Top Six Employing Agencies (Fiscal Year 2006)

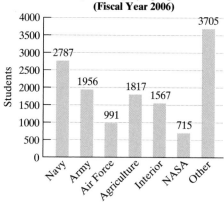

Objective 5: Perimeter

For Exercises 90–97, find the perimeter. **(See Example 11.)**

90.

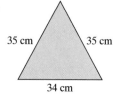

35 cm   35 cm

34 cm

91.

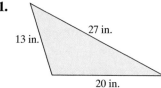

27 in.

13 in.

20 in.

92. Find the perimeter of an NBA basketball court.

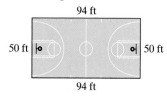

94 ft

50 ft   50 ft

94 ft

93.

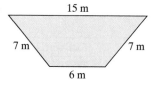

15 m

7 m   7 m

6 m

94.

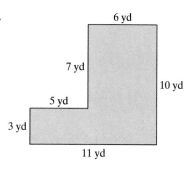

6 yd

7 yd

10 yd

5 yd

3 yd

11 yd

95.

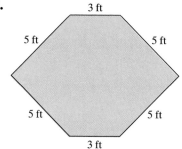

3 ft

5 ft   5 ft

5 ft   5 ft

3 ft

96.

21 m 20 m
18 m
21 m
11 m 19 m

97. A major league baseball diamond is in the shape of a square. Find the distance a batter must run if he hits a home run.
(See Example 12.)

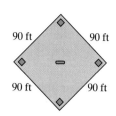

90 ft   90 ft

90 ft   90 ft

Calculator Connections

Topic: Adding on a calculator

The following keystrokes demonstrate the procedure to add numbers on a calculator. The ⌜Enter⌝ key (or, on some calculators, the ⌜=⌝ key or ⌜Exe⌝ key) tells the calculator to complete the calculation. Notice that commas used in large numbers are not entered into the calculator.

Expression	Keystrokes	Result
92,406 + 83,168	92406 ⌜+⌝ 83168 ⌜Enter⌝	175574

↑
Your calculator may use the ⌜=⌝ key or ⌜Exe⌝ key instead.

Calculator Exercise

For Exercises 98–101, add by using a calculator.

98. 9,084,037 + 452,903

99. 899,382 + 9406

100.
```
   45,418
   81,990
    9,063
+ 56,309
```

101.
```
  9,300,050
  7,803,513
  3,480,009
+   907,822
```

102. The number of viewers for four television programs for a selected week is given in the table. What is the total number of viewers?

Program	Number of Viewers
ABC premier event	17,457,000
American Idol	17,164,000
CSI	17,004,000
Law and Order	15,717,000

103. The number of votes tallied for the leading Presidential candidates for the 2004 election is given in the table. Find the total number of votes for these three candidates.

Candidate	Number of Votes
Nader	411,304
Kerry	59,028,109
Bush	62,040,606

section 1.3   Subtraction of Whole Numbers

1. Introduction to Subtraction

Jeremy bought a case of 12 sodas, and on a hot afternoon he drank 3 of the sodas. We can use the operation of subtraction to find the number of sodas remaining.

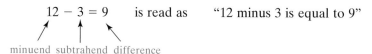

12 sodas − 3 sodas   =   9 sodas

The symbol − between two numbers is a subtraction sign, and the result of a subtraction is called the **difference**. The number being subtracted (in this case, 3) is called the **subtrahend**. The number 12 from which 3 is subtracted is called the **minuend**.

$$12 - 3 = 9$$ is read as   "12 minus 3 is equal to 9"

minuend subtrahend difference

Subtraction is the reverse operation of addition. To find the number of sodas that remain after Jeremy takes 3 sodas away from 12 sodas, we ask the following question:

"3 added to what number equals 12?"

That is,

$$12 - 3 = ?$$ is equivalent to $? + 3 = 12$

Subtraction can also be visualized on the number line. To evaluate $7 - 4$, start from the point on the number line corresponding to the minuend (7 in this case). Then move to the *left* 4 units. The resulting position on the number line is the difference.

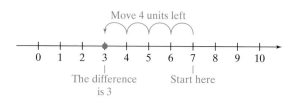

Move 4 units left

0 1 2 3 4 5 6 7 8 9 10

The difference is 3   Start here

To check the result, we can use addition.

$$7 - 4 = 3$$ because $3 + 4 = 7$

example 1   Subtracting Whole Numbers

Subtract and check the answer, using addition.

a. $8 - 2$ **b.** $10 - 6$ **c.** $5 - 0$ **d.** $3 - 3$

Solution:

a. $8 - 2 = 6$ because $6 + 2 = 8$

b. $10 - 6 = 4$ because $4 + 6 = 10$

c. $5 - 0 = 5$ because $5 + 0 = 5$

d. $3 - 3 = 0$ because $0 + 3 = 3$

2. Subtraction of Whole Numbers

When subtracting large numbers, it is usually more convenient to write the numbers vertically. We write the minuend on top and the subtrahend below it. Starting from the ones column, we subtract digits having corresponding place values.

---

example 2   Subtracting Whole Numbers Without Borrowing

Subtract and check the answer by using addition.

a. $\begin{array}{r} 976 \\ -\ 124 \\ \hline \end{array}$ **b.** $\begin{array}{r} 2498 \\ -\ 197 \\ \hline \end{array}$

Solution:

a. $\begin{array}{r} 976 \\ -\ 124 \\ \hline 852 \end{array}$ Check: $\begin{array}{r} 852 \\ +\ 124 \\ \hline 976 \ \checkmark \end{array}$

┌─Subtract the ones column digits
├─Subtract the tens column digits
└─Subtract the hundreds column digits

b. $\begin{array}{r} 2498 \\ -\ 197 \\ \hline 2301 \end{array}$ Check: $\begin{array}{r} 2301 \\ +\ 197 \\ \hline 2498 \ \checkmark \end{array}$

Skill Practice

Subtract. Check by using addition.

5. $\begin{array}{r} 472 \\ -\ 261 \\ \hline \end{array}$ **6.** $\begin{array}{r} 3947 \\ -\ 137 \\ \hline \end{array}$

When a digit in the subtrahend is larger than the corresponding digit in the minuend, we must "regroup" or borrow a value from the column to the left.

$\begin{array}{l} 92 = 9 \text{ tens} + 2 \text{ ones} \\ -74 = 7 \text{ tens} + 4 \text{ ones} \\ \hline \end{array}$ In the ones column, we cannot take 4 away from 2. We will regroup by borrowing 1 ten from the minuend. Furthermore, 1 ten = 10 ones.

$\begin{array}{l} \overset{8\ +10}{9}\ \overset{8}{2} = \overset{8}{9} \text{ tens} + \overset{+10 \text{ ones}}{2} \text{ ones} \Big\} \\ -7\ 4 = 7 \text{ tens} + 4 \text{ ones} \end{array}$ We now have 12 ones in the minuend.

$\begin{array}{l} \overset{8}{9} \overset{12}{2} = \overset{8}{9} \text{ tens} + 12 \text{ ones} \\ -7 4 = 7 \text{ tens} + \ \ 4 \text{ ones} \\ \hline 1 8 = 1 \text{ ten} + \ \ 8 \text{ ones} \end{array}$

Tip: The process of *borrowing* in subtraction is the reverse operation of *carrying* in addition.

Concept Connections

7. Which subtraction (a or b) requires borrowing?

a. $\begin{array}{r} 76 \\ -\ 24 \\ \hline \end{array}$ **b.** $\begin{array}{r} 76 \\ -\ 49 \\ \hline \end{array}$

---

example 3   Subtracting Whole Numbers With Borrowing

Subtract and check the result with addition.

a. $\begin{array}{r} 134,616 \\ -\ 53,438 \\ \hline \end{array}$ **b.** $500 - 247$

Answers

5. 211   6. 3810   7. b

Solution:

a.
$$
\begin{array}{r}
\overset{\scriptstyle 0\ 16}{134,6\cancel{1}\cancel{6}} \\
-\ 53,438 \\
\hline
8
\end{array}
$$

In the ones place, 8 is greater than 6. In the minuend, we borrow 1 ten from the tens place.

$$
\begin{array}{r}
\overset{\scriptstyle 5\ \overset{10}{\cancel{0}}\ 16}{134,6\cancel{1}\cancel{6}} \\
-\ 53,438 \\
\hline
78
\end{array}
$$

In the tens place, 3 is greater than 0. In the minuend, we borrow 1 hundred from the hundreds place.

$$
\begin{array}{r}
\overset{\scriptstyle 0\ 13\quad 5\ \overset{10}{\cancel{0}}\ 16}{\cancel{1}\cancel{3}4,6\cancel{1}\cancel{6}} \\
-\ 53,438 \\
\hline
81,178
\end{array}
$$

In the ten-thousands place, 5 is greater than 3. We borrow 1 hundred-thousand from the hundred-thousands place.

Check:
$$
\begin{array}{r}
\overset{\scriptstyle 1\quad 1\ 1}{81,178} \\
+\ 53,438 \\
\hline
134,616\ \checkmark
\end{array}
$$

b.
$$
\begin{array}{r}
500 \\
-\ 247 \\
\end{array}
$$

In the ones place, 7 is greater than 0. We try to borrow 1 ten from the tens place. However, the tens place digit is 0. Therefore we must first borrow from the hundreds place.

$$
\begin{array}{r}
\overset{\scriptstyle 4\ 10}{\cancel{5}\cancel{0}\ 0} \\
-\ 2\ 4\ 7 \\
\end{array}
$$

$$
\begin{array}{r}
\overset{\scriptstyle \quad 9}{\overset{\scriptstyle 4\ \cancel{10}\ 10}{\cancel{5}\cancel{0}\cancel{0}}} \\
-\ 2\ 4\ 7 \\
\hline
2\ 5\ 3
\end{array}
$$

←Now we can borrow 1 ten to add to the ones place.

Subtract.

Check:
$$
\begin{array}{r}
\overset{\scriptstyle 1\ 1}{253} \\
+\ 247 \\
\hline
500\ \checkmark
\end{array}
$$

3. Translations and Applications Involving Subtraction

In applications of mathematics, several words and phrases imply subtraction. A partial list is provided in Table 1-2.

table 1-2

Word/Phrase	Example	In Symbols
Minus	15 minus 10	15 − 10
Difference	The difference of 10 and 2	10 − 2
Decreased by	9 decreased by 1	9 − 1
Less than	5 less than 12	12 − 5
Subtract . . . from	Subtract 3 from 8	8 − 3

In Table 1-2, make a note of the last two entries. The phrases *less than* and *subtract . . . from* imply a specific order in which the subtraction is performed. In both cases, begin with the second number listed and subtract the first number listed.

---

example 4   Translating an English Phrase to a Mathematical Statement

Translate the English phrase to a mathematical statement and simplify.

a. The difference of 150 and 38

b. 30 subtracted from 82

Solution:

a. From Table 1-2, the *difference* of 150 and 38 implies that the first number (150) is the minuend and the second number (38) is the subtrahend. Therefore, we have 150 − 38.

$$
\begin{array}{r}
\overset{4\ 10}{1\cancel{5}0} \\
-\ \ 38 \\
\hline
112
\end{array}
$$

b. The phrase "30 subtracted from 82" implies that 30 is taken away from 82. Therefore, we must start with 82 as the minuend and subtract 30. We have 82 − 30.

$$
\begin{array}{r}
82 \\
-\ 30 \\
\hline
52
\end{array}
$$

Skill Practice

Translate the English phrase into a mathematical statement and simplify.

11. Twelve decreased by eight

12. Subtract three from nine.

In Section 1.2 we saw that the operation of addition is commutative. That is, the order in which two numbers are added does not affect the sum. This is *not* true for subtraction. For example, 82 − 30 is not equal to 30 − 82. The symbol ≠ means "is not equal to." Thus, 82 − 30 ≠ 30 − 82.

Most applications of subtraction generally fall into two categories.

1. The first type is phrased as a subtraction problem in which the minuend and subtrahend are given.

Example: Shawn has $52 and then spends $40. How much money does he have left? (In this problem, we subtract $40 from $52.)

$52 − $40 = $12

2. The second type is phrased as an addition problem with a missing addend.

Example: Maria received 72 points on her last math test, but needed 90 points to receive an A. How many more points would she have needed to earn an A? (In this problem, the addition problem can be translated to subtraction.)

72 + ? = 90   is equivalent to   90 − 72 = ?

Because 90 − 72 = 18, Maria would have needed 18 more points.

Answers

11. 12 − 8; 4
12. 9 − 3; 6

Skill Practice

13. The temperature at 1:00 P.M. in Denver was 47°F. Three hours later, the temperature was 34°F. By how much did the temperature drop?

---

example 5   Solving an Application Problem

A biology class started with 35 students. By mid-semester, 7 students had dropped. How many students are still in the class?

Solution:

$35 - 7 = 28$ There are 28 students still in the class.

Skill Practice

14. Teresa earned test scores of 98, 84, and 90 on her first three exams. How many points must she score on the fourth exam to earn a total of 360 points?

---

example 6   Solving an Application Problem

A surveyor knows that the perimeter of the lot shown is 620 ft. Find the length of the missing side. See Figure 1-5.

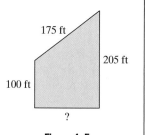

175 ft
205 ft
100 ft
?

Figure 1-5

Solution:

Recall that the perimeter of a polygon is the sum of the lengths of its sides. The sum of the three known sides in Figure 1-5 is 480 ft:

$$
\begin{array}{r}
\overset{1}{1}00 \\
175 \\
+\ 205 \\
\hline
480
\end{array}
$$

This value plus the length of the fourth side equals the perimeter: 480 ft + ? = 620 ft. Equivalently, we can subtract 480 ft from the perimeter to find the length of the missing side:

$$620 \text{ ft} - 480 \text{ ft} = ?$$

$$
\begin{array}{r}
\overset{5}{\cancel{6}}\overset{12}{2}0 \\
-\ 480 \\
\hline
140
\end{array}
$$

The missing side is 140 ft long.

A third application of subtraction is to compute a change (increase or decrease) in an amount.

Skill Practice

15. At Houston Community College, the total enrollment for the fall semester in 2000 was 49,520 students. In 2001, the fall semester enrollment was 53,565.

  a. Has the enrollment increased or decreased?

  b. Determine the amount of increase or decrease.

---

example 7   Solving an Application Problem

The number of reported robberies in the United States has fluctuated each year as shown in the graph.

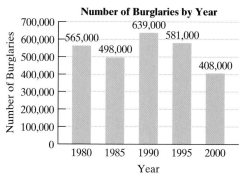

Number of Burglaries by Year

Number of Burglaries

700,000
600,000 — 565,000 — 639,000
500,000   498,000   581,000
400,000   408,000
300,000
200,000
100,000
0
      1980   1985   1990   1995   2000
                  Year

Answers

13. 13°F   14. 88 points
15. a. Increased   b. 4045

a. Find the increase in the number of reported robberies from the year 1985 to 1990.

b. Find the decrease in the number of reported robberies from the year 1995 to 2000.

Solution:

For the purpose of finding an amount of increase or decrease, we will subtract the smaller number from the larger number.

a. Because the number of robberies went *up* from 1985 to 1990, there was an *increase*. To find the amount of the increase, we subtract the smaller number from the larger number.

$$\begin{array}{r} \overset{5\ 13}{6\,3\,9,0\,0\,0} \\ -\ 4\,9\,8,0\,0\,0 \\ \hline 1\,4\,1,0\,0\,0 \end{array}$$

From 1985 to 1990, there was an increase of 141,000 reported robberies in the United States.

b. Because the number of robberies went *down* from 1995 to 2000, there was a *decrease*. To find the amount of the decrease, we subtract the smaller number from the larger number.

$$\begin{array}{r} \overset{7\ 11}{5\,8\,1,0\,0\,0} \\ -\ 4\,0\,8,0\,0\,0 \\ \hline 1\,7\,3,0\,0\,0 \end{array}$$

From 1995 to 2000 there was a decrease of 173,000 reported robberies in the United States.

section 1.3   Practice Exercises

Boost *your* GRADE at mathzone.com!

MathZone

- Practice Problems
- Self-Tests
- NetTutor
- e-Professors
- Videos

Study Skills Exercises

1. It is very important to attend class every day. Math is cumulative in nature, and you must master the material learned in the previous class to understand today's lesson. Because this is so important, many instructors tie attendance into the final grade. Write down the attendance policy for your class.

2. Define the key terms.

   a. Difference   **b. Subtrahend**   **c. Minuend**

Review Exercises

For Exercises 3–5, add.

3. $330 + 821$

4.
$$
\begin{array}{r}
782 \\
21 \\
+\ 1046 \\
\hline
\end{array}
$$

5.
$$
\begin{array}{r}
46 \\
804 \\
+\ 49 \\
\hline
\end{array}
$$

6. Circle the true statement:

$14 > 21, 14 < 21$

7. Circle the true statement:

$0 < 10, 0 > 10$

8. Write the inequality in words:

$22 < 25$

Objective 1: Introduction to Subtraction

For Exercises 9–14, identify the minuend, subtrahend, and the difference.

9. $12 - 8 = 4$

10. $6 - 1 = 5$

11. $21 - 12 = 9$

12. $32 - 2 = 30$

13.
$$
\begin{array}{r}
9 \\
-\ 6 \\
\hline
3
\end{array}
$$

14.
$$
\begin{array}{r}
17 \\
-\ 3 \\
\hline
14
\end{array}
$$

For Exercises 15–18, write the subtraction problem as a related addition problem. For example, $19 - 6 = 13$ can be written as $13 + 6 = 19$.

15. $27 - 9 = 18$

16. $20 - 8 = 12$

17. $102 - 75 = 27$

18. $211 - 45 = 166$

For Exercises 19–24, subtract, then check the answer by using addition. **(See Example 1.)**

19. $8 - 3$ Check: $\boxed{} + 3 = 8$

20. $7 - 2$ Check: $\boxed{} + 2 = 7$

21. $4 - 1$ Check: $\boxed{} + 1 = 4$

22. $9 - 1$ Check: $\boxed{} + 1 = 9$

23. $6 - 0$ Check: $\boxed{} + 0 = 6$

24. $3 - 0$ Check: $\boxed{} + 0 = 3$

Objective 2: Subtraction of Whole Numbers

For Exercises 25–38, subtract and check the answer by using addition. **(See Example 2.)**

25.
$$
\begin{array}{r}
68 \\
-\ 23 \\
\hline
\end{array}
$$

26.
$$
\begin{array}{r}
54 \\
-\ 31 \\
\hline
\end{array}
$$

27.
$$
\begin{array}{r}
88 \\
-\ 27 \\
\hline
\end{array}
$$

28.
$$
\begin{array}{r}
75 \\
-\ 50 \\
\hline
\end{array}
$$

29.
$$
\begin{array}{r}
1347 \\
-\ 221 \\
\hline
\end{array}
$$

30.
$$
\begin{array}{r}
4865 \\
-\ 713 \\
\hline
\end{array}
$$

31.
$$
\begin{array}{r}
1525 \\
-\ 1204 \\
\hline
\end{array}
$$

32.
$$
\begin{array}{r}
8843 \\
-\ 5612 \\
\hline
\end{array}
$$

33. $12,806 - 2802$

34. $12,771 - 1240$

35. $14,356 - 13,253$

36. $34,550 - 31,450$

37. $95,432 - 61,101$

38. $80,529 - 20,117$

For Exercises 39–62, subtract the whole numbers involving borrowing. **(See Example 3.)**

39. 76
     − 59

40. 64
     − 48

41. 87
     − 38

42. 94
     − 75

43. 240
     − 136

44. 360
     − 225

45. 710
     − 189

46. 850
     − 303

47. 4350
     − 4327

48. 7293
     − 7255

49. 6002
     − 1238

50. 3000
     − 2356

51. 10,425
     − 9,122

52. 23,901
     − 8,164

53. 62,088
     − 59,871

54. 32,112
     − 28,334

55. 470 − 92

56. 674 − 89

57. 3709 − 2987

58. 8052 − 2788

59. 32,439 − 1498

60. 21,335 − 4123

61. 8,007,234 − 2,345,115

62. 3,045,567 − 1,871,495

Objective 3: Translations and Applications Involving Subtraction

For Exercises 63–72, translate the English phrase into a mathematical statement and simplify. **(See Example 4.)**

63. 78 minus 23

64. 45 minus 17

65. 78 decreased by 6

66. 50 decreased by 12

67. Subtract 100 from 422.

68. Subtract 42 from 89.

69. 72 less than 1090

70. 60 less than 3111

71. The difference of 50 and 13

72. The difference of 405 and 103

For Exercises 73–76, write an English phrase for the mathematical statement. (Answers will vary.)

73. 93 − 27

74. 80 − 20

75. 165 − 85

76. 171 − 42

77. Use the expression 7 − 4 to explain why subtraction is not commutative.

78. Is subtraction associative? Use the numbers 10, 6, 2 to explain.

79. A $50 bill was used to purchase $17 worth of gasoline. Find the amount of change received. **(See Example 5.)**

80. There are 55 DVDs to shelve one evening at a video rental store. If Jason puts away 39 before leaving for the day, how many are left for Patty to handle?

81. The songwriting team of John Lennon and Paul McCartney had 118 chart hits while Mick Jagger and Keith Richards had 63. How many more chart hits did Lennon and McCartney have than Jagger and Richards?

82. In 2005 it was estimated that the urban population of China was about 536 million people while the urban population of India was about 313 million people. What was the difference in the populations of China and India in 2005?

83. In landscaping a yard, Lily would like 26 plants for a border. If she has 18 plants in her truck, how many more will she need to finish the job?

84. A collection is taken to buy flowers for a co-worker who is in the hospital. If $30 has been collected and the flower arrangement costs $43, how much more needs to be collected?

85. At the time of John Elway's retirement from football, his total passing yardage was 51,475 yd. Brett Favre had 42,285 yd as of 2002. How many more yards would Favre need to reach Elway's total?

86. The musical *Cats* has the record of being the longest-running musical on Broadway with 7485 performances. *The Phantom of the Opera* had performed 6231 times as of January 1, 2003. How many more performances must there be of *Phantom* to equal the record?

For Exercises 87 and 88, for each figure find the missing length.

87. The perimeter of the triangle is 39 m.

88. The perimeter of the figure is 547 cm.

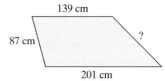

89. A homeowner knows that the perimeter of his backyard is 56 yd. Find the length of the missing side. **(See Example 6.)**

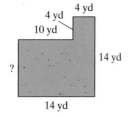

90. Barbara has 15 ft of molding to install in her bathroom, as shown in the figure. What is the missing length? *Note*: There will be no molding by the tub or door.

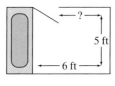

For Exercises 91–94, use the information from the graph on page 33. **(See Example 7.)**

91. What is the difference in the number of marriages for the 20-year period from 1980 to 2000?

92. Of the years presented in the graph, which year had the greatest number of marriages? Which year had the least?

93. What is the difference in the number of marriages between the year having the greatest and the year having the least?

94. Between which two 5-year periods did the greatest increase in the number of marriages occur? What is the increase?

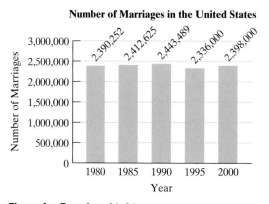

Figure for Exercises 91–94

Calculator Connections

Topic: Subtracting on a calculator

To subtract numbers on a calculator, use the subtraction key $\boxed{-}$. Do not confuse the subtraction key with the $\boxed{(-)}$ key. The $\boxed{(-)}$ is presented later to enter negative numbers.

Expression	Keystrokes	Result
345,899 − 43,018	345899 $\boxed{-}$ 43018 $\boxed{\text{Enter}}$	$\boxed{302881}$

Calculator Exercises

For Exercises 95 and 96, subtract by using a calculator.

95. 4,905,620
   − 458,318

96. 953,400,415
   − 56,341,902

For Exercises 97–100, refer to the table showing the land area for five states.

State	Land Area (mi²)
Rhode Island	1,045
Tennessee	41,217
West Virginia	24,078
Wisconsin	54,310
Colorado	103,718

97. Find the difference in land area between Colorado and Wisconsin.

98. Find the difference in land area between Tennessee and West Virginia.

99. Find the difference in land area between the state with the greatest land area and the state with the least land area.

100. How much more land area does Wisconsin have than Tennessee?

Objectives

1. Rounding
2. Estimation
3. Using Estimation in Applications

section 1.4   Rounding and Estimating

1. Rounding

Rounding a whole number is a common practice when we do not require an exact value. For example, a recent enrollment figure for the College of DuPage in Glyn Ellyn, Illinois, was 29,423 students. We might round this number to the nearest thousand and say that there were approximately 29,000 students. In mathematics we use the symbol ≈ to read "is approximately equal to." Hence 29,423 ≈ 29,000.

A number line is a helpful tool to understand rounding. For example, the number 48 is closer to 50 than it is to 40. Therefore, 48 rounded to the nearest ten is 50.

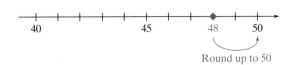

The number 43, on the other hand, is closer to 40 than to 50. Therefore, 43 rounded to the nearest ten is 40.

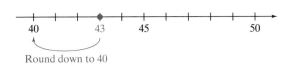

The number 45 is halfway between 40 and 50. In such a case, our convention will be to round *up* to the next-larger ten.

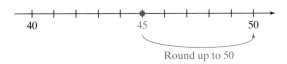

The decision to round up or down to a given place value is determined by the digit to the *right* of the given place value. The following steps outline the procedure.

Rounding Whole Numbers

1. Identify the digit one position to the right of the given place value.

2. If the digit in step 1 is a 5 or greater, add 1 to the digit in the given place value. Then replace each digit to the right of the given place value by 0.

3. If the digit in step 1 is less than 5, replace it and each digit to its right by 0. Note that in this case, the digit in the original given place value does not change.

example 1   Rounding a Whole Number

Round 3741 to the nearest hundred.

Solution:

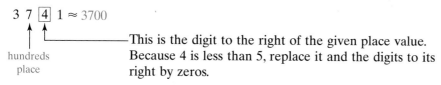

$$3\,7\,\boxed{4}\,1 \approx 3700$$

This is the digit to the right of the given place value. Because 4 is less than 5, replace it and the digits to its right by zeros.

hundreds place

The number 3700 is 3741 rounded to the nearest hundred.

■

Example 1 could also have been solved by drawing a number line. Use the part of a number line showing multiples of 100 on either side of 3741.

3700   3741 3750   3800

Round down to 3700

---

example 2   Rounding a Whole Number

Round 1,790,641 to the nearest hundred-thousand.

Solution:

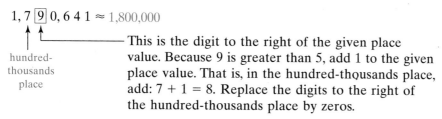

$$1,7\,\boxed{9}\,0,6\,4\,1 \approx 1,800,000$$

This is the digit to the right of the given place value. Because 9 is greater than 5, add 1 to the given place value. That is, in the hundred-thousands place, add: $7 + 1 = 8$. Replace the digits to the right of the hundred-thousands place by zeros.

hundred-thousands place

The number 1,800,000 is 1,790,641 rounded to the nearest hundred-thousand.

■

Skill Practice

4. Round 147,316 to the nearest ten-thousand.

---

example 3   Rounding a Whole Number

Round 1503 to the nearest thousand.

Solution:

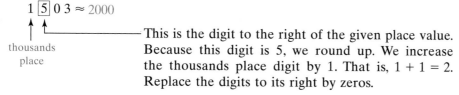

$$1\,\boxed{5}\,0\,3 \approx 2000$$

This is the digit to the right of the given place value. Because this digit is 5, we round up. We increase the thousands place digit by 1. That is, $1 + 1 = 2$. Replace the digits to its right by zeros.

thousands place

The number 2000 is 1503 rounded to the nearest thousand.

■

Skill Practice

5. Round 7,521,460 to the nearest million.

---

example 4   Rounding a Whole Number

Round the number 24,961 to the hundreds place.

Skill Practice

6. Round 39,823 to the nearest thousand.

Answers

4. 150,000   5. 8,000,000   6. 40,000

Solution:

$24,9\boxed{6}1 \approx 25,000$

This value is greater than 5. Therefore, add 1 to the hundreds place digit. Replace the digits to the right of the hundreds place with 0.

$24,\overset{+1}{9}00$ which equals $25,000$

The number 25,000 is 24,961 rounded to the nearest hundred.

2. Estimation

We use the process of rounding to estimate the result of numerical calculations. For example, to estimate the following sum, we can round each addend to the nearest ten.

31	rounds to →	30
12	rounds to →	10
+ 49	rounds to →	+ 50
		90

The estimated sum is 90 (the actual sum is 92).

Skill Practice

7. Estimate the sum by rounding each number to the nearest hundred.

3162 + 4931 + 2206

example 5   Estimating a Sum

Estimate the sum by rounding to the nearest thousand.

$$6109 + 976 + 4842 + 11,619$$

Solution:

6,109	rounds to →	$\overset{1}{6,000}$
976	rounds to →	1,000
4,842	rounds to →	5,000
+ 11,619	rounds to →	+ 12,000
		24,000

The estimated sum is 24,000 (the actual sum is 23,546).

Skill Practice

8. Estimate the difference by rounding each number to the nearest million.

35,264,000 − 21,906,210

example 6   Estimating a Difference

Estimate the difference 4817 − 2106 by rounding each number to the nearest hundred.

Solution:

4817	rounds to →	4800
− 2106	rounds to →	− 2100
		2700

Answers
7. 10,300
8. 13,000,000

The estimated difference is 2700 (the actual difference is 2711).

3. Using Estimation in Applications

example 7	Estimating a Sum in an Application

A driver for a delivery service must drive from Chicago, Illinois, to Dallas, Texas, and make several stops on the way. The driver follows the route given on the map. Estimate the total mileage by rounding each distance to the nearest ten miles.

Solution:

541	rounds to $\longrightarrow$	$\overset{1\,1}{540}$
418	rounds to $\longrightarrow$	420
344	rounds to $\longrightarrow$	340
+ 205	rounds to $\longrightarrow$	+ 210
		1510

The driver traveled approximately 1510 mi.

example 8	Estimating a Difference in an Application

In a recent year, the U.S. Census Bureau reported that the number of males over the age of 18 was 100,994,367. The same year, the number of females over 18 was 108,133,727. Round each value to the nearest million. Estimate how many more females over 18 there were than males over 18.

Solution:

The number of males was approximately 101,000,000. The number of females was approximately 108,000,000.

$$\begin{array}{r} 108,000,000 \\ - \ 101,000,000 \\ \hline 7,000,000 \end{array}$$

There were approximately 7 million more women over age 18 in the United States than men.

section 1.4   Practice Exercises

Study Skills Exercises

1. Purchase a three-ring binder for your math notes and homework. Use section dividers to separate each chapter that you cover in the text. Keep your homework and notes in the appropriate section. What other course materials might you keep organized in your notebook?

2. Define the key term **rounding**.

Review Exercises

For Exercises 3–5, add or subtract as indicated.

3.   59   4.   130   5.   4009   6.   12,033
    − 33   − 98   + 998   + 23,441

7. Determine the place value of the digit 6 in the number 1,860,432.

8. Determine the place value of the digit 4 in the number 1,860,432.

Objective 1: Rounding

9. Explain how to round a whole number to the hundreds place.

10. Explain how to round a whole number to the tens place.

For Exercises 11–32, round each number to the given place value. **(See Examples 1–4.)**

11. 342; tens   12. 834; tens   13. 725; tens

14. 445; tens   15. 9384; hundreds   16. 8363; hundreds

17. 8539; hundreds   18. 9817; hundreds   19. 9982; hundreds

20. 7974; hundreds   21. 2578; thousands   22. 3511; thousands

23. 34,992; thousands   24. 76,831; thousands   25. 109,337; thousands

26. 437,208; thousands   **27.** 489,090; ten-thousands   **28.** 388,725; ten-thousands

29. In the first five months after its release, the movie *Harry Potter and the Sorcerer's Stone* grossed $317,093,502. Round this number to the millions place.

30. The year 1999 saw the highest number of computer viruses. There were 26,193. Round this number to the nearest thousand.

31. The largest English dictionary contains 21,543 words. Round this number to the thousands place.

32. A shopping center in Edmonton, Alberta, Canada, covers an area of 492,000 square meters (m^2). Round this number to the hundred-thousands place.

Objective 2: Estimation

For Exercises 33–36, estimate the sum by first rounding each number to the nearest ten. **(See Example 5.)**

33.	**34.**	**35.**	**36.**
57	33	41	29
82	78	12	73
+ 21	+ 41	+ 129	+ 113

For Exercises 37–40, estimate the difference by first rounding each number to the nearest hundred. **(See Example 6.)**

37.	**38.**	**39.**	**40.**
898	731	412	771
− 422	− 584	− 252	− 544

Objective 3: Using Estimation in Applications

41. The number of women in the 40–44 age group who gave birth in 1981 is 23,326. By 2001 this number increased to 92,813. Round each value to the nearest thousand to estimate how many more women in the 40–44 age group gave birth in 2001.

42. The number of women in the 45–49 age group who gave birth in 1981 is 1190. By 2001 this number increased to 4844. Round each value to the nearest thousand to estimate how many more women in the 45–49 age group gave birth in 2001.

43. The table shows the sales of the top five candy bars for the year 2001.

Brand	Manufacturer	Sales ($)
M&Ms	Mars	97,404,576
Hershey's Milk Chocolate	Hershey Chocolate	81,296,784
Reese's Peanut Butter Cups	Hershey Chocolate	54,391,268
Snickers	Mars	53,695,428
KitKat	Hershey Chocolate	38,168,580

Round the sales to the nearest million to estimate the total sales brought in by the Mars company. **(See Example 7.)**

44. Refer to the chart in Exercise 43. Round the sales to the nearest million to estimate the total sales brought in by the Hershey Chocolate Company.

For Exercises 45–48, use the given table.

45. Round the revenue to the nearest hundred-thousand to estimate the total revenue for the years 1996 through 1999.

46. Round the revenue to the nearest hundred-thousand to estimate the total revenue for the years 2000 through 2003.

47. a. Determine the year with the greatest revenue. Round this revenue to the nearest hundred-thousand.

    b. Determine the year with the least revenue. Round this revenue to the nearest hundred-thousand.

Beach Parking Revenue for Daytona Beach, Florida	
Year	**Revenue**
1994	$3,603,462
1995	3,152,743
1996	3,499,468
1997	3,257,846
1998	3,235,061
1999	3,514,777
2000	3,316,897
2001	3,272,028
2002	3,360,289
2003	3,470,295

Table for Exercises 45–48

48. Estimate the difference between the year with the greatest revenue and the year with the least revenue.

For Exercises 49–52, use the graph provided.

49. Determine the state with the greatest number of students enrolled in grades 6–12. Round this number to the nearest thousand.

50. Determine the state with the least number of students enrolled in grades 6–12. Round this number to the nearest thousand.

51. Use the information in Exercises 49 and 50 to estimate the difference between the number of students in the state with the highest enrollment and that of the lowest enrollment.
(See Example 8.)

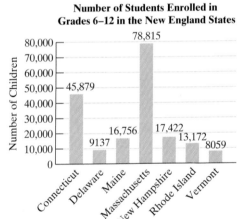

Number of Students Enrolled in Grades 6–12 in the New England States

52. Estimate the total number of students enrolled in grades 6–12 in the New England states by first rounding the number of students to the thousands place.

Figure for Exercises 49–52

53. If you were to estimate the following sum, what place value would you round to and why?

$$389,220 + 2988 + 12,824 + 101,333$$

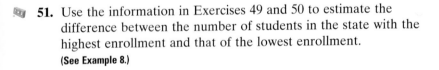

54. Identify the place value that you would round to when estimating the answer to the following problem. Then round the values and estimate the answer.

$$4208 - 932 + 1294$$

Expanding Your Skills

For Exercises 55–58, round the numbers to estimate the perimeter of each figure. (Answers may vary.)

55.

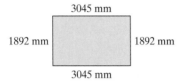

3045 mm

1892 mm   1892 mm

3045 mm

56.

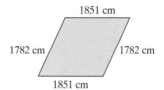

1851 cm

1782 cm   1782 cm

1851 cm

57.

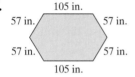

105 in.

57 in.   57 in.

57 in.   57 in.

105 in.

58.

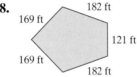

182 ft

169 ft

121 ft

169 ft

182 ft

---

chapter 1 | midchapter review

For Exercises 1–4, add or subtract.

1. $35 + 998$

2. $6723 - 3342$

3. $590 - 489$

4. $9110 + 432$

For Exercises 5–8, determine the place value for the underlined digit.

5. 2\underline{3},981

6. 87\underline{3}9

7. \underline{7}83,870

8. 3,\underline{3}24,921

For Exercises 9–10, estimate the answer by rounding as indicated.

9. $23,981 - 8739$; thousands

10. $783,870 + 3,324,921$; hundred-thousands

For Exercises 11–14, use your knowledge of adding and subtracting to find the number.

11. Find a number that when decreased by 23 yields 245.

12. Find a number that when increased by 23 yields 245.

13. Find a number that when increased by 51 yields 72.

14. Find a number that when decreased by 51 yields 72.

section 1.5   # Multiplication of Whole Numbers

1. Introduction to Multiplication

Suppose that Carmen buys three cartons of eggs to prepare a large family brunch. If there are 12 eggs per carton, then the total number of eggs can be found by adding three 12s.

$$\begin{array}{r} 12 \text{ eggs} \\ 12 \text{ eggs} \\ +\ 12 \text{ eggs} \\ \hline 36 \text{ eggs} \end{array}$$

When each addend in a sum is the same, we have what is called *repeated* addition. Repeated addition is also called **multiplication**. We use the multiplication sign $\times$ to express repeated addition more concisely.

$$12 + 12 + 12 \quad \text{is equal to} \quad 3 \times 12$$

The expression 3×12 is read "3 times 12" to signify that the number 12 is added 3 times. The numbers 3 and 12 are called **factors**, and the number 36 is called the **product**.

The symbol $\cdot$ may also be used to denote multiplication such as in the expression $3 \cdot 12 = 36$. Two factors written adjacent to each other with no other operator between them also implies multiplication. The quantity $2y$, for example, is understood to be 2 times y. If we use this notation to multiply two numbers, parentheses are used to group one or both factors. For example,

$$3(12) = 36 \qquad (3)12 = 36 \qquad \text{and} \qquad (3)(12) = 36$$

all represent the product of 3 and 12.

> **Tip:** In the expression $3(12)$, the parentheses are necessary because two adjacent factors written together with no grouping symbol would look like the number 312.

The products of one-digit numbers such as $4 \times 5 = 20$ and $2 \times 7 = 14$ are basic facts. All products of one-digit numbers should be memorized (see Exercise 6).

example 1   ### Identifying Factors and Products

Identify the factors and the product.

a. $6 \times 3 = 18$ **b.** $5 \times 2 \times 7 = 70$

Solution:

a. Factors: 6, 3; product: 18   **b.** Factors: 5, 2, 7; product: 70

2. Properties of Multiplication

Recall from Section 1.2 that the order in which two numbers are added does not affect the sum. The same is true for multiplication. This is stated formally as the *commutative property of multiplication*.

Commutative Property of Multiplication

Changing the order of two factors does not affect the product.

Example: 2×5 is equivalent to 5×2

The following rectangular arrays help us visualize the commutative property of multiplication.

$2 \times 5 = 10$ 2 rows of 5

$5 \times 2 = 10$ 5 rows of 2

Multiplication is also an associative operation.

Associative Property of Multiplication

The manner in which factors are grouped under multiplication does not affect the product.

Example: $(3 \times 5) \times 2$ is equivalent to $3 \times (5 \times 2)$

example 2   Applying Properties of Multiplication

a. Rewrite the expression 3×9, using the commutative property of multiplication. Then find the product.

b. Rewrite the expression $(4 \times 2) \times 3$, using the associative property of multiplication. Then find the product.

Solution:

a. $3 \times 9 = 9 \times 3$. The product is 27.

b. $(4 \times 2) \times 3 = 4 \times (2 \times 3)$.

To find the product, we have

$$4 \times (2 \times 3)$$
$$= 4 \times (6)$$
$$= 24$$

The product is 24.

Two other important properties of multiplication involve factors of 0 and factors of 1.

Skill Practice

5. Rewrite the expression 6×5, using the commutative property of multiplication. Then find the product.

6. Rewrite the expression $3 \times (1 \times 7)$, using the associative property of multiplication. Then find the product.

Answers

5. 5×6; product is 30
6. $(3 \times 1) \times 7$; product is 21

Multiplication Property of 0

The product of any number and 0 is 0.

Examples:
$$5 \times 0 = 0$$
$$0 \times 12 = 0$$

The product $5 \times 0 = 0$ can easily be understood by writing the product as repeated addition.

$$\underbrace{0 + 0 + 0 + 0 + 0}_{\text{add 0 five times}} = 0$$

Multiplication Property of 1

The product of any number and 1 is that number.

Examples:
$$1 \times 4 = 4$$
$$3 \times 1 = 3$$

These examples can be understood by considering rectangular arrays.

$$1 \times 4 = 4 \quad \text{one row of 4}$$
$$3 \times 1 = 3 \quad \text{three rows of 1}$$

The last property of multiplication involves both addition and multiplication. First consider the expression $2(4 + 3)$. By performing the operation within parentheses first, we have

$$2(4 + 3) = 2(7) = 14$$

We get the same result by multiplying 2 times each addend within the parentheses:

$$2(4 + 3) = (2 \times 4) + (2 \times 3) = 8 + 6 = 14$$

This result illustrates the **distributive property of multiplication over addition** (sometimes we simply say *distributive property* for short).

Skill Practice

Apply the distributive property and simplify.

7. $2(6 + 4)$

8. $5(0 + 8)$

 example 3   Applying the Distributive Property of Multiplication Over Addition

Apply the distributive property and simplify.

a. $3(4 + 8)$ **b.** $7(3 + 0)$

Solution:

a. $3(4 + 8) = (3 \times 4) + (3 \times 8) = 12 + 24 = 36$

b. $7(3 + 0) = (7 \times 3) + (7 \times 0) = 21 + 0 = 21$

Answers

7. $(2 \times 6) + (2 \times 4)$; 20
8. $(5 \times 0) + (5 \times 8)$; 40

3. Multiplying Many-Digit Whole Numbers

When multiplying numbers with several digits, it is sometimes necessary to carry. To see why, consider the product 3×29. By writing the factors in expanded form, we can apply the distributive property. In this way we see that 3 is multiplied by both 20 and 9.

$$3 \times 29 = 3(20 + 9) = (3 \times 20) + (3 \times 9)$$
$$= 60 + 27$$
$$= 6 \text{ tens} + 2 \text{ tens} + 7 \text{ ones}$$
$$= 8 \text{ tens} + 7 \text{ ones}$$
$$= 87$$

Now we will multiply 29×3 in vertical form.

$$\begin{array}{r} \overset{2}{2}\,9 \\ \times \quad 3 \\ \hline 7 \end{array}$$

Multiply $3 \times 9 = 27$. Write the 7 in the ones column and carry the 2.

$$\begin{array}{r} \overset{2}{2}\,9 \\ \times \quad 3 \\ \hline 8\,7 \end{array}$$

Multiply 3×2 tens $= 6$ tens. Add the carry: 6 tens + 2 tens = 8 tens. Write the 8 in the tens place.

---

example 4	Multiplying a Many-Digit Number by a One-Digit Number

Multiply.

$$\begin{array}{r} 368 \\ \times \quad 5 \\ \hline \end{array}$$

Solution:

Using the distributive property, we have

$$5(300 + 60 + 8) = 1500 + 300 + 40 = 1840$$

This can be written vertically as:

$$\begin{array}{r} 368 \\ \times \quad 5 \\ \hline 40 \\ 300 \\ + \ 1500 \\ \hline 1840 \end{array}$$

Multiply 5×8.
Multiply 5×60.
Multiply 5×300.
Add.

The numbers 40, 300, and 1500 are called *partial sums*. The product of 386 and 5 is found by adding the partial sums. The product is 1840.

The solution to Example 4 can also be found by using a shorter form of multiplication. We outline the procedure:

$$\begin{array}{r} \overset{4}{3}68 \\ \times \quad 5 \\ \hline 0 \end{array}$$

Multiply $5 \times 8 = 40$. Write the 0 in the ones place and carry the 4.

Answer

9. 741

$$\begin{array}{r} {\scriptstyle 3\,4} \\ 368 \\ \times \quad 5 \\ \hline 40 \end{array}$$

Multiply 5×6 tens = 300. Add the carry. $300 + 4$ tens = 340. Write the 4 in the tens place and carry the 3.

$$\begin{array}{r} {\scriptstyle 3\,4} \\ 368 \\ \times \quad 5 \\ \hline 1840 \end{array}$$

Multiply 5×3 hundreds = 1500. Add the carry. $1500 + 3$ hundreds = 1800. Write the 8 in the hundreds place and the 1 in the thousands place.

The next example demonstrates the process to multiply two factors with many digits.

<table>
<tr><td>

Skill Practice

10. Multiply.

$$\begin{array}{r} 59 \\ \times\ 26 \end{array}$$

</td></tr>
</table>

example 5   Multiplying a Many-Digit Number by a Many-Digit Number

Multiply:

$$\begin{array}{r} 72 \\ \times\ 83 \end{array}$$

Solution:

Writing the problem vertically and computing the partial sums, we have

$$\begin{array}{r} 72 \\ \times\ 83 \\ \hline 216 \\ +\ 5760 \\ \hline 5976 \end{array}$$

Multiply 3×72.
Multiply 80×72.
Add.

The product is 5976.

The procedure to use the short form of multiplication is as follows.

Step 1:

$$\begin{array}{r} 72 \\ \times\ 83 \\ \hline 216 \end{array}$$

Multiply 3×2. Write the product, 6, in the ones column.
Multiply 3×7 tens = 210. Write the 1 in the tens column. Write the 2 in the hundreds column.

Step 2:

$$\begin{array}{r} {\scriptstyle 1} \\ 72 \\ \times\ 83 \\ \hline 216 \\ 5760 \end{array}$$

Multiply 8 tens $\times$ 2 = 160. Write the 0 in the ones column and the 6 in the tens column. Carry the 1.
Multiply 8 tens $\times$ 7 tens = 5600.
Add the carry: $5600 + 1$ hundred = 5700.
Write the 7 in the hundreds place. Write the 5 in the thousands place.

Step 3:

$$\begin{array}{r} {\scriptstyle 1} \\ 72 \\ \times\ 83 \\ \hline 216 \\ +\ 5760 \\ \hline 5976 \end{array}$$

Add.

Answer

10. 1534

example 6 Multiplying Two Multidigit Whole Numbers

Use the short-form procedure to compute 368×497.

Solution:

$$
\begin{array}{r}
{\scriptstyle 2\,3} \\
{\scriptstyle 6\,7} \\
{\scriptstyle 4\,5} \\
368 \\
\times\ 497 \\
\hline
2576 \\
33120 \\
+\ 147200 \\
\hline
182{,}896
\end{array}
$$

4. Estimating Products by Rounding

A special pattern occurs when one or more factors in a product ends in zero. Consider the following products:

$12 \times 20 = 240$		$120 \times 20 = 2400$
$12 \times 200 = 2400$		$1200 \times 20 = 24{,}000$
$12 \times 2000 = 24{,}000$		$12{,}000 \times 20 = 240{,}000$

Notice in each case the product is $12 \times 2 = 24$ followed by the total number of zeros from each factor. Consider the product 1200×20.

$$
\begin{array}{r}
12\,|\,00 \\
\times\ \ 2\,|\,0 \\
\hline
24\,|\,000
\end{array}
$$

Shift the numbers 1200 and 20 so that the zeros appear to the right of the multiplication process. Multiply $12 \times 2 = 24$.
Write the product 24 followed by the total number of zeros from each factor.

example 7 Estimating a Product

Estimate the product 795×4060 by rounding 795 to the nearest hundred and 4060 to the nearest thousand.

Solution:

795	rounds to $\longrightarrow$	800	$8\,|\,00$
4060	rounds to $\longrightarrow$	4000	$\times\ \ 4\,|\,000$
			$\overline{32\,|\,00000}$

The product is approximately 3,200,000.

example 8 Estimating a Product in an Application

For a trip from Atlanta to Los Angeles, the average cost of a plane ticket was $495. If the plane carried 218 passengers, estimate the total revenue for the airline. (*Hint*: Round each number to the hundreds place and find the product.)

Solution:

$495   rounds to ⟶ $ 5 | 00
218   rounds to ⟶   × 2 | 00
                            $10 | 0000

The airline received approximately $100,000 in revenue.

5. Translations and Applications Involving Multiplication

In English there are many different words that imply multiplication. A partial list is given in Table 1-3.

table 1-3		
Word/Phrase	**Example**	**In Symbols**
Product	The product of 4 and 7	4×7
Times	8 times 4	8×4
Multiply … by…	Multiply 6 by 3	6×3

Multiplication may also be warranted in applications involving unit rates. In Example 8, we multiplied the cost per customer ($495) by the number of customers (218). The value $495 is a unit rate because it gives the cost per one customer (per one unit).

example 9   Solving an Application Involving Multiplication

The average weekly income for production workers is $489. How much does a production worker make in 1 year (assume 52 weeks in 1 year).

Solution:

The value $489 per week is a unit rate. The total earnings for 1 year are given by $489 × 52.

$$\begin{array}{r} {\scriptstyle 4\,4} \\ {\scriptstyle 1\,1} \\ 489 \\ \times\ 52 \\ \hline 978 \\ +\ 24450 \\ \hline 25428 \end{array}$$

The yearly earnings are $25,428.

Tip: This product can be estimated quickly by rounding the factors.

489   rounds to ⟶   5 | 00
52   rounds to ⟶   × 5 | 0
                          25 | 000

The total yearly income is approximately $25,000. Estimating gives a quick approximation of a product. Furthermore, it also checks for the reasonableness of our exact product. In this case $25,000 is close to our exact value of $25,428.

6. Area of a Rectangle

Another application of multiplication of whole numbers lies in finding the area of a region. **Area** measures the amount of surface contained within the region. For example, a square that is 1 in. by 1 in. occupies an area of 1 square inch, denoted as 1 in.^{2}. Similarly, a square that is 1 centimeter (cm) by 1 cm occupies an area of 1 square centimeter. This is denoted by 1 cm^2.

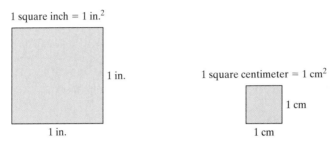

1 square inch = 1 in.^{2}

1 in.

1 in.

1 square centimeter = 1 cm^2

1 cm

1 cm

The units of square inches and square centimeters (in.^{2} and cm^2) are called *square units*. For larger regions, we measure the number of square units occupied in that region. For example, the region in Figure 1-6 occupies 6 cm^2.

Area = 6 cm^2

2 cm

— 3 cm —

Figure 1-6

The 3-cm by 2-cm region in Figure 1-6 suggests that to find the **area of a rectangle**, multiply the length by the width. If the area is represented by A, the length is represented by l, and the width is represented by w, then we have

$$\text{Area of rectangle} = (\text{length}) \times (\text{width})$$

$$A = l \times w$$

The letters A, l, and w are called **variables** because their values *vary* as they are replaced by different numbers.

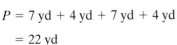 **example 10**   Finding the Area of a Rectangle

Find the area and perimeter of the rectangle.

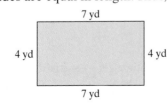

4 yd

7 yd

Solution:

Area:

$A = l \times w$

$A = (7 \text{ yd}) \times (4 \text{ yd})$

$\quad = 28 \text{ yd}^2$

Recall from Section 1.2 that the perimeter of a polygon is the sum of the lengths of the sides. In a rectangle the opposite sides are equal in length. Thus,

Perimeter:

$P = 7 \text{ yd} + 4 \text{ yd} + 7 \text{ yd} + 4 \text{ yd}$

$\quad = 22 \text{ yd}$

7 yd

4 yd   4 yd

7 yd

The area is 28 yd^2 and the perimeter is 22 yd.

Skill Practice

16. Find the area and perimeter of the rectangle.

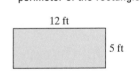

12 ft

5 ft

Avoiding Mistakes: Notice that area is measured in square units (such as yd^2) and perimeter is measured in units of length (such as yd). It is important to apply the correct units of measurement.

Answer

16. Area: 60 ft^2; perimeter: 34 ft

Skill Practice

17. A house sits on a rectangular lot that is 154 ft by 86 ft. Find the area of the lot.

---

example 11   Finding Area in an Application

The state of Wyoming is approximately the shape of a rectangle (Figure 1-7). Its length is 355 mi and its width is 276 mi. Approximate the total area of Wyoming by rounding the length and width to the nearest ten.

Figure 1-7

Solution:

$$
\begin{array}{rcl}
355 & \text{rounds to} \longrightarrow & \overset{\overset{1}{4}}{36}\,\big|\,0 \\
276 & \text{rounds to} \longrightarrow & \times\,28\,\big|\,0 \\
\hline
 & & 288 \\
 & & 720 \\
\hline
 & & 1008\,\big|\,00
\end{array}
$$

The area of Wyoming is approximately 100,800 mi².

Answer

17. 13,244 ft²

section 1.5   Practice Exercises

Boost *your* GRADE at mathzone.com!

- Practice Problems
- Self-Tests
- NetTutor
- e-Professors
- Videos

Study Tips

1. List the materials that you need to bring to class every day (for example, paper, pencil, etc.).

2. Define the key terms.

    a. Multiplication   **b. Factor**   **c. Product**

    d. Distributive property of multiplication over addition

    e. Area   **f. Area of a rectangle**   **g. Variable**

Review Exercises

For Exercises 3–5, estimate the answer by rounding to the indicated place value.

3. $869{,}240 + 34{,}921 + 108{,}332$; ten-thousands

4. $907{,}801 - 413{,}560$; hundred-thousands

5. $8821 - 3401$; hundreds

Objective 1: Introduction to Multiplication

6. Fill out the chart of multiplication facts.

×	0	1	2	3	4	5	6	7	8	9
0										
1										
2										
3										
4										
5										
6										
7										
8										
9										

For Exercises 7–10, write the repeated addition as multiplication and simplify.

7. $5 + 5 + 5 + 5 + 5 + 5$

8. $2 + 2 + 2 + 2 + 2 + 2 + 2 + 2 + 2$

9. $9 + 9 + 9$

10. $7 + 7 + 7 + 7$

For Exercises 11–16, identify the factors and the product. **(See Example 1.)**

11. $6 \times 4 = 24$

12. $5 \times 8 = 40$

13. $13 \times 42 = 546$

14. $26 \times 9 = 234$

15. $3 \cdot 5 \cdot 2 = 30$

16. $4 \cdot 1 \cdot 8 = 32$

17. Write the product of 5 and 12, using three different notations. (Answers may vary.)

18. Write the product of 23 and 14, using three different notations. (Answers may vary.)

Objective 2: Properties of Multiplication

For Exercises 19–24, match the property with the expression.

19. $8 \times 1 = 8$

a. Commutative property of multiplication

20. $6 \cdot 13 = 13 \cdot 6$

b. Associative property of multiplication

21. $2(6 + 12) = 2 \cdot 6 + 2 \cdot 12$

c. Multiplication property of 0

22. $5 \cdot (3 \cdot 2) = (5 \cdot 3) \cdot 2$

d. Multiplication property of 1

23. $0 \times 4 = 0$

e. Distributive property of multiplication over addition

24. $7(14) = 14(7)$

For Exercises 25–30, rewrite the expression, using the indicated property. **(See Examples 2–3.)**

25. 14×8; commutative property of multiplication   **26.** 3×9; commutative property of multiplication

27. $6 \times (2 \times 10)$; associative property of multiplication   **28.** $(4 \times 15) \times 5$; associative property of multiplication

29. $5(7 + 4)$; distributive property of multiplication over addition

30. $3(2 + 6)$; distributive property of multiplication over addition

Objective 3: Multiplying Many-Digit Whole Numbers

For Exercises 31–60, multiply. **(See Examples 4–6.)**

31. $\begin{array}{r} 24 \\ \times\ 6 \\ \hline \end{array}$ **32.** $\begin{array}{r} 18 \\ \times\ 5 \\ \hline \end{array}$ **33.** $\begin{array}{r} 26 \\ \times\ 2 \\ \hline \end{array}$ **34.** $\begin{array}{r} 71 \\ \times\ 3 \\ \hline \end{array}$

35. $\begin{array}{r} 131 \\ \times\ 5 \\ \hline \end{array}$ **36.** $\begin{array}{r} 720 \\ \times\ 3 \\ \hline \end{array}$ **37.** $\begin{array}{r} 344 \\ \times\ 4 \\ \hline \end{array}$ **38.** $\begin{array}{r} 105 \\ \times\ 9 \\ \hline \end{array}$

39. $\begin{array}{r} 1410 \\ \times\ 8 \\ \hline \end{array}$ **40.** $\begin{array}{r} 2016 \\ \times\ 6 \\ \hline \end{array}$ **41.** $\begin{array}{r} 3312 \\ \times\ 7 \\ \hline \end{array}$ **42.** $\begin{array}{r} 4801 \\ \times\ 5 \\ \hline \end{array}$

43. $\begin{array}{r} 42{,}014 \\ \times\ 9 \\ \hline \end{array}$ **44.** $\begin{array}{r} 51{,}006 \\ \times\ 8 \\ \hline \end{array}$ **45.** $\begin{array}{r} 32 \\ \times\ 14 \\ \hline \end{array}$ **46.** $\begin{array}{r} 41 \\ \times\ 21 \\ \hline \end{array}$

47. $68 \cdot 24$

48. $55 \cdot 41$

49. $72 \cdot 12$

50. $13 \cdot 46$

51. $(143)(17)$

52. $(722)(28)$

53. $(349)(19)$

54. $(512)(31)$

55. $\begin{array}{r} 151 \\ \times\ 127 \\ \hline \end{array}$

56. $\begin{array}{r} 703 \\ \times\ 146 \\ \hline \end{array}$

57. $\begin{array}{r} 222 \\ \times\ 841 \\ \hline \end{array}$

58. $\begin{array}{r} 387 \\ \times\ 506 \\ \hline \end{array}$

59. $\begin{array}{r} 3532 \\ \times\ 6014 \\ \hline \end{array}$

60. $\begin{array}{r} 2810 \\ \times\ 1039 \\ \hline \end{array}$

Objective 4: Estimating Products by Rounding

For Exercises 61–68, multiply the numbers, using the method found on page 47. **(See Example 7.)**

61. $\begin{array}{r} 600 \\ \times\ 40 \\ \hline \end{array}$

62. $\begin{array}{r} 900 \\ \times\ 50 \\ \hline \end{array}$

63. $\begin{array}{r} 3000 \\ \times\ 700 \\ \hline \end{array}$

64. $\begin{array}{r} 4000 \\ \times\ 400 \\ \hline \end{array}$

65. $\begin{array}{r} 8000 \\ \times\ 9000 \\ \hline \end{array}$

66. $\begin{array}{r} 1000 \\ \times\ 2000 \\ \hline \end{array}$

67. $\begin{array}{r} 90,000 \\ \times\ 400 \\ \hline \end{array}$

68. $\begin{array}{r} 50,000 \\ \times\ 6000 \\ \hline \end{array}$

For Exercises 69–72, estimate the product by first rounding the number to the indicated place value.

69. $11,784 \times 5201$; thousands place

70. $45,046 \times 7812$; thousands place

71. $82,941 \times 29,740$; ten-thousands place

72. $630,229 \times 71,907$; ten-thousands place

73. Suppose a hotel room costs $189 per night. Round this number to the nearest hundred to estimate the cost for a five-night stay. **(See Example 8.)**

74. The science department of Comstock High School must purchase a set of calculators for a class. If the cost of one calculator is $129, estimate the cost of 28 calculators by rounding the numbers to the nearest tens place.

75. The average price for a ticket to see U2 during their 2001 Elevation tour was $78 (rounded). If a concert stadium seats 10,256 fans, estimate the amount of money made during that performance by rounding the number of seats to the nearest ten-thousand.

76. A breakfast buffet at a local restaurant serves 48 people. Estimate the maximum revenue for one week (7 days) if the price of a breakfast is $12.

Objective 5: Translation and Applications Involving Multiplication

77. If it takes 15 pounds (lb) of grapes to make 1 gallon (gal) of red wine, how many pounds of grapes would be needed for 25 gal? **(See Example 9.)**

78. Dustin's monthly homeowner's association dues are $82. How much will he pay the association in 1 year (12 months)?

79. It costs about $45 for a cat to have a medical exam. If a humane society has 37 cats, find the cost of medical exams for their cats.

80. A can of Coke contains 12 fluid ounces (fl oz). Find the number of ounces in a case of Coke containing 12 cans.

81. PaperWorld shipped 115 cases of copy paper to a business. There are 5 reams of paper in each case and 500 sheets of paper in each ream. Find the number of sheets of paper delivered to the business.

82. A dietary supplement bar has 14 grams (g) of protein. If Kathleen eats 2 bars a day for 6 days, how many grams of protein will she get from this supplement?

83. Tylee's car gets 31 miles per gallon (mpg) on the highway. How many miles can he travel if he has a full tank of gas (12 gal)?

84. Sherica manages a small business called Pizza Express. She has 23 employees who work an average of 32 hours (hr) per week. How many hours of work does Sherica have to schedule each week?

Objective 6: Area of a Rectangle

For Exercises 85–88, find the area of the rectangle. **(See Example 10.)**

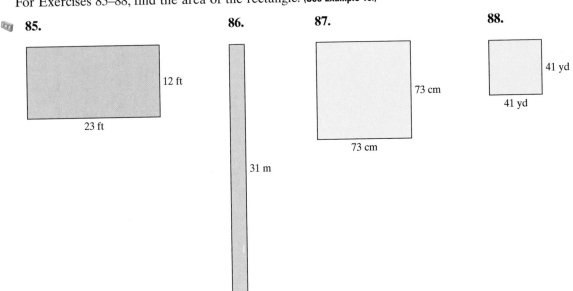

85.
12 ft
23 ft

86.
31 m
2 m

87.
73 cm
73 cm

88.
41 yd
41 yd

89. Mr. Beckwith wants to paint his garage door that is 8 ft by 16 ft. To decide how much paint to buy, he must find the area of the door. What is the area of the door? **(See Example 11.)**

90. Mrs. Patel must have her driveway pressure-cleaned. The cost of the job depends on the area of the driveway. Find the area of the driveway given that it is a rectangle with a length of 80 ft and a width of 12 ft.

91. The front of a building has windows that are 44 in. by 58 in.

    a. Find the area of one window.

    b. If the building has 3 floors and each floor has 14 windows, how many windows are there?

    c. What is the total area of all the windows?

92. A Monopoly game board is 19 in. by 19 in. Find the area of the game board.

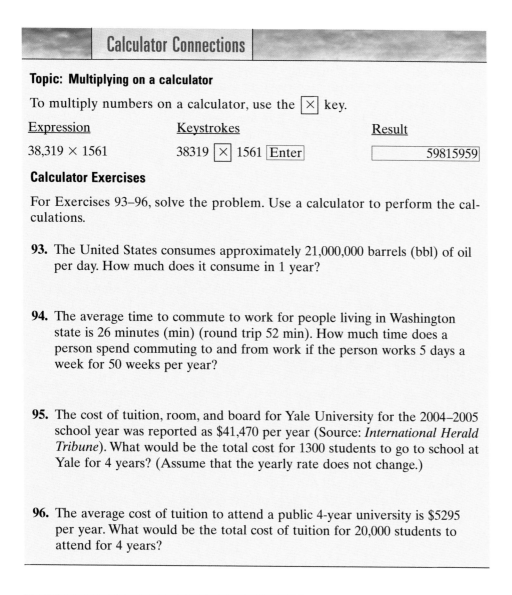

Calculator Connections

Topic: Multiplying on a calculator

To multiply numbers on a calculator, use the ☒ key.

Expression	Keystrokes	Result
38,319 × 1561	38319 ☒ 1561 Enter	59815959

Calculator Exercises

For Exercises 93–96, solve the problem. Use a calculator to perform the calculations.

93. The United States consumes approximately 21,000,000 barrels (bbl) of oil per day. How much does it consume in 1 year?

94. The average time to commute to work for people living in Washington state is 26 minutes (min) (round trip 52 min). How much time does a person spend commuting to and from work if the person works 5 days a week for 50 weeks per year?

95. The cost of tuition, room, and board for Yale University for the 2004–2005 school year was reported as $41,470 per year (Source: *International Herald Tribune*). What would be the total cost for 1300 students to go to school at Yale for 4 years? (Assume that the yearly rate does not change.)

96. The average cost of tuition to attend a public 4-year university is $5295 per year. What would be the total cost of tuition for 20,000 students to attend for 4 years?

section 1.6   Division of Whole Numbers

1. Introduction to Division

Suppose 12 pieces of pizza are to be divided evenly among 4 children (Figure 1-8). The number of pieces that each child would receive is given by $12 \div 4$, read "12 divided by 4."

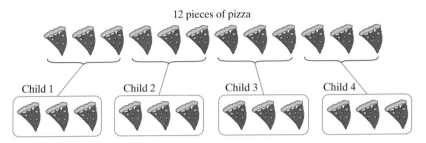

12 pieces of pizza

Child 1   Child 2   Child 3   Child 4

Figure 1-8

The process of separating 12 pieces of pizza among 4 children is called **division**. The statement $12 \div 4 = 3$ indicates that each child receives 3 pieces of pizza. The number 12 is called the **dividend**. It represents the number to be divided. The number 4 is called the **divisor**, and it represents the number of groups. The result of the division (in this case 3) is called the **quotient**. It represents the number of items in each group.

Division may be represented in several ways. For example, the following are all equivalent statements.

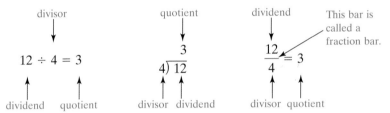

Recall that subtraction is the reverse operation of addition. In the same way, division is the reverse operation of multiplication. For example, we say $12 \div 4 = 3$ because $3 \times 4 = 12$.

example 1   Identifying the Dividend, Divisor, and Quotient

Simplify each expression. Then identify the dividend, divisor, and quotient.

a. $48 \div 6$ **b.** $9\overline{)36}$ **c.** $\dfrac{63}{7}$

Solution:

a. $48 \div 6 = 8$ because $8 \times 6 = 48$
The dividend is 48, the divisor is 6, and the quotient is 8.

b. $9\overline{)36}^{\;4}$ because $4 \times 9 = 36$

The dividend is 36, the divisor is 9, and the quotient is 4.

c. $\dfrac{63}{7} = 9$ because $9 \times 7 = 63$

The dividend is 63, the divisor is 7, and the quotient is 9.

2. Properties of Division

Example 2 illustrates some of the interesting properties of division.

example 2	Dividing Whole Numbers

Divide.

a. $8 \div 8$ **b.** $\dfrac{6}{6}$ **c.** $5 \div 1$

d. $1\overline{)7}$ **e.** $0 \div 6$ **f.** $\dfrac{0}{4}$

Solution:

a. $8 \div 8 = 1$ because $1 \times 8 = 8$

b. $\dfrac{6}{6} = 1$ because $1 \times 6 = 6$

c. $5 \div 1 = 5$ because $5 \times 1 = 5$

d. $\overset{7}{1\overline{)7}}$ because $7 \times 1 = 7$

e. $0 \div 6 = 0$ because $0 \times 6 = 0$

f. $\dfrac{0}{4} = 0$ because $0 \times 4 = 0$

Skill Practice

Divide.

4. $3\overline{)3}$ **5.** $5 \div 5$

6. $\dfrac{4}{1}$ **7.** $8 \div 1$

8. $\dfrac{0}{7}$ **9.** $3\overline{)0}$

Properties of Division

1. Any number divided by itself is 1. See Examples 2(a) and 2(b).
2. Any number divided by 1 is the number itself. See Examples 2(c) and 2(d).
3. Zero divided by any nonzero number is zero. See Examples 2(e) and 2(f).

Note that $0 \div 6 = 0$. However, reversing the dividend and divisor produces an undefined quotient. That is,

$$6 \div 0 \text{ is undefined}$$

This is so because there is no number that when multiplied by 0, will produce a product of 6.

You should also note that unlike addition and multiplication, division is neither commutative nor associative. In other words, reversing the order of the dividend and divisor may produce a different quotient. Similarly, changing the manner in which numbers are grouped with division may affect the outcome. See Exercises 31 and 32.

Concept Connections

10. Which expression is undefined?

$$\dfrac{5}{0} \quad \text{or} \quad \dfrac{0}{5}$$

11. Which expression is equal to zero?

$$0\overline{)4} \quad \text{or} \quad 4\overline{)0}$$

3. Long Division

To divide larger numbers we use a process called **long division**. This process uses a series of estimates to find the quotient. We illustrate long division in Example 3.

Answers

4. 1   5. 1   6. 4   7. 8

8. 0   9. 0   10. $\dfrac{5}{0}$ 11. $4\overline{)0}$

Skill Practice

12. Divide.

$8\overline{)136}$

---

example 3   Using Long Division

Divide.

$$7\overline{)161}$$

Solution:

Estimate $7\overline{)161}$ by first estimating $7\overline{)16}$ and writing the result in the tens place of the quotient. Since $7 \times 2 = 14$, there are at least 2 sevens in 16.

```
      2
 7)161        The 2 in the tens place represents 20 in the quotient.
-140    ←—Multiply 7 × 20 and write the result under the dividend.
  21          Subtract 140. We see that our estimate leaves 21.
```

Repeat the process. Now divide $7\overline{)21}$ and write the result in the ones place of the quotient.

```
     23
 7)161
 -140
   21
  -21  ←——Multiply 7 × 3.
    0        Subtract.
```

The quotient is 23.   Check: 23
                                    $\times 7$
                                    161 ✔

We can streamline the process of long division by "bringing down" digits of the dividend one at a time.

Skill Practice

13. Divide.

$2891 \div 7$

---

example 4   Using Long Division

Divide.

$$6138 \div 9$$

Solution:

```
    682
 9)6138
 -54↓       9 × 6 = 54 and subtract.
   73       Bring down the 3.
  -72↓      9 × 8 = 72 and subtract.
   18       Bring down the 8.
  -18       9 × 2 = 18 and subtract.
    0
```

The quotient is 682.   Check: $\overset{71}{682}$
                                    $\times\ 9$
                                    6138 ✔

Answers

12. 17
13. 413

In many instances, quotients do not come out evenly. For example, suppose we had 13 pieces of pizza to distribute among 4 children (Figure 1-9).

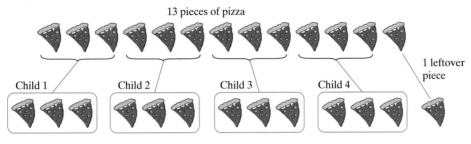

13 pieces of pizza

Child 1   Child 2   Child 3   Child 4

1 leftover piece

Figure 1-9

The mathematical term given to the "leftover" piece is called the **remainder**. The division process may be written as

$$\begin{array}{r} 3\ R1 \\ 4\overline{)13} \\ -12 \\ \hline 1 \end{array}$$

The remainder is written next to the 3.

The **whole part of the quotient** is 3, and the remainder is 1. Notice that the remainder is written next to the whole part of the quotient.

We can check a division problem that has a remainder. To do so, multiply the divisor by the whole part of the quotient and then add the remainder. The result must equal the dividend. That is,

(Divisor)(whole part of quotient) + remainder = dividend

Thus,

$$(4)(3) + 1 \stackrel{?}{=} 13$$
$$12 + 1 \stackrel{?}{=} 13$$
$$13 = 13 \ ✔$$

| **example 5** | **Using Long Division** |

Divide.

$$1595 \div 6$$

Solution:

$$\begin{array}{r} 265\ R5 \\ 6\overline{)1595} \\ -12 \\ \hline 39 \\ -36 \\ \hline 35 \\ -30 \\ \hline 5 \end{array}$$

$6 \times 2 = 12$ and subtract.
Bring down the 9.
$6 \times 6 = 36$ and subtract.
Bring down the 5.
$6 \times 5 = 30$ and subtract.
The remainder is 5.

To check, verify that $6 \times 265 + 5 = 1595$. ✔

Skill Practice

14. Divide.

  $1482 \div 5$

Answer

14. 296 R2

4. Dividing by a Many-Digit Divisor

When the divisor has more than one digit, we still use a series of estimations to find the quotient.

example 6   Dividing by a Two-Digit Number

Divide.

$$32\overline{)1259}$$

Solution:

To estimate the leading digit of the quotient, estimate the number of times 30 will go into 125. Since $30 \cdot 4 = 120$, our estimate is 4.

$$
\begin{array}{r}
4 \\
32\overline{)1259} \\
-128
\end{array}
$$

$32 \times 4 = 128$ is too big. We cannot subtract 128 from 125. Revise the estimate in the quotient to 3.

$$
\begin{array}{r}
3 \\
32\overline{)1259} \\
-96 \\
\hline
299
\end{array}
$$

$32 \times 3 = 96$ and subtract.
Bring down the 9.

Now estimate the number of times 30 will go into 299. Because $30 \times 9 = 270$, our estimate is 9.

$$
\begin{array}{r}
39 \ \text{R}11 \\
32\overline{)1259} \\
-96 \\
\hline
299 \\
-288 \\
\hline
11
\end{array}
$$

$32 \times 9 = 288$ and subtract.
The remainder is 11.

To check, verify that $32 \times 39 + 11 = 1259.$ ✔

example 7   Dividing by a Many-Digit Number

Divide.

$$\frac{82,705}{602}$$

Solution:

$$
\begin{array}{r}
137 \ \text{R}231 \\
602\overline{)82,705} \\
-602 \\
\hline
2250 \\
-1806 \\
\hline
4445 \\
-4214 \\
\hline
231
\end{array}
$$

$602 \times 1 = 602$ and subtract.
Bring down the 0.
$602 \times 3 = 1806$ and subtract.
Bring down the 5.
$602 \times 7 = 4214$ and subtract.
The remainder is 231.

To check, verify that $602 \times 137 + 231 = 82,705.$ ✔

5. Translations and Applications Involving Division

Several words and phrases imply division. A partial list is given in Table 1-4.

table 1-4

Word/Phrase	Example	In Symbols
Divide	Divide 12 by 3	$12 \div 3$ or $\dfrac{12}{3}$ or $3\overline{)12}$
Quotient	The quotient of 20 and 2	$20 \div 2$ or $\dfrac{20}{2}$ or $2\overline{)20}$
Per	110 mi per 2 hr	$110 \div 2$ or $\dfrac{110}{2}$ or $2\overline{)110}$
Divides into	4 divides into 28	$28 \div 4$ or $\dfrac{28}{4}$ or $4\overline{)28}$
Divided, or shared equally among	64 shared equally among 4	$64 \div 4$ or $\dfrac{64}{4}$ or $4\overline{)64}$

---

example 8   Solving an Application Involving Division

A painting business employs 3 painters. The business collects $1950 for painting a house. If all painters are paid equally, how much does each person make?

Solution:

This is an example where $1950 is shared equally among 3 people. Therefore, we divide.

$$
\begin{array}{r}
650 \\
3\overline{)1950} \\
\end{array}
$$

 $-18\downarrow$ $3 \times 6 = 18$ and subtract.

  15 Bring down the 5.

 $-15\downarrow$ $3 \times 5 = 15$ and subtract.

  00 Bring down the 0. The remainder is 0.

Each painter makes $650.

---

example 9   Solving an Application Involving Division with Estimation

Elaine and Max drove from South Bend, Indiana, to Bonita Springs, Florida. The total driving distance was 1089 mi, and the driving time was approximately 20 hr. Estimate the average speed by rounding the distance to the nearest hundred.

Skill Practice

17. Four players play Hearts with a standard 52-card deck of cards. If the cards are equally distributed, how many cards does each player get?

Skill Practice

18. A college has budgeted $4800 to buy graphing calculators. Each calculator costs $119. Estimate the number of calculators that the college can buy by rounding the cost to the nearest ten.

Answers

17. 13 cards   18. 40 calculators

Solution:

1089 mi rounds to 1100 mi. The speed is represented by 1100 mi per 20 hr, or

$$
\begin{array}{r}
55 \\
20\overline{)1100} \\
-100 \\
\hline
100 \\
-100 \\
\hline
0
\end{array}
$$

20 × 5 = 100 and subtract.

Bring down the 0.

20 × 5 = 100 and subtract.

Max and Elaine averaged approximately 55 miles per hour (mph).

Skill Practice

19. The cost for four different types of pastry at a French bakery is shown in the graph.

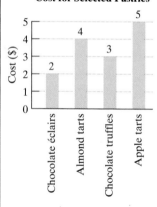

Cost for Selected Pastries

Melissa has $360 to spend on desserts.

a. If she spends all the money on chocolate éclairs, how many can she buy?

b. If she spends all the money on apple tarts, how many can she buy?

---

example 10   Solving an Application Involving Division

The chart in Figure 1-10 depicts the number of calories burned per hour for selected activities.

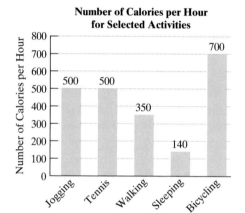

Figure 1-10

a. Janie wants to burn 3500 calories per week exercising. For how many hours must she jog?

b. For how many hours must Janie bicycle to burn 3500 calories?

Solution:

a. The total number of calories must be distributed in 500-calorie increments. Thus, the number of hours required is given by 3500 ÷ 500.

$$
\begin{array}{r}
7 \\
500\overline{)3500} \\
-3500 \\
\hline
0
\end{array}
$$

Janie requires 7 hr of jogging to burn 3500 calories.

b. 3500 calories must be distributed in 700-calorie increments. The number of hours required is given by 3500 ÷ 700.

$$
\begin{array}{r}
5 \\
700\overline{)3500} \\
-3500 \\
\hline
0
\end{array}
$$

Janie requires 5 hr of bicycling to burn 3500 calories.

Answers

19. a. 180 chocolate éclairs
    b. 72 apple tarts

section 1.6   Practice Exercises

Boost *your* GRADE at
mathzone.com!

MathZone

• Practice Problems   • e-Professors
• Self-Tests   • Videos
• NetTutor

Study Skills Exercises

1. In your next math class, take notes by drawing a vertical line about three-fourths of the way across the paper, as shown. On the left side, write down what your instructor puts on the board or overhead. On the right side, make your own comments about important words, procedures, or questions that you have.

2. Define the key terms.

   a. **Division**   b. **Dividend**   c. **Divisor**   d. **Quotient**

   e. **Long division**   f. **Remainder**   g. **Whole part of the quotient**

Review Exercises

For Exercises 3–10, add, subtract, or multiply as indicated.

3. $48 \cdot 103$ 4. $678 - 83$ 5. $1008 + 245$ 6. $14(220)$

7. 5230×127 8. $789(25)$ 9. $4890 - 3988$ 10. $38,002 + 3902$

Objective 1: Introduction to Division

For Exercises 11–16, simplify each expression. Then identify the dividend, divisor, and quotient. **(See Example 1.)**

11. $72 \div 8$ 12. $32 \div 4$ 13. $8\overline{)64}$

14. $5\overline{)35}$ 15. $\dfrac{45}{9}$ 16. $\dfrac{20}{5}$

Objective 2: Properties of Division

17. In your own words, explain the difference between dividing a number by zero and dividing zero by a number.

18. Explain what happens when a number is either divided or multiplied by 1.

For Exercises 19–30, use the properties of division to simplify the expression, if possible. **(See Example 2.)**

19. $15 \div 1$

20. $21\overline{)21}$

21. $0 \div 10$

22. $\dfrac{0}{3}$

23. $0\overline{)9}$

24. $4 \div 0$

25. $\dfrac{20}{20}$

26. $1\overline{)9}$

27. $\dfrac{16}{0}$

28. $\dfrac{5}{1}$

29. $8\overline{)0}$

30. $13 \div 13$

31. Show that $6 \div 3 = 2$ but $3 \div 6 \neq 2$ by using multiplication to check.

32. Show that division is not associative, using the numbers 36, 12, and 3.

Objective 3: Long Division

33. Explain the process for checking a division problem when there is no remainder.

34. Show how checking by multiplication can help us remember that $0 \div 5 = 0$ and that $5 \div 0$ is undefined.

For Exercises 35–46, divide and check by multiplying. **(See Examples 3 and 4.)**

35. $78 \div 6$

36. $364 \div 7$

37. $5\overline{)205}$

38. $8\overline{)152}$

39. $\dfrac{972}{2}$

40. $\dfrac{582}{6}$

41. $1227 \div 3$

42. $236 \div 4$

43. $4\overline{)3808}$

44. $3\overline{)2895}$

45. $\dfrac{4932}{6}$

46. $\dfrac{3619}{7}$

For Exercises 47–54, check the following division problems. If it does not check, find the correct answer.

47. $4\overline{)224}^{\,56}$

48. $7\overline{)574}^{\,82}$

49. $761 \div 3 = 253 \text{ R2}$

50. $604 \div 5 = 120 \text{ R4}$

51. $\dfrac{1021}{9} = 113 \text{ R4}$

52. $\dfrac{1311}{6} = 218 \text{ R3}$

53. $8\overline{)203}^{\,25 \text{ R6}}$

54. $7\overline{)821}^{\,117 \text{ R5}}$

For Exercises 55–70, divide and check the answer. **(See Example 5.)**

55. $61 \div 8$

56. $89 \div 3$

57. $9\overline{)92}$

58. $5\overline{)74}$

59. $\dfrac{55}{2}$

60. $\dfrac{49}{3}$

61. $593 \div 3$

62. $801 \div 4$

63. $\dfrac{382}{9}$ **64.** $\dfrac{428}{8}$ **65.** $3115 \div 2$ **66.** $4715 \div 6$

67. $6014 \div 8$ **68.** $9013 \div 7$ **69.** $6\overline{)5012}$ **70.** $2\overline{)1101}$

Objective 4: Dividing by a Many-Digit Divisor

For Exercises 71–82, divide. **(See Examples 6 and 7.)**

71. $9110 \div 19$ **72.** $3505 \div 13$ **73.** $24\overline{)1051}$ **74.** $41\overline{)8104}$

75. $\dfrac{8008}{26}$ **76.** $\dfrac{9180}{15}$ **77.** $68{,}012 \div 54$ **78.** $92{,}013 \div 35$

79. $69{,}712 \div 304$ **80.** $51{,}107 \div 221$ **81.** $114\overline{)34{,}428}$ **82.** $421\overline{)87{,}989}$

Objective 5: Translations and Applications Involving Division

For Exercises 83–88, for each English sentence, write a mathematical expression and simplify.

83. Find the quotient of 497 and 71.

84. Find the quotient of 1890 and 45.

85. Divide 877 by 14.

86. Divide 722 by 53.

87. Divide 6 into 42.

88. Divide 9 into 108.

89. There are 392 students signed up for Anatomy 101. If each classroom can hold 28 students, find the number of classrooms that are needed. **(See Example 8.)**

90. A wedding reception is planned to take place in the fellowship hall of a church. The bride anticipates 120 guests, and each table will seat 8 people. How many tables should be set up for the reception to accommodate all the guests?

91. A case of tomato sauce contains 32 cans. If a grocer has 168 cans, how many cases can he fill completely? How many cans will be left over?

92. Austin has $425 to spend on dining room chairs. If each chair costs $52, does he have enough to purchase 8 chairs? If so, will he have any money left over?

93. Pauline drove 312 mi in 6 hr. Find Pauline's average speed (in miles per hour).

94. A house cleaning company charges $144 to clean a 3-room apartment. At this rate, how much does it cost to clean 1 room?

95. If it takes 2200 lb of grapes to make 100 gal of white wine, how many pounds are needed for 1 gal?

96. There are 7280 acres of ferns in Florida that are owned by 260 farmers. Find the average size of each farm.

97. A group of 18 people go to a concert. Ticket prices are given in the chart. If the group has $450, can they all attend the concert? If so, which type of seats can they buy? **(See Example 10.)**

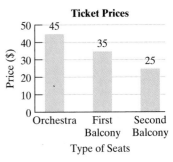

Ticket Prices

Figure for Exercise 97

98. The chart gives the average annual income for four professions: teacher, professor, CEO, and programmer. Find the monthly income for each of the four professions.

99. Suppose Genny can type 1234 words in 22 min. Round each number to estimate her rate in words per minute. **(See Example 9.)**

100. On a trip to California from Illinois, Lavu drove 2780 mi. The gas tank in his car allows him to travel 405 mi. Round each number to the hundreds place to estimate the number of tanks of gas needed for the trip.

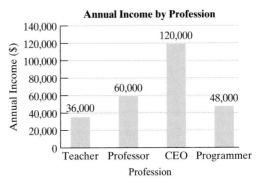

Annual Income by Profession

Figure for Exercise 98

Calculator Connections

Topic: Dividing on a calculator

To divide numbers on a calculator, use the ÷ key.

Expression	Keystrokes	Result
2,449,216 ÷ 6248	2449216 ÷ 6248 Enter	392

Calculator Exercises

For Exercises 101–104, use a calculator to divide.

101. 3,437,226 ÷ 14,689

102. 982)625,534

103. The budget for the U.S. federal government for 2006 is approximately $2160 billion dollars. How much could the government spend each month and still stay within its budget?

104. At a weigh station, a truck carrying 96 crates weighs in at 34,080 lb. If the truck weighs 9600 lb when empty, how much does each crate weigh?

section 1.7   Exponents and the Order of Operations

Objectives

1. Exponents
2. Square Roots
3. Order of Operations
4. Computing a Mean (Average)

1. Exponents

Thus far in the text we have learned to add, subtract, multiply, and divide whole numbers. We now present the concept of an **exponent** to represent repeated multiplication. For example, the product

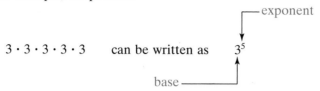

$$3 \cdot 3 \cdot 3 \cdot 3 \cdot 3 \quad \text{can be written as} \quad 3^5$$

The expression 3^5 is written in exponential form. The exponent, or **power**, is 5 and represents the number of times the **base**, 3, is multiplied. The expression 3^5 is read as "three to the fifth power." Other expressions in exponential form are shown below.

5^2	is read as	"five squared" or "five to the second power"
5^3	is read as	"five cubed" or "five to the third power"
5^4	is read as	"five to the fourth power"
5^5	is read as	"five to the fifth power"

Tip: The expression $5^1 = 5$. Any number without an exponent explicitly written is assumed to be to the first power.

Concept Connections

1. Write the expression in exponential form:
   $2 \cdot 2 \cdot 2$.

2. How would you read the expression 7^3?

Exponential form is a shortcut notation for repeated multiplication. However, to simplify an expression in exponential form, we often write out the individual factors.

example 1   Evaluating Exponential Expressions

Evaluate.

a. 6^2 **b.** 5^3 **c.** 2^4

Solution:

a. $6^2 = 6 \cdot 6$ The exponent, 2, indicates the number of times the
       $= 36$ base, 6, is multiplied.

b. $5^3 = 5 \cdot 5 \cdot 5$ When three factors are multiplied, we can group the first
            two factors and perform the multiplication.

$= (\underline{5 \cdot 5}) \cdot 5$

$= (25) \cdot 5$ Then multiply the product of the first two factors by
            the last factor.

$= 125$

c. $2^4 = 2 \cdot 2 \cdot 2 \cdot 2$

$= (\underline{2 \cdot 2}) \cdot 2 \cdot 2$ Group the first two factors.

$= 4 \cdot 2 \cdot 2$ Multiply the first two factors.

$= (\underline{4 \cdot 2}) \cdot 2$ Multiply the product by the next factor to the right.

$= 8 \cdot 2$

$= 16$

Skill Practice

Evaluate.

3. 8^2 **4.** 4^3 **5.** 2^5

Answers
1. 2^3
2. "Seven cubed" or "seven to the third power"
3. 64   4. 64   5. 32

One important application of exponents lies in recognizing **powers of 10**, that is, 10 raised to a whole-number power. For example, consider the following expressions.

$$10^1 = 10$$

$$10^2 = 10 \cdot 10 = 100$$

$$10^3 = 10 \cdot 10 \cdot 10 = 1000$$

$$10^4 = 10 \cdot 10 \cdot 10 \cdot 10 = 10{,}000$$

$$10^5 = 10 \cdot 10 \cdot 10 \cdot 10 \cdot 10 = 100{,}000$$

$$10^6 = 10 \cdot 10 \cdot 10 \cdot 10 \cdot 10 \cdot 10 = 1{,}000{,}000$$

From these examples, we see that a power of 10 results in a 1 followed by several zeros. The number of zeros is the same as the exponent on the base of 10.

Skill Practice

Evaluate.

6. 10^8

7. 10^{13}

2. Square Roots

To square a number means that we multiply the base times itself. For example, $5^2 = 5 \cdot 5 = 25$.

To find a positive **square root** of a number means that we reverse the process of squaring. For example, finding the square root of 25 is equivalent to asking, What positive number when squared, equals 25? The symbol $\sqrt{}$, (called a *radical sign*) is used to denote the positive square root of a number. Therefore, $\sqrt{25}$ is the positive number that when squared, equals 25. Thus, $\sqrt{25} = 5$ because $(5)^2 = 25$.

Skill Practice

Find the square roots.

8. $\sqrt{4}$

9. $\sqrt{100}$

10. $\sqrt{81}$

example 2	Evaluating Square Roots

Find the square roots.

a. $\sqrt{9}$ **b.** $\sqrt{64}$ **c.** $\sqrt{1}$ **d.** $\sqrt{0}$

Solution:

a. $\sqrt{9} = 3$ because $(3)^2 = 3 \cdot 3 = 9$

b. $\sqrt{64} = 8$ because $(8)^2 = 8 \cdot 8 = 64$

c. $\sqrt{1} = 1$ because $(1)^2 = 1 \cdot 1 = 1$

d. $\sqrt{0} = 0$ because $(0)^2 = 0 \cdot 0 = 0$

Tip: To simplify square roots, it is advisable to become familiar with the following squares and square roots.

$$0^2 = 0 \longrightarrow \sqrt{0} = 0 \qquad 7^2 = 49 \longrightarrow \sqrt{49} = 7$$

$$1^2 = 1 \longrightarrow \sqrt{1} = 1 \qquad 8^2 = 64 \longrightarrow \sqrt{64} = 8$$

$$2^2 = 4 \longrightarrow \sqrt{4} = 2 \qquad 9^2 = 81 \longrightarrow \sqrt{81} = 9$$

$$3^2 = 9 \longrightarrow \sqrt{9} = 3 \qquad 10^2 = 100 \longrightarrow \sqrt{100} = 10$$

$$4^2 = 16 \longrightarrow \sqrt{16} = 4 \qquad 11^2 = 121 \longrightarrow \sqrt{121} = 11$$

$$5^2 = 25 \longrightarrow \sqrt{25} = 5 \qquad 12^2 = 144 \longrightarrow \sqrt{144} = 12$$

$$6^2 = 36 \longrightarrow \sqrt{36} = 6 \qquad 13^2 = 169 \longrightarrow \sqrt{169} = 13$$

Answers

6. 100,000,000
7. 10,000,000,000,000
8. 2
9. 10
10. 9

3. Order of Operations

A numerical expression may contain more than one operation. For example, the following expression contains both multiplication and subtraction.

$$18 - 5(2)$$

The order in which the multiplication and subtraction are performed will affect the overall outcome.

Multiplying first yields	Subtracting first yields
$18 - 5(2) = 18 - 10$	$18 - 5(2) = 13(2)$
$= 8$ (correct)	$= 26$ (incorrect)

To avoid confusion, mathematicians have outlined the proper order of operations. In particular, multiplication is performed before addition or subtraction. The guidelines for the order of operations are given below. These rules must be followed in all cases.

Order of Operations

1. Perform all operations inside parentheses first.
2. Simplify any expressions containing exponents or square roots.
3. Perform multiplication or division in the order that they appear from left to right.
4. Perform addition or subtraction in the order that they appear from left to right.

example 3   Using the Order of Operations

Simplify.

a. $15 - 10 \div 2 + 3$ **b.** $(5 - 2) \cdot 7 - 1$ **c.** $\sqrt{100} - 2^3$

Solution:

a. $15 - 10 \div 2 + 3$

$= 15 - 5 + 3$ Perform the division $10 \div 2$ first.

$=\quad 10 + 3$ Perform addition and subtraction from left to right.

$=\quad 13$ Add.

b. $(5 - 2) \cdot 7 - 1$

$= (3) \cdot 7 - 1$ Perform the operation inside parentheses first.

$=\quad 21 - 1$ Perform multiplication before subtraction.

$=\quad 20$ Subtract.

c. $\sqrt{100} - 2^3$

$= 10 - 8$ Simplify any expressions with exponents or square roots. Note that $\sqrt{100} = 10$, and $2^3 = 2 \cdot 2 \cdot 2 = 8$.

$= 2$ Subtract.

example 4   Using the Order of Operations

Simplify.

   a. $300 \div (7 - 2)^2 - 2^2$ **b.** $36 + (7^2 - 3)$

Solution:

  a. $300 \div (7 - 2)^2 - 2^2$

$$= 300 \div (5)^2 - 2^2 \qquad \text{Perform the operation within parentheses first.}$$

$$= 300 \div 25 - 4 \qquad \text{Simplify exponents: } 5^2 = 5 \cdot 5 = 25 \text{ and } 2^2 = 2 \cdot 2 = 4.$$

$$= \quad 12 - 4 \qquad \text{Perform division before subtraction.}$$

$$= \quad\quad 8 \qquad \text{Subtract.}$$

  b. $\quad 36 + (7^2 - 3)$

$$= 36 + (49 - 3) \qquad \text{Perform the operation within parentheses first. The guidelines indicate that we simplify the expression with the exponent before we subtract: } 7^2 = 49.$$

$$= 36 + \quad 46 \qquad \text{Continue simplifying within parentheses.}$$

$$= 82 \qquad \text{Add.}$$

4. Computing a Mean (Average)

The order of operations must be used when we compute an average. The technical term for the average of a list of numbers is the **mean** of the numbers. To find the mean of a set of numbers, first compute the sum of the values. Then divide the sum by the number of values. This is represented by the formula

$$\text{Mean} = \frac{\text{sum of the values}}{\text{number of values}}$$

example 5   Computing a Mean

Six drivers were stopped for speeding in a 25-mph zone. The speed for each driver (in miles per hour) is given below. Find the mean speed.

$$45, 38, 42, 50, 41, 54$$

Solution:

$$\text{Mean speed} = \frac{45 + 38 + 42 + 50 + 41 + 54}{6}$$

$$= \frac{270}{6} \qquad \text{Add the values in the list first.}$$

$$= 45 \qquad \text{Divide.} \qquad \begin{array}{r} 45 \\ 6\overline{)270} \\ -24 \\ \hline 30 \\ -30 \\ \hline 0 \end{array}$$

The mean speed is 45 mph.

section 1.7   Practice Exercises

Study Skills Exercises

1. Look over the notes that you took today. Do you understand what you wrote? If there were any rules, definitions, or formulas, highlight them so that they can be easily found when studying for the test.

2. Define the key terms.

   a. Exponent   **b. Power**   **c. Base**

   d. Power of 10   **e. Square root**   **f. Mean**

Review Exercises

For Exercises 3–8, write true or false for each statement.

3. Addition is commutative; for example, $5 + 3 = 3 + 5$.

4. Subtraction is commutative; for example, $5 - 3 = 3 - 5$.

5. $6 \cdot 0 = 6$ **6.** $0 \div 8 = 0$ **7.** $0 \cdot 8 = 0$ **8.** $5 \div 0$ is undefined

Objective 1: Exponents

9. Write an exponential expression with 9 as the base and 4 as the exponent.

10. Write an exponential expression with 3 as the base and 8 as the exponent.

11. Write an exponential expression with 7 as the exponent and 2 as the base.

12. Write an exponential expression with 5 as the exponent and 6 as the base.

For Exercises 13–16, write the repeated multiplication in exponential form. Do not simplify.

13. $3 \cdot 3 \cdot 3 \cdot 3 \cdot 3 \cdot 3$ **14.** $7 \cdot 7 \cdot 7 \cdot 7$ **15.** $4 \cdot 4 \cdot 4 \cdot 4 \cdot 2 \cdot 2 \cdot 2$ **16.** $5 \cdot 5 \cdot 5 \cdot 10 \cdot 10 \cdot 10$

For Exercises 17–20, expand the exponential expression as a repeated multiplication. Do not simplify.

17. 8^4 **18.** 2^6 **19.** 4^8 **20.** 6^2

For Exercises 21–36, evaluate the exponential expressions. **(See Example 1.)**

21. 2^3

22. 4^2

23. 3^2

24. 5^2

25. 3^3

26. 11^2

27. 5^3

28. 4^3

29. 2^5

30. 6^3

31. 3^4

32. 5^4

33. 1^2

34. 1^3

35. 1^4

36. 1^5

37. Explain what happens when the number 1 is raised to any power. **(See Exercises 33–36.)**

For Exercises 38–41, evaluate the powers of 10.

38. 10^2

39. 10^3

40. 10^4

41. 10^5

42. Explain how to get 10^9 *without* doing the repeated multiplication. **(See Exercises 38–41.)**

Objective 2: Square Roots

For Exercises 43–50, evaluate the square roots. **(See Example 2.)**

43. $\sqrt{4}$

44. $\sqrt{9}$

45. $\sqrt{36}$

46. $\sqrt{81}$

47. $\sqrt{100}$

48. $\sqrt{49}$

49. $\sqrt{0}$

50. $\sqrt{16}$

Objective 3: Order of Operations

51. Does the order of operations indicate that addition is always performed before subtraction? Explain.

52. Does the order of operations indicate that multiplication is always performed before division? Explain.

For Exercises 53–84, simplify using the order of operations. **(See Examples 3–4.)**

53. $6 + 10 \cdot 2$

54. $4 + 3 \cdot 7$

55. $10 - 3^2$

56. $11 - 2^2$

57. $(10 - 3)^2$

58. $(11 - 2)^2$

59. $36 \div 2 \div 6$

60. $48 \div 4 \div 2$

61. $15 - (5 + 8)$

62. $41 - (13 + 8)$

63. $(13 - 2) \cdot 5$

64. $(8 + 4) \cdot 6$

65. $4 + 12 \div 3$

66. $9 + 15 \div \sqrt{25}$

67. $30 \div 2 \cdot \sqrt{9}$

68. $55 \div 11 \cdot 5$

69. $7^2 - 5^2$

70. $3^3 - 2^3$

71. $(7 - 5)^2$

72. $(3 - 2)^3$

73. $\sqrt{81} + 2(9 - 1)$ **74.** $\sqrt{121} + 3(8 - 3)$ **75.** $36 \div (2^2 + 5)$ **76.** $42 \div (3^2 - 2)$

77. $80 - (20 \div 4) + 6$ **78.** $120 - (48 \div 8) - 40$ **79.** $(43 - 26) \cdot 2 - 4^2$ **80.** $(51 - 48) \cdot 3 + 7^2$

81. $(18 - 5) - (23 - \sqrt{100})$ **82.** $(\sqrt{36} + 11) - (31 - 16)$ **83.** $80 \div (9^2 - 7 \cdot 11)^2$

84. $108 \div (3^3 - 6 \cdot 4)^2$

Objective 4: Computing a Mean (Average)

For Exercises 85–90, find the mean (average) of each set of numbers. **(See Example 5.)**

85. 5, 8, 4, 3, 10

86. 7, 2, 4, 8, 1, 2

87. 32, 41, 68, 51

88. 19, 21, 18, 21, 16

89. 105, 114, 123, 101, 100, 111

90. 1480, 1102, 1032, 1002

91. Neelah took 6 quizzes and received the following scores: 19, 20, 18, 19, 18, 14. Find her quiz average.

92. Shawn's scores on his last 4 tests were 83, 95, 87, and 91. What is his test average?

93. At a certain grocery store, Jessie notices that the price of bananas varies from week to week. During a 3-week period she buys bananas for 33¢ per pound, 39¢ per pound, and 42¢ per pound. What does Jessie pay on average per pound?

94. On a trip, Stephen had his car washed 4 times and paid $7, $10, $8, and $7. What was the average amount spent per wash?

95. The monthly rainfall for Seattle, Washington, is given in the table. All values are in millimeters (mm).

	Jan.	Feb.	Mar.	Apr.	May	Jun.	Jul.	Aug.	Sep.	Oct.	Nov.	Dec.
Rainfall	122	94	80	52	47	40	15	21	44	90	118	123

Find the average monthly rainfall for the winter months of November, December, and January.

96. The monthly snowfall for Alpena, Michigan, is given in the table. All values are in inches.

	Jan.	Feb.	Mar.	Apr.	May	Jun.	Jul.	Aug.	Sep.	Oct.	Nov.	Dec.
Snowfall	22	16	13	5	1	0	0	0	0	1	9	20

Find the average monthly snowfall for the winter months of November, December, January, February, and March.

Expanding Your Skills

Sometimes an expression will have parentheses within parentheses. This is called *nested parentheses*. Often different shapes such as $(\ )$, $[\ ]$, or $\{\ \}$ are used to make it easier to match up the pairs of parentheses, for example,

$$\{300 - 4[4 + (5 + 2)^2] + 8\} - 31$$

It is important to note that the symbols $(\ )$, $[\ ]$, or $\{\ \}$ all represent parentheses and are used for grouping. When nested parentheses occur, simplify the innermost set first. Then work your way out. For example, simplify

$$\{300 - 4[4 + (5 + 2)^2] + 8\} - 31$$

The solution is

$\{300 - 4[4 + (5 + 2)^2] + 8\} - 31$

$= \{300 - 4[4 + (7)^2] + 8\} - 31$ Simplify within the innermost parentheses first $(\ )$.

$= \{300 - 4[4 + 49] + 8\} - 31$ Simplify the exponent.

$= \{300 - 4[53] + 8\} - 31$ Simplify within the next innermost parentheses $[\ ]$.

$= \{300 - 212 + 8\} - 31$ Multiply before adding.

$= \{88 + 8\} - 31$ Subtract and add in order from left to right within the parentheses $\{\ \}$.

$= 96 - 31$ Simplify within the parentheses $\{\ \}$.

$= 65$ Simplify.

For Exercises 97–100, simplify the expressions with nested parentheses.

97. $3[4 + (6 - 3)^2] - 15$ **98.** $2[5(4 - 1) + 3] \div 6$

99. $5\{21 - [3^2 - (4 - 2)]\}$ **100.** $4\{18 - [(10 - 8) + 2^3]\}$

Calculator Connections

Topic: Evaluating expressions with exponents on a calculator

Many calculators use the $\boxed{x^2}$ key to square a number. To raise a number to a higher power, use the $\boxed{\wedge}$ key (or on some calculators, the $\boxed{x^y}$ key or $\boxed{y^x}$ key).

Expression	Keystrokes	Result
26^2	$26\ \boxed{x^2}\ \boxed{\text{Enter}}$	676

$\uparrow$
On some calculators, you
do not need to press $\boxed{\text{Enter}}$

3^7	$3\ \boxed{\wedge}\ 7\ \boxed{\text{Enter}}$	2187
	or $3\ \boxed{y^x}\ 7\ \boxed{=}$	2187

Calculator Exercises

For Exercises 101–104, use a calculator to perform the indicated operations.

101. 156^2 **102.** 418^2 **103.** 12^5 **104.** 35^4

For Exercises 105–110, simplify the expressions by using the order of operations. For each step use the calculator to simplify the given operation.

105. $8126 - 54{,}978 \div 561$

106. $92{,}168 + 6954 \times 29$

107. $(3548 - 3291)^2$

108. $(7500 \div 625)^3$

109. $\dfrac{89{,}880}{384 + 2184}$

110. $\dfrac{54{,}137}{3393 - 2134}$

---

section 1.8   Problem-Solving Strategies

Objectives

1. Problem-Solving Strategies
2. Applications Involving One Operation
3. Applications Involving Multiple Operations

1. Problem-Solving Strategies

In this section we offer additional practice with applications of whole numbers. Keep in mind that all word problems are different and that there is no magic "trick" to solve an application problem. However, we can offer the following guidelines.

Guidelines for Problem Solving

1. Read the problem carefully and familiarize yourself with the situation. If possible, draw a diagram or write down an appropriate formula. Sometimes you may be able to estimate a reasonable answer.

2. Write down what information is given and what must be found.

3. Form a strategy. Identify what mathematical operation applies (addition, subtraction, multiplication, or division). Sometimes a combination of operations is necessary.

4. Perform the mathematical operations to solve for the unknown.

5. Check the answer. If the answer is reasonable and checks, state the answer in words.

2. Applications Involving One Operation

We illustrate these guidelines with a variety of examples. To assist with step 3 where we must identify an appropriate mathematical operation, we summarize some of our key words and phrases. See Table 1-5.

table 1-5

Operation	Key Word or Phrase
Addition	Sum, added to, increased by, more than, plus, total of
Subtraction	Difference, minus, decreased by, less, subtract
Multiplication	Product, times, multiply
Division	Quotient, divide, per, shared equally

Concept Connections

1. The odometer of a car read 24,316 mi last year. This year the reading is 37,134. How many miles was the car driven during the year?

example 1   Solving a Travel Application

Kent travels from Columbus, Ohio, to Indianapolis, Indiana, and then on to Springfield, Illinois. The total distance he drives is 351 mi. The distance between Columbus and Indianapolis is 168 mi. Find the distance between Indianapolis and Springfield.

Solution:

Familiarize and draw a picture.

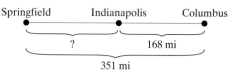

Given:	In this case, we know the total distance and one of the parts.
Find:	Find the second distance (between Indianapolis and Springfield).
Operation:	This problem can be phrased as an addition problem with a missing addend or as an equivalent subtraction problem.

$$168 + ? = 351 \quad \text{or} \quad 351 - 168 = ?$$

Subtracting yields

$$351 - 168 = 183$$

The distance between Indianapolis and Springfield is 183 mi.

Tip: The answer is reasonable because the sum of the distances equals the total distance.

$$183 \text{ mi} + 168 \text{ mi} = 351 \text{ mi}$$

Skill Practice

Refer to the chart in Example 2.

2. Find the total number of trucks sold during this 3-month period.

3. How many more vehicles were sold in September than in August?

example 2   Solving a Sales Application

A used car business keeps records of vehicle sales by type of vehicle and month.

	July	August	September
Cars	23	28	32
Trucks	13	8	10
SUVs	15	18	21

Find the total number of vehicles sold in July.

Solution:

In this problem, we can use the chart as our diagram. We are looking for the total number of vehicles sold in July, so we might highlight the July column.

	July	August	September
Cars	23	28	32
Trucks	13	8	10
SUVs	15	18	21

Given:	The number of each type of vehicle sold in July (highlighted in red).
Find:	The total number of vehicles sold in July.

Answers

1. 12,818 mi
2. 31 trucks
3. 9

Operation: The word *total* indicates addition.

$$Total = 23 + 13 + 15$$
$$= 51$$

There were 51 vehicles sold in July.

---

example 3   Solving a Business Application

A ream of paper holds 500 sheets. Gail purchases 24 reams for her office. How many sheets of paper is this?

Solution:

Familiarize and draw a picture.

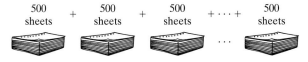

$$\underset{\text{sheets}}{500} + \underset{\text{sheets}}{500} + \underset{\text{sheets}}{500} + \cdots + \underset{\text{sheets}}{500}$$

This situation calls for repeated addition. Therefore, we will multiply.

$$24(500) = 12,000$$

There are 12,000 sheets of paper.

Skill Practice

4. One page of print in a book contains 48 lines of text. How many lines of text are in one chapter containing 21 pages?

Tip: We might also reason that each pair of 2 reams produces 1000 sheets of paper. Since there are 12 pairs of 2 in 24, there must be 12 thousand sheets of paper.

---

example 4   Solving a Consumer Application

A 5-speed Jeep Cherokee gets 23 mpg (miles per gallon) on the highway. How many gallons of gas would be required for a 667-mi drive from El Paso to Dallas?

Solution:

Familiarize and draw a picture.

```
      23 mi  23 mi  23 mi  23 mi        23 mi  23 mi
El Paso ●━━━━━━━━━━━━━━━━━━━━  ⋯  ━━━━━━━━━━● Dallas
        ├─────────── 667 mi ───────────┤
```

Given: The total distance, 667 mi, and the gas mileage, 23 mpg.

Find: How many increments of 23 mi would be required for the trip?

This is a situation where 667 mi must be divided into 23-mi increments. Use the operation of division.

$$
\begin{array}{r}
29 \\
23\overline{)667} \\
-46 \\
\hline
207 \\
-207 \\
\hline
0
\end{array}
$$

The drive from El Paso to Dallas in a Jeep Cherokee will require 29 gal of gas.

Skill Practice

5. A vat of flour at a food distributor holds 580 lb of flour. How many 5-lb bags of flour can be filled from one vat?

Tip: The solution to Example 4 can be checked by multiplication. Twenty-nine gallons of gas at 23 mpg produces

$$(29 \text{ gal})(23 \text{ mi/gal}) = 667 \text{ mi}$$

---

3. Applications Involving Multiple Operations

Sometimes more than one operation is needed to solve an application problem.

Answers

4. 1008 lines
5. 116 bags

example 5   Solving a Consumer Application

Jorge bought a car for $18,340. He paid $2500 down and then paid the rest in equal monthly payments over a 4-year period. Find the amount of Jorge's monthly payment (not including interest).

Solution:

Familiarize and draw a picture.

Given: total price: $18,340
          down payment: $2500

          payment plan: 4 years
          (48 months)

Find: monthly payment

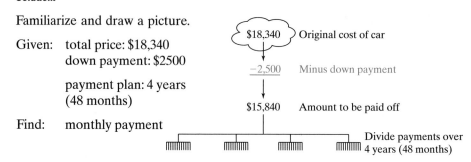

$18,340   Original cost of car

−2,500   Minus down payment

$15,840   Amount to be paid off

Divide payments over 4 years (48 months)

Operations:

1. The amount of the loan to be paid off is equal to the original cost of the car minus the down payment. We use subtraction:

$$\begin{array}{r} \$18,340 \\ -\ 2,500 \\ \hline \$15,840 \end{array}$$

2. This money is distributed in equal payments over a 4-year period. Because there are 12 months in 1 year, there are $4 \times 12 = 48$ months in a 4-year period. To distribute $15,840 among 48 equal payments, we divide.

$$\begin{array}{r} 330 \\ 48)\overline{15,840} \\ -144 \\ \hline 144 \\ -144 \\ \hline 00 \end{array}$$

Jorge's monthly payments will be $330.

Tip: The solution to Example 5 can be checked by multiplication. Forty-eight payments of $330 each amount to 48($330) = $15,840. This added to the down payment totals $18,340 as desired.

example 6   Solving a Travel Application

Linda must drive from Clayton to Oakley. She can travel directly from Clayton to Oakley on a mountain road, but will only average 40 mph. On the route through Pearson, she travels on highways and can average 60 mph. Which route will take less time?

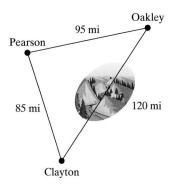

Oakley

95 mi

Pearson

85 mi

120 mi

Clayton

Solution:

Read and familiarize: A map is presented in the problem.

Given: The distance for each route and the speed traveled along each route.

Find: Find the time required for each route. Then compare the times to determine which will take less time.

Operations:

1. First note that the total distance of the route through Pearson is found by using addition.

$$85 \text{ mi} + 95 \text{ mi} = 180 \text{ mi}$$

2. The speed of the vehicle gives us an increment of distance traveled per hour. Therefore, the time of travel equals the total distance divided by the speed.

From Clayton to Oakley through the mountains, we divide 120 mi by 40-mph increments to determine the number of hours.

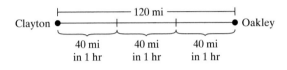

$$\text{Time} = \frac{120 \text{ mi}}{40 \text{ mph}} = 3 \text{ hr}$$

From Clayton to Oakley through Pearson, we divide 180 mi by 60-mph increments to determine the number of hours.

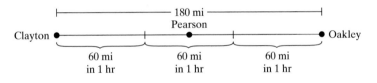

$$\text{Time} = \frac{180 \text{ mi}}{60 \text{ mph}} = 3 \text{ hr}$$

Therefore, each route takes the same amount of time, 3 hr.

---

example 7   **Solving a Construction Application**

A rancher must fence the corral shown in Figure 1-11. However, no fencing is required on the side adjacent to the barn. If fencing costs $4 per foot, what is the total cost?

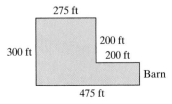

Figure 1-11

Skill Practice

8. Alain wants to put molding around the base of the room shown in the figure. No molding is needed where the door, closet, and bathroom are located. Find the total cost if molding is $2 per foot.

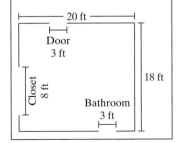

Answer
8. $124

Solution:

Read and familiarize: A figure is provided.

Strategy

With some application problems, it helps to work backward from your final goal. In this case our final goal is to find the total cost. However, to find the total cost, we must first find the total distance to be fenced. To find the total distance, we add the lengths of the sides that are being fenced.

$$
\begin{array}{r}
\overset{1\,1}{275} \text{ ft} \\
200 \text{ ft} \\
200 \text{ ft} \\
475 \text{ ft} \\
+\ 300 \text{ ft} \\
\hline
1450 \text{ ft}
\end{array}
$$

Therefore,

$$
\begin{pmatrix} \text{Total cost} \\ \text{of fencing} \end{pmatrix} = \begin{pmatrix} \text{total} \\ \text{distance} \\ \text{in feet} \end{pmatrix} \begin{pmatrix} \text{cost} \\ \text{per foot} \end{pmatrix}
$$

$$
= (1450 \text{ ft})(\$4 \text{ per ft})
$$

$$
= \$5800
$$

The total cost of fencing is $5800.

---

section 1.8   Practice Exercises

Study Skills Exercise

1. Sometimes you may run into a problem with homework, or you find that you are having trouble keeping up with the pace of the class. A tutor can be a good resource. Answer the following questions.

   a. Does your college offer tutoring?

   b. Is it free?

   c. Where would you go to sign up for a tutor?

Review Exercises

For Exercises 2–11, translate the English phrase into a mathematical statement and simplify.

2. 89 decreased by 66

3. 71 increased by 14

4. 16 more than 42

5. Twice 14

6. The difference of 93 and 79

7. Subtract 32 from 102

8. Divide 12 into 60

9. The product of 10 and 13

10. The total of 12, 14, and 15

11. The quotient of 24 and 6

Objective 1: Problem-Solving Strategies

12. In your own words, list the guidelines or strategy that you would use to solve an application problem.

For Exercises 13–16, write two or more key words or phrases that represent the given operation. Answers may vary.

13. Addition

14. Multiplication

15. Subtraction

16. Division

Objective 2: Applications Involving One Operation

17. A graphing calculator screen consists of an array of rectangular dots called *pixels*. If the screen has 96 rows of pixels and 126 pixels in each row, how many pixels are in the whole screen? **(See Example 3.)**

18. The floor of a rectangular room has 62 rows of tile with 38 tiles in each row. How many total tiles are there?

19. The Honda Hybrid gets 60 miles per gallon (mpg) in stop-and-go traffic. How many gallons will it use in 540 mi of stop-and-go driving?

20. A couple travels an average speed of 52 mph for a cross-country trip. If the couple drove 1352 mi, how many hours was the trip?

21. White Mountain Peak in California is 14,246 ft high. Denali in Alaska is 20,320 ft high. How much higher is Denali than White Mountain Peak? **(See Example 1.)**

22. In a recent year, *Reader's Digest* was the best-selling U.S. magazine with 12,212,000 yearly subscriptions. *Sports Illustrated* was 15th overall and had 3,252,900 yearly subscriptions. How many more subscriptions did *Reader's Digest* have than *Sports Illustrated*?

23. Jeannette has two children who each attended college in Boston. Her son Ricardo attended Bunker Hill Community College where the yearly tuition and fees came to $2600. Her daughter Ricki attended M.I.T. where the yearly tuition and fees totaled $26,960. If Jeannette paid the full amount for both children to go to school, what was her total expense for tuition and fees for one year? **(See Example 2.)**

24. Clyde and Mason each leave a rest area on the Florida Turnpike. Clyde travels north and Mason travels south. After 2 hr, Clyde has gone 138 mi and Mason, who ran into heavy traffic, traveled only 96 mi. How far apart are they?

25. The Honda Insight gets 66 mpg on the highway. How many miles can it go on 20 gal?

26. A 3 credit-hour class at a certain college meets 3 hr per week. If a semester is 16 weeks long, how many hours will the class meet during the semester?

27. At one time, Tidewater Community College in Virginia had 3000 students who registered for Beginning Algebra. If the average class size is 25 students, how many Beginning Algebra classes will the college have to offer? **(See Example 4.)**

28. Eight people are to share equally in an inheritance of $84,480. How much money will each person receive?

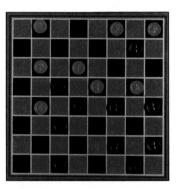

29. A movie theater has 70 rows and 45 seats in a row. What is the maximum seating capacity?

30. A square checkerboard has 8 boxes per row and 8 rows. What is the total number of boxes?

Objective 3: Applications Involving Multiple Operations

31. The balance in Gina's checking account is $278. If she writes checks for $82, $59, and $101, how much will be left over?

32. The balance in Jose's checking account is $3455. If he write checks for $587, $36, and $156, how much will be left over?

33. A community college bought 72 new computers and 6 new printers for a computer lab. If computers were purchased for $2118 each and the printers for $256 each, what was the total bill (not including tax)?

34. Tickets to the San Diego Zoo in California cost $14 for children aged 3–11 and $21 for adults. How much money is required to buy tickets for a class of 33 children and 6 adult chaperones?

35. A discount music store buys used CDs from its customers for $3. Furthermore, a customer can buy any used CD in the store for $8. Latayne sells 16 CDs.

    a. How much money does she receive by selling the 16 CDs?

    b. How many CDs can she then purchase with the money?

36. Shevona earns $8 per hour and works a 40-hr workweek. At the end of the week, she cashes her paycheck and then buys two tickets to a Janet Jackson concert.

    a. How much money is her paycheck worth?

    b. If the concert tickets cost $64 each, how much money does she have left over from her paycheck after buying the tickets?

37. During his 13-year career with the Chicago Bulls, Michael Jordan scored 12,192 field goals (worth 2 points each). He scored 581 three-point shots and 7327 free-throws (worth 1 point each). How many total points did he score during his career with the Bulls?

38. A.J. is a manager for a surf shop. One month he bought 80 T-shirts that cost $6 each, 35 bathing suits that cost $12 each, and 20 pairs of men's shorts that cost $18 each. How much money did he spend?

39. In a recent year, Atlanta's Hartsfield Airport was the busiest airport in the world with an estimated 75,858,500 passengers. In the same year, Chicago's O'Hare Airport was the second busiest with 67,448,000 passengers.

    a. What was the difference between the numbers of passengers traveling through Hartsfield Airport and O'Hare Airport?

    b. What was the total number of passengers for the two airports?

40. Recently, the American Medical Association reported that there were 618,233 male doctors and 195,537 female doctors in the United States.

    a. What is the difference between the number of male doctors and the number of female doctors?

    b. What is the total number of doctors?

41. On a map, each inch represents 60 mi.

    a. If Las Vegas and Salt Lake City are approximately 6 in. apart on the map, what is the actual distance between the cities?

    b. If Madison, Wisconsin, and Dallas, Texas, are approximately 840 mi apart, how many inches would this represent on the map?

42. On a map, each inch represents 40 mi.

    a. If Wichita, Kansas, and Des Moines, Iowa, are approximately 8 in. apart on the map, what is the actual distance between the cities?

    b. If Seattle, Washington and Sacramento, California are approximately 600 mi apart, how many inches would this represent on the map?

43. A textbook company ships books in boxes containing a maximum of 12 books. If a bookstore orders 1250 books, how many boxes can be filled completely? How many books will be left over?

44. A farmer sells eggs in containers holding a dozen eggs. If he has 4257 eggs, how many containers will be filled completely? How many eggs will be left over?

45. Marc pays for an $84 dinner with $20 bills.

    a. How many bills must he use?

    b. How much change will he receive?

46. Shawn buys 3 CDs for a total of $54 and pays with $10 bills.

    a. How many bills must he use?

    b. How much change will he receive?

47. Jackson purchased a car for $16,540. He paid $2500 down and paid the rest in equal monthly payments over a 36-month period. How much were his monthly payments? **(See Example 5.)**

48. Lucio purchased a refrigerator for $1170. He paid $150 at the time of purchase and then paid off the rest in equal monthly payments over 1 year. How much was his monthly payment?

49. Monika must drive from Watertown to Utica. She can travel directly from Watertown to Utica on a small county road, but will only average 40 mph. On the route through Syracuse, she travels on highways and can average 60 mph. Which route will take less time? **(See Example 6.)**

Figure for Exercise 49

50. It takes Rex 4 hr to travel from Oklahoma City to Fort Smith. If the distance between Oklahoma City and Fort Smith is 180 mi, what is his average speed (in miles per hour).

51. If you wanted to line the outside of a garden with a decorative border, would you need to know the area of the garden or the perimeter of the garden?

52. If you wanted to know how much sod to lay down within a rectangular backyard, would you need to know the area of the yard or the perimeter of the yard?

53. A homeowner wants to fence her rectangular backyard. The yard is 75 ft by 90 ft. If fencing costs $5 per foot, how much will it cost to fence the yard?

54. Alexis wants to buy molding for a room that is 12 ft by 11 ft. No molding is needed for the doorway which measures 3 ft. See the figure. If molding costs $2 per foot, how much money will it cost? **(See Example 7.)**

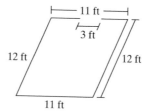

55. What is the cost to carpet the room whose dimensions are shown in the figure? Assume that carpeting costs $34 per square yard and that there is no waste.

56. What is the cost to tile the room whose dimensions are shown in the figure? Assume that tile costs $3 per square foot.

57. Ling has three jobs. He works for a lawn maintenance service 4 days a week. He also tutors math and works as a waiter on weekends. His hourly wage and the number of hours for each job are given for a 1-week period. How much money did Ling earn for the week?

	Hourly Wage	Number of Hours
Tutor	$30/hr	4
Waiter	10/hr	16
Lawn maintenance	8/hr	30

58. An electrician, a plumber, a mason, and a carpenter work at a certain construction site. The hourly wage and the number of hours each person worked are summarized in the table. What was the total amount paid for all four workers?

	Hourly Wage	Number of Hours
Electrician	$36/hr	18
Plumber	28/hr	15
Mason	26/hr	24
Carpenter	22/hr	48

chapter 1 | summary

section 1.1 Introduction to Whole Numbers

Key Concepts

The place value for each **digit** of a number is shown in the chart.

Billions Period			Millions Period			Thousands Period			Ones Period		
Hundred-billions	Ten-billions	Billions	Hundred-millions	Ten-millions	Millions	Hundred-thousands	Ten-thousands	Thousands	Hundreds	Tens	Ones
		3,	4	0	9,	1	1	2			

Numbers can be written in different forms, for example:

Standard Form: 3,409,112

Expanded Form: 3 millions + 4 hundred-thousands + 9 thousands + 1 hundred + 1 ten + 2 ones

Words: three million, four hundred nine thousand, one hundred twelve

The order of the whole numbers can be visualized by placement on a number line.

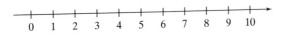

Examples

Example 1

The digit 9 in the number 24,891,321 is in the ten-thousands place.

Example 2

The standard form of the number forty-one million, three thousand, fifty-six is 41,003,056.

Example 3

The expanded form of the number 76,903 is 7 ten-thousands + 6 thousands + 9 hundreds + 3 ones.

Example 4

In words the number 2504 is two thousand, five hundred four.

Example 5

To show that $8 > 4$, note the placement on the number line: 8 is to the right of 4.

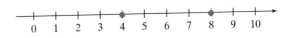

section 1.2 Addition of Whole Numbers

Key Concepts

The **sum** is the result of adding numbers called **addends**.

Addition is performed with and without carrying.

Addition Property of Zero:
The sum of any number and zero is that number.

Commutative Property of Addition:
Changing the order of the addends does not affect the sum.

Associative Property of Addition:
The manner in which the addends are grouped does not affect the sum.

There are several words and phrases that indicate addition, such as *sum, added to, increased by, more than, plus,* and *total of.*

The **perimeter** of a **polygon** is the distance around the outside of the figure. To find perimeter, take the sum of the lengths of all sides of the figure.

Examples

Example 1
For $2 + 7 = 9$, the addends are 2 and 7, and the sum is 9.

Example 2

$$
\begin{array}{r} 23 \\ + 41 \\ \hline 64 \end{array} \qquad
\begin{array}{r} {}^{1\,1}189 \\ + 76 \\ \hline 265 \end{array}
$$

Example 3
$16 + 0 = 16$

Example 4
$3 + 12 = 12 + 3$

Example 5
$2 + (19 + 3) = (2 + 19) + 3$

Example 6
The sum of 6 and 18 translates to $6 + 18$.

Example 7
The expression $5 + 4$ can be translated as 5 increased by 4, or 4 more than 5.

Example 8
The perimeter is found by adding the lengths of all sides.

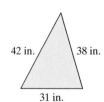

42 in.   38 in.

31 in.

Perimeter $= 42$ in. $+ 38$ in. $+ 31$ in. $= 111$ in.

section 1.3 Subtraction of Whole Numbers

Key Concepts

The **difference** is the result of subtracting the **subtrahend** from the **minuend**.

Subtracting numbers with and without borrowing.

There are several words and phrases that indicate subtraction, such as *minus, difference, decreased by, less than,* and *subtract from.*

Example 5 is an application involving subtraction.

Examples

Example 1

For $19 - 13 = 6$, the minuend is 19, the subtrahend is 13, and the difference is 6.

Example 2

$$
\begin{array}{r}
398 \\
-\,227 \\
\hline
171
\end{array}
\qquad
\begin{array}{r}
\overset{9}{}\overset{1\;\cancel{10}}{2\cancel{0}4} \\
-\,88 \\
\hline
116
\end{array}
$$

Example 3

The difference of 15 and 7 translates to $15 - 7$.

Example 4

The expression $31 - 20$ can be translated to 31 decreased by 20, or subtract 20 from 31.

Example 5

Henry has to drive to his in-law's house 185 mi away. If he drives 105 mi today, how many miles will he have to drive tomorrow?

Solution:
$$105 + \boxed{?} = 185$$
$$185 - 105 = \boxed{80}$$

He must drive 80 mi tomorrow.

section 1.4 Rounding and Estimating

Key Concepts

To **round a number**, follow these steps.

1. Identify the digit one position to the right of the given place value.
2. If the digit in step 1 is a 5 or greater, add 1 to the digit in the given place value. Then replace each digit to the right of the given place value by 0.
3. If the digit in step 1 is less than 5, replace it and each digit to its right by 0.

Round to estimate sums and differences.

Examples

Example 1

Round each number to the indicated place.

a. 4942; hundreds place
b. 3712; thousands place
c. 135; tens place

Solution:

a. 4900   b. 4000   c. 140

Example 2

Round to the thousands place to estimate the sum: $3929 + 2528 + 5452$.

Solution: $4000 + 3000 + 5000 = 12,000$

The sum is approximately 12,000.

section 1.5 Multiplication of Whole Numbers

Key Concepts	Examples
Multiplication is repeated addition.	**Example 1** $16 + 16 + 16 + 16 = 4 \times 16 = 64$
The **product** is the result of multiplying **factors**.	**Example 2** For $3 \times 13 \times 2 = 78$ the factors are 3, 13, and 2, and the product is 78.
Commutative Property of Multiplication: Changing the order of the factors does not affect the product.	**Example 3** $4(7) = 7(4)$
Associative Property of Multiplication: The manner in which the factors are grouped does not affect the product.	**Example 4** $6 \times (5 \times 7) = (6 \times 5) \times 7$
Multiplication Property of 0: The product of any number and 0 is 0.	**Example 5** $43 \times 0 = 0$
Multiplication Property of 1: The product of any real number and 1 is that number.	**Example 6** $290 \times 1 = 290$
Distributive Property of Multiplication Over Addition: $a(b + c) = (a \times b) + (a \times c)$	**Example 7** $5 \times (4 + 8) = (5 \times 4) + (5 \times 8)$

Multiplying whole numbers.

Example 8

$3 \times 14 = 42 \qquad 7(4) = 28$

$$
\begin{array}{r}
312 \\
\times\ 23 \\
\hline
936 \\
6240 \\
\hline
7176
\end{array}
$$

Estimating products by rounding.

Example 9

$3102 \times 698 \approx 3000 \times 700 = 2{,}100{,}000$

There are several words and phrases that indicate multiplication, such as *product*, *times*, and *multiply by*.

Example 10

The product of 25 and 3 translates to 25(3).

Example 11

The expression $78 \cdot 12$ can be translated to 78 times 12, or 78 multiplied by 12.

The **area of a rectangle** with length l and width w is given by $A = l \cdot w$.

Example 12

Find the area of the rectangle.

23 cm ⬚
70 cm

Solution:

$$A = (23\ \text{cm}) \cdot (70\ \text{cm}) = 1610\ \text{cm}^2$$

section 1.6 Division of Whole Numbers

Key Concepts

A **quotient** is the result of dividing the **dividend** by the **divisor**.

Properties of Division:

1. Any number divided by itself is 1.
2. Any number divided by 1 is the number itself.
3. Zero divided by any nonzero number is zero.

Note: A number divided by zero is undefined.

Long division, with and without a **remainder**.

There are several words and phrases that indicate division, such as *divide, quotient, per, divides into,* and *shared equally*.

Example 7 is an application of division.

Examples

Example 1

For $36 \div 4 = 9$, the dividend is 36, the divisor is 4, and the quotient is 9.

Example 2

1. $13 \div 13 = 1$

2. $\dfrac{37}{1)\overline{37}}$

3. $\dfrac{0}{2} = 0$

Example 3

$\dfrac{2}{0}$ is undefined

Example 4

$$
\begin{array}{r}
263 \\
3)\overline{789} \\
-6 \\
\hline
18 \\
-18 \\
\hline
09 \\
-9 \\
\hline
0
\end{array}
\qquad
\begin{array}{r}
41 \text{ R } 12 \\
21)\overline{873} \\
-84 \\
\hline
33 \\
-21 \\
\hline
12
\end{array}
$$

Example 5

The quotient of 72 and 9 translates to $72 \div 9$.

Example 6

The expression $4)\overline{84}$ can be translated to 84 divided by 4, or 4 divides into 84.

Example 7

Rwanda has an area of 10,169 mi^2 and a population of 7,398,000 people. The population density of Rwanda is the number of people per square mile. Round the numbers to the nearest ten-thousand to estimate the population density of Rwanda.

Solution: $7,400,000 \div 10,000 = 740$

There are approximately 740 people per square mile.

section 1.7 Exponents and Order of Operations

Key Concepts

A number raised to an **exponent** represents repeated multiplication.

For 6^3, 6 is the **base** and 3 is the exponent or **power**.

The **square root** of 16 is 4 because $4^2 = 16$. That is, $\sqrt{16} = 4$.

Order of Operations

1. Perform all operations inside parentheses first.
2. Simplify any expressions containing exponents or square roots.
3. Perform multiplication or division in the order that they appear from left to right.
4. Perform addition or subtraction in the order that they appear from left to right.

Powers of 10 can be expressed as the number 1 followed by zeros. The number of zeros is the same as the exponent on the base of 10.

$10^1 = 10$

$10^2 = 100$

$10^3 = 1000$ and so on.

The **mean** is the average of a set of numbers. To find the mean, add all the values and divide by the number of values.

Examples

Example 1

$9^4 = 9 \cdot 9 \cdot 9 \cdot 9 = 6561$

Example 2

$\sqrt{49} = 7$

Example 3

$19 - 32 \div 2^4 + 21$

$= 19 - 32 \div 16 + 21$

$= 19 - 2 + 21$

$= 17 + 21$

$= 38$

Example 4

$(17 - 12)^2 - \sqrt{16}(10 - 2 \cdot 4)$

$= (17 - 12)^2 - 4(10 - 2 \cdot 4)$

$= (5)^2 - 4(10 - 8)$

$= (5)^2 - 4(2)$

$= 25 - 4(2)$

$= 25 - 8$

$= 17$

Example 5

$10^5 = 10,000$ 1 followed by 5 zeros

Example 6

Find the mean of Michael's scores from his homework assignments.

40, 41, 48, 38, 42, 43

Solution:

$$\frac{40 + 41 + 48 + 38 + 42 + 43}{6} = \frac{252}{6} = 42$$

The mean is 42.

section 1.8 Problem-Solving Strategies

Key Concepts

Guidelines for Problem Solving

1. Read the problem carefully. Draw a diagram or write an appropriate formula. Estimate a reasonable answer.
2. Write down what information is given and what must be found.
3. Form a strategy. Identify what mathematical operation or operations apply.
4. Perform the mathematical operations to solve for the unknown.
5. Check the answer.

Examples

Example 1

Nolan received a doctor's bill for $984. His insurance will pay $200, and the balance can be paid in 4 equal monthly payments. How much will each payment be?

Solution:

To find the amount not paid by insurance, subtract $200 from the total bill.

$$984 - 200 = 784$$

To find Nolan's 4 equal payments, divide the amount not covered by insurance by 4.

$$784 \div 4 = 196$$

Nolan must make 4 payments of $196 each.

---

chapter 1 | review exercises

Section 1.1

For Exercises 1–2, determine the place value for each underlined digit.

1. 10,024

2. 821,811

For Exercises 3–4, convert the numbers to standard form.

3. 9 ten-thousands + 2 thousands + 4 tens + 6 ones

4. 5 hundred-thousands + 3 thousands + 1 hundred + 6 tens

For Exercises 5–6, convert the numbers to expanded form.

5. 3,400,820

6. 30,554

For Exercises 7–8, write the numbers in words.

7. 245

8. 30,861

For Exercises 9–10, write the numbers in standard form.

9. Three thousand, six-hundred two

10. Eight hundred thousand, thirty-nine

For Exercises 11–12, place the numbers on the number line.

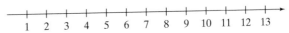

11. 2

12. 7

For Exercises 13–14, determine if the inequality is true or false.

13. $3 < 10$

14. $10 > 12$

chapter 1 | test

1. Determine the place value for the underlined digit.

   a. 4<u>9</u>2   **b.** 2<u>3</u>,441   **c.** <u>2</u>,340,711   **d.** 340,<u>5</u>92

2. Fill in the table with either the word name for the number or the number in standard form.

State / Province	Population	
	Standard Form	Word Name
a. Kentucky		Four million, sixty-five thousand
b. Texas	21,325,000	
c. Pennsylvania	12,287,000	
d. New Brunswick, Canada		Seven hundred twenty-nine thousand
e. Ontario, Canada	11,410,000	

3. Translate the phrase by writing the numbers in standard form and inserting the appropriate inequality. Choose from $<$ or $>$.

   a. Fourteen is greater than six.

   b. Seventy-two is less than eighty-one.

For Exercises 4–17, perform the indicated operation.

4.   51
       $+ 78$

5.   82
       $\times 4$

6.   154
       $- 41$

7. $4\overline{)908}$

8. $58 \cdot 49$

9. $149 + 298$

10. $324 \div 15$

11. $3002 - 2456$

12. $10{,}984 - 2881$

13. $\dfrac{840}{42}$

14. $(500{,}000)(3000)$

15. $34 + 89 + 191 + 22$

16. $403(0)$

17. $0\overline{)16}$

18. For each of the mathematical statements, identify the property used. Choose from the commutative property of multiplication and the associative property of multiplication. Explain your answer.

   a. $(11 \cdot 6) \cdot 3 = 11 \cdot (6 \cdot 3)$

   b. $(11 \cdot 6) \cdot 3 = 3 \cdot (11 \cdot 6)$

19. Round each number to the indicated place value.

   a. 4850; hundreds   **b.** 12,493; thousands

   c. 7,963,126; hundred-thousands

20. The attendance to the Van Gogh and Gauguin exhibit in Chicago was 690,951. The exhibit moved to Amsterdam, and the attendance was 739,117. Round the numbers to the ten-thousands place to estimate the total attendance of this exhibit.

For Exercises 21–23, simplify, using the order of operations.

21. $8^2 \div 2^4$

22. $26 \cdot \sqrt{4} - 4(8 - 1)$

23. $36 \div 3(14 - 10)$

24. Brittany and Jennifer are taking an online course in business management. Brittany has taken 6 quizzes worth 30 points each and received the following scores: 29, 28, 24, 27, 30, and 30. Jennifer has only taken 5 quizzes so far, and her scores are 30, 30, 29, 28, and 28. At this point in the course, which student has a higher average?

25. The number of foreign adoptions by U.S. citizens rose by 862 children from the year 2001 to 2002. If there were 19,237 foreign adoptions in 2001, how many were there in 2002?

26. The use of the cell phone has grown every year for the past 13 years. See the figure.

  a. Find the change in the number of phones used from 2001 to 2002.

  b. Of the years presented in the chart, between which two years was the increase the greatest?

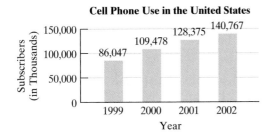

Cell Phone Use in the United States

27. The table gives the number of calls to three fire departments during a selected number of weeks. Find the number of calls per week of each department to determine which department is the busiest.

	Number of Calls	Time Period (Number of Weeks)
North Side Fire Department	80	16
South Side Fire Department	72	18
East Side Fire Department	84	28

28. Find the perimeter of the figure.

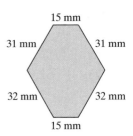

29. Find the perimeter and the area of the rectangle.

30. Round to the nearest hundred to estimate the area of the rectangle.

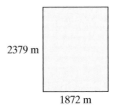

Fractions and Mixed Numbers: Multiplication and Division

2

In this chapter we study the concept of a fraction and a mixed number. We learn how to simplify fractions by reducing to lowest terms. Multiplication and division of fractions and mixed numbers are also presented along with a variety of applications. For example, suppose Ricardo buys a house for $240,000. The bank requires $\frac{1}{10}$ of the cost of the house as a down payment. Ricardo's mother pays $\frac{2}{3}$ of the down payment as a gift. Find out how much Ricardo and his mother each pay toward the down payment of the house in Exercise 93 in Section 2.5.

chapter 2 | preview

The exercises in this chapter preview contain concepts that have not yet been presented. These exercises are provided for students who want to compare their levels of understanding before and after studying the chapter. Alternatively, you may prefer to work these exercises when the chapter is completed and before taking the exam.

Section 2.1

1. Identify the fractions as proper or improper.

   a. $\dfrac{4}{5}$ b. $\dfrac{16}{8}$ c. $\dfrac{15}{15}$

2. Write $4\frac{3}{5}$ as an improper fraction.

3. Write $\frac{39}{7}$ as a mixed number.

4. Write a fraction that represents the shaded area.

   a.   b.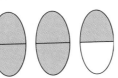

5. There are 8 different brands of wine on the wine list at a restaurant. Of these wines, 5 are red wines and the rest are white wines. What fraction represents the white wines?

Section 2.2

6. Is the number 1092 divisible by 2, 3, or 5? Explain your answers.

7. List all the factors of 45.

8. Write the prime factorization of 630.

Section 2.3

9. Which of the following fractions is simplified to lowest terms?

   a. $\dfrac{16}{25}$ b. $\dfrac{12}{14}$ c. $\dfrac{30}{15}$

Section 2.4

For Exercises 10–12, multiply and simplify the answer to lowest terms.

10. $\dfrac{9}{13} \times \dfrac{39}{27}$ 11. $\left(\dfrac{7}{12}\right)\left(\dfrac{6}{35}\right)$ 12. $12 \cdot \dfrac{77}{84}$

13. Find the area of the triangle.

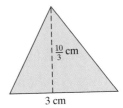

Section 2.5

For Exercises 14–16, divide. Simplify the answer to lowest terms.

14. $\dfrac{64}{21} \div 8$ 15. $\dfrac{33}{20} \div \dfrac{44}{15}$ 16. $\dfrac{3}{0}$

17. George painted $\frac{2}{3}$ of a wall that measures 18 ft by 10 ft. How much area did he paint?

18. If a recipe requires $2\frac{1}{2}$ cups of flour for one batch of cookies, how many batches can be made from 10 cups of flour?

Section 2.6

For Exercises 19–21, multiply or divide the mixed numbers. Write the answer as a mixed number or a whole number.

19. $1\frac{3}{4} \cdot 9\frac{5}{7}$ 20. $8\frac{5}{6} \div 2\frac{1}{2}$ 21. $4\frac{1}{3} \cdot 2\frac{7}{10} \div 1\frac{4}{5}$

section 2.1   **Introduction to Fractions and Mixed Numbers**

Objectives

1. Definition of a Fraction
2. Proper and Improper Fractions
3. Mixed Numbers
4. Fractions and the Number Line

1. Definition of a Fraction

In Chapter 1, we studied operations on whole numbers. In this chapter we work with numbers that represent part of a whole. When a whole unit is divided into equal parts, we call the parts **fractions** of a whole. For example, the pie in Figure 2-1 is divided into 5 equal parts. One-fifth $\left(\frac{1}{5}\right)$ of the pie has been eaten, and four-fifths $\left(\frac{4}{5}\right)$ of the pie remains.

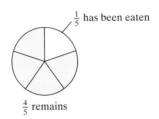

$\frac{1}{5}$ has been eaten

$\frac{4}{5}$ remains

Figure 2-1

Tip: The fraction $\frac{a}{b}$ may also be written as $^a/_b$. However, we discourage the use of the "slanted" fraction bar. In later applications of algebra, the slanted fraction bar can cause confusion.

A fraction is written in the form $\frac{a}{b}$, where a and b are whole numbers and $b \neq 0$. In the fraction $\frac{5}{8}$, the "top" number, 5, is called the *numerator*. The bottom number, 8, is called the *denominator*.

numerator $\longrightarrow$ $\dfrac{5}{8}$
denominator $\longrightarrow$

example 1   Identifying the Numerator and Denominator of a Fraction

For each fraction, identify the numerator and denominator.

a. $\dfrac{3}{5}$ **b.** $\dfrac{1}{8}$ **c.** $\dfrac{8}{1}$

Solution:

a. $\dfrac{3}{5}$ The numerator is 3. The denominator is 5.

b. $\dfrac{1}{8}$ The numerator is 1. The denominator is 8.

c. $\dfrac{8}{1}$ The numerator is 8. The denominator is 1.

Skill Practice

Identify the numerator and denominator.

1. $\dfrac{4}{11}$ **2.** $\dfrac{0}{5}$ **3.** $\dfrac{6}{1}$

The **denominator** of a fraction denotes the number of equal pieces into which a whole unit is divided. The **numerator** denotes the number of pieces being considered.

Answers

1. Numerator: 4, denominator: 11
2. Numerator: 0, denominator: 5
3. Numerator: 6, denominator: 1

For example, the garden in Figure 2-2 is divided into 10 equal parts. Three sections contain tomato plants. Therefore, $\frac{3}{10}$ of the garden contains tomato plants.

$\frac{3}{10}$ tomato plants

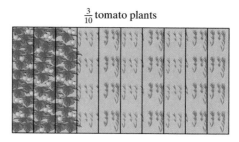

Figure 2-2

Skill Practice

4. Write a fraction for the shaded portion and a fraction for the unshaded portion.

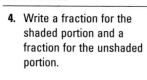

example 2   Writing Fractions

Write a fraction for the shaded portion and a fraction for the unshaded portion of the figure.

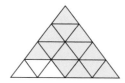

Solution:

Shaded portion: $\dfrac{13}{16}$ ⟵ 13 pieces are shaded.
ㅤㅤㅤㅤㅤㅤㅤㅤㅤㅤㅤ ⟵ The triangle is divided into 16 equal pieces.

Unshaded portion: $\dfrac{3}{16}$ ⟵ 3 pieces are not shaded.
ㅤㅤㅤㅤㅤㅤㅤㅤㅤㅤㅤ ⟵ The triangle is divided into 16 equal pieces.

Skill Practice

5. The graph categorizes a sample of people by blood type. What portion of the sample represents people with type O blood?

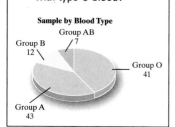

Sample by Blood Type

Group AB 7
Group B 12
Group O 41
Group A 43

example 3   Writing Fractions

What portion of the group of celebrities shown below is female?

Solution:

The group is divided among 5 members. Therefore, the denominator is 5. There are 2 women being considered. Thus, $\frac{2}{5}$ of the group is female.

Answers

4. Shaded portion: $\frac{3}{8}$; unshaded portion: $\frac{5}{8}$
5. Group O: $\frac{41}{103}$

In Section 1.6 we learned that fractions represent division. For example, note that the fraction $\frac{5}{1} = 5 \div 1 = 5$. In general, a fraction of the form $\frac{n}{1} = n$. This implies that any whole number may be written as a fraction by writing the whole number over 1.

Further recall that for $a \neq 0$, $0 \div a = 0$ and $a \div 0$ is undefined. Therefore, a fraction of the form $\frac{0}{a} = 0$ and $\frac{a}{0}$ is undefined. For example,

$$\frac{0}{5} = 0 \text{ whereas } \frac{5}{0} \text{ is undefined}$$

2. Proper and Improper Fractions

If the numerator is less than the denominator in a fraction, then the fraction is called a **proper fraction**. Furthermore, a proper fraction represents a number less than 1 whole unit. The following are proper fractions.

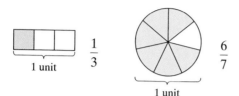

An **improper fraction** is a fraction in which the numerator is greater than or equal to the denominator. For example:

numerator greater ⟶ $\frac{4}{3}$ and $\frac{7}{7}$ ⟵ numerator equal
than denominator   to denominator

An improper fraction represents a quantity greater than a whole unit or equal to a whole unit.

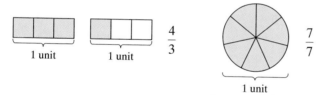

---

example 4   **Categorizing Fractions**

Identify each fraction as proper or improper.

a. $\frac{12}{5}$ **b.** $\frac{5}{12}$ **c.** $\frac{12}{12}$

Skill Practice

Identify each fraction as proper or improper.

8. $\frac{10}{10}$ **9.** $\frac{7}{9}$ **10.** $\frac{9}{7}$

Solution:

a. $\frac{12}{5}$ Improper fraction (numerator is greater than denominator)

b. $\frac{5}{12}$ Proper fraction (numerator is less than denominator)

c. $\frac{12}{12}$ Improper fraction (numerator is equal to denominator)

Answers

6. Undefined   7. 0
8. Improper   9. Proper
10. Improper

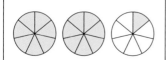
Avoiding Mistakes: In Example 5, each whole unit is divided into 8 pieces. Therefore the screw is $\frac{11}{8}$ in., not $\frac{11}{16}$ in.

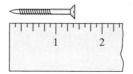 **example 5**   Writing Improper Fractions

Write an improper fraction to represent the fractional part of an inch for the screw shown in the figure.

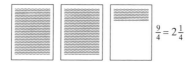

Solution:

Each 1-in. unit is divided into 8 parts, and the screw extends for 11 parts. Therefore, the screw is $\frac{11}{8}$ in.

3. Mixed Numbers

Sometimes a mixed number is used instead of an improper fraction to denote a quantity greater than one whole. For example, suppose a typist typed $\frac{9}{4}$ pages of a report. We would be more likely to say that the typist typed $2\frac{1}{4}$ pages (read as "two and one-fourth pages"). The number $2\frac{1}{4}$ is called a *mixed number* and represents 2 wholes plus $\frac{1}{4}$ of a whole.

$$\frac{9}{4} = 2\frac{1}{4}$$

In general, a **mixed number** is a sum of a whole number and a fractional part of a whole. However, by convention the plus sign is left out.

$$3\frac{1}{2} \quad \text{means} \quad 3 + \frac{1}{2}$$

Suppose we want to change a mixed number to an improper fraction. From Figure 2-3, we see that the mixed number $3\frac{1}{2}$ is the same as $\frac{7}{2}$.

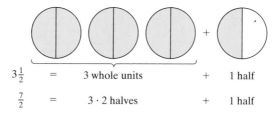

$3\frac{1}{2}$	=	3 whole units	+	1 half
$\frac{7}{2}$	=	$3 \cdot 2$ halves	+	1 half

Figure 2-3

This process to convert a mixed number to an improper fraction can be summarized as follows.

Changing a Mixed Number to an Improper Fraction

1. Multiply the whole number by the denominator.

2. Add the result to the numerator.

3. Write the result from step 2 over the denominator.

Answer

11. $\dfrac{15}{7}$

For example,

Multiply the whole
number by the
denominator.

Add the
numerator.

$$3\frac{1}{2} = \frac{3 \times 2 + 1}{2} = \frac{7}{2}$$

Write the result over
the denominator.

example 6   Converting Mixed Numbers to Fractions

Convert the mixed number to an improper fraction.

a. $7\frac{1}{4}$ **b.** $8\frac{2}{5}$

Solution:

a. $7\frac{1}{4} = \frac{7 \times 4 + 1}{4}$

$= \frac{28 + 1}{4}$

$= \frac{29}{4}$

b. $8\frac{2}{5} = \frac{8 \times 5 + 2}{5}$

$= \frac{40 + 2}{5}$

$= \frac{42}{5}$

Skill Practice

Convert the mixed number to
an improper fraction.

12. $10\frac{5}{8}$ **13.** $15\frac{1}{2}$

Now suppose we want to convert an improper fraction to a mixed number. In Figure 2-4, the improper fraction $\frac{13}{5}$ represents 13 slices of pie where each slice is $\frac{1}{5}$ of a whole pie. If we divide the 13 pieces into groups of 5, we make 2 whole pies with 3 pieces left over. Thus,

$$\frac{13}{5} = 2\frac{3}{5}$$

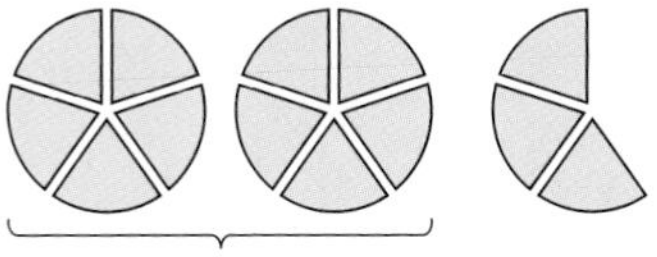

13 pieces =   2 groups of 5   + 3 left over

$\frac{13}{5} =$ 2   + $\frac{3}{5}$

Figure 2-4

This process can be accomplished by division.

$$\frac{13}{5} \longrightarrow \begin{array}{r} 2 \\ 5\overline{)13} \\ -10 \\ \hline 3 \end{array} \quad 2\frac{3}{5} \begin{array}{l} \text{remainder} \\ \\ \text{divisor} \end{array}$$

Changing an Improper Fraction to a Mixed Number

1. Divide the numerator by the denominator to obtain the quotient and remainder.

2. The mixed number is then given by

$$\text{Quotient} + \frac{\text{remainder}}{\text{divisor}}$$

Answers

12. $\frac{85}{8}$ **13.** $\frac{31}{2}$

example 7   Converting an Improper Fraction to a Mixed Number

Convert to a mixed number.

a. $\dfrac{25}{6}$ **b.** $\dfrac{162}{41}$

Solution:

a. $\dfrac{25}{6}$ $\longrightarrow$

$$\begin{array}{r} 4 \\ 6\overline{)25} \\ -24 \\ \hline 1 \end{array}$$

$4\dfrac{1}{6}$ (remainder / divisor)

b. $\dfrac{162}{41}$ $\longrightarrow$

$$\begin{array}{r} 3 \\ 41\overline{)162} \\ -123 \\ \hline 39 \end{array}$$

$3\dfrac{39}{41}$ (remainder / divisor)

The process to convert an improper fraction to a mixed number indicates that the result of a division problem can be written as a mixed number.

example 8   Writing a Quotient as a Mixed Number

Divide. Write the quotient as a mixed number.

$$28\overline{)4217}$$

Solution:

$$\begin{array}{r} 150 \\ 28\overline{)4217} \\ -28 \\ \hline 141 \\ -140 \\ \hline 17 \\ -0 \\ \hline 17 \end{array}$$

$150\dfrac{17}{28}$ (remainder / divisor)

4. Fractions and the Number Line

Fractions can be visualized on a number line. For example, to graph the fraction $\frac{3}{4}$, divide the distance between 0 and 1 into 4 equal parts. To plot the number $\frac{3}{4}$, start at 0 and count over 3 parts.

| example 9 | Plotting Fractions on a Number Line |

Plot the point on the number line corresponding to each fraction.

a. $\dfrac{1}{2}$ **b.** $\dfrac{5}{6}$ **c.** $\dfrac{21}{5}$

Solution:

a. $\dfrac{1}{2}$ Divide the distance between 0 and 1 into 2 equal parts.

b. $\dfrac{5}{6}$ Divide the distance between 0 and 1 into 6 equal parts.

c. $\dfrac{21}{5} = 4\dfrac{1}{5}$ Write $\frac{21}{5}$ as a mixed number.

Thus, $\frac{21}{5} = 4\frac{1}{5}$ is located one-fifth of the way between 4 and 5 on the number line.

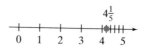

Skill Practice

Plot the numbers on a number line.

17. $\dfrac{4}{5}$ **18.** $\dfrac{1}{3}$

19. $\dfrac{13}{4}$ **20.** $\dfrac{20}{7}$

Answers

17.

18.

19.

20.

| section 2.1 | Practice Exercises |

Boost *your* GRADE at mathzone.com!

MathZone

- Practice Problems
- Self-Tests
- NetTutor
- e-Professors
- Videos

Study Skills Exercises

1. After doing a section of homework, check the odd answers in the back of the text. Choose a method to identify the exercises that you got wrong or had trouble with (i.e., circle the number or put a star by the number). List some reasons why it is important to label these problems.

2. Define the key terms.

   a. Fraction

   b. Numerator

   c. Denominator

   d. Proper fraction

   e. Improper fraction

   f. Mixed number

Objective 1: Definition of a Fraction

For Exercises 3–10, write a fraction that represents the shaded area. **(See Example 2.)**

3.

4.

 5.

6.

7.

8.

9.

10.

11. Write a fraction to represent the portion of gas in a gas tank represented by the gauge.

12. Write a fraction that represents the portion of medicine left in the bottle.

For Exercises 13–16, identify the numerator and the denominator for each fraction.
(See Example 1.)

13. $\dfrac{2}{3}$ 14. $\dfrac{8}{9}$ 15. $\dfrac{12}{11}$ 16. $\dfrac{1}{2}$

For Exercises 17–24, write the fraction as a division problem and simplify, if possible.

17. $\dfrac{6}{1}$ 18. $\dfrac{9}{1}$ 19. $\dfrac{2}{2}$ 20. $\dfrac{8}{8}$

 21. $\dfrac{0}{3}$ 22. $\dfrac{0}{7}$ 23. $\dfrac{2}{0}$ 24. $\dfrac{11}{0}$

25. What fraction of the umbrellas is yellow?
    (See Example 3.)

26. Write a fraction representing the boats in the marina that are sailboats.

27. A class has 21 children—11 girls and 10 boys. What fraction of the class is made up of boys?

28. A restaurant has 33 tables. Of the total, 10 are reserved for customers who smoke, and 23 are for nonsmokers. Write a fraction representing the tables reserved for the smokers.

Objective 2: Proper and Improper Fractions

For Exercises 29–34, label the fraction as proper or improper. **(See Example 4.)**

29. $\dfrac{7}{8}$ **30.** $\dfrac{2}{3}$ **31.** $\dfrac{10}{10}$ **32.** $\dfrac{3}{3}$

33. $\dfrac{7}{2}$ **34.** $\dfrac{21}{20}$

For Exercises 35–38, write an improper fraction for the shaded portion of each group of figures. **(See Example 5.)**

35.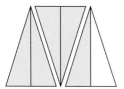

36.

37.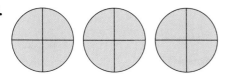

38.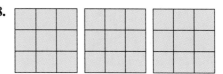

Objective 3: Mixed Numbers

For Exercises 39–40, write an improper fraction and a mixed number for the shaded portion of each group of figures.

39.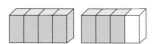

40.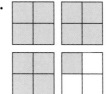

41. Write an improper fraction and a mixed number that represent the fraction of the length of the ribbon.

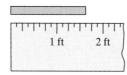

42. Write an improper fraction and a mixed number that represent the fraction of the amount of sugar needed for a batch of cookies as indicated in the figure.

For Exercises 43–58, convert the mixed number to an improper fraction. **(See Example 6.)**

43. $1\dfrac{3}{4}$

44. $6\dfrac{1}{3}$

45. $4\dfrac{2}{9}$

46. $3\dfrac{1}{5}$

47. $3\dfrac{3}{7}$

48. $8\dfrac{2}{3}$

49. $7\dfrac{1}{4}$

50. $10\dfrac{3}{5}$

51. $11\dfrac{5}{12}$

52. $12\dfrac{1}{6}$

53. $21\dfrac{3}{8}$

54. $15\dfrac{1}{2}$

55. $8\dfrac{5}{16}$

56. $7\dfrac{4}{15}$

57. $13\dfrac{9}{20}$

58. $9\dfrac{17}{18}$

59. How many eighths are in $2\dfrac{3}{8}$?

60. How many fifths are in $2\dfrac{3}{5}$?

61. How many fourths are in $1\dfrac{3}{4}$?

62. How many thirds are in $5\dfrac{2}{3}$?

For Exercises 63–78, convert the improper fraction to a mixed number. **(See Example 7.)**

63. $\dfrac{37}{8}$

64. $\dfrac{13}{7}$

65. $\dfrac{39}{5}$

66. $\dfrac{19}{4}$

67. $\dfrac{27}{10}$

68. $\dfrac{43}{18}$

69. $\dfrac{52}{9}$

70. $\dfrac{67}{12}$

71. $\dfrac{133}{11}$

72. $\dfrac{51}{10}$

73. $\dfrac{23}{6}$

74. $\dfrac{115}{7}$

75. $\dfrac{68}{9}$

76. $\dfrac{40}{17}$

77. $\dfrac{65}{8}$

78. $\dfrac{101}{15}$

For Exercises 79–84, divide. Write the quotient as a mixed number. **(See Example 8.)**

79. $7\overline{)309}$

80. $4\overline{)921}$

81. $5281 \div 5$

82. $7213 \div 8$

83. $8913 \div 11$

84. $4257 \div 23$

Objective 4: Fractions and the Number Line

For Exercises 85–94, plot the fraction on the number line. **(See Example 9.)**

85. $\dfrac{3}{4}$

86. $\dfrac{1}{2}$

87. $\dfrac{1}{3}$

88. $\dfrac{1}{5}$

89. $\dfrac{2}{3}$

90. $\dfrac{5}{6}$

91. $\dfrac{7}{6}$

92. $\dfrac{7}{5}$

93. $\dfrac{5}{3}$

94. $\dfrac{3}{2}$

Expanding Your Skills

95. True or false? Whole numbers can be written both as proper and improper fractions.

96. True or false? Suppose m and n are whole numbers where $m > n$. Then $\frac{m}{n}$ is an improper fraction.

97. True or false? Suppose m and n are whole numbers where $m > n$. Then $\frac{n}{m}$ is a proper fraction.

98. True or false? Suppose m and n are whole numbers where $m > n$. Then $\frac{n}{3m}$ is a proper fraction.

Calculator Connections

Topic: Converting mixed numbers to improper fractions

Calculator Exercises

For Exercises 99–102, convert the mixed number to an improper fraction. Use a calculator to help you with the calculations.

99. $21\dfrac{39}{407}$

100. $184\dfrac{17}{91}$

101. $48\dfrac{23}{112}$

102. $25\dfrac{59}{73}$

section 2.2   Prime Numbers and Factorization

1. Factors and Factorizations

Recall from Section 1.5 that two numbers multiplied to form a product are called factors. For example, $2 \cdot 3 = 6$ indicates that 2 and 3 are factors of 6. Likewise, because $1 \cdot 6 = 6$, the numbers 1 and 6 are factors of 6. In general, a **factor** of a number n is a nonzero whole number that divides evenly into n.

The products $2 \cdot 3$ and $1 \cdot 6$ are called factorizations of 6. In general, a **factorization** of a number n is a product of factors that equals n.

Skill Practice

Find four different factorizations of the given number.

1. 18   2. 30

example 1   Finding Factorizations of a Number

Find four different factorizations of 12.

Solution:

$$12 = \begin{cases} 1 \cdot 12 \\ 2 \cdot 6 \\ 3 \cdot 4 \\ 2 \cdot 2 \cdot 3 \end{cases}$$

Tip: Notice that a factorization may include more than two factors.

2. Divisibility Rules

The number 20 is said to be divisible by 5 because 5 divides evenly into 20. To determine whether one number is divisible by another, we can perform the division and note whether the remainder is zero. However, there are several rules by which we can quickly determine whether a number is divisible by 2, 3, 5, or 10. These are called divisibility rules.

Divisibility Rules for 2, 3, 5, and 10

- *Divisibility by 2.* A whole number is divisible by 2 if it is an even number. That is, the ones-place digit is 0, 2, 4, 6, or 8.
    Examples: 26 and 384
- *Divisibility by 5.* A whole number is divisible by 5 if its ones-place digit is 5 or 0.
    Examples: 45 and 260
- *Divisibility by 10.* A whole number is divisible by 10 if its ones-place digit is 0.
    Examples: 30 and 170
- *Divisibility by 3.* A whole number is divisible by 3 if the sum of its digits is divisible by 3.
    Example: 312   (sum of digits is $3 + 1 + 2 = 6$ which is divisible by 3)

We address other divisibility rules for 4, 6, 8, and 9 in the Expanding Your Skills portion of the exercises. However, these divisibility rules are harder to remember, and it is often easier simply to perform division to test for divisibility.

---

example 2   Applying the Divisibility Rules

Determine whether the given number is divisible by 2, 3, 5, or 10.

a. 624   **b.** 82   **c.** 720

Solution:

	Test for divisibility		
a. 624	By 2:	Yes.	The number 624 is even.
	By 3:	Yes.	The sum $6 + 2 + 4 = 12$ is divisible by 3.
	By 5:	No.	The ones-place digit is not 5 or 0.
	By 10:	No.	The ones-place digit is not 0.
b. 82	By 2:	Yes.	The number 82 is even.
	By 3:	No.	The sum $8 + 2 = 10$ is not divisible by 3.
	By 5:	No.	The ones-place digit is not 5 or 0.
	By 10:	No.	The ones-place digit is not 0.
c. 720	By 2:	Yes.	The number 720 is even.
	By 3:	Yes.	The sum $7 + 2 + 0 = 9$ is divisible by 3.
	By 5:	Yes.	The ones-place digit is 0.
	By 10:	Yes.	The ones-place digit is 0.

Tip: When in doubt about divisibility, you can check by performing the division. For instance, in Example 2(a), we can verify that 624 is divisible by 3.

$$\begin{array}{r} 208 \\ 3\overline{)624} \\ -6 \\ \hline 24 \\ -24 \\ \hline 0 \end{array}$$

3. Prime and Composite Numbers

Two important classifications of whole numbers are prime numbers and composite numbers.

Definition of Prime and Composite Numbers

- A **prime number** is a whole number greater than 1 that has only two factors (itself and 1).

- A **composite number** is a whole number greater than 1 that is not prime. That is, a composite number will have at least one factor other than 1 and the number itself.

Note: The whole numbers 0 and 1 are neither prime nor composite.

---

example 3   Identifying Prime and Composite Numbers

Determine whether the number is prime, composite, or neither.

a. 19   **b.** 51   **c.** 1

Tip: The number 2 is the only even prime number.

Solution:

a. The number 19 is prime because its only factors are 1 and 19.

b. The number 51 is composite because $3 \cdot 17 = 51$. That is, 51 has factors other than 1 and 51.

c. The number 1 is neither prime nor composite by definition.

Prime numbers are used in a variety of skills in mathematics. We advise you to become familiar with the first several prime numbers: 2, 3, 5, 7, 11, 13, 17, 19, 23, 29, . . .

4. Prime Factorization

In Example 1 we found four factorizations of 12.

$$1 \cdot 12$$
$$2 \cdot 6$$
$$3 \cdot 4$$
$$2 \cdot 2 \cdot 3$$

The last factorization $2 \cdot 2 \cdot 3$ consists of only prime-number factors. Therefore, we say $2 \cdot 2 \cdot 3$ is the prime factorization of 12. Note that the order in which we write the factors within a factorization does not affect its product (this is so because multiplication is commutative). Therefore, the products $2 \cdot 2 \cdot 3$, $2 \cdot 3 \cdot 2$, and $3 \cdot 2 \cdot 2$ are all equivalent and all represent the prime factorization of 12.

> ### Prime Factorization
>
> The **prime factorization** of a number is the factorization in which every factor is a prime number.
>
> *Note:* The order in which the factors are written does not affect the product.

Prime factorizations of numbers will be particularly helpful when we add, subtract, multiply, divide, and simplify fractions to lowest terms.

example 4	Determining the Prime Factorization of a Number

Find the prime factorization of 220.

Solution:

One method to factor a whole number is to make a factor tree. Begin by determining any two numbers that when multiplied equal 220. Then continue factoring each factor until the branches "end" in prime numbers.

←Branches end in prime numbers.

> **Tip:** The prime factorization from Example 4 can also be expressed by using exponents as $2^2 \cdot 5 \cdot 11$.

Therefore, the prime factorization of 220 is $2 \cdot 2 \cdot 5 \cdot 11$.

In Example 4, note that the result of a prime factorization does not depend on the original two-number factorization. Similarly, the order in which the factors are written does not affect the product, for example,

$$220 = 2 \cdot 2 \cdot 5 \cdot 11 \qquad 220 = 2 \cdot 2 \cdot 5 \cdot 11 \qquad 220 = 11 \cdot 2 \cdot 2 \cdot 5$$

> **Tip:** You can check the prime factorization of any number by multiplying the factors.

Concept Connections

9. Is the product $2 \cdot 3 \cdot 10$ the prime factorization of 60? Explain.

10. Which is the prime factorization of 70?

$2 \cdot 5 \cdot 7$ or $2 \cdot 7 \cdot 5$
or $5 \cdot 7 \cdot 2$

Concept Connections

11. How would you write the factorization, $2 \cdot 2 \cdot 2 \cdot 2 \cdot 3 \cdot 5 \cdot 5$ using exponents?

Avoiding Mistakes: Make sure that the end of each branch is a prime number.

Answers
9. No. The factor 10 is not a prime number. The prime factorization of 60 is $2 \cdot 2 \cdot 3 \cdot 5$.
10. All three factorizations represent the prime factorization. The order in which we write the factors does not affect the product.
11. $2^4 \cdot 3 \cdot 5^2$

Another technique to find the prime factorization of a number is to divide the number by the smallest known prime factor. Then divide the quotient by its smallest known prime factor. Continue dividing in this fashion until the quotient is a prime number. The prime factorization is the product of divisors and the final quotient. For example,

the last quotient is prime ⟶ 11
5 is the smallest prime factor of 55 ⟶ 5)$\overline{55}$
2 is the smallest prime factor of 110 ⟶ 2)$\overline{110}$
2 is the smallest prime factor of 220 ⟶ 2)$\overline{220}$

Therefore, the prime factorization of 220 is $2 \cdot 2 \cdot 5 \cdot 11$ or $2^2 \cdot 5 \cdot 11$.

---

example 5   Determining Prime Factorizations

Find the prime factorization.

a. 198   **b.** 153

Solution:

a.

$$\begin{array}{r} 11 \\ 3)\overline{33} \\ 3)\overline{99} \\ 2)\overline{198} \end{array}$$

The sum of the digits
$9 + 9 = 18$ is divisible by 3.

Because 198 is even, we ⟶ know it is divisible by 2.

The prime factorization of 198 is $2 \cdot 3 \cdot 3 \cdot 11$ or $2 \cdot 3^2 \cdot 11$.

b.

$$\begin{array}{r} 17 \\ 3)\overline{51} \\ 3)\overline{153} \end{array}$$

The prime factorization of 153 is $3 \cdot 3 \cdot 17$ or $3^2 \cdot 17$.

Skill Practice

Find the prime factorization of the given number.

12. 168   **13.** 990

5. Identifying All Factors of a Whole Number

Sometimes it is necessary to identify all factors (both prime and other) of a number. Take the number 30, for example. A list of all factors of 30 is a list of all whole numbers that divide evenly into 30.

Factors of 30:   1, 2, 3, 5, 6, 10, 15, and 30

---

example 6   Listing All Factors of a Number

List all factors of 36.

Solution:

Begin by listing all the two-number factorizations of 36. This can be accomplished by systematically dividing 36 by 1, 2, 3, and so on. Notice, however, that after the product $6 \cdot 6$, the two-number factorizations are repetitious, and we can stop the process.

Skill Practice

List all the factors of the given number.

14. 45   **15.** 52

Answers

12. $2 \cdot 2 \cdot 2 \cdot 3 \cdot 7$ or $2^3 \cdot 3 \cdot 7$
13. $2 \cdot 3 \cdot 3 \cdot 5 \cdot 11$ or $2 \cdot 3^2 \cdot 5 \cdot 11$
14. 1, 3, 5, 9, 15, 45
15. 1, 2, 4, 13, 26, 52

Tip: When listing a set of factors, it is not necessary to write the numbers in any specified order. However, in general we list the factors in order from smallest to largest.

$1 \cdot 36$
$2 \cdot 18$
$3 \cdot 12$
$4 \cdot 9$
$6 \cdot 6$
$9 \cdot 4$
$12 \cdot 3$
$18 \cdot 2$
$36 \cdot 1$

These products are repetitious of the factorizations above. Therefore, we can stop at $6 \cdot 6$.

The list of all factors of 36 consists of the individual factors in the products. The factors are 1, 2, 3, 4, 6, 9, 12, 18, 36.

section 2.2   Practice Exercises

Boost *your* GRADE at mathzone.com!

 MathZone

• Practice Problems
• Self-Tests
• NetTutor

• e-Professors
• Videos

Study Skills Exercises

1. A rule of thumb is that 2 to 3 hours of study time per week is needed for each 1 hour per week of class time. Based on the number of hours you are in class this semester, how many hours per week should you be studying?

2. Define the key terms.

   a. **Factor**

   b. **Factorization**

   c. **Prime number**

   d. **Composite number**

   e. **Prime factorization**

Review Exercises

For Exercises 3–5, write two fractions, one representing the shaded area and one representing the unshaded area.

3.

   0   1

4.

5.

6. Write a fraction with numerator 6 and denominator 5. Is this fraction proper or improper?

7. Write a fraction with denominator 12 and numerator 7. Is this fraction proper or improper?

8. Write a fraction with denominator 6 and numerator 6. Is this fraction proper or improper?

9. Write the improper fraction $\frac{23}{5}$ as a mixed number.   **10.** Write the mixed number $6\frac{2}{7}$ as an improper fraction.

Objective 1: Factors and Factorization

For Exercises 11–16, find two different factorizations of each number. (Answers may vary.) **(See Example 1.)**

11. 8   **12.** 20   🖩 **13.** 24   **14.** 14

15. 32   **16.** 54

17. Find two factors whose product is the number in the top row and whose sum is the number in the bottom row. The first column is done for you as an example.

Product	36	42	30	15	81
Factor	12				
Factor	3				
Sum	15	13	31	16	30

18. Find two factors whose product is the number in the top row and whose difference is the number in the bottom row. The first column is done for you as an example.

Product	36	42	45	72	24
Factor	9				
Factor	4				
Difference	5	1	12	14	5

Objective 2: Divisibility Rules

19. State the divisibility rule for dividing by 2.   **20.** State the divisibility rule for dividing by 10.

21. State the divisibility rule for dividing by 3.   **22.** State the divisibility rule for dividing by 5.

For Exercises 23–32, determine if the number is divisible by

a. 2   **b.** 3   **c.** 5   **d.** 10 **(See Example 2.)**

23. 45   **24.** 100   **25.** 72   **26.** 57

🖩 **27.** 108   **28.** 1040   **29.** 3140   **30.** 2115

31. 137   **32.** 241

33. Ms. Haefele has 28 students in her class. Can she distribute a package of 84 candies evenly to her students?

34. Mr. Dietz has 22 students in an algebra class. He has 110 sheets of graph paper. Can he distribute the graph paper evenly among his students?

Objective 3: Prime and Composite Numbers

35. Are there any whole numbers that are not prime or composite? If so, list them.

36. True or false? The square of any prime number is also a prime number.

37. True or false? All odd numbers are prime.   **38.** True or false? All even numbers are composite.

39. One method for finding prime numbers is the *sieve of Eratosthenes*. The natural numbers from 2 to 50 are shown in the table. Start at the number 2 (the smallest prime number). Leave the number 2 and cross out every second number after the number 2. This will eliminate all numbers that are multiples of 2. Then go back to the beginning of the chart and leave the number 3, but cross out every third number after the number 3 (thus eliminating the multiples of 3). Begin at the next open number and continue this process. The numbers that remain are prime numbers. Use this process to find the prime numbers less than 50.

	2	3	4	5	6	7	8	9	10
11	12	13	14	15	16	17	18	19	20
21	22	23	24	25	26	27	28	29	30
31	32	33	34	35	36	37	38	39	40
41	42	43	44	45	46	47	48	49	50

40. Use the sieve of Eratosthenes to find the prime numbers less than 80.

	2	3	4	5	6	7	8	9	10
11	12	13	14	15	16	17	18	19	20
21	22	23	24	25	26	27	28	29	30
31	32	33	34	35	36	37	38	39	40
41	42	43	44	45	46	47	48	49	50
51	52	53	54	55	56	57	58	59	60
61	62	63	64	65	66	67	68	69	70
71	72	73	74	75	76	77	78	79	80

For Exercises 41–56, determine whether the number is prime, composite, or neither. **(See Example 3.)**

41. 7   **42.** 17   **43.** 10   **44.** 21

45. 51   **46.** 57   **47.** 23   **48.** 31

49. 1   **50.** 0   **51.** 121   **52.** 69

53. 19   **54.** 29   **55.** 39   **56.** 49

Objective 4: Prime Factorization

For Exercises 57–60, determine whether or not the factorization represents the prime factorization. If not, explain why.

57. $36 = 2 \cdot 2 \cdot 9$ **58.** $48 = 2 \cdot 3 \cdot 8$ **59.** $210 = 5 \cdot 2 \cdot 7 \cdot 3$ **60.** $126 = 3 \cdot 7 \cdot 3 \cdot 2$

For Exercises 61–72, find the prime factorization. **(See Examples 4 and 5.)**

61. 70   **62.** 495   **63.** 260   **64.** 175

65. 147   **66.** 102   **67.** 138   **68.** 231

69. 616   **70.** 364   **71.** 47   **72.** 41

Objective 5: Identifying All Factors of a Whole Number

For Exercises 73–80, list all the factors of the number. **(See Example 6.)**

73. 12   **74.** 18   **75.** 32   **76.** 55

77. 81   **78.** 60   **79.** 48   **80.** 72

Expanding Your Skills

For Exercises 81–84, determine whether the number is divisible by 4. Use the following divisibility rule: A whole number is divisible by 4 if the number formed by its last two digits is divisible by 4.

81. 230   **82.** 1046   **83.** 4616   **84.** 10,264

For Exercises 85–88, determine whether the number is divisible by 8. Use the following divisibility rule: A whole number is divisible by 8 if the number formed by its last three digits is divisible by 8.

85. 1032   **86.** 2520   **87.** 17,126   **88.** 25,058

For Exercises 89–92, determine whether the number is divisible by 9. Use the following divisibility rule: A whole number is divisible by 9 if the sum of its digits is divisible by 9.

89. 396   **90.** 414   **91.** 8453   **92.** 1587

For Exercises 93–96, determine whether the number is divisible by 6. Use the following divisibility rule: A whole number is divisible by 6 if it is divisible by both 2 and 3 (use the divisibility rules for 2 and 3 together).

93. 522   **94.** 546   **95.** 5917   **96.** 6394

section 2.3   Simplifying Fractions to Lowest Terms

1. Equivalent Fractions

The fractions $\frac{3}{6}$, $\frac{2}{4}$, and $\frac{1}{2}$ all represent the same portion of a whole. See Figure 2-5. Therefore, we say that the fractions are *equivalent*.

$$\frac{3}{6} \quad = \quad \frac{2}{4} \quad = \quad \frac{1}{2}$$

Figure 2-5

Avoiding Mistakes: The test to determine whether two fractions are equivalent is not the same process as multiplying fractions. Multiplying of fractions is covered in Section 2.4.

One method to show that two fractions are equivalent is to calculate their cross products. For example, to show that $\frac{3}{6} = \frac{2}{4}$, we have

$$\frac{3}{6} \quad \diagdown\!\!\!\!\diagup \quad \frac{2}{4}$$

$$3 \times 4 \overset{?}{=} 6 \times 2$$

$$12 = 12 \qquad \text{Yes. The fractions are equivalent.}$$

Skill Practice

Fill in the blank ☐ with = or ≠.

1. $\dfrac{13}{24} \ \square\ \dfrac{6}{11}$

2. $\dfrac{9}{4} \ \square\ \dfrac{54}{24}$

---

example 1   Determining Whether Two Fractions Are Equivalent

Fill in the blank ☐ with = or ≠.

a. $\dfrac{18}{39} \ \square\ \dfrac{6}{13}$ b. $\dfrac{5}{7} \ \square\ \dfrac{7}{9}$

Solution:

a. $\dfrac{18}{39} \ \diagdown\!\!\!\!\diagup\ \dfrac{6}{13}$ b. $\dfrac{5}{7} \ \diagdown\!\!\!\!\diagup\ \dfrac{7}{9}$

$18 \times 13 \overset{?}{=} 39 \times 6$ $5 \times 9 \overset{?}{=} 7 \times 7$

$234 = 234$ $45 \neq 49$

Therefore, $\dfrac{18}{39} \boxed{=} \dfrac{6}{13}$.   Therefore, $\dfrac{5}{7} \boxed{\neq} \dfrac{7}{9}$.

2. Simplifying Fractions to Lowest Terms

In Figure 2-5 we see that $\frac{3}{6}$, $\frac{2}{4}$, and $\frac{1}{2}$ all represent equal quantities. However, the fraction $\frac{1}{2}$ is said to be in **lowest terms** because the numerator and denominator share no common factor other than 1.

To simplify a fraction to lowest terms, we use the following important principle.

The Fundamental Principle of Fractions

Consider the fraction $\dfrac{a}{b}$ and the nonzero number c. Then

$$\frac{a}{b} = \frac{a \div c}{b \div c}$$

Answers

1. ≠
2. =

The fundamental principle of fractions indicates that dividing both the numerator and the denominator by the same nonzero number results in an equivalent fraction. For example, the numerator and denominator of the fraction $\frac{3}{6}$ both share a common factor of 3. To simplify $\frac{3}{6}$, we will divide both the numerator and denominator by the common factor 3.

$$\frac{3}{6} = \frac{3 \div 3}{6 \div 3} = \frac{1}{2}$$

Before applying the fundamental principle of fractions, it is helpful to write the prime factorization of both the numerator and the denominator. This will allow us to find the common factors. For example, to simplify $\frac{35}{42}$ to lowest terms, begin by writing

$$\frac{35}{42} = \frac{5 \cdot 7}{2 \cdot 3 \cdot 7}$$

In this form, it is clear that 7 is the common factor. Use the fundamental principle of fractions to divide the numerator and denominator by 7:

$$\frac{5 \cdot 7 \div 7}{2 \cdot 3 \cdot 7 \div 7} = \frac{5}{2 \cdot 3} = \frac{5}{6}$$

Because there are no other common factors, we say that $\frac{5}{6}$ is simplified to lowest terms.

A shorthand notation of writing the division by 7 is to strike out the common factors with "cancel lines." Then replace the common factor of 7 by the new common factor of 1.

$$\frac{35}{42} = \frac{5 \cdot 7}{2 \cdot 3 \cdot 7} = \frac{5 \cdot \overset{1}{\cancel{7}}}{2 \cdot 3 \cdot \underset{1}{\cancel{7}}} = \frac{5 \cdot 1}{2 \cdot 3 \cdot 1} = \frac{5}{6}$$

Tip: Simplifying a fraction is also called reducing a fraction to lowest terms. For example, the simplified (or reduced) form of $\frac{35}{42}$ is $\frac{5}{6}$.

| example 2 | **Simplifying Fractions to Lowest Terms** |

Simplify to lowest terms. Write the answer as a fraction or whole number.

a. $\dfrac{30}{20}$ **b.** $\dfrac{8}{24}$ **c.** $\dfrac{110}{99}$ **d.** $\dfrac{75}{25}$

Skill Practice

Simplify to lowest terms.

3. $\dfrac{15}{35}$ **4.** $\dfrac{48}{12}$

5. $\dfrac{14}{84}$ **6.** $\dfrac{26}{195}$

Solution:

a. $\dfrac{30}{20} = \dfrac{2 \cdot 3 \cdot \overset{1}{\cancel{5}}}{2 \cdot 2 \cdot \underset{1}{\cancel{5}}} = \dfrac{1 \cdot 3 \cdot 1}{1 \cdot 2 \cdot 1} = \dfrac{3}{2}$

Avoiding Mistakes: Don't forget to write the 1's when you strike out common factors. This is particularly important when all the factors in the numerator "cancel."

b. $\dfrac{8}{24} = \dfrac{\overset{1}{\cancel{2}} \cdot \overset{1}{\cancel{2}} \cdot \overset{1}{\cancel{2}}}{\underset{1}{\cancel{2}} \cdot \underset{1}{\cancel{2}} \cdot \underset{1}{\cancel{2}} \cdot 3} = \dfrac{1 \cdot 1 \cdot 1}{1 \cdot 1 \cdot 1 \cdot 3} = \dfrac{1}{3}$

c. $\dfrac{110}{99} = \dfrac{2 \cdot 5 \cdot \overset{1}{\cancel{11}}}{3 \cdot 3 \cdot \underset{1}{\cancel{11}}} = \dfrac{2 \cdot 5}{3 \cdot 3} = \dfrac{10}{9}$

d. $\dfrac{75}{25} = \dfrac{3 \cdot \overset{1}{\cancel{5}} \cdot \overset{1}{\cancel{5}}}{\underset{1}{\cancel{5}} \cdot \underset{1}{\cancel{5}}} = \dfrac{3 \cdot 1 \cdot 1}{1 \cdot 1} = \dfrac{3}{1} = 3$

Tip: Recall that any fraction of the form $\frac{n}{1} = n$. Therefore, $\frac{3}{1}$ equals the whole number 3.

Another method to simplify a fraction to lowest terms is to identify the greatest factor shared by both the numerator and denominator (called the *greatest*

Answers

3. $\dfrac{3}{7}$ 4. 4   5. $\dfrac{1}{6}$ 6. $\dfrac{2}{15}$

common factor). For example, with the fraction $\frac{48}{32}$, you might notice that 16 is the greatest number that divides evenly into both the numerator and the denominator. Therefore, we can factor the numerator and denominator by using 16 as one of the factors. Then we divide the numerator and denominator by 16.

$$\frac{48}{32} = \frac{3 \cdot 16}{2 \cdot 16} = \frac{3 \cdot \cancel{16}^{1}}{2 \cdot \cancel{16}_{1}} = \frac{3}{2}$$

The drawback to this method is that students don't always divide by the *greatest* common factor from the numerator and denominator. For example, suppose we had incorrectly thought that 8 was the greatest number that divides into the numerator and denominator. We show that our final answer is not simplified completely.

$$\frac{48}{32} = \frac{6 \cdot 8}{4 \cdot 8} = \frac{6 \cdot \cancel{8}^{1}}{4 \cdot \cancel{8}_{1}} = \frac{6}{4} \quad \longleftarrow \quad \begin{array}{l} \text{6 and 4 still share a} \\ \text{common factor of 2.} \end{array}$$

The fraction $\frac{6}{4}$ is only *partially simplified* because we did not divide by the *greatest* common factor. To complete the simplification, we must reduce again by dividing the numerator and denominator by the common factor of 2.

$$\frac{6}{4} = \frac{2 \cdot 3}{2 \cdot 2} = \frac{\cancel{2}^{1} \cdot 3}{\cancel{2}_{1} \cdot 2} = \frac{3}{2}$$

3. Simplifying Fractions by Powers of 10

Consider the fraction $\frac{50}{70}$. Both the numerator and the denominator are divisible by 10 because the ones-place digit ends in 0. To simplify this fraction, we can divide both numerator and denominator by 10.

$$\frac{50}{70} = \frac{5 \cdot 10}{7 \cdot 10} = \frac{5 \cdot \cancel{10}^{1}}{7 \cdot \cancel{10}_{1}} = \frac{5}{7}$$

Notice that dividing numerator and denominator by 10 has the effect of eliminating the 0 in the ones place from each number.

$$\frac{5\cancel{0}}{7\cancel{0}} = \frac{5}{7}$$

This is a quick way to simplify, or partially simplify, a fraction when the numerator and denominator share a common factor of 10, 100, 1000, and so on. This is demonstrated in Example 3.

Skill Practice

Simplify to lowest terms by first reducing by 10, 100, or 1000.

8. $\dfrac{630}{190}$ **9.** $\dfrac{1300}{52,000}$

10. $\dfrac{21,000}{35,000}$

example 3   Simplifying Fractions by 10, 100, and 1000

Simplify each fraction to lowest terms by first reducing by 10, 100, or 1000. Write the answer as a fraction.

a. $\dfrac{170}{30}$ **b.** $\dfrac{2500}{7500}$ **c.** $\dfrac{5000}{130,000}$

Solution:

a. $\dfrac{170}{30} = \dfrac{17\cancel{0}}{3\cancel{0}}$ Both 170 and 30 are divisible by 10. "Strike through" one zero.

$\phantom{\dfrac{170}{30}} = \dfrac{17}{3}$ The fraction $\frac{17}{3}$ is simplified completely.

Answers

7. The fraction $\frac{39}{52}$ can be simplified further to $\frac{3}{4}$.

8. $\dfrac{63}{19}$ 9. $\dfrac{1}{40}$ 10. $\dfrac{3}{5}$

b. $\dfrac{2500}{7500} = \dfrac{25\cancel{00}}{75\cancel{00}}$ Both 2500 and 7500 are divisible by 100. Strike through two zeros.

$= \dfrac{25}{75}$ The fraction is partially simplified.

$= \dfrac{\cancel{5} \cdot \cancel{5}}{3 \cdot \cancel{5} \cdot \cancel{5}}$ Factor and simplify further.

$= \dfrac{1}{3}$

c. $\dfrac{5000}{130{,}000} = \dfrac{5\cancel{000}}{130{,}\cancel{000}}$ The numbers 5000 and 130,000 are both divisible by 1000. Strike through three zeros.

$= \dfrac{5}{130}$

$= \dfrac{\cancel{5}}{2 \cdot \cancel{5} \cdot 13}$ Factor and simplify further.

$= \dfrac{1}{26}$

Concept Connections

11. How many zeros may be eliminated from the numerator and denominator of the fraction $\frac{430{,}000}{154{,}000{,}000}$?

4. Applications of Simplifying Fractions

example 4   Simplifying Fractions in an Application

Madeleine got 28 out of 35 problems correct on an algebra exam. David got 27 out of 45 questions correct on a different algebra exam.

a. What fractional part of the exam did each student answer correctly?

b. Which student performed better?

Solution:

a. Fractional part correct for Madeleine:

$$\frac{28}{35} \quad \text{or equivalently} \quad \frac{28}{35} = \frac{2 \cdot 2 \cdot \cancel{7}}{5 \cdot \cancel{7}} = \frac{4}{5}$$

Fractional part correct for David:

$$\frac{27}{45} \quad \text{or equivalently} \quad \frac{27}{45} = \frac{\cancel{3} \cdot \cancel{3} \cdot 3}{\cancel{3} \cdot \cancel{3} \cdot 5} = \frac{3}{5}$$

b. From the simplified form of each fraction, we see that Madeleine performed better because $\frac{4}{5} > \frac{3}{5}$. That is, 4 parts out of 5 is greater than 3 parts out of 5. This is also easily verified on a number line.

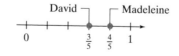

Skill Practice

12. Joanne planted 77 seeds in her garden and 55 sprouted. Geoff planted 140 seeds and 80 sprouted.

    a. What fractional part of the seeds sprouted for Joanne and what part sprouted for Geoff?

    b. For which person did a greater portion of seeds sprout?

Answers

11. Four zeros; the numerator and denominator are both divisible by 10,000.
12. a. Joanne: $\frac{5}{7}$; Geoff: $\frac{4}{7}$
    b. Joanne had a greater portion of seeds sprout.

section 2.3   Practice Exercises

Study Skills Exercises

1. Write down the page number(s) for the Midchapter Review for this chapter. _____ Explain the purpose of the Midchapter Review.

2. Define the key term **lowest terms**.

Review Exercises

For Exercises 3–9, write the prime factorization for each number.

3. 145	**4.** 114	**5.** 92	**6.** 153

7. 85	**8.** 120	**9.** 195

Objective 1: Equivalent Fractions

For Exercises 10–13, shade the second figure so that it expresses a fraction equivalent to the first figure.

10.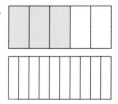

11.

12.

13.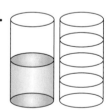

14. True or false? The fractions $\frac{1}{3}$ and $\frac{3}{1}$ are equivalent.   **15.** True or false? The fractions $\frac{4}{5}$ and $\frac{5}{4}$ are equivalent.

16. In your own words, explain the concept of equivalent fractions.

For Exercises 17–24, determine if the fractions are equivalent. Then fill in the blank with either $=$ or $\neq$.
(See Example 1.)

17. $\frac{2}{3} \square \frac{3}{5}$ **18.** $\frac{1}{4} \square \frac{2}{9}$ **19.** $\frac{1}{2} \square \frac{3}{6}$ **20.** $\frac{6}{16} \square \frac{3}{8}$

21. $\dfrac{12}{16}\,\square\,\dfrac{3}{4}$

22. $\dfrac{4}{5}\,\square\,\dfrac{12}{15}$

23. $\dfrac{8}{9}\,\square\,\dfrac{20}{27}$

24. $\dfrac{5}{6}\,\square\,\dfrac{12}{18}$

Objective 2: Simplifying Fractions to Lowest Terms

For Exercises 25–54, simplify the fraction to lowest terms. Write the answer as a fraction or a whole number.
(See Example 2.)

25. $\dfrac{12}{24}$

26. $\dfrac{15}{18}$

27. $\dfrac{6}{18}$

28. $\dfrac{21}{24}$

29. $\dfrac{36}{20}$

30. $\dfrac{49}{42}$

31. $\dfrac{15}{12}$

32. $\dfrac{30}{25}$

33. $\dfrac{20}{25}$

34. $\dfrac{8}{16}$

35. $\dfrac{14}{14}$

36. $\dfrac{8}{8}$

37. $\dfrac{50}{25}$

38. $\dfrac{24}{6}$

39. $\dfrac{9}{9}$

40. $\dfrac{2}{2}$

41. $\dfrac{105}{140}$

42. $\dfrac{84}{126}$

43. $\dfrac{33}{11}$

44. $\dfrac{65}{5}$

45. $\dfrac{77}{110}$

46. $\dfrac{85}{153}$

47. $\dfrac{130}{150}$

48. $\dfrac{70}{120}$

49. $\dfrac{385}{195}$

50. $\dfrac{39}{130}$

51. $\dfrac{34}{85}$

52. $\dfrac{69}{92}$

53. $\dfrac{145}{58}$

54. $\dfrac{114}{95}$

Objective 3: Simplifying Fractions by Powers of 10

For Exercises 55–62, simplify to lowest terms by first reducing the powers of 10. **(See Example 3.)**

55. $\dfrac{120}{160}$

56. $\dfrac{720}{800}$

57. $\dfrac{3000}{1800}$

58. $\dfrac{2000}{1500}$

59. $\dfrac{42{,}000}{22{,}000}$

60. $\dfrac{50{,}000}{65{,}000}$

61. $\dfrac{5100}{30{,}000}$

62. $\dfrac{9800}{28{,}000}$

Objective 4: Application of Simplifying Fractions

63. Aundrea tossed a coin 48 times and heads came up 20 times. What fractional part of the tosses came up heads? What fractional part came up tails?

64. **a.** What fraction of the alphabet is made up of vowels? (Include the letter y as a vowel, not a consonant.)

 b. What fraction of the alphabet is made up of consonants?

65. Of the 88 constellations that can be seen in the night sky, 12 are associated with astrological horoscopes. The names of as many as 36 constellations are associated with animals or mythical creatures.

 a. Of the 88 constellations, what fraction is associated with horoscopes?

 b. What fraction of the constellations have names associated with animals or mythical creatures?

66. At Pizza Company, Lee made 70 pizzas one day. There were 105 pizzas sold that day. What fraction of the pizzas did Lee make?

67. Jonathan and Jared sell candy bars for a fund-raiser. Jonathan sold 25 of his 35 candy bars, and Jared sold 24 of his 28 candy bars. **(See Example 4.)**

 a. What fractional part of his total number of candy bars did each boy sell?

 b. Which boy sold the greater fractional part?

68. Lynette and Lisa are taking online courses. Lisa has completed 14 out of 16 assignments in her course while Lynette has completed 15 out of 24 assignments.

 a. What fractional part of her total number of assignments did each woman complete?

 b. Which woman has completed more of her course?

69. Raymond read 720 pages of a 792-page book. His roommate, Travis, read 540 pages from a 660-page book.

 a. What fractional part of the book did each person read?

 b. Which of the roommates read a greater fraction of his book?

70. Mr. Bishop and Ms. Waymire both gave exams today. By mid-afternoon, Mr. Bishop had finished grading 16 out of 36 exams, and Ms. Waymire had finished grading 15 out of 27 exams.

    a. What fractional part of her total has Ms. Waymire completed?

    b. What fractional part of his total has Mr. Bishop completed?

Expanding Your Skills

71. Write three fractions equivalent to $\frac{3}{4}$.

72. Write three fractions equivalent to $\frac{1}{3}$.

73. Write three fractions equivalent to $\frac{12}{18}$.

74. Write three fractions equivalent to $\frac{80}{100}$.

chapter 2 | midchapter review

1. Write a definition of an improper fraction.

2. Write a definition of a proper fraction.

3. Of the fractions $\frac{2}{3}$ and $\frac{3}{2}$, which one is proper and which one is improper?

4. Draw a figure that represents the fraction $\frac{2}{3}$. Answers may vary.

5. Draw a figure that represents the fraction $\frac{3}{2}$. Answers may vary.

6. List all the factors of the given number.

    a. 16   **b.** 63

    c. 40   **d.** 30

7. Write the prime factorization of each number.

    a. 16   **b.** 63

    c. 40   **d.** 30

For Exercises 8–13, simplify the fraction to lowest terms and write the answer as a fraction.

8. $\dfrac{16}{30}$ **9.** $\dfrac{20}{30}$ **10.** $\dfrac{20}{16}$

11. $\dfrac{30}{24}$ **12.** $\dfrac{24}{16}$ **13.** $\dfrac{20}{24}$

For Exercises 14–16, simplify the fraction and write the answer as a mixed number.

14. $\dfrac{30}{12}$ **15.** $\dfrac{22}{8}$ **16.** $\dfrac{12}{9}$

Objectives

1. Multiplication of Fractions
2. Fractions and the Order of Operations
3. Area of a Triangle
4. Applications of Multiplying Fractions

Concept Connections

1. What fraction is $\frac{1}{2}$ of $\frac{1}{4}$ of a whole?

section 2.4   Multiplication of Fractions and Applications

1. Multiplication of Fractions

Suppose Elija takes $\frac{1}{3}$ of a cake and then gives $\frac{1}{2}$ of this portion to his friend Max. Max gets $\frac{1}{2}$ of $\frac{1}{3}$ of the cake. This is equivalent to the expression $\frac{1}{2} \cdot \frac{1}{3}$. See Figure 2-6.

Elija takes $\frac{1}{3}$

Max gets $\frac{1}{2}$ of $\frac{1}{3} = \frac{1}{6}$

Figure 2-6

From the illustration, the product $\frac{1}{2} \cdot \frac{1}{3} = \frac{1}{6}$. Notice that the product $\frac{1}{6}$ is found by multiplying the numerators and multiplying the denominators. This is true in general to multiply fractions.

Multiplication of Fractions

To multiply fractions, write the product of the numerators over the product of the denominators. Then simplify the resulting fraction, if possible.

The rule for multiplying fractions can be expressed symbolically as follows.

$$\frac{a}{b} \cdot \frac{c}{d} = \frac{a \cdot c}{b \cdot d} \qquad \text{provided } b \text{ and } d \text{ are not equal to } 0$$

Skill Practice

Multiply. Write the answer as a fraction.

2. $\frac{2}{3} \cdot \frac{5}{9}$ **3.** $\frac{7}{12} \times 11$

example 1   Multiplying Fractions

Multiply.

a. $\frac{2}{5} \cdot \frac{4}{7}$ **b.** $\frac{8}{3} \times 5$

Solution:

a. $\frac{2}{5} \cdot \frac{4}{7} = \frac{2 \cdot 4}{5 \cdot 7} = \frac{8}{35}$ ← Multiply the numerators.
← Multiply the denominators.

Notice that the product $\frac{8}{35}$ is simplified completely because there are no common factors shared by 8 and 35.

b. $\frac{8}{3} \times 5 = \frac{8}{3} \times \frac{5}{1}$ First write the whole number as a fraction.

$= \frac{8 \times 5}{3 \times 1}$ Multiply the numerators. Multiply the denominators.

$= \frac{40}{3}$ The product is not reducible because there are no common factors shared by 40 and 3.

Answers

1. $\frac{1}{8}$ 2. $\frac{10}{27}$ 3. $\frac{77}{12}$

Example 2 illustrates a case where the product of fractions must be simplified.

---

example 2   Multiplying and Simplifying Fractions

Multiply the fractions and simplify if possible.

$$\frac{4}{30} \cdot \frac{5}{14}$$

Solution:

$$\frac{4}{30} \cdot \frac{5}{14} = \frac{4 \cdot 5}{30 \cdot 14}$$ Multiply the numerators. Multiply the denominators.

$$= \frac{20}{420}$$ The fraction $\frac{20}{420}$ is not simplified.
To simplify, write the prime factorization of 20 and 420.

$$\begin{array}{r} 5 \\ 2\overline{)10} \\ 2\overline{)20} \end{array} \qquad \begin{array}{r} 7 \\ 5\overline{)35} \\ 3\overline{)105} \\ 2\overline{)210} \\ 2\overline{)420} \end{array}$$

$$20 = 2 \cdot 2 \cdot 5 \qquad 420 = 2 \cdot 2 \cdot 3 \cdot 5 \cdot 7$$

$$\frac{20}{420} = \frac{\overset{1}{\cancel{2}} \cdot \overset{1}{\cancel{2}} \cdot \overset{1}{\cancel{5}}}{\underset{1}{\cancel{2}} \cdot \underset{1}{\cancel{2}} \cdot 3 \cdot \underset{1}{\cancel{5}} \cdot 7}$$

$$= \frac{1 \cdot 1 \cdot 1}{1 \cdot 1 \cdot 3 \cdot 1 \cdot 7}$$

$$= \frac{1}{21}$$

Skill Practice

Multiply and simplify. Write the answer as a fraction.

4. $\dfrac{7}{20} \cdot \dfrac{4}{3}$ **5.** $\dfrac{12}{8}\left(\dfrac{5}{6}\right)$

It is often easier to factor the numerator and denominator of a fraction *before* multiplying. Consider the product from Example 2. The numbers 4, 5, 30, and 14 can be factored more easily than the larger numbers of 20 and 420.

$$\frac{4}{30} \cdot \frac{5}{14} = \frac{2 \cdot 2}{3 \cdot 2 \cdot 5} \cdot \frac{5}{2 \cdot 7}$$ First factor the numbers in the original fractions.

$$= \frac{2 \cdot 2}{3 \cdot 2 \cdot \underset{1}{\cancel{5}}} \cdot \frac{\overset{1}{\cancel{5}}}{2 \cdot 7}$$ We can simplify *before* multiplying and obtain the same result.

$$= \frac{1}{21}$$

As a general rule, this method is used most often in the text.

---

example 3   Multiplying and Simplifying Fractions

Multiply and simplify.

$$\frac{10}{18} \times \frac{21}{55}$$

Answers

4. $\dfrac{7}{15}$ **5.** $\dfrac{5}{4}$

Solution:

$$\frac{10}{18} \times \frac{21}{55} = \frac{2 \cdot 5}{2 \cdot 3 \cdot 3} \times \frac{3 \cdot 7}{5 \cdot 11} \qquad \text{Factor the numerators and denominators.}$$

$$= \frac{2 \cdot \overset{1}{\cancel{5}}}{\underset{1}{\cancel{2}} \cdot \underset{1}{\cancel{3}} \cdot 3} \times \frac{\overset{1}{\cancel{3}} \cdot 7}{\underset{1}{\cancel{5}} \cdot 11} \qquad \text{Simplify.}$$

$$= \frac{7}{33} \qquad \text{Multiply.}$$

Sometimes you may recognize factors common to both the numerator and the denominator without writing the prime factorizations first. In such a case, you may opt to simplify without factoring the individual numerators or denominators. For example, consider the product:

$$\frac{10}{18} \times \frac{21}{55} = \frac{\overset{2}{\cancel{10}}}{\underset{6}{\cancel{18}}} \times \frac{\overset{7}{\cancel{21}}}{\underset{11}{\cancel{55}}} \qquad \begin{array}{l}\text{10 and 55 share a common factor of 5.}\\ \text{18 and 21 share a common factor of 3.}\end{array}$$

$$= \frac{\overset{\overset{1}{\cancel{2}}}{\cancel{10}}}{\underset{\underset{3}{\cancel{6}}}{\cancel{18}}} \times \frac{\overset{7}{\cancel{21}}}{\underset{11}{\cancel{55}}} \qquad \begin{array}{l}\text{We can simplify further because 2}\\ \text{and 6 share a common factor of 2.}\end{array}$$

$$= \frac{7}{33}$$

example 4   Multiplying and Simplifying Fractions

Multiply and simplify. Write the answer as a fraction.

a. $6\left(\dfrac{3}{8}\right)$ **b.** $\dfrac{21}{25} \cdot \dfrac{65}{24} \cdot \dfrac{15}{39}$

Solution:

a. $6\left(\dfrac{3}{8}\right) = \dfrac{6}{1} \cdot \dfrac{3}{8}$ \qquad Write the whole number as a fraction.

$$= \frac{2 \cdot 3}{1} \cdot \frac{3}{\underset{1}{\cancel{2}} \cdot 2 \cdot 2} \qquad \begin{array}{l}\text{Factor the numerators and denominators.}\\ \text{Simplify.}\end{array}$$

$$= \frac{9}{4} \qquad \text{Multiply.}$$

b. $\dfrac{21}{25} \cdot \dfrac{65}{24} \cdot \dfrac{15}{39} = \dfrac{3 \cdot 7}{5 \cdot 5} \cdot \dfrac{5 \cdot 13}{2 \cdot 2 \cdot 2 \cdot 3} \cdot \dfrac{3 \cdot 5}{3 \cdot 13}$ \qquad Factor.

$$= \frac{\overset{1}{\cancel{3}} \cdot 7}{\underset{1}{\cancel{5}} \cdot \underset{1}{\cancel{5}}} \cdot \frac{\overset{1}{\cancel{5}} \cdot \overset{1}{\cancel{13}}}{2 \cdot 2 \cdot 2 \cdot \underset{1}{\cancel{3}}} \cdot \frac{\overset{1}{\cancel{3}} \cdot \overset{1}{\cancel{5}}}{\underset{1}{\cancel{3}} \cdot \underset{1}{\cancel{13}}} \qquad \text{Simplify.}$$

$$= \frac{7}{8} \qquad \text{Multiply.}$$

2. Fractions and the Order of Operations

In Section 1.7 we learned to recognize powers of 10. These are $10^1 = 10$, $10^2 = 100$, and so on. In this section, we learn to recognize the **powers of one-tenth**, that is, $\frac{1}{10}$ raised to a whole-number power. For example, consider the following expressions.

$$\left(\frac{1}{10}\right)^1 = \frac{1}{10}$$

$$\left(\frac{1}{10}\right)^2 = \frac{1}{10} \cdot \frac{1}{10} = \frac{1}{100}$$

$$\left(\frac{1}{10}\right)^3 = \frac{1}{10} \cdot \frac{1}{10} \cdot \frac{1}{10} = \frac{1}{1000}$$

$$\left(\frac{1}{10}\right)^4 = \frac{1}{10} \cdot \frac{1}{10} \cdot \frac{1}{10} \cdot \frac{1}{10} = \frac{1}{10,000}$$

$$\left(\frac{1}{10}\right)^5 = \frac{1}{10} \cdot \frac{1}{10} \cdot \frac{1}{10} \cdot \frac{1}{10} \cdot \frac{1}{10} = \frac{1}{100,000}$$

$$\left(\frac{1}{10}\right)^6 = \frac{1}{10} \cdot \frac{1}{10} \cdot \frac{1}{10} \cdot \frac{1}{10} \cdot \frac{1}{10} \cdot \frac{1}{10} = \frac{1}{1,000,000}$$

From these examples, we see that a power of one-tenth results in a fraction with a 1 in the numerator. The denominator has a 1 followed by the same number of zeros as the exponent on the base of $\frac{1}{10}$.

For problems with more than one operation, the order of operations must still be considered.

---

example 5   Simplifying Expressions

Simplify.

a. $\left(\frac{2}{5}\right)^3$ **b.** $\left(\frac{2}{15} \cdot \frac{3}{4}\right)^2$

Solution:

a. $\left(\frac{2}{5}\right)^3 = \frac{2}{5} \cdot \frac{2}{5} \cdot \frac{2}{5}$ With an exponent of 3, multiply 3 factors of the base.

$= \frac{2 \cdot 2 \cdot 2}{5 \cdot 5 \cdot 5}$ Multiply the numerators. Multiply the denominators.

$= \frac{8}{125}$

b. $\left(\frac{2}{15} \cdot \frac{3}{4}\right)^2 = \left(\frac{\overset{1}{2}}{3 \cdot 5} \cdot \frac{\overset{1}{3}}{2 \cdot 2}\right)^2$ Perform the multiplication within the parentheses. Simplify.

$= \left(\frac{1}{10}\right)^2$ Multiply fractions within parentheses.

$= \frac{1}{100}$

3. Area of a Triangle

Recall that the area of a rectangle with length l and width w is given by

$$A = l \times w$$

Area of a Triangle

The formula for the area of a triangle is given by $A = \frac{1}{2}bh$, read "one-half base times height."

The value of b is the measure of the base of the triangle. The value of h is the measure of the height of the triangle. The base b may be chosen as the length of any of the sides of the triangle. However, once you have chosen the base, the height must be measured as the shortest distance from the base to the opposite vertex (or point) of the triangle. For example, Figure 2-7 shows the same triangle with different choices for the base. Figure 2-8 shows a situation in which the height must be drawn "outside" the triangle. In such a case, notice that the height is drawn down to an imaginary extension of the base line.

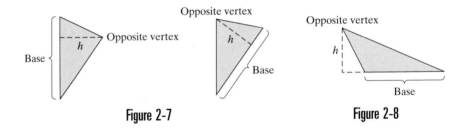

Figure 2-7   **Figure 2-8**

In Example 6 we demonstrate how to apply the formula to find the area of a triangle.

---

example 6   Finding the Area of a Triangle

Find the area of the triangle.

a.

4 m

6 m

b.

$\frac{3}{4}$ ft

$\frac{5}{3}$ ft

Concept Connections

Identify the measure of the base and height.

14.

8 m

5 m

15.

$\frac{4}{3}$ ft

2 ft

Answers

14. Base is 8 m; height is 5 m
15. Base is 2 ft; height is $\frac{4}{3}$ ft

Solution:

a. $b = 6\,\text{m}$ and $h = 4\,\text{m}$ Identify the measure of the base and the height.

$A = \dfrac{1}{2}bh$

$= \dfrac{1}{2}(6\,\text{m})(4\,\text{m})$ Apply the formula for the area of a triangle.

$= \dfrac{1}{2}\left(\dfrac{6}{1}\,\text{m}\right)\left(\dfrac{4}{1}\,\text{m}\right)$ Write the whole numbers as fractions.

$= \dfrac{1}{2}\left(\dfrac{\overset{3}{6}}{1}\,\text{m}\right)\left(\dfrac{4}{1}\,\text{m}\right)$ Simplify.

$= \dfrac{12}{1}\,\text{m}^2$ Multiply numerators. Multiply denominators.

$= 12\,\text{m}^2$ The area of the triangle is 12 square meters (m²).

b. $b = \dfrac{5}{3}\,\text{ft}$ and $h = \dfrac{3}{4}\,\text{ft}$ Identify the measure of the base and the height.

$A = \dfrac{1}{2}bh$

$= \dfrac{1}{2}\left(\dfrac{5}{3}\,\text{ft}\right)\left(\dfrac{3}{4}\,\text{ft}\right)$ Apply the formula for the area of a triangle.

$= \dfrac{1}{2}\left(\dfrac{5}{\overset{}{\underset{1}{3}}}\,\text{ft}\right)\left(\dfrac{\overset{1}{3}}{4}\,\text{ft}\right)$ Simplify.

$= \dfrac{5}{8}\,\text{ft}^2$ The area of the triangle is $\dfrac{5}{8}$ square feet (ft²).

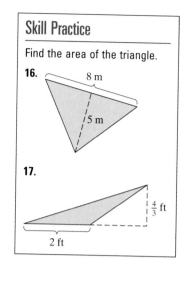
---

example 7   Find the Area of a Composite Geometric Figure

Find the area.

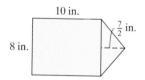

10 in.

8 in.

$\dfrac{7}{2}$ in.

Solution:

The total area is the sum of the areas of the rectangular region and the triangular region. That is,

Total area =

10 in.

8 in.

$\dfrac{7}{2}$ in.

$+$ 8 in.

(area of rectangle) + (area of triangle)
$(l \times w)$ $(\tfrac{1}{2}b \times h)$

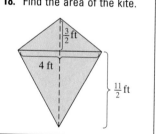

$$= (10 \text{ in.})(8 \text{ in.}) + \frac{1}{2}(8 \text{ in.})\left(\frac{7}{2} \text{ in.}\right)$$

$$= 80 \text{ in.}^2 + \frac{1}{2}\left(\frac{8}{1} \text{ in.}\right)\left(\frac{7}{2} \text{ in.}\right)$$

$$= 80 \text{ in.}^2 + \frac{1}{2}\left(\frac{\overset{1}{2} \cdot \overset{1}{2} \cdot 2}{1} \text{ in.}\right)\left(\frac{7}{\underset{1}{2}} \text{ in.}\right)$$

$$= 80 \text{ in.}^2 + 14 \text{ in.}^2$$

$$= 94 \text{ in.}^2$$

The total area of the region is 94 square inches (in.^{2}).

4. Applications of Multiplying Fractions

example 8   Multiplying Fractions in an Application

In 2005, the population of Texas comprised roughly $\frac{3}{40}$ of the population of the United States. If the U.S. population was approximately 292,000,000, approximate the population of Texas.

Solution:

We must find $\frac{3}{40}$ of the U.S. population. This translates to

$$\frac{3}{40} \cdot 292,000,000 = \frac{3}{40} \cdot \frac{292,000,000}{1}$$

$$= \frac{876,000,000}{40} \quad \longleftarrow \quad \text{Multiply the numerators.}$$
$$\phantom{= \frac{876,000,000}{40}} \quad \longleftarrow \quad \text{Multiply the denominators.}$$

$$= \frac{876,000,0\cancel{0}0}{4\cancel{0}} \qquad \text{Simplify by a factor of 10.}$$

$$= \frac{87,600,000}{4} \qquad \text{Simplify by first writing the fraction as a division problem: } 87,600,000 \div 4.$$

$$\begin{array}{r} 21,900,000 \\ 4\overline{)87,600,000} \\ \underline{-8} \\ 7 \\ \underline{-4} \\ 36 \\ \underline{-36} \\ 0 \end{array}$$

$$= 21,900,000 \qquad \text{Divide.}$$

The population of Texas was approximately 21,900,000.

section 2.4   Practice Exercises

Study Skills Exercises

1. Write down the page number(s) for the Chapter Summary for this chapter. _____
Describe one way in which you can use the summary found at the end of each chapter.

2. Define the key term **power of one-tenth**.

Review Exercises

For Exercises 3–7, identify the numerator and the denominator. Then simplify the fraction to lowest terms.

3. $\dfrac{10}{14}$ **4.** $\dfrac{32}{36}$ **5.** $\dfrac{25}{15}$ **6.** $\dfrac{2100}{7000}$ **7.** $\dfrac{7200}{90,000}$

Objective 1: Multiplication of Fractions

8. Shade the portion of the figure that represents $\frac{1}{3}$ of $\frac{1}{2}$.

9. Shade the portion of the figure that represents $\frac{1}{4}$ of $\frac{1}{4}$.

10. Shade the portion of the figure that represents $\frac{1}{3}$ of $\frac{1}{4}$.

11. Find $\frac{1}{2}$ of $\frac{1}{4}$.   **12.** Find $\frac{2}{3}$ of $\frac{1}{5}$.   **13.** Find $\frac{3}{4}$ of 8.   **14.** Find $\frac{2}{5}$ of 20.

For Exercises 15–26, multiply the fractions. Write the answer as a fraction. **(See Example 1.)**

15. $\dfrac{1}{2} \times \dfrac{3}{8}$ **16.** $\dfrac{2}{3} \times \dfrac{1}{3}$ **17.** $\dfrac{14}{9} \cdot \dfrac{1}{9}$ **18.** $\dfrac{1}{8} \cdot \dfrac{9}{8}$

19. $\left(\dfrac{12}{7}\right)\left(\dfrac{2}{5}\right)$

20. $\left(\dfrac{9}{10}\right)\left(\dfrac{7}{4}\right)$

21. $8 \cdot \left(\dfrac{1}{11}\right)$

22. $3 \cdot \left(\dfrac{2}{7}\right)$

23. $\dfrac{4}{5} \cdot 6$

24. $\dfrac{5}{8} \cdot 5$

25. $\dfrac{13}{9} \times \dfrac{5}{4}$

26. $\dfrac{6}{5} \times \dfrac{7}{5}$

For Exercises 27–50, multiply the fractions and simplify to lowest terms. Write the answer as a fraction or whole number. (See Examples 2–4.)

27. $\dfrac{2}{9} \times \dfrac{3}{5}$

28. $\dfrac{1}{8} \times \dfrac{4}{7}$

29. $\dfrac{5}{6} \times \dfrac{3}{4}$

30. $\dfrac{7}{12} \times \dfrac{18}{5}$

31. $\dfrac{21}{5} \cdot \dfrac{25}{12}$

32. $\dfrac{16}{25} \cdot \dfrac{15}{32}$

33. $\dfrac{24}{15} \cdot \dfrac{5}{3}$

34. $\dfrac{49}{24} \cdot \dfrac{6}{7}$

35. $\left(\dfrac{6}{11}\right)\left(\dfrac{22}{15}\right)$

36. $\left(\dfrac{12}{45}\right)\left(\dfrac{5}{4}\right)$

37. $\left(\dfrac{17}{9}\right)\left(\dfrac{72}{17}\right)$

38. $\left(\dfrac{39}{11}\right)\left(\dfrac{11}{13}\right)$

39. $\dfrac{21}{4} \cdot \dfrac{16}{7}$

40. $\dfrac{85}{6} \cdot \dfrac{12}{10}$

41. $12 \times \dfrac{15}{42}$

42. $4 \times \dfrac{8}{92}$

43. $\dfrac{9}{15} \times \dfrac{16}{3} \times \dfrac{25}{8}$

44. $\dfrac{49}{8} \times \dfrac{4}{5} \times \dfrac{20}{7}$

45. $\dfrac{5}{2} \times \dfrac{10}{21} \times \dfrac{7}{5}$

46. $\dfrac{55}{9} \times \dfrac{18}{32} \times \dfrac{24}{11}$

47. $\dfrac{7}{10} \cdot \dfrac{3}{28} \cdot 5$

48. $\dfrac{11}{18} \cdot \dfrac{2}{20} \cdot 15$

49. $\dfrac{100}{49} \times 21 \times \dfrac{14}{25}$

50. $\dfrac{38}{22} \times 11 \times \dfrac{5}{19}$

Objective 2: Fractions and the Order of Operations

51. Find the powers of $\dfrac{1}{10}$.

    a. $\left(\dfrac{1}{10}\right)^3$ **b.** $\left(\dfrac{1}{10}\right)^4$ **c.** $\left(\dfrac{1}{10}\right)^6$

For Exercises 52–63, simplify. Write the answer as a fraction or whole number. (See Example 5.)

52. $\left(\dfrac{1}{9}\right)^2$

53. $\left(\dfrac{1}{4}\right)^2$

54. $\left(\dfrac{3}{2}\right)^3$

55. $\left(\dfrac{4}{3}\right)^3$

56. $\left(4 \cdot \dfrac{3}{4}\right)^3$

57. $\left(5 \cdot \dfrac{2}{5}\right)^3$

58. $\left(\dfrac{1}{9} \cdot \dfrac{3}{5}\right)^2$

59. $\left(\dfrac{10}{3} \cdot \dfrac{1}{100}\right)^2$

60. $\dfrac{1}{3} \cdot \left(\dfrac{21}{4} \cdot \dfrac{8}{7}\right)$

61. $\dfrac{1}{6} \cdot \left(\dfrac{24}{5} \cdot \dfrac{30}{8}\right)$

62. $\dfrac{16}{9} \cdot \left(\dfrac{1}{2}\right)^3$

63. $\dfrac{28}{6} \cdot \left(\dfrac{3}{2}\right)^2$

Objective 3: Area of a Triangle

For Exercises 64–67, label the height with h and the base with b as shown in the figure.

64.

65.

66.

67.

For Exercises 68–77, find the area of the figure. **(See Example 6.)**

68.
8 cm
11 cm

69.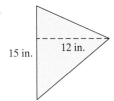
15 in.   12 in.

70.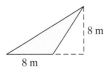
8 m
8 m

71.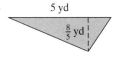
5 yd
$\frac{8}{5}$ yd

72.
1 ft
$\frac{7}{4}$ ft

73.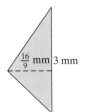
$\frac{16}{9}$ mm 3 mm

74.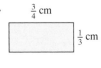
$\frac{3}{4}$ cm
$\frac{1}{3}$ cm

75.
3 m
$\frac{8}{3}$ m

76.
$\frac{15}{16}$ in.
$\frac{13}{16}$ in.

77.
$\frac{3}{4}$ ft
$\frac{23}{24}$ ft

For Exercises 78–81, find the area of the shaded region. **(See Example 7.)**

78.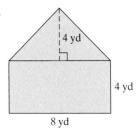
4 yd
4 yd
8 yd

79.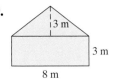
3 m
3 m
8 m

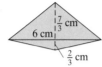

80.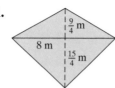

81.

Objective 4: Applications of Multiplying Fractions

82. Ms. Robbins' car holds 16 gallons (gal) of gas. If the fuel gauge indicates that there is $\frac{5}{8}$ of a tank left, how many gallons of gas are left in the tank? **(See Example 8.)**

83. Land in a rural part of Bowie County, Texas, sells for $11,000 per acre. If Mr. Stembridge purchased $\frac{5}{4}$ acre, how much did it cost?

84. Jim has half a pizza left over from dinner. If he eats $\frac{1}{4}$ of what's left for breakfast, how much pizza did he eat for breakfast?

85. In a certain sample of individuals, $\frac{2}{5}$ are known to have blood type O. Of the individuals with blood type O, $\frac{1}{4}$ are Rh-negative. What fraction of the individuals in the sample have O negative blood?

86. A recipe for chocolate chip cookies calls for $\frac{2}{3}$ cup of sugar. If Erin triples the recipe, how many cups of sugar should she use?

87. Nancy spends $\frac{3}{4}$ hour 3 times a day walking and playing with her dog. What is the total time she spends walking and playing with the dog each day?

88. The Bishop Gaming Center hosts a football pool. There is $1200 in prize money. The first-place winner receives $\frac{2}{3}$ of the prize money. The second-place winner receives $\frac{1}{4}$ of the prize money, and the third-place winner receives $\frac{1}{12}$ of the prize money. How much money does each person get?

89. Frankie's lawn measures 40 yd by 36 yd. In the morning he mowed $\frac{2}{3}$ of the lawn. How many square yards of lawn did he already mow? How much is left to be mowed?

Expanding Your Skills

90. Evaluate.

  a. $\left(\frac{1}{6}\right)^2$ **b.** $\sqrt{\frac{1}{36}}$

91. Evaluate.

  a. $\left(\frac{2}{7}\right)^2$ **b.** $\sqrt{\frac{4}{49}}$

For Exercises 92–95, evaluate the square roots.

92. $\sqrt{\frac{1}{25}}$ **93.** $\sqrt{\frac{1}{100}}$ **94.** $\sqrt{\frac{64}{81}}$ **95.** $\sqrt{\frac{9}{4}}$

96. Find the next number in the sequence: $\frac{1}{2}, \frac{1}{4}, \frac{1}{8}, \frac{1}{16},$ _____

97. Find the next number in the sequence: $\frac{2}{3}, \frac{2}{9}, \frac{2}{27},$ _____

98. Which is greater, $\frac{1}{2}$ of $\frac{1}{8}$ or $\frac{1}{8}$ of $\frac{1}{2}$?

99. Which is greater, $\frac{2}{3}$ of $\frac{1}{4}$ or $\frac{1}{4}$ of $\frac{2}{3}$?

Calculator Connections

Topic: Multiplying fractions

Calculator Exercises

For Exercises 100–103, use a calculator to multiply the numerators and to multiply the denominators. Do not simplify the result to lowest terms.

100. $\dfrac{341}{415} \times \dfrac{71}{91}$

101. $\dfrac{37}{52} \cdot \dfrac{15}{103}$

102. $461 \cdot \dfrac{28}{313}$

103. $\dfrac{593}{225} \cdot 464$

---

section 2.5   Division of Fractions and Applications

1. Reciprocal of a Fraction

Two numbers whose product is 1 are said to be *reciprocals* of each other. For example, consider the product of $\frac{3}{8}$ and $\frac{8}{3}$.

$$\frac{3}{8} \cdot \frac{8}{3} = \frac{\overset{1}{\cancel{3}}}{\underset{1}{\cancel{8}}} \cdot \frac{\overset{1}{\cancel{8}}}{\underset{1}{\cancel{3}}} = 1$$

Because the product equals 1, we say that $\frac{3}{8}$ is the reciprocal of $\frac{8}{3}$ and vice versa.

To divide fractions, first we need to learn how to find the reciprocal of a fraction.

Finding the Reciprocal of a Fraction

To find the **reciprocal** of a nonzero fraction, interchange the numerator and denominator of the fraction. Thus, the reciprocal of $\frac{a}{b}$ is $\frac{b}{a}$ (provided $a \neq 0$ and $b \neq 0$).

Objectives

1. Reciprocal of a Fraction
2. Division of Fractions
3. Order of Operations
4. Applications of Multiplication and Division of Fractions

Concept Connections

Fill in the blank.

1. The product of a number and its reciprocal is _____.

Answer

1. 1

example 1   Finding Reciprocals

Find the reciprocal.

a. $\dfrac{2}{5}$ **b.** $\dfrac{1}{9}$ **c.** 5   **d.** 0

Solution:

a. The reciprocal of $\frac{2}{5}$ is $\frac{5}{2}$.

b. The reciprocal of $\frac{1}{9}$ is $\frac{9}{1}$, or 9.

c. First write the whole number 5 as the improper fraction $\frac{5}{1}$. The reciprocal of $\frac{5}{1}$ is $\frac{1}{5}$.

d. The number 0 has no reciprocal because $\frac{1}{0}$ is undefined.

■

2. Division of Fractions

To understand the division of fractions, we draw an analogy to the division of whole numbers. The statement $6 \div 2$ asks, How many groups of 2 can be found among 6 wholes? The answer is 3.

$$6 \div 2 = 3$$

In fractional form, the statement $6 \div 2 = 3$ can be written as $\frac{6}{2} = 3$. This result can also be found by multiplying.

$$6 \cdot \frac{1}{2} = \frac{6}{1} \cdot \frac{1}{2} = \frac{6}{2} = 3$$

That is, to divide by 2 is equivalent to multiplying by the reciprocal $\frac{1}{2}$.

Now let's look at an analogy where we have a fraction divided by a fraction. The statement $\frac{2}{3} \div \frac{1}{6}$ asks, How many increments of $\frac{1}{6}$ can be found within $\frac{2}{3}$ of a whole? The answer is 4.

From the figure,

$$\frac{2}{3} \div \frac{1}{6} = 4$$

4 increments of $\frac{1}{6}$

$\frac{2}{3}$ of a whole

As with the division of whole numbers, the quotient $\frac{2}{3} \div \frac{1}{6}$ can be found by multiplying: $\frac{2}{3} \cdot \frac{6}{1} = \frac{12}{3} = 4$. That is, division by $\frac{1}{6}$ is equivalent to multiplication by $\frac{6}{1}$.

Dividing Fractions

To divide two fractions, multiply the dividend (the "first" fraction) by the reciprocal of the divisor (the "second" fraction).

The process to divide fractions can be written symbolically as

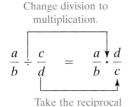

Change division to
multiplication.

$$\frac{a}{b} \div \frac{c}{d} = \frac{a}{b} \cdot \frac{d}{c}$$ provided b, c, and d are not 0

Take the reciprocal
of the divisor.

example 2   Dividing Fractions

Divide and simplify, if possible. Write the answer as a fraction.

a. $\dfrac{2}{5} \div \dfrac{7}{4}$ **b.** $\dfrac{2}{27} \div \dfrac{8}{15}$ **c.** $\dfrac{35}{14} \div 7$ **d.** $12 \div \dfrac{8}{3}$

Solution:

a. $\dfrac{2}{5} \div \dfrac{7}{4} = \dfrac{2}{5} \cdot \dfrac{4}{7}$ Multiply by the reciprocal of the divisor ("second" fraction).

$= \dfrac{2 \cdot 4}{5 \cdot 7}$ Multiply numerators. Multiply denominators.

$= \dfrac{8}{35}$

b. $\dfrac{2}{27} \div \dfrac{8}{15} = \dfrac{2}{27} \cdot \dfrac{15}{8}$ Multiply by the reciprocal of the divisor ("second" fraction).

$= \dfrac{\overset{1}{2}}{\underset{1}{3 \cdot 3 \cdot 3}} \cdot \dfrac{\overset{1}{3} \cdot 5}{\underset{1}{2 \cdot 2 \cdot 2}}$ Factor and simplify.

$= \dfrac{5}{36}$ Multiply.

c. $\dfrac{35}{14} \div 7 = \dfrac{35}{14} \div \dfrac{7}{1}$ Write the whole number 7 as an improper fraction *before* multiplying by the reciprocal.

$= \dfrac{35}{14} \cdot \dfrac{1}{7}$ Multiply by the reciprocal of the divisor.

$= \dfrac{5 \cdot \overset{1}{7}}{2 \cdot \underset{1}{7}} \cdot \dfrac{1}{7}$ Factor and simplify.

$= \dfrac{5}{14}$ Multiply.

Avoiding Mistakes: Do not try to simplify until after taking the reciprocal of the divisor. In Example 2(a) it would be incorrect to "cancel" the 2 and the 4 in the expression $\frac{2}{5} \div \frac{7}{4}$.

d. $12 \div \dfrac{8}{3} = \dfrac{12}{1} \div \dfrac{8}{3}$ Write the whole number 12 as an improper fraction.

$= \dfrac{12}{1} \cdot \dfrac{3}{8}$ Multiply by the reciprocal of the divisor.

$= \dfrac{\overset{1}{2} \cdot \overset{1}{2} \cdot 3}{1} \cdot \dfrac{3}{\underset{1 \quad 1}{2 \cdot 2 \cdot 2}}$ Factor and simplify.

$= \dfrac{9}{2}$ Multiply.

3. Order of Operations

When simplifying fractional expressions with more than one operation, be sure to follow the order of operations. Simplify within parentheses first. Then simplify expressions with exponents, followed by multiplication or division in the order of appearance from left to right.

example 3   Applying the Order of Operations

Simplify. Write the answer as a fraction.

a. $\dfrac{2}{3} \div \dfrac{4}{9} \div 6$ **b.** $\left(\dfrac{3}{5} \div \dfrac{2}{15} \right)^2$

Solution:

a. $\dfrac{2}{3} \div \dfrac{4}{9} \div 6$

$= \left(\dfrac{2}{3} \div \dfrac{4}{9} \right) \div 6$ We will divide from left to right. To emphasize this order, we can insert parentheses around the first two fractions.

$= \left(\dfrac{\overset{1}{2}}{\underset{1}{3}} \cdot \dfrac{\overset{3}{9}}{\underset{2}{4}} \right) \div 6$ Simplify within parentheses.

$= \left(\dfrac{3}{2} \right) \div \dfrac{6}{1}$ Simplify within parentheses and write the whole number as an improper fraction.

$= \left(\dfrac{3}{2} \right) \cdot \dfrac{1}{6}$ Multiply by the reciprocal of the divisor.

$= \dfrac{\overset{1}{3}}{2} \cdot \dfrac{1}{\underset{2}{6}}$ Simplify.

$= \dfrac{1}{4}$ Multiply.

Tip: In Example 3(a) we could also have written each division as multiplication of the reciprocal right from the start.

$\dfrac{2}{3} \div \dfrac{4}{9} \div 6 = \left(\dfrac{2}{3} \cdot \dfrac{9}{4} \right) \cdot \dfrac{1}{6}$

$= \dfrac{\overset{1}{2}}{\underset{1}{3}} \cdot \dfrac{\overset{1}{3} \cdot \overset{1}{3}}{\underset{1}{2 \cdot 2}} \cdot \dfrac{1}{\underset{1}{2 \cdot 3}}$

Factor and simplify.

$= \dfrac{1}{4}$ Multiply.

b. $\left(\dfrac{3}{5} \div \dfrac{2}{15}\right)^2$ Perform operations within parentheses first.

$= \left(\dfrac{3}{5} \cdot \dfrac{15}{2}\right)^2$ Multiply by the reciprocal of the divisor.

$= \left(\dfrac{3}{\cancel{5}} \cdot \dfrac{\overset{3}{\cancel{15}}}{2}\right)^2$ Simplify.

$= \left(\dfrac{9}{2}\right)^2$ Multiply within parentheses.

$= \dfrac{9}{2} \cdot \dfrac{9}{2}$ With an exponent of 2, multiply 2 factors of the base.

$= \dfrac{81}{4}$ Multiply.

4. Applications of Multiplication and Division of Fractions

Sometimes it is difficult to determine whether multiplication or division is appropriate to solve an application problem. Division is generally used for a problem that requires you to separate or "split up" a quantity into pieces. Multiplication is generally used if it is necessary to take a fractional part of a quantity.

---

example 4   Using Division in an Application

A road crew must mow the grassy median along a stretch of highway I-95. If they can mow $\frac{5}{8}$ mile (mi) in 1 hr, how long will it take them to mow a 15-mi stretch?

Solution:

Read and familiarize.

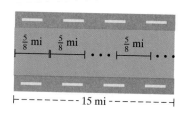

Strategy/operation: From the figure, we must separate or "split up" a 15-mi stretch of highway into pieces that are $\frac{5}{8}$ mi in length. Therefore, we must divide 15 by $\frac{5}{8}$.

$15 \div \dfrac{5}{8} = \dfrac{15}{1} \cdot \dfrac{8}{5}$ Write the whole number as a fraction. Multiply by the reciprocal of the divisor.

$= \dfrac{\overset{3}{\cancel{15}}}{1} \cdot \dfrac{8}{\cancel{5}}$

$= 24$

The 15-mi stretch of highway will take 24 hr to mow.

Skill Practice

14. A cookie recipe requires $\frac{2}{5}$ package of chocolate chips for each batch of cookies. If a restaurant has 20 packages of chocolate chips, how many batches of cookies can it make?

Answer

14. 50 batches

Skill Practice

15. A $\frac{25}{2}$-yd ditch will be dug to put in a new water line. If piping comes in segments of $\frac{5}{4}$ yd, how many segments are needed to line the ditch?

---

example 5   Using Division in an Application

A $\frac{9}{4}$-ft length of wire must be cut into pieces of equal length that are $\frac{3}{8}$ ft long. How many pieces can be cut?

Solution:

Read and familiarize.
Operation: Here we divide the total length of wire into pieces of equal length.

$$\frac{9}{4} \div \frac{3}{8} = \frac{9}{4} \cdot \frac{8}{3} \qquad \text{Multiply by the reciprocal of the divisor.}$$

$$= \frac{\overset{3}{\cancel{9}}}{\underset{1}{\cancel{4}}} \cdot \frac{\overset{2}{\cancel{8}}}{\underset{1}{\cancel{3}}} \qquad \text{Simplify.}$$

$$= 6$$

Six pieces of wire can be cut.

Skill Practice

16. A new school will cost $20,000,000 to build, and the state will pay $\frac{3}{5}$ of the cost.

   a. How much will the state pay?

   b. How much will the state not pay?

   c. The county school district issues bonds to pay $\frac{4}{5}$ of the money not covered by the state. How much money will be covered by bonds?

---

example 6   Using Multiplication in an Application

Carson estimates that his total cost for college for 1 year is $12,600. He has scholarship money to pay $\frac{2}{3}$ of the cost.

   a. How much money is the scholarship worth?

   b. How much money will Carson have to pay?

   c. If Carson's parents help him by paying $\frac{1}{3}$ of the amount not paid by the scholarship, how much money will be paid by Carson's parents?

Solution:

   a. Carson's scholarship will pay $\frac{2}{3}$ of $12,600. Because we are looking for a fraction of a quantity, we multiply.

$$\frac{2}{3} \cdot 12{,}600 = \frac{2}{3} \cdot \frac{12{,}600}{1}$$

$$= \frac{2}{\underset{1}{\cancel{3}}} \cdot \frac{\overset{4200}{\cancel{12{,}600}}}{1}$$

$$= 8400$$

The scholarship will pay $8400.

   b. Carson will have to pay the remaining portion of the cost. This can be found by subtraction.

$$\$12{,}600 - \$8400 = \$4200$$

Carson will have to pay $4200.

Answers

15. 10 segments of piping
16. a. $12,000,000
    b. $8,000,000
    c. $6,400,000

Tip: The answer to Example 6(b) could also have been found by noting that the scholarship paid $\frac{2}{3}$ of the cost. This means that Carson must pay $\frac{1}{3}$ of the cost, or

$$\frac{1}{3} \cdot \frac{\$12{,}600}{1} = \frac{1}{\overset{1}{3}} \cdot \frac{\$\overset{4200}{12{,}600}}{1}$$

$$= \$4200$$

c. Carson's parents will pay $\frac{1}{3}$ of $4200.

$$\frac{1}{\overset{1}{3}} \cdot \frac{\overset{1400}{4200}}{1}$$

Carson's parents will pay $1400.

---

example 7	Using Multiplication in an Application

Three-fifths of the students in the freshman class are female. Of these students, $\frac{5}{9}$ are over the age of 25. What fraction of the freshman class is female over the age of 25?

Solution:

Read and familiarize.
Strategy/operation: We must find $\frac{5}{9}$ of $\frac{3}{5}$ of one whole freshman class. This implies multiplication.

$$\frac{5}{9} \times \frac{3}{5} = \frac{\overset{1}{5}}{\underset{3}{9}} \times \frac{\overset{1}{3}}{\underset{1}{5}} = \frac{1}{3}$$

One-third of the freshman class consists of female students over the age of 25.

---

section 2.5	**Practice Exercises**

Boost *your* GRADE at
mathzone.com!

MathZone

- Practice Problems
- Self-Tests
- NetTutor
- e-Professors
- Videos

Study Skills Exercises

1. Find the page numbers for the Chapter Review Exercises, the Chapter Test, and the Cumulative Review Exercises for this chapter.

Chapter Review Exercises, page(s) _____.

Chapter Test, page(s) _____.

Cumulative Review Exercise(s) _____.

Compare these features and state the advantages of each.

2. Define the key term **reciprocal**.

Review Exercises

For Exercises 3–11, multiply and simplify to lowest terms. Write the answer as a fraction or whole number.

3. $\dfrac{9}{11} \times \dfrac{22}{5}$

4. $\dfrac{24}{7} \cdot \dfrac{7}{8}$

5. $\dfrac{34}{5} \cdot \dfrac{5}{17}$

6. $3 \cdot \left(\dfrac{7}{6}\right)$

7. $8 \cdot \left(\dfrac{5}{24}\right)$

8. $\left(\dfrac{2}{7}\right)\left(\dfrac{7}{2}\right)$

9. $\left(\dfrac{9}{5}\right)\left(\dfrac{5}{9}\right)$

10. $\dfrac{1}{10} \times 10$

11. $\dfrac{1}{3} \times 3$

Objective 1: Reciprocal of a Fraction

12. For each number, determine whether the number has a reciprocal.

   a. $\dfrac{1}{2}$ **b.** $\dfrac{5}{3}$ **c.** 6 **d.** 0

For Exercises 13–20, find the reciprocal of the number, if it exists. **(See Example 1.)**

13. $\dfrac{7}{8}$

14. $\dfrac{5}{6}$

15. $\dfrac{10}{9}$

16. $\dfrac{14}{5}$

17. 4

18. 9

19. 0

20. $\dfrac{0}{4}$

Objective 2: Division of Fractions

For Exercises 21–24, fill in the blank.

21. Dividing by 3 is the same as multiplying by _____.   **22.** Dividing by 5 is the same as multiplying by _____.

23. Dividing by 8 is the same as _____ by $\dfrac{1}{8}$.   **24.** Dividing by 12 is the same as _____ by $\dfrac{1}{12}$.

For Exercises 25–50, divide and simplify the answer to lowest terms. Write the answer as a fraction or whole number.
(See Example 2.)

25. $\dfrac{2}{15} \div \dfrac{5}{12}$

26. $\dfrac{11}{3} \div \dfrac{6}{5}$

27. $\dfrac{7}{13} \div \dfrac{2}{5}$

28. $\dfrac{8}{7} \div \dfrac{3}{10}$

29. $\dfrac{14}{3} \div \dfrac{6}{5}$

30. $\dfrac{11}{2} \div \dfrac{3}{4}$

31. $\dfrac{15}{2} \div \dfrac{3}{2}$

32. $\dfrac{9}{10} \div \dfrac{9}{2}$

33. $\dfrac{3}{4} \div \dfrac{3}{4}$

34. $\dfrac{6}{5} \div \dfrac{6}{5}$

35. $7 \div \dfrac{2}{3}$

36. $4 \div \dfrac{3}{5}$

37. $\dfrac{10}{9} \div \dfrac{1}{18}$

38. $\dfrac{4}{3} \div \dfrac{1}{3}$

39. $12 \div \dfrac{3}{4}$

40. $24 \div \dfrac{8}{5}$

41. $\dfrac{12}{5} \div 4$

42. $\dfrac{20}{6} \div 5$

43. $\dfrac{9}{50} \div \dfrac{18}{25}$

44. $\dfrac{30}{40} \div \dfrac{15}{8}$

45. $\dfrac{9}{100} \div \dfrac{13}{1000}$

46. $\dfrac{1000}{17} \div \dfrac{10}{3}$

47. $\dfrac{36}{5} \div \dfrac{9}{25}$

48. $\dfrac{13}{5} \div \dfrac{17}{10}$

49. $\dfrac{44}{3} \div \dfrac{2}{7}$

50. $\dfrac{31}{15} \div \dfrac{10}{3}$

Mixed Exercises

For Exercises 51–66, multiply or divide as indicated. Write the answer as a fraction or whole number.

51. $\dfrac{7}{8} \div \dfrac{1}{4}$

52. $\dfrac{7}{12} \div \dfrac{5}{3}$

53. $\dfrac{5}{8} \cdot \dfrac{2}{9}$

54. $\dfrac{1}{16} \cdot \dfrac{4}{3}$

55. $6 \cdot \dfrac{4}{3}$

56. $12 \cdot \dfrac{5}{6}$

57. $\dfrac{16}{5} \div 8$

58. $\dfrac{42}{11} \div 7$

59. $\dfrac{16}{3} \div \dfrac{2}{5}$

60. $\dfrac{17}{8} \div \dfrac{1}{4}$

61. $\dfrac{1}{8} \cdot 16$

62. $\dfrac{2}{3} \cdot 9$

63. $\dfrac{22}{7} \cdot \dfrac{5}{16}$

64. $\dfrac{40}{21} \cdot \dfrac{18}{25}$

65. $8 \div \dfrac{16}{3}$

66. $5 \div \dfrac{15}{4}$

Objective 3: Order of Operations

67. Explain the difference in the process to evaluate $\frac{2}{3} \cdot 6$ versus $\frac{2}{3} \div 6$. Then evaluate each expression.

68. Explain the difference in the process to evaluate $8 \cdot \frac{2}{3}$ versus $8 \div \frac{2}{3}$. Then evaluate each expression.

For Exercises 69–78, simplify by using the order of operations. Write the answer as a fraction or whole number.
(See Example 3.)

69. $\dfrac{54}{21} \div \dfrac{2}{3} \div \dfrac{9}{7}$

70. $\dfrac{48}{56} \div \dfrac{3}{8} \div \dfrac{8}{7}$

71. $\left(\dfrac{3}{5} \div \dfrac{6}{7}\right) \cdot \dfrac{5}{3}$

72. $\left(\dfrac{5}{8} \div \dfrac{35}{16}\right) \cdot \dfrac{1}{4}$

73. $\left(\dfrac{3}{8}\right)^2 \div \dfrac{9}{14}$

74. $\dfrac{7}{8} \div \left(\dfrac{1}{2}\right)^2$

75. $\left(\dfrac{2}{5} \div \dfrac{8}{3}\right)^2$

76. $\left(\dfrac{5}{12} \div \dfrac{2}{3}\right)^2$

77. $\left(\dfrac{63}{8} \div \dfrac{9}{4}\right)^2 \cdot 4$

78. $\left(\dfrac{25}{3} \div \dfrac{50}{9}\right)^2 \cdot 8$

Objective 4: Applications of Multiplication and Division of Fractions

79. How many eighths are in $\frac{9}{4}$?

80. How many sixths are in $\frac{4}{3}$?

81. If one cup is $\frac{1}{16}$ gal, how many cups of orange juice can be filled from $\frac{3}{2}$ gal? **(See Example 5.)**

82. If 1 centimeter (cm) is $\frac{1}{100}$ meter (m), how many centimeters are a $\frac{5}{4}$-m piece of rope?

83. During the month of December, a department store wraps packages free of charge. Each package requires $\frac{2}{3}$ yd of ribbon. If Li used up a 36-yd roll of ribbon, how many packages were wrapped? **(See Example 4.)**

84. A developer sells lots of land in increments of $\frac{3}{4}$ acre. If the developer has 60 acres, how many lots can be sold?

85. Dorci buys 16 sheets of plywood, each $\frac{3}{4}$ in. thick, to cover her windows in the event of a hurricane. She stacks the wood in the garage. How high will the stack be?

86. Davey built a bookshelf 36 in. long. Can the shelf hold a set of encyclopedias if there are 24 books and each book averages $\frac{5}{4}$ in. thick? Explain your answer.

87. A radio station allows 18 minutes (min) of advertising each hour. How many 40-second ($\frac{2}{3}$-min) commercials can be run in

  a. 1 hr   **b.** 1 day

88. A television station has 20 min of advertising each hour. How many 30-sec ($\frac{1}{2}$-min) commercials can be run in

  a. 1 hr   **b.** 1 day

89. A landowner has $\frac{9}{4}$ acres of land. She plans to sell $\frac{1}{3}$ of the land. **(See Example 7.)**

  a. How much land will she sell?   **b.** How much land will she retain?

90. Josh must read 24 pages for his English class and 18 pages for psychology. He has read $\frac{1}{6}$ of the pages.

  a. How many pages has he read?   **b.** How many pages does he still have to read?

91. A lab technician has $\frac{7}{4}$ liters (L) of alcohol. If she needs samples of $\frac{1}{8}$ L, how many samples can she prepare?

92. Troy has a $\frac{7}{8}$-in. nail that he must hammer into a board. Each strike of the hammer moves the nail $\frac{1}{16}$ in. into the board. How many strikes of the hammer must he make?

93. Ricardo wants to buy a new house for $240,000. The bank requires $\frac{1}{10}$ of the cost of the house as a down payment. As a gift, Ricardo's mother will pay $\frac{2}{3}$ of the down payment. **(See Example 6.)**

  a. How much money will Ricardo's mother pay toward the down payment?

  b. How much money will Ricardo have to pay toward the down payment?

  c. How much is left over for Ricardo to finance?

94. Althea wants to buy a Toyota Camry for a total cost of $18,000. The dealer requires $\frac{1}{12}$ of the money as a down payment. Althea's parents have agreed to pay one-half of the down payment for her.

  a. How much money will Althea's parents pay toward the down payment?

  b. How much will Althea pay toward the down payment?   **c.** How much will Althea have to finance?

Expanding Your Skills

95. The rectangle shown here has an area of 30 ft². Find the length.

$\frac{5}{2}$ ft

?

96. The rectangle shown here has an area of 8 m². Find the width.

?

14 m

Calculator Connections

Topic: Dividing fractions

Calculator Exercises

For Exercises 97–100, use a calculator to divide. Do not simplify the result to lowest terms.

97. $\dfrac{177}{37} \div \dfrac{23}{226}$

98. $\dfrac{412}{337} \div \dfrac{77}{53}$

99. $\dfrac{681}{214} \div 112$

100. $584 \div \dfrac{3317}{25}$

section 2.6   Multiplication and Division of Mixed Numbers

1. Multiplication of Mixed Numbers

To multiply mixed numbers, we follow these steps.

Steps to Multiply Mixed Numbers

1. Change each mixed number to an improper fraction.

2. Multiply the improper fractions and simplify to lowest terms, if possible (see Section 2.4).

Answers greater than 1 may be written as an improper fraction or as a mixed number depending on the directions of the problem.

Example 1 demonstrates this process.

Skill Practice

Multiply and write the answer as a mixed number or whole number.

1. $\left(4\frac{3}{5}\right)\left(5\frac{5}{6}\right)$

2. $16\frac{1}{2} \cdot 3\frac{7}{11}$

3. $7\frac{1}{6} \cdot 10$

example 1   Multiplying Mixed Numbers

Multiply and write the answer as a mixed number or whole number.

a. $\left(3\frac{1}{5}\right)\left(4\frac{3}{4}\right)$ b. $25\frac{1}{2} \cdot 4\frac{2}{3}$ c. $12 \cdot 8\frac{7}{9}$

Solution:

a. $\left(3\frac{1}{5}\right)\left(4\frac{3}{4}\right) = \frac{16}{5} \cdot \frac{19}{4}$ Write each mixed number as an improper fraction.

$= \frac{\overset{4}{\cancel{16}}}{5} \cdot \frac{19}{\underset{1}{\cancel{4}}}$ Simplify.

$= \frac{76}{5}$ Multiply.

$= 15\frac{1}{5}$ Write the improper fraction as a mixed number.

$$
\begin{array}{r}
15 \\
5\overline{)76} \\
-5 \\
\hline
26 \\
-25 \\
\hline
1
\end{array}
$$

Tip: To check whether the answer from Example 1(a) is reasonable, we can round each factor and estimate the product.

$3\frac{1}{5}$ rounds to 3.

$4\frac{3}{4}$ rounds to 5.

Thus, $\left(3\frac{1}{5}\right)\left(4\frac{3}{4}\right) \approx (3)(5) = 15$, which is close to $15\frac{1}{5}$.

Answers

1. $26\frac{5}{6}$

2. 60

3. $71\frac{2}{3}$

b. $25\frac{1}{2} \cdot 4\frac{2}{3} = \frac{51}{2} \cdot \frac{14}{3}$ Write each mixed number as an improper fraction.

$= \frac{\overset{17}{51}}{\underset{1}{2}} \cdot \frac{\overset{7}{14}}{\underset{1}{3}}$ Simplify.

$= \frac{119}{1}$ Multiply.

$= 119$

c. $12 \cdot 8\frac{7}{9} = \frac{12}{1} \cdot \frac{79}{9}$ Write the whole number and mixed number as improper fractions.

$= \frac{\overset{4}{12}}{1} \cdot \frac{79}{\underset{3}{9}}$ Simplify.

$= \frac{316}{3}$ Multiply.

$= 105\frac{1}{3}$ Write the improper fraction as a mixed number.

$$\begin{array}{r} 105 \\ 3\overline{)316} \\ -3 \\ \hline 16 \\ -15 \\ \hline 1 \end{array}$$

Avoiding Mistakes: Do not try to multiply mixed numbers by multiplying the whole-number parts and multiplying the fractional parts. You will not get the correct answer.
For the expression $25\frac{1}{2} \cdot 4\frac{2}{3}$, it would be incorrect to multiply $(25)(4)$ and $\frac{1}{2} \cdot \frac{2}{3}$. Notice that these values do not equal 119.

Concept Connections

4. Explain how you could check whether the answer to Example 1(c) is reasonable.

2. Division of Mixed Numbers

To divide mixed numbers, we use the following steps.

Steps to Divide Mixed Numbers

1. Change each mixed number to an improper fraction.
2. Divide the improper fractions and simplify to lowest terms, if possible. Recall that to divide fractions, we multiply the dividend by the reciprocal of the divisor (see Section 2.5).

Answers greater than 1 may be written as an improper fraction or as a mixed number depending on the directions of the problem.

example 2   Dividing Mixed Numbers

Divide and write the answer as a mixed number or whole number.

a. $7\frac{1}{2} \div 4\frac{2}{3}$ **b.** $6 \div 5\frac{1}{7}$ **c.** $13\frac{5}{6} \div 7$

Skill Practice

Divide and write the answer as a mixed number or whole number.

5. $10\frac{1}{3} \div 2\frac{5}{6}$ 6. $8 \div 4\frac{4}{5}$

7. $12\frac{4}{9} \div 8$

Answers

4. Round $8\frac{7}{9}$ to 9. Then $12 \cdot 8\frac{7}{9} \approx 12 \cdot 9 = 108$ which is close to $105\frac{1}{3}$.

5. $3\frac{11}{17}$ 6. $1\frac{2}{3}$ 7. $1\frac{5}{9}$

Solution:

Avoiding Mistakes: Be sure to take the reciprocal *after* the mixed number is changed to an improper fraction.

a. $7\dfrac{1}{2} \div 4\dfrac{2}{3} = \dfrac{15}{2} \div \dfrac{14}{3}$ Write the mixed numbers as improper fractions.

$= \dfrac{15}{2} \cdot \dfrac{3}{14}$ Multiply by the reciprocal of the divisor.

$= \dfrac{45}{28}$ Multiply.

$= 1\dfrac{17}{28}$ Write the improper fraction as a mixed number.

b. $6 \div 5\dfrac{1}{7} = \dfrac{6}{1} \div \dfrac{36}{7}$ Write the whole number and mixed number as improper fractions.

$= \dfrac{6}{1} \cdot \dfrac{7}{36}$ Multiply by the reciprocal of the divisor.

$= \dfrac{\overset{1}{\cancel{6}}}{1} \cdot \dfrac{7}{\underset{6}{\cancel{36}}}$ Simplify.

$= \dfrac{7}{6}$ Multiply.

$= 1\dfrac{1}{6}$ Write the improper fraction as a mixed number.

Avoiding Mistakes: Be sure to take the reciprocal *after* the whole number is changed to an improper fraction.

c. $13\dfrac{5}{6} \div 7 = \dfrac{83}{6} \div \dfrac{7}{1}$ Write the whole number and mixed number as improper fractions.

$= \dfrac{83}{6} \cdot \dfrac{1}{7}$ Multiply by the reciprocal of the divisor.

$= \dfrac{83}{42}$ Multiply.

$= 1\dfrac{41}{42}$ Write the improper fraction as a mixed number.

3. Applications of Multiplication and Division of Mixed Numbers

Examples 3 and 4 demonstrate multiplication and division of mixed numbers in day-to-day applications.

Skill Practice

8. A recipe calls for $2\dfrac{3}{4}$ cups of flour. How much flour is required for $2\dfrac{1}{2}$ times the recipe?

example 3   Applying Multiplication of Mixed Numbers

Sometimes homeowners tape the windows in their homes before a hurricane to prevent glass from shattering. Antonio must buy masking tape to tape the windows of his house as shown (Figure 2-9). Each diagonal of the window is $5\dfrac{2}{5}$ ft. If Antonio has 8 windows of this size, how much masking tape does he need?

Figure 2-9

Answer

8. $6\dfrac{7}{8}$ cups of flour

Solution:

One approach is to find the amount of tape required for each window. Then multiply by the number of windows.

The length of tape needed for each window:

$$2 \cdot \left(5\frac{2}{5}\ \text{ft}\right) = \frac{2}{1} \cdot \frac{27}{5}\ \text{ft} \qquad \text{Write the whole number and mixed number as improper fractions.}$$

$$= \frac{54}{5}\ \text{ft} \qquad \text{Multiply.}$$

Amount needed for 8 windows:

$$8 \cdot \left(\frac{54}{5}\ \text{ft}\right) = \frac{8}{1} \cdot \frac{54}{5}\ \text{ft}$$

$$= \frac{432}{5}\ \text{ft}$$

$$= 86\frac{2}{5}\ \text{ft}$$

The homeowner requires $86\frac{2}{5}$ ft of tape.

Tip: The solution to Example 3 can be computed quickly by estimating. In this case, the homeowner might want to *overestimate* the answer, to be sure that he doesn't run short of tape before the hurricane. We can round the value $5\frac{2}{5}$ ft to 6 ft.

Two strips are needed for each window, and there are 8 windows. Therefore our estimate is

$$2(6\ \text{ft})(8) = 96\ \text{ft}$$

---

example 4	Applying Division of Mixed Numbers

A construction site brings in $6\frac{2}{3}$ tons of soil. Each truck holds $\frac{2}{3}$ ton. How many truckloads are necessary?

Solution:

The $6\frac{2}{3}$ tons of soil must be distributed in $\frac{2}{3}$-ton increments. This will require division.

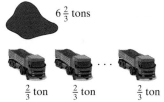

$6\frac{2}{3}$ tons

$\frac{2}{3}$ ton $\frac{2}{3}$ ton $\cdots$ $\frac{2}{3}$ ton

$$6\frac{2}{3} \div \frac{2}{3} = \frac{20}{3} \div \frac{2}{3} \qquad \text{Write the mixed number as an improper fraction.}$$

$$= \frac{20}{3} \cdot \frac{3}{2} \qquad \text{Multiply by the reciprocal of the divisor.}$$

$$= \frac{\overset{10}{\cancel{20}}}{\underset{1}{\cancel{3}}} \cdot \frac{\overset{1}{\cancel{3}}}{\underset{1}{2}} \qquad \text{Simplify.}$$

$$= \frac{10}{1} \qquad \text{Multiply.}$$

$$= 10$$

A total of 10 truckloads of soil will be required.

Skill Practice

9. A department store wraps packages for $2 each. Ribbon $2\frac{5}{8}$ ft long is used to wrap each package. How many packages can be wrapped from a roll of ribbon 168 ft long?

Answer

9. 64 packages

section 2.6   Practice Exercises

Study Skills Exercise

1. Sometimes, test anxiety can be eliminated by adequate preparation and practice. List some places where you can find extra problems for practice.

Review Exercises

For Exercises 2–7, multiply or divide the fractions. Write your answers as fractions.

2. $\dfrac{5}{6} \cdot \dfrac{2}{9}$

3. $\dfrac{13}{5} \cdot \dfrac{10}{9}$

4. $\dfrac{20}{9} \div \dfrac{10}{3}$

5. $\dfrac{42}{11} \div \dfrac{7}{2}$

6. $\dfrac{32}{15} \div 4$

7. $\dfrac{52}{18} \div 13$

8. Explain the process to change a mixed number to an improper fraction.

For Exercises 9–16, write the mixed number as an improper fraction.

9. $3\dfrac{2}{5}$

10. $2\dfrac{7}{10}$

11. $1\dfrac{4}{7}$

12. $4\dfrac{1}{8}$

13. $12\dfrac{5}{6}$

14. $5\dfrac{2}{11}$

15. $9\dfrac{3}{4}$

16. $15\dfrac{1}{2}$

Objective 1: Multiplication of Mixed Numbers

For Exercises 17–36, multiply the mixed numbers. Write the answer as a mixed number or whole number.
(See Example 1.)

17. $\left(2\dfrac{2}{5}\right)\left(3\dfrac{1}{12}\right)$

18. $\left(5\dfrac{1}{5}\right)\left(3\dfrac{3}{4}\right)$

19. $2\dfrac{1}{3} \cdot \dfrac{5}{7}$

20. $6\dfrac{1}{8} \cdot \dfrac{4}{7}$

21. $4\dfrac{2}{9} \cdot 9$

22. $3\dfrac{1}{3} \cdot 6$

23. $\left(5\dfrac{3}{16}\right)\left(5\dfrac{1}{3}\right)$

24. $\left(8\dfrac{2}{3}\right)\left(2\dfrac{1}{13}\right)$

25. $\dfrac{2}{3} \cdot 2\dfrac{7}{10}$

26. $\dfrac{4}{3} \cdot 5\dfrac{1}{8}$

27. $\left(7\dfrac{1}{4}\right) \cdot 10$

28. $\left(2\dfrac{2}{3}\right) \cdot 3$

29. $4\frac{5}{8} \cdot 0$ **30.** $0 \cdot 6\frac{1}{10}$ **31.** $\left(3\frac{1}{2}\right)\left(2\frac{1}{7}\right)$ **32.** $\left(1\frac{3}{10}\right)\left(1\frac{1}{4}\right)$

33. $\left(5\frac{2}{5}\right)\left(\frac{2}{9}\right)\left(1\frac{4}{5}\right)$ **34.** $\left(6\frac{1}{8}\right)\left(2\frac{3}{4}\right)\left(\frac{8}{7}\right)$ **35.** $\left(3\frac{2}{5}\right)\left(\frac{7}{34}\right)\left(3\frac{3}{4}\right)$ **36.** $\left(5\frac{1}{6}\right)\left(1\frac{4}{7}\right)\left(\frac{14}{33}\right)$

Objective 2: Division of Mixed Numbers

For Exercises 37–54, divide the mixed numbers. Write the answer as a mixed number, proper fraction, or whole number. **(See Example 2.)**

37. $1\frac{7}{10} \div 2\frac{3}{4}$ **38.** $5\frac{1}{10} \div \frac{3}{4}$ **39.** $5\frac{8}{9} \div 1\frac{1}{3}$ **40.** $12\frac{4}{5} \div 2\frac{3}{5}$

41. $2\frac{1}{2} \div 1\frac{1}{16}$ **42.** $7\frac{3}{5} \div 1\frac{7}{12}$ **43.** $4\frac{1}{2} \div 2\frac{1}{4}$ **44.** $5\frac{5}{6} \div 2\frac{1}{3}$

45. $0 \div 6\frac{7}{12}$ **46.** $0 \div 1\frac{9}{11}$ **47.** $2\frac{5}{6} \div \frac{1}{6}$ **48.** $6\frac{1}{2} \div \frac{1}{2}$

49. $1\frac{1}{3} \div \frac{2}{7}$ **50.** $2\frac{1}{7} \div \frac{5}{13}$ **51.** $3\frac{1}{2} \div 2$ **52.** $4\frac{2}{3} \div 3$

53. $7\frac{1}{8} \div 1\frac{1}{3} \div 2\frac{1}{4}$ **54.** $3\frac{1}{8} \div 5\frac{5}{7} \div 1\frac{5}{16}$

Objective 3: Applications of Multiplication and Division of Mixed Numbers

55. Tabitha charges $8 per hour for baby sitting. If she works for $4\frac{3}{4}$ hr, how much should she be paid? **(See Example 3.)**

56. Kurt bought $2\frac{2}{3}$ acres of land. If land costs $10,500 per acre, how much will the land cost him?

57. The age of a small kitten can be approximated by the following rule. The kitten's age is given as 1 week for every quarter pound of weight. **(See Example 4.)**

   a. Approximately how old is a $1\frac{3}{4}$-lb kitten?

   b. Approximately how old is a $2\frac{1}{8}$-lb kitten?

58. Richard's estate is to be split equally among his three children. If his estate is worth $1\frac{3}{4}$ million, how much will each child inherit?

59. Lucy earns $14 per hour and Ricky earns $10 per hour. Suppose Lucy worked $35\frac{1}{2}$ hr last week and Ricky worked $42\frac{1}{2}$ hr.

    a. Who earned more money and by how much?

    b. How much did they earn altogether?

60. A roll of wallpaper covers an area of 28 ft². If the roll is $1\frac{17}{24}$ ft wide, how long is the roll?

Mixed Exercises

For Exercises 61–74, perform the indicated operation. Write the answer as a mixed number, proper fraction, or whole number.

61. $2\frac{1}{5} \div 1\frac{1}{10}$

62. $3\frac{3}{4} \cdot 1\frac{5}{6}$

63. $6 \div 1\frac{1}{8}$

64. $8 \div 2\frac{1}{3}$

65. $4\frac{1}{12} \cdot 0$

66. $5\frac{1}{3} \cdot 6$

67. $10\frac{1}{2} \div 9$

68. $\frac{2}{7} \cdot 1\frac{8}{9}$

69. $0 \div 9\frac{2}{3}$

70. $\frac{3}{8} \div 2\frac{1}{2}$

71. $12 \cdot \frac{1}{8}$

72. $20 \cdot \frac{2}{15}$

73. $6\frac{8}{9} \div 0$

74. $0 \cdot 2\frac{1}{8}$

Expanding Your Skills

75. A landscaper will use a decorative concrete border around the cactus garden shown. Each concrete brick is $1\frac{1}{4}$ ft long and costs $3. What is the total cost of the border?

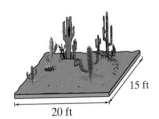

15 ft

20 ft

76. Sara drives a total of $64\frac{1}{2}$ mi to work and back. Her car gets $21\frac{1}{2}$ miles per gallon (mpg) of gas. If gas is $2 per gallon, how much does it cost her to commute to and from work each day?

For Exercises 76–79, simplify by using the order of operations. Write the answer as a fraction.

76. $\left(\dfrac{2}{19} \div \dfrac{8}{19}\right)^3$

77. $\left(\dfrac{12}{5}\right)^2 \div \dfrac{36}{5}$

78. $\dfrac{81}{55} \div \dfrac{3}{11} \div \dfrac{3}{2}$

79. $\dfrac{4}{13} \cdot \left(\dfrac{1}{2}\right)^3 \div 2$

For Exercises 80–81, translate to a mathematical statement. Then simplify.

80. How much is $\frac{4}{5}$ of 20?

81. How many $\frac{2}{3}$'s are in 18?

82. How many $\frac{2}{3}$-lb bags of candy can be filled from a 24-lb sack of candy?

83. Amelia worked only $\frac{4}{5}$ of her normal 40-hr workweek. If she makes $18 per hour, how much money did she earn for the week?

84. A small patio floor will be made from square pieces of tile that are $\frac{4}{3}$ ft on a side. See the figure. Find the area of the patio (in square feet) if its dimensions are 10 tiles by 12 tiles.

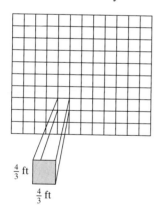

$\frac{4}{3}$ ft

$\frac{4}{3}$ ft

85. Chuck is an elementary school teacher and needs 22 pieces of wood, $\frac{3}{8}$ ft long, for a class project. If he has a 9-ft board from which to cut the pieces, will he have enough $\frac{3}{8}$-ft pieces for his class? Explain.

Section 2.6

For Exercises 86–96, multiply or divide as indicated.

86. $\left(3\dfrac{2}{3}\right)\left(6\dfrac{2}{5}\right)$

87. $\left(11\dfrac{1}{3}\right)\left(2\dfrac{3}{34}\right)$

88. $6\dfrac{1}{2} \cdot 1\dfrac{3}{13}$

89. $4 \cdot \left(5\dfrac{5}{8}\right)$

90. $45\dfrac{5}{13} \cdot 0$

91. $4\dfrac{5}{16} \div 2\dfrac{7}{8}$

92. $3\dfrac{5}{11} \div 3\dfrac{4}{5}$

93. $7 \div 1\dfrac{5}{9}$

94. $4\dfrac{6}{11} \div 2$

95. $10\dfrac{1}{5} \div 17$

96. $0 \div 3\dfrac{5}{12}$

97. It takes $1\frac{1}{4}$ gal of paint for Neva to paint her living room. If her great room (including the dining area) is $2\frac{1}{2}$ times larger than the living room, how many gallons will it take to paint that room?

98. A roll of ribbon contains $12\frac{1}{2}$ yd. How many pieces of length $1\frac{1}{4}$ yd can be cut from this roll?

chapter 2 | test

1. a. Write a fraction that represents the shaded portion of the figure.

b. Is the fraction proper or improper?

2. a. Write a fraction that represents the total shaded portion of the 3 figures.

b. Is the fraction proper or improper?

3. Write an improper fraction and a mixed number that represent the shaded region.

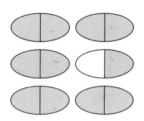

4. Is the fraction $\frac{7}{7}$ a proper or an improper fraction? Explain.

5. a. Write $\frac{44}{12}$ as a mixed number.

b. Write $3\frac{7}{9}$ as an improper fraction.

For Exercises 6–9, plot the fraction on the number line.

6. $\frac{1}{2}$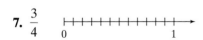

7. $\frac{3}{4}$

8. $\frac{7}{12}$

9. $\frac{13}{5}$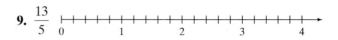

10. Label the following numbers as prime, composite, or neither.

a. 15   **b.** 0

c. 53   **d.** 1

e. 29   **f.** 39

11. a. List all the factors of 80.

b. Write the prime factorization of 80.

12. a. What is the divisibility rule for 3?

b. Is 1,981,011 divisible by 3?

13. Determine whether 1155 is divisible by

a. 2   **b.** 3

c. 5   **d.** 10

For Exercises 14–15, determine if the fractions are equivalent. Then fill in the blank with either = or ≠ .

14. $\frac{15}{12} \square \frac{5}{4}$ **15.** $\frac{2}{5} \square \frac{4}{25}$

For Exercises 16–17, simplify the fractions to lowest terms.

16. $\frac{150}{105}$ **17.** $\frac{1,200,000}{1,400,000}$

18. Christine and Brad are putting their photographs in scrapbooks. Christine has placed 15 of her 25 photos and Brad has placed 16 of his 20 photos.

a. What fractional part of the total photos has each person placed?

b. Which person has a greater fractional part completed?

For Exercises 19–26, multiply or divide as indicated. Simplify the fraction to lowest terms.

19. $\dfrac{2}{9} \times \dfrac{57}{46}$

20. $\left(\dfrac{75}{24}\right) \cdot 4$

21. $\dfrac{28}{24} \div \dfrac{21}{8}$

22. $\dfrac{105}{42} \div 5$

23. $\dfrac{2}{18} \times \dfrac{9}{25} \times \dfrac{40}{6}$

24. $\dfrac{600}{1200} \div \dfrac{50}{65} \div \dfrac{13}{15}$

25. $\dfrac{10}{21} \div 4\dfrac{1}{6}$

26. $4\dfrac{4}{17} \cdot 2\dfrac{4}{15}$

27. Perform the order of operations. Simplify the fraction to lowest terms.

$$\dfrac{52}{72} \div \left[\left(\dfrac{1}{2}\right)^2 \cdot \dfrac{8}{3}\right]$$

28. Find the area of the triangle.

$\frac{11}{3}$ cm

8 cm

29. Which is greater, $20 \cdot \frac{1}{4}$ or $20 \div \frac{1}{4}$?

30. How many "quarter-pounders" can be made from 12 lb of ground beef?

31. The Humane Society has 120 dogs. Of the 120, $\frac{5}{8}$ are female. Among the female dogs, $\frac{1}{15}$ are pure breeds. How many of the dogs are female and pure breeds?

32. A zoning requirement indicates that a house built on less than 1 acre of land may take up no more than one-half of the land. If Liz and George purchased a $\frac{4}{5}$-acre lot of land, what is the maximum land area that they can use to build the house?

chapters 1 and 2 | cumulative review

1. Fill out the table with either the word name for the number or the number in standard form.

Mountain	Height (ft)	
	Standard Form	Words
Mt. Foraker (Alaska)		Seventeen thousand, four hundred
Mt. Kilimanjaro (Tanzania)	19,340	
El Libertador (Argentina)		Twenty-two thousand, forty-seven
Mont Blanc (France-Italy)	15,771	

For Exercises 2–13, perform the indicated operation.

2. $432 + 998$

3. $572 - 433$

4. 4122×52

5. $384 \div 16$

6. $23(81)$

7. $4\overline{)74}$

8. $\begin{array}{r} 3{,}000{,}000 \\ \times\, 40{,}000 \end{array}$

9. $\begin{array}{r} 1007 \\ -\ 823 \end{array}$

10. $\dfrac{48}{8}$

11. $6 + 2 \cdot 8$

12. $5^2 - 3^2$

13. $(5 - 3)^2$

For Exercises 14–18, match the algebraic expression with the property that it demonstrates.

14. $5 \cdot 8 = 8 \cdot 5$

    a. Commutative property of addition

15. $4(3 + 2)$
   $= 4 \cdot 3 + 4 \cdot 2$

    b. Associative property of addition

16. $(12 + 3) + 5$
   $= 12 + (3 + 5)$

    c. Distributive property of multiplication over addition

17. $8 \cdot (7 \cdot 2)$
   $= (8 \cdot 7) \cdot 2$

    d. Commutative property of multiplication

18. $32 + 9$
   $= 9 + 32$

    e. Associative property of multiplication

19. Write a fraction that represents the shaded area.

    a.

    b.

20. Identify each fraction as proper or improper.

    a. $\dfrac{7}{8}$ **b.** $\dfrac{8}{7}$ **c.** $\dfrac{8}{8}$

21. a. List all the factors of 30.

    b. Write the prime factorization of 30.

22. Simplify the fraction to lowest terms.

    a. $\dfrac{144}{84}$ **b.** $\dfrac{60,000}{150,000}$

23. Multiply and simplify to lowest terms. $\dfrac{35}{27} \cdot \dfrac{51}{95}$

24. Divide and simplify to lowest terms. $5\frac{2}{3} \div 6\frac{4}{5}$

25. Is multiplication of fractions a commutative operation? Explain, using the fractions $\frac{8}{13}$ and $\frac{5}{16}$.

26. Is multiplication of fractions an associative operation? Explain, using the fractions $\frac{1}{2}, \frac{2}{9}$, and $\frac{5}{3}$.

27. Simplify, using the order of operations. Simplify the answer to lowest terms. $\left(\frac{5}{6} \cdot \frac{12}{25}\right)^2 \div \frac{2}{3}$

28. Find the area of the rectangle.

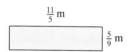

29. Find the area of the triangle.

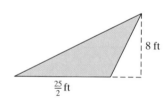

30. At one college $\frac{3}{4}$ of the students are male, and of the males, $\frac{1}{10}$ are from out of state. What fraction of the students are males who are from out of state?

Fractions and Mixed Numbers: Addition and Subtraction

3

In this chapter we learn about addition and subtraction of fractions as well as operations on mixed numbers. For example, suppose a student works 3 part-time jobs. She spends $8\frac{2}{3}$ hr per week delivering newspapers. She also spends $4\frac{1}{2}$ hr per week tutoring and $3\frac{3}{4}$ hr per week taking notes for a blind student. See Exercise 86 in Section 3.4 to determine the total number of hours per week that the student works.

chapter 3 | preview

The exercises in this chapter preview contain concepts that have not yet been presented. These exercises are provided for students who want to compare their levels of understanding before and after studying the chapter. Alternatively, you may prefer to work these exercises when the chapter is completed and before taking the exam.

Section 3.1

For Exercises 1–3, add or subtract the like fractions. Write the answer as a fraction or whole number simplified to lowest terms.

1. $\dfrac{53}{12} + \dfrac{25}{12}$ **2.** $\dfrac{28}{9} - \dfrac{10}{9}$ **3.** $\dfrac{19}{12} - \dfrac{5}{12} + \dfrac{7}{12}$

Section 3.2

4. a. List eight multiples of 9. Answers may vary.

b. List eight multiples of 12. Answers may vary.

c. From the lists from parts (a) and (b), list two common multiples of 9 and 12.

d. Identify the least common multiple (LCM) of 9 and 12.

5. What is the LCM of the numbers 8, 12, and 18?

6. Rewrite each fraction with the indicated denominator.

a. $\dfrac{8}{15} = \dfrac{}{60}$ **b.** $\dfrac{3}{5} = \dfrac{}{60}$

c. $\dfrac{11}{20} = \dfrac{}{60}$ **d.** $\dfrac{7}{12} = \dfrac{}{60}$

7. Rank the fractions from Exercise 6 from least to greatest.

Section 3.3

For Exercises 8–11, add or subtract the fractions. Write the answer as a fraction or whole number, and simplify to lowest terms.

8. $\dfrac{23}{5} + \dfrac{13}{10}$ **9.** $\dfrac{31}{16} - \dfrac{5}{4}$

10. $6 - \dfrac{5}{4}$ **11.** $\dfrac{23}{18} - \dfrac{19}{36} + \dfrac{3}{4}$

Section 3.4

For Exercises 12–14, add and subtract the mixed numbers. Write the answer as a mixed number.

12. $14\dfrac{9}{10} + 2\dfrac{49}{100}$ **13.** $7 - 4\dfrac{13}{14}$

14. $15\dfrac{3}{8} - 12\dfrac{5}{8} + 1\dfrac{3}{4}$

Section 3.5

For Exercises 15–16, simplify the expressions by using the order of operations. Simplify the answer to lowest terms.

15. $\left(1\dfrac{3}{8} - \dfrac{15}{16}\right) \div \left(\dfrac{3}{4}\right)^2$ **16.** $1\dfrac{1}{9} + \left(\dfrac{10}{27} \cdot 1\dfrac{4}{5}\right)^3$

17. Lou wants to paint the front of his cottage. Find the area of the front of the house, given the figure.

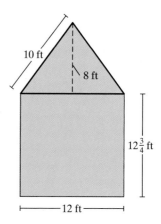

section 3.1   Addition and Subtraction of Like Fractions

Objectives

1. Addition of Like Fractions
2. Subtraction of Like Fractions
3. Order of Operations
4. Applications of Addition and Subtraction of Fractions

1. Addition of Like Fractions

In Chapter 2 we learned how to multiply and divide fractions. The main focus of this chapter is to add and subtract fractions. The operation of addition can be thought of as combining like groups of objects. For example:

$$3 \text{ apples} + 1 \text{ apple} = 4 \text{ apples}$$

three-fifths + one-fifth = four-fifths

$$\frac{3}{5} + \frac{1}{5} = \frac{4}{5}$$

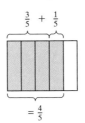

The fractions $\frac{3}{5}$ and $\frac{1}{5}$ are said to be **like fractions** because their denominators are the same. That is, their denominators represent the same part of a whole. In general, two or more like fractions may be added according to the following procedure.

Adding Like Fractions

1. Add the numerators.
2. Write the sum over the common denominator.
3. Simplify the fraction to lowest terms, if possible.

Concept Connections

Determine whether the fractions are like or unlike.

1. $\frac{4}{7}$ and $\frac{7}{3}$ 2. $\frac{9}{8}$ and $\frac{1}{8}$

---

example 1   Adding Like Fractions

Add. Write the answer as a fraction or whole number.

a. $\frac{1}{4} + \frac{5}{4}$ **b.** $\frac{3}{10} + \frac{7}{10}$ **c.** $\frac{7}{15} + \frac{2}{15} + \frac{1}{15}$

Solution:

a. $\dfrac{1}{4} + \dfrac{5}{4} = \dfrac{1+5}{4}$ Add the numerators.

$= \dfrac{6}{4}$ Write the sum over the common denominator.

$= \dfrac{\overset{3}{6}}{\underset{2}{4}}$ Simplify to lowest terms.

$= \dfrac{3}{2}$

> **Avoiding Mistakes:** Notice that when adding fractions, we do not add the denominators. We add *only* the numerators.

b. $\dfrac{3}{10} + \dfrac{7}{10} = \dfrac{3+7}{10}$ Add the numerators.

$= \dfrac{10}{10}$ Write the sum over the common denominator.

$= 1$ Simplify to lowest terms.

Skill Practice

Add. Write the answer as a fraction or whole number.

3. $\frac{2}{9} + \frac{4}{9}$ 4. $\frac{11}{5} + \frac{4}{5}$

5. $\frac{7}{12} + \frac{5}{12} + \frac{11}{12}$

Answers

1. Unlike   2. Like   3. $\frac{2}{3}$

4. 3   5. $\frac{23}{12}$

c. $\dfrac{7}{15} + \dfrac{2}{15} + \dfrac{1}{15} = \dfrac{7 + 2 + 1}{15}$ Add the numerators.

$\qquad\qquad = \dfrac{10}{15}$ Write the sum over the common denominator.

$\qquad\qquad = \dfrac{2}{3}$ Simplify to lowest terms.

Concept Connections

6. Which is the correct sum for $\frac{2}{3} + \frac{5}{3}$?

$\dfrac{7}{6}$ or $\dfrac{7}{3}$

7. Which is the correct product for $\frac{2}{3} \cdot \frac{5}{3}$?

$\dfrac{10}{9}$ or $\dfrac{10}{3}$

Avoiding Mistakes: Note that the process to add fractions is different from the process to multiply fractions.

$$\frac{2}{7} \times \frac{3}{7} = \frac{6}{49} \qquad \text{but} \qquad \frac{2}{7} + \frac{3}{7} = \frac{5}{7}$$

2. Subtraction of Like Fractions

Subtracting like fractions is performed in a manner similar to adding like fractions.

Subtracting Like Fractions

1. Subtract the numerators.

2. Write the difference over the common denominator.

3. Simplify the fraction to lowest terms, if possible.

Skill Practice

Subtract. Write the answer as a fraction or whole number.

8. $\dfrac{7}{2} - \dfrac{3}{2}$ **9.** $\dfrac{14}{11} - \dfrac{8}{11}$

10. $\dfrac{5}{6} + \dfrac{7}{6} - \dfrac{2}{6}$

---

example 2   **Subtracting Like Fractions**

Subtract. Write the answer as a fraction or whole number.

a. $\dfrac{13}{9} - \dfrac{2}{9}$ **b.** $\dfrac{7}{3} - \dfrac{1}{3}$

Solution:

a. $\dfrac{13}{9} - \dfrac{2}{9} = \dfrac{13 - 2}{9}$ Subtract the numerators.

$\qquad\qquad = \dfrac{11}{9}$ Write the difference over the common denominator. The fraction is already in lowest terms because 11 and 9 share no common factors.

b. $\dfrac{7}{3} - \dfrac{1}{3} = \dfrac{7 - 1}{3}$ Subtract the numerators.

$\qquad\qquad = \dfrac{6}{3}$ Write the difference over the common denominator.

$\qquad\qquad = 2$

Answers

6. $\dfrac{7}{3}$ 7. $\dfrac{10}{9}$ 8. 2

9. $\dfrac{6}{11}$ 10. $\dfrac{5}{3}$

3. Order of Operations

Example 3 reviews the order of operations. Simplify within parentheses first. Then simplify expressions with exponents, followed by multiplication or division in the order they appear from left to right. Addition or subtraction is performed last in the order of appearance from left to right.

example 3   Applying the Order of Operations

Simplify.

a. $\left(\dfrac{2}{7} + \dfrac{1}{7}\right)^2$ **b.** $\dfrac{3}{5} \div \dfrac{9}{10} + \dfrac{1}{3}$ **c.** $\dfrac{7}{15} - \dfrac{3}{15} + \dfrac{2}{15}$

Solution:

a. $\left(\dfrac{2}{7} + \dfrac{1}{7}\right)^2 = \left(\dfrac{2+1}{7}\right)^2$ Add fractions within parentheses first.

$= \left(\dfrac{3}{7}\right)^2$

$= \dfrac{3}{7} \cdot \dfrac{3}{7}$ Square the fraction $\frac{3}{7}$.

$= \dfrac{9}{49}$ The fraction is in lowest terms.

b. $\dfrac{3}{5} \div \dfrac{9}{10} + \dfrac{1}{3} = \left(\dfrac{3}{5} \div \dfrac{9}{10}\right) + \dfrac{1}{3}$ We can insert parentheses to emphasize that division is performed before addition.

$= \left(\dfrac{3}{5} \cdot \dfrac{10}{9}\right) + \dfrac{1}{3}$ Multiply by the reciprocal of the divisor.

$= \left(\dfrac{\overset{1}{\cancel{3}}}{\cancel{5}} \cdot \dfrac{\overset{2}{\cancel{10}}}{\cancel{9}}\right) + \dfrac{1}{3}$ Simplify.

$= \left(\dfrac{2}{3}\right) + \dfrac{1}{3}$ Multiply the fractions.

$= \dfrac{3}{3}$ Add the fractions.

$= 1$ Simplify.

c. $\dfrac{7}{15} - \dfrac{3}{15} + \dfrac{2}{15} = \dfrac{7 - 3 + 2}{15}$ Subtract and add the numerators.

$= \dfrac{6}{15}$ Write the result over the common denominator.

$= \dfrac{\overset{2}{\cancel{6}}}{\underset{5}{\cancel{15}}}$ Simplify to lowest terms.

$= \dfrac{2}{5}$

Skill Practice

Simplify.

11. $\left(\dfrac{3}{10} + \dfrac{2}{10}\right)^2$

12. $\dfrac{2}{7} \div \dfrac{4}{5} + \dfrac{3}{14}$

13. $\dfrac{8}{11} - \dfrac{3}{11} + \dfrac{7}{11}$

Answers

11. $\dfrac{1}{4}$ **12.** $\dfrac{4}{7}$ **13.** $\dfrac{12}{11}$

4. Applications of Addition and Subtraction of Fractions

Recall that the perimeter of a polygon is found by adding the lengths of the sides.

Skill Practice

14. Find the perimeter.

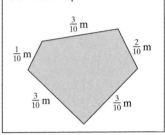

example 4   Finding Perimeter

Find the perimeter of the figure.

$\frac{10}{12}$ yd

$\frac{5}{12}$ yd $\frac{5}{12}$ yd

$\frac{15}{12}$ yd

Solution:

$$\text{Perimeter} = \frac{10}{12} + \frac{5}{12} + \frac{15}{12} + \frac{5}{12}$$

$$= \frac{10 + 5 + 15 + 5}{12}$$

$$= \frac{35}{12} \quad \text{or} \quad 2\frac{11}{12}$$

The perimeter is $2\frac{11}{12}$ yd.

Skill Practice

15. Jamie mixed $\frac{5}{8}$ gal of green paint with $\frac{7}{8}$ gal of white paint. Then she used $\frac{3}{8}$ gal of the mixture to paint a mural. How much paint is left over?

example 5   Applying Addition and Subtraction of Fractions

On Monday, a stock rose by $\frac{11}{16}$ point. On Tuesday it rose $\frac{3}{16}$ point, and on Wednesday it dropped $\frac{9}{16}$ point. What was the net gain for these 3 days?

Solution:

The net change in the stock is given by $\frac{11}{16} + \frac{3}{16} - \frac{9}{16}$.

$$\frac{11}{16} + \frac{3}{16} - \frac{9}{16} = \frac{11 + 3 - 9}{16}$$

$$= \frac{5}{16}$$

The stock rose by $\frac{5}{16}$ point.

Answers

14. $\frac{6}{5}$ or $1\frac{1}{5}$ m

15. $\frac{9}{8}$ or $1\frac{1}{8}$ gal

section 3.1   Practice Exercises

Study Skills Exercises

1. How can you utilize the margin exercises in the text?

2. Define the key term **like fractions**.

Objective 1: Addition of Like Fractions

For Exercises 3–7, add the like units.

3. 3 ft + 5 ft

4. 7 chairs + 2 chairs

5. 7 m + 13 m

6. 8 thirds + 2 thirds

7. 1 fourth + 6 fourths

For Exercises 8–9, shade in the portion of the third figure that represents the addition of the first two figures.

8.

9.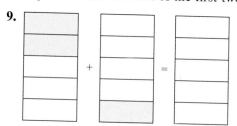

10. Explain the difference between evaluating the two expressions $\frac{2}{5} \times \frac{7}{5}$ and $\frac{2}{5} + \frac{7}{5}$.

For Exercises 11–22, add the like fractions. Write the answer as a fraction or whole number. **(See Example 1.)**

11. $\dfrac{6}{11} + \dfrac{7}{11}$

12. $\dfrac{5}{3} + \dfrac{2}{3}$

13. $\dfrac{6}{5} + \dfrac{3}{5}$

14. $\dfrac{3}{10} + \dfrac{4}{10}$

15. $\dfrac{1}{4} + \dfrac{3}{4}$

16. $\dfrac{1}{8} + \dfrac{3}{8}$

17. $\dfrac{2}{9} + \dfrac{4}{9}$

18. $\dfrac{3}{2} + \dfrac{5}{2}$

19. $\dfrac{3}{20} + \dfrac{8}{20} + \dfrac{15}{20}$

20. $\dfrac{5}{8} + \dfrac{4}{8} + \dfrac{9}{8}$

21. $\dfrac{18}{14} + \dfrac{11}{14} + \dfrac{6}{14}$

22. $\dfrac{7}{18} + \dfrac{22}{18} + \dfrac{10}{18}$

23. Bethany pours $\frac{1}{4}$ cup of bleach into a container and then adds $\frac{9}{4}$ cups of water. How many cups of bleach and water mixture does she have?

24. Austin rode his bike $\frac{7}{6}$ mi before he got a flat tire. He then had to walk another $\frac{1}{6}$ mi. How far did Austin travel?

Objective 2: Subtraction of Like Fractions

For Exercises 25–28, subtract the like units.

25. 15 baskets − 4 baskets   **26.** 52 cards − 13 cards   **27.** 7 fifths − 1 fifth   **28.** 18 tenths − 11 tenths

For Exercises 29–30, shade in the portion of the third figure that represents the subtraction of the first two figures.

29.   **30.**

For Exercises 31–42, subtract the like fractions. Write the answer as a fraction or whole number. **(See Example 2.)**

31. $\frac{9}{8} - \frac{6}{8}$

32. $\frac{7}{9} - \frac{6}{9}$

33. $\frac{9}{2} - \frac{6}{2}$

34. $\frac{10}{4} - \frac{5}{4}$

35. $\frac{13}{3} - \frac{7}{3}$

36. $\frac{13}{10} - \frac{3}{10}$

37. $\frac{23}{12} - \frac{15}{12}$

38. $\frac{13}{6} - \frac{5}{6}$

39. $\frac{28}{25} - \frac{14}{25} - \frac{4}{25}$

40. $\frac{34}{15} - \frac{6}{15} - \frac{3}{15}$

41. $\frac{10}{16} - \frac{1}{16} - \frac{5}{16}$

42. $\frac{31}{40} - \frac{14}{40} - \frac{12}{40}$

43. A chemist has $\frac{5}{8}$ grams (g) of NaCl (salt). If she uses $\frac{3}{8}$ g, how much is left?

44. Jason bought $\frac{11}{4}$ acres of land and then sold $\frac{3}{4}$ acre. How much land does he have left?

Mixed Exercises

For Exercises 45–54, add or subtract as indicated. Write the answer as a fraction or whole number.

45. $\frac{7}{8} + \frac{5}{8}$

46. $\frac{1}{21} + \frac{13}{21}$

47. $\frac{14}{5} - \frac{2}{5}$

48. $\frac{5}{3} - \frac{2}{3}$

49. $\frac{6}{13} + \frac{7}{13}$

50. $\frac{20}{35} + \frac{12}{35}$

51. $\frac{14}{15} + \frac{2}{15} - \frac{4}{15}$

52. $\frac{19}{6} - \frac{11}{6} + \frac{5}{6}$

53. $\frac{7}{2} - \frac{3}{2} + \frac{1}{2}$

54. $\frac{8}{3} + \frac{2}{3} - \frac{1}{3}$

Objective 3: Order of Operations

For Exercises 55–64, simplify the expression by using the order of operations. Write the answer as a fraction or whole number. **(See Example 3.)**

55. $\dfrac{6}{5} + \dfrac{7}{5} - \dfrac{4}{5}$

56. $\dfrac{10}{3} - \dfrac{2}{3} + \dfrac{5}{3}$

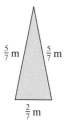 **57.** $\dfrac{5}{4} \div \dfrac{3}{2} + \dfrac{5}{6}$

58. $\dfrac{1}{7} \div \dfrac{2}{21} + \dfrac{5}{2}$

59. $\dfrac{3}{7} + \dfrac{13}{14} \cdot 2$

60. $\dfrac{13}{6} - \dfrac{5}{18} \cdot 3$

61. $\left(\dfrac{7}{3} - \dfrac{5}{3}\right)^3$

62. $\left(\dfrac{11}{10} - \dfrac{2}{10}\right)^2$

63. $\left(\dfrac{2}{21} + \dfrac{11}{21}\right) \div \dfrac{1}{7}$

64. $\left(\dfrac{17}{30} - \dfrac{12}{30}\right) \div \dfrac{5}{6}$

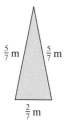 **65.** Gail mixed $\frac{1}{10}$ gal of red paint with $\frac{7}{10}$ gal of white paint. She used $\frac{3}{10}$ gal of the mixture to paint a room. How much mixture was left over? **(See Example 5.)**

66. Emeril mixed $\frac{3}{8}$ cup balsamic vinegar with $\frac{4}{8}$ cup oil to make a salad dressing. Then he used $\frac{1}{8}$ cup of the mixture for a large salad. How much oil and vinegar mixture was left over?

67. A chemist mixed $\frac{5}{8}$ liter (L) of water with $\frac{7}{8}$ L of alcohol. Then he used one-quarter of the mixture in an experiment. How much mixture did he use?

68. Malcom planted tomatoes in $\frac{2}{7}$ of his garden. He planted cucumbers in $\frac{3}{7}$ of the garden and cabbage in $\frac{1}{7}$. The remaining $\frac{1}{7}$ still has not yet been planted. A deer came in one night and ate $\frac{1}{3}$ of the plants in the planted area. What fraction of the garden did the deer eat?

Objective 4: Applications of Addition and Subtraction of Fractions

For Exercises 69–70, find the perimeter.

69.

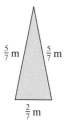

$\frac{5}{7}$ m $\frac{5}{7}$ m

$\frac{2}{7}$ m

70.

$\frac{20}{9}$ ft $\frac{23}{9}$ ft

$\frac{11}{9}$ ft

71. Find the perimeter of the stamp. **(See Example 4.)**

$\frac{13}{16}$ in.

$\frac{15}{16}$ in.

Australia 90c

72. Find the perimeter of the top of the table.

$\frac{4}{3}$ yd

$\frac{8}{3}$ yd

73. Thilan has taken up a new exercise program. He walks 6 days per week. One week he walked the distances given in the table.

    a. Find the total distance he walked for the week.

    b. Find the average distance walked per day.

Day	Distance
Monday	$\frac{4}{10}$ mi
Tuesday	$\frac{7}{10}$ mi
Wednesday	$\frac{9}{10}$ mi
Thursday	$\frac{5}{10}$ mi
Friday	$\frac{13}{10}$ mi
Saturday	$\frac{17}{10}$ mi

74. Denzel recorded the weekly rainfall for his town for 4 weeks of summer.

Week	Amount of rainfall
1	$\frac{2}{10}$ in.
2	$\frac{7}{10}$ in.
3	$\frac{9}{10}$ in.
4	$\frac{17}{10}$ in.

    a. Find the total amount of rainfall for this 4-week period.

    b. Find the average rainfall per week.

For Exercises 75–78, find the perimeter and the area.

75.

$\frac{3}{8}$ ft

$\frac{5}{8}$ ft

76.

$\frac{7}{8}$ m

$\frac{15}{8}$ m

77.

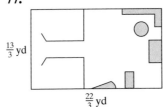

$\frac{13}{3}$ yd

$\frac{22}{3}$ yd

78.

May						
Sun	Mon	Tues	Wed	Thur	Fri	Sat

$\frac{25}{4}$ in.

$\frac{30}{4}$ in.

For Exercises 79–82, translate the phrase to a mathematical expression, then simplify.

79. The sum of three-fifths and two-fifths

80. Seven-ninths more than five-ninths

81. The difference of eleven-fifteenths and eight-fifteenths

82. Two-sevenths subtracted from five-sevenths

section 3.2   Least Common Multiple

1. Least Common Multiple

In Section 3.1 we learned how to add and subtract like fractions. To add or subtract fractions with different denominators, we must learn how to convert unlike fractions into like fractions. An essential concept in this process is the idea of a least common multiple of two or more numbers.

When we multiply a number by the whole numbers 1, 2, 3, and so on, we form the **multiples** of the number. For example, some of the multiples of 6 and 9 are shown below.

Multiples of 6	Multiples of 9
$6 \times 1 = 6$	$9 \times 1 = 9$
$6 \times 2 = 12$	$9 \times 2 = 18$
$6 \times 3 = 18$	$9 \times 3 = 27$
$6 \times 4 = 24$	$9 \times 4 = 36$
$6 \times 5 = 30$	$9 \times 5 = 45$
$6 \times 6 = 36$	$9 \times 6 = 54$
$6 \times 7 = 42$	$9 \times 7 = 63$
$6 \times 8 = 48$	$9 \times 8 = 72$
$6 \times 9 = 54$	$9 \times 9 = 81$

The **least common multiple (LCM)** of two given numbers is the smallest whole number that is a multiple of each given number. For example, the LCM of 6 and 9 is 18.

Multiples of 6:   6, 12, 18, 24, 30, 36, 42, . . .

Multiples of 9:   9, 18, 27, 36, 45, 54, 63, . . .

Tip: There are infinitely many numbers that are common multiples of both 6 and 9. These include 18, 36, 54, 72, and so on. However, 18 is the smallest, and is therefore the *least* common multiple.

If one number is a multiple of another number, then the LCM is the larger of the two numbers. For example, the LCM of 4 and 8 is 8. Similarly, the LCM of 3 and 6 is 6.

Multiples of 4:   4, 8, 12, 16, . . .   Multiples of 3:   3, 6, 9, 12, . . .

Multiples of 8:   8, 16, 24, 32, . . .   Multiples of 6:   6, 12, 18, 24, . . .

example 1   Finding the LCM by Listing Multiples

Find the LCM of the given numbers by listing several multiples of each number.

a. 15 and 12   **b.** 10, 15, and 8

Solution:

a. Multiples of 15:   15, 30, 45, 60
    Multiples of 12:   12, 24, 36, 48, 60

   The LCM of 15 and 12 is 60.

Objectives

1. Least Common Multiple
2. Finding the LCM by Using Prime Factors
3. Finding the LCM by Using Division by Primes (Optional)
4. Applications of the LCM
5. Ordering Fractions

Concept Connections

1. Explain the difference between a multiple of a number and a factor of a number.

Skill Practice

Find the LCM by listing several multiples of each number.

2. 15 and 25   **3.** 4, 6, and 10

Answers

1. A multiple of a number is the product of the number and a whole number 1 or greater. A factor of a number is a value that divides evenly into the number.
2. 75   3. 60

b. Multiples of 10:   10, 20, 30, 40, 50, 60, 70, 80, 90, 100, 110, 120
   Multiples of 15:   15, 30, 45, 60, 75, 90, 105, 120
   Multiples of 8:   8, 16, 24, 32, 40, 48, 56, 64, 72, 80, 88, 96, 104, 112, 120

The LCM of 10, 15, and 8 is 120.

2. Finding the LCM by Using Prime Factors

In Example 1 we used the method of listing multiples to find the LCM of two or more numbers. As you can see, the solution to Example 1(b) required several long lists of multiples. Here we offer another method to find the LCM of two given numbers by using their prime factors.

Using Prime Factors to Find the LCM of Two Numbers

1. Write each number as a product of prime factors.
2. The LCM is the product of unique prime factors from both numbers. If a factor is repeated within the factorization of either number, use that factor the maximum number of times it appears in either factorization.

This process is demonstrated in Example 2.

Skill Practice

Find the LCM by using prime factors.

4. 9 and 24   **5.** 16 and 9

6. 36, 42, and 30

example 2   Finding the LCM by Using Prime Factors

Find the LCM.

a. 15 and 12   **b.** 18 and 8   **c.** 45, 54, and 10

Solution:

a. $15 = 3 \cdot 5$ Write each number as a product of
   $12 = 2 \cdot 2 \cdot 3$ prime factors.

The factors 3 and 5 each occur a maximum of one time within a list of factors. Note that the factor 2 occurs twice in the second list of factors.

The LCM is $2 \cdot 2 \cdot 3 \cdot 5 = 60$.   The LCM is the product of the factors 2, 3, and 5, where 2 is repeated twice. Note that this is the same answer as in Example 1(a).

b. $18 = 2 \cdot 3 \cdot 3$ Write each number as a product of
   $8 = 2 \cdot 2 \cdot 2$ prime factors.

Note that the factor 2 occurs most often (3 times) in the second list of factors. Note that the factor 3 occurs most often (2 times) in the first list of factors.

The LCM is $2 \cdot 2 \cdot 2 \cdot 3 \cdot 3 = 72$.   The LCM is the product of the factors 2 and 3, where 2 is repeated 3 times and 3 is repeated twice.

c. $45 = 3 \cdot 3 \cdot 5$ Write each number as a product of
   $54 = 2 \cdot 3 \cdot 3 \cdot 3$ prime factors.
   $10 = 2 \cdot 5$

Note that the factor 3 occurs most often (3 times) in the second list of factors. The factors 2 and 5 each occur a maximum of 1 time within a list of factors.

The LCM is $2 \cdot 3 \cdot 3 \cdot 3 \cdot 5 = 270$.

Answers

4. 72   5. 144   6. 1260

3. Finding the LCM by Using Division by Primes (Optional)

We present a third method for finding least common multiples. We systematically divide by prime numbers to determine which will be a factor of the LCM. This method is particularly helpful if three or more numbers are involved. Try each method, and then you and your instructor can decide which method works best for you.

| example 3 | Finding the LCM by Using Division by Primes |

Find the LCM of 32, 48, and 30 by using division of prime factors.

Solution:

To begin this process, find any prime number that divides evenly into any of the numbers. Then divide and write the quotient as shown. We begin by dividing by the smallest prime number, 2.

$$2)\overline{32\ \ 48\ \ 30}$$
$$16\ \ 24\ \ 15$$

Repeat this process and bring down any number that is not divisible by the chosen prime.

$$2)\overline{32\ \ 48\ \ 30}$$
$$2)\overline{16\ \ 24\ \ 15}$$
$$\overline{8\ \ 12\ \ 15}\ \ \longleftarrow \text{Bring down the 15.}$$

Continue until all quotients are 1. The LCM is the product of the prime factors at the left.

$$2)\overline{32\ \ 48\ \ 30}$$
$$2)\overline{16\ \ 24\ \ 15}$$
$$2)\overline{8\ \ 12\ \ 15}$$
$$2)\overline{4\ \ 6\ \ 15}$$
$$2)\overline{2\ \ 3\ \ 15}$$
$$3)\overline{1\ \ 3\ \ 15}\ \ \longleftarrow$$
$$5)\overline{1\ \ 1\ \ 5}$$
$$1\ \ 1\ \ 1$$

At this point, the prime number 2 does not divide evenly into any of the quotients. We try the next-greater prime number, 3.

The LCM is $2 \cdot 2 \cdot 2 \cdot 2 \cdot 2 \cdot 3 \cdot 5 = 480$.

4. Applications of the LCM

| example 4 | Using the LCM in an Application |

A tile wall is to be made from 6-in., 8-in., and 12-in. square tiles. A design is made by alternating rows with different-size tiles. The first row uses only 6-in. tiles, the second row uses only 8-in. tiles, and the third row uses only 12-in. tiles. Neglecting the grout seams, what is the shortest length of wall space that can be covered using only whole tiles?

Skill Practice

Find the LCM by using division by prime factors.

7. 20, 36, and 15

8. 30, 22, and 45

Skill Practice

9. Three runners run on an oval track. One runner takes 60 sec to complete the loop. The second runner requires 75 sec, and the third runner requires 90 sec. Suppose the runners begin "lined up" at the same point on the track. Find the minimum amount of time required for all three runners to be lined up again.

Answers

7. 180   8. 990
9. After 900 sec (15 min) the runners will again be "lined up."

Solution:

The length of the first row must be a multiple of 6 in., the length of the second row must be a multiple of 8 in., and the length of the third row must be a multiple of 12 in. Therefore, the shortest-length wall that can be covered is given by the LCM of 6, 8, and 12.

$$6 = 2 \cdot 3$$

$$8 = 2 \cdot 2 \cdot 2$$

$$12 = 2 \cdot 2 \cdot 3$$

The LCM is $2 \cdot 2 \cdot 2 \cdot 3 = 24$. The shortest-length wall is 24 in.

This means that four 6-in. tiles can be placed on the first row, three 8-in. tiles can be placed on the second row, and two 12-in. tiles can be placed in the third row. See Figure 3-1.

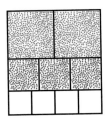

Figure 3-1

5. Ordering Fractions

The concept of the least common multiple is important when we compare the size of two fractions.

Comparing the fractions $\frac{3}{5}$ and $\frac{2}{5}$ is relatively easy because 3 parts out of 5 is clearly greater than 2 parts out of 5. Thus,

 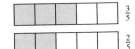

$$\frac{3}{5} > \frac{2}{5}$$

However, to compare the fractions $\frac{3}{5}$ and $\frac{4}{7}$ is more difficult. We have 3 pieces that are each one-fifth of a whole and 4 pieces that are each one-seventh of a whole.

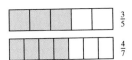

Because the pieces are of different sizes, it is difficult to make a comparison. For this reason, we want to express the fractions $\frac{3}{5}$ and $\frac{4}{7}$ as equivalent fractions with the same denominator, called a common denominator. The **least common denominator (LCD)** of two fractions is the LCM of the denominators of the fractions. Thus, the LCD of $\frac{3}{5}$ and $\frac{4}{7}$ is 35.

To convert $\frac{3}{5}$ and $\frac{4}{7}$ to equivalent fractions with a denominator of 35, we use the multiplication principle of fractions. This says that we can multiply the numerator and denominator of a fraction by the same nonzero number, and the value of the fraction remains the same.

Concept Connections

10. Shade the figures to determine which fraction represents a larger portion of a whole, $\frac{5}{6}$ or $\frac{7}{9}$.

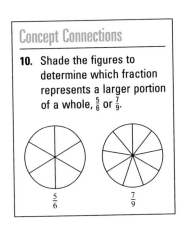

$$\frac{5}{6} \qquad \frac{7}{9}$$

Answer

10.

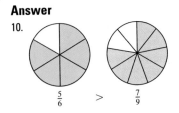

$$\frac{5}{6} \quad > \quad \frac{7}{9}$$

Tip: When we multiply the numerator and denominator of the fraction $\frac{3}{5}$, we are actually multiplying the fraction by 1. This is so because $\frac{7}{7} = 1$. Hence,

$$\frac{3}{5} = \frac{3}{5} \times 1 = \frac{3}{5} \times \frac{7}{7} = \frac{3 \times 7}{5 \times 7} = \frac{21}{35}$$

$$\frac{3}{5} = \frac{}{35}$$

What number must we multiply 5 by to get 35?

$$\frac{3 \times 7}{5 \times 7} = \frac{21}{35}$$

Multiply numerator and denominator by 7.

$$\frac{4}{7} = \frac{}{35}$$

What number must we multiply 7 by to get 35?

$$\frac{4 \times 5}{7 \times 5} = \frac{20}{35}$$

Multiply numerator and denominator by 5.

Comparing the fractions $\frac{3}{5}$ and $\frac{4}{7}$ is equivalent to comparing $\frac{21}{35}$ and $\frac{20}{35}$. Therefore, we have $\frac{21}{35} > \frac{20}{35}$, which means that $\frac{3}{5} > \frac{4}{7}$.

example 5   Comparing Two Fractions

Fill in the blank with $<$, $>$, or $=$.

$$\frac{9}{8} \ \square \ \frac{7}{6}$$

Solution:

The fractions have different denominators and cannot be compared by inspection. The LCD is 24. We need to convert each fraction to an equivalent fraction with a denominator of 24.

$$\frac{9}{8} = \frac{9 \times 3}{8 \times 3} = \frac{27}{24}$$ Multiply numerator and denominator by 3, because $8 \times 3 = 24$.

$$\frac{7}{6} = \frac{7 \times 4}{6 \times 4} = \frac{28}{24}$$ Multiply numerator and denominator by 4, because $6 \times 4 = 24$.

Because $\frac{27}{24} < \frac{28}{24}$, then $\frac{9}{8} \ \boxed{<} \ \frac{7}{6}$.

The relationship between $\frac{9}{8}$ and $\frac{7}{6}$ is shown on the number lines in Figure 3-2.

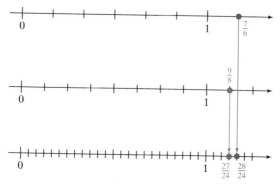

Figure 3-2

Skill Practice

13. Rank the fractions from least to greatest.

$$\frac{5}{9}, \frac{8}{15}, \text{and} \frac{3}{5}$$

Concept Connections

14. Determine which fraction is greater by observation.

a. $\frac{3}{5}$ or $\frac{2}{5}$ **b.** $\frac{3}{5}$ or $\frac{3}{4}$

c. $\frac{5}{12}$ or $\frac{7}{12}$ **d.** $\frac{9}{14}$ or $\frac{9}{16}$

Answers

13. $\frac{8}{15}, \frac{5}{9}, \frac{3}{5}$

14. a. $\frac{3}{5}$ b. $\frac{3}{4}$ c. $\frac{7}{12}$ d. $\frac{9}{14}$

---

example 6   Ranking Fractions in Order from Least to Greatest

Rank the fractions from least to greatest.

$$\frac{9}{20}, \frac{7}{15}, \frac{4}{9}$$

Solution:

We want to convert each fraction to an equivalent fraction with a common denominator. The least common denominator is the LCM of 20, 15, and 9.

$$\left.\begin{array}{l} 20 = 2 \cdot 2 \cdot 5 \\ 15 = 3 \cdot 5 \\ 9 = 3 \cdot 3 \end{array}\right\} \quad \text{The least common denominator is } 2 \cdot 2 \cdot 3 \cdot 3 \cdot 5 = 180.$$

Now convert each fraction to an equivalent fraction with a denominator of 180.

$$\frac{9}{20} = \frac{9 \times 9}{20 \times 9} = \frac{81}{180} \qquad \begin{array}{l}\text{Multiply numerator and denominator by 9} \\ \text{because } 20 \times 9 = 180.\end{array}$$

$$\frac{7}{15} = \frac{7 \times 12}{15 \times 12} = \frac{84}{180} \qquad \begin{array}{l}\text{Multiply numerator and denominator by 12} \\ \text{because } 15 \times 12 = 180.\end{array}$$

$$\frac{4}{9} = \frac{4 \times 20}{9 \times 20} = \frac{80}{180} \qquad \begin{array}{l}\text{Multiply numerator and denominator by 20} \\ \text{because } 9 \times 20 = 180.\end{array}$$

Ranking the fractions from least to greatest, we have $\frac{80}{180}, \frac{81}{180}, \frac{84}{180}$. This is equivalent to $\frac{4}{9}, \frac{9}{20}, \frac{7}{15}$.

---

section 3.2   Practice Exercises

Boost **your** GRADE at mathzone.com!

- Practice Problems
- Self-Tests
- NetTutor
- e-Professors
- Videos

Study Skills Exercises

1. Where do you usually do your homework? Is this the best place for you to concentrate? Explain.

2. Define the key terms.

   a. Multiple   **b. Least common multiple (LCM)**   **c. Least common denominator (LCD)**

Review Exercises

For Exercises 3–8, add and subtract as indicated. Write the answer as a whole number or fraction simplified to lowest terms.

3. $\frac{19}{6} - \frac{16}{6}$

4. $\frac{28}{4} - \frac{22}{4}$

5. $\frac{31}{15} + \frac{2}{15} - \frac{8}{15}$

6. $\frac{8}{5} + \frac{12}{5}$

7. $\frac{11}{3} + \frac{7}{3}$

8. $\frac{5}{19} - \frac{2}{19}$

Objective 1: Least Common Multiple

9. **a.** Circle the multiples of 24: 4, 8, 48, 72, 12, 240

   b. Circle the factors of 24: 4, 8, 48, 72, 12, 240

10. **a.** Circle the multiples of 30: 15, 90, 120, 3, 5, 60

    b. Circle the factors of 30: 15, 90, 120, 3, 5, 60

11. **a.** Circle the multiples of 36: 72, 6, 360, 12, 9, 108

    b. Circle the factors of 36: 72, 6, 360, 12, 9, 108

12. **a.** Circle the multiples of 28: 7, 4, 2, 56, 140, 280

    b. Circle the factors of 28: 7, 4, 2, 56, 140, 280

For Exercises 13–18, list five multiples of the given number. (Answers may vary.)

13. 5   **14.** 7   **15.** 14

16. 18   **17.** 16   **18.** 20

For Exercises 19–24, find the LCM by listing several multiples of each number. **(See Example 1.)**

19. 10 and 25   **20.** 21 and 14   **21.** 16 and 12

22. 20 and 12   **23.** 8, 10, and 12   **24.** 4, 6, and 14

Objective 2: Finding the LCM by Using Prime Factors

For Exercises 25–30, find the prime factorization.

25. 24   **26.** 42   **27.** 40

28. 80   **29.** 36   **30.** 64

For Exercises 31–40, find the LCM by using the prime factorization of each number. **(See Example 2.)**

31. 18 and 24   **32.** 9 and 30   **33.** 12 and 15   **34.** 27 and 45

35. 15 and 25   **36.** 16 and 24   **37.** 20, 18, and 27   **38.** 9, 15, and 42

39. 12, 15, and 20   **40.** 20, 30, and 40

Objective 3: Finding the LCM by Using Division by Primes

For Exercises 41–48, find the LCM by dividing by prime numbers. **(See Example 3.)**

41. 24 and 30

42. 14 and 35

43. 42 and 70

44. 6 and 21

45. 16, 24, and 30

46. 20, 42, and 35

47. 6, 12, 18, and 20

48. 21, 35, 50, and 75

Mixed Exercises

For Exercises 49–66, find the LCM by using any method.

49. 8 and 32

50. 7 and 14

51. 40 and 24

52. 21 and 28

53. 36 and 45

54. 48 and 36

55. 16 and 10

56. 6 and 15

57. 9 and 24

58. 32 and 40

59. 4, 6, and 14

60. 15, 30, and 45

61. 8, 18, and 20

62. 18, 15, and 20

63. 20, 30, and 40

64. 8, 10, and 12

65. 5, 15, 18, and 20

66. 28, 10, 21, and 35

Objective 4: Applications of the LCM

67. A tile floor is to be made from 10-in., 12-in., and 15-in. square tiles. A design is made by alternating rows with different-size tiles. The first row uses only 10-in. tiles, the second row uses only 12-in. tiles, and the third row uses only 15-in. tiles. Neglecting the grout seams, what is the shortest length of floor space that can be covered evenly by each row? **(See Example 4.)**

68. Four satellites revolve around the earth once every 6, 8, 10, and 15 hr, respectively. If the satellites are initially "lined up," how many hours must pass before they will again be lined up?

69. Mercury, Venus, and Earth revolve around the Sun approximately once every 3 months, 7 months, and 12 months, respectively (see the figure). If the planets begin "lined up," what is the minimum number of months required for them to be aligned again? (Assume that the planets lie roughly in the same plane.)

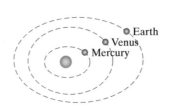

70. A bricklayer lays bricks of size 6, 8, and 10 in. She plans to lay one row of 6-in. bricks, a second row above of 8-in. bricks, and a third row of 10-in. bricks.

    a. Neglecting the mortar seams, what is the shortest-length wall that can be covered?

    b. Can a wall of length 12 ft (144 in.) be covered evenly, using this design?

Objective 5: Ordering Fractions

For Exercises 71–76, rewrite each fraction with the indicated denominators.

71. $\dfrac{2}{3} = \dfrac{}{21}$

72. $\dfrac{7}{4} = \dfrac{}{32}$

73. $\dfrac{5}{8} = \dfrac{}{16}$

74. $\dfrac{2}{9} = \dfrac{}{27}$

75. $\dfrac{3}{4} = \dfrac{}{16}$

76. $\dfrac{3}{10} = \dfrac{}{50}$

For Exercises 77–82, fill in the blanks with $<$, $>$, or $=$. **(See Example 5.)**

77. $\dfrac{7}{8} \,\square\, \dfrac{3}{4}$

78. $\dfrac{7}{15} \,\square\, \dfrac{11}{20}$

79. $\dfrac{13}{10} \,\square\, \dfrac{22}{15}$

80. $\dfrac{15}{4} \,\square\, \dfrac{21}{6}$

81. $\dfrac{3}{12} \,\square\, \dfrac{2}{8}$

82. $\dfrac{5}{20} \,\square\, \dfrac{4}{16}$

83. Which of the following fractions has the greatest value? $\dfrac{2}{3}, \dfrac{7}{8}, \dfrac{5}{6}, \dfrac{1}{2}$

84. Which of the following fractions has the least value? $\dfrac{1}{6}, \dfrac{1}{4}, \dfrac{2}{15}, \dfrac{2}{9}$

For Exercises 85–90, rank the fractions from least to greatest. **(See Example 6.)**

85. $\dfrac{7}{8}, \dfrac{2}{3}, \dfrac{3}{4}$

86. $\dfrac{5}{12}, \dfrac{3}{8}, \dfrac{2}{3}$

87. $\dfrac{5}{16}, \dfrac{3}{8}, \dfrac{1}{4}$

88. $\dfrac{2}{5}, \dfrac{3}{10}, \dfrac{5}{6}$

89. $\dfrac{4}{3}, \dfrac{13}{12}, \dfrac{17}{15}$

90. $\dfrac{5}{7}, \dfrac{11}{21}, \dfrac{18}{35}$

91. Susan buys $\frac{2}{3}$ lb of smoked turkey, $\frac{3}{5}$ lb of ham, and $\frac{5}{8}$ lb of roast beef. Which type of meat did she buy in the greatest amount? Which type did she buy in the least amount?

92. For a party, Aman had $\frac{3}{4}$ lb of cheddar cheese, $\frac{7}{8}$ lb of Swiss cheese, and $\frac{4}{5}$ lb of pepper jack cheese. Which type of cheese is in the least amount? Which type is in the greatest amount?

Expanding Your Skills

93. Which of the following fractions is between $\frac{1}{4}$ and $\frac{5}{6}$? Identify all that apply.

    a. $\dfrac{5}{12}$ **b.** $\dfrac{2}{3}$ **c.** $\dfrac{1}{8}$

94. Which of the following fractions is between $\frac{1}{3}$ and $\frac{11}{15}$? Identify all that apply.

    a. $\dfrac{2}{3}$ **b.** $\dfrac{4}{5}$ **c.** $\dfrac{2}{5}$

Objectives

1. Addition and Subtraction of Unlike Fractions
2. Order of Operations
3. Applications Involving Unlike Fractions

section 3.3   Addition and Subtraction of Unlike Fractions

1. Addition and Subtraction of Unlike Fractions

In this section we use the concept of the LCD to help us add and subtract unlike fractions. The first step in adding or subtracting unlike fractions is to identify the LCD. Then we change the unlike fractions to like fractions having the LCD as the denominator.

Skill Practice

Add.

1. $\dfrac{1}{10} + \dfrac{1}{15}$

2. $\dfrac{4}{7} + \dfrac{3}{14}$

example 1   Adding Unlike Fractions

Add.

$$\frac{1}{6} + \frac{3}{4}$$

Solution:

The LCD of $\frac{1}{6}$ and $\frac{3}{4}$ is 12. We can convert each individual fraction to an equivalent fraction with 12 as the denominator.

$$\frac{1}{6} = \frac{1 \cdot 2}{6 \cdot 2} = \frac{2}{12} \qquad$$ Multiply numerator and denominator by 2 because $6 \cdot 2 = 12$.

$$\frac{3}{4} = \frac{3 \cdot 3}{4 \cdot 3} = \frac{9}{12} \qquad$$ Multiply numerator and denominator by 3 because $4 \cdot 3 = 12$.

Thus, $\frac{1}{6} + \frac{3}{4}$ becomes $\frac{2}{12} + \frac{9}{12} = \frac{11}{12}$.

Tip: In Example 1, we multiplied the fraction $\frac{1}{6}$ by $\frac{2}{2}$. This is equivalent to multiplying $\frac{1}{6}$ by 1 and does not change the value.

$$\frac{1}{6} = \frac{1}{6} \cdot 1 = \frac{1}{6} \cdot \frac{2}{2} = \frac{2}{12}$$

The fraction $\frac{2}{12}$ is equivalent to $\frac{1}{6}$.

Answers

1. $\dfrac{1}{6}$

2. $\dfrac{11}{14}$

Adding fractions can be visualized by using a diagram. For example, the sum $\frac{1}{2} + \frac{1}{3}$ is illustrated in Figure 3-3.

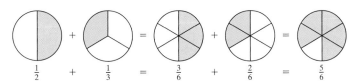

$$\begin{array}{ccccccccc} \frac{1}{2} & + & \frac{1}{3} & = & \frac{3}{6} & + & \frac{2}{6} & = & \frac{5}{6} \end{array}$$

Figure 3-3

The general procedure to add or subtract unlike fractions is outlined as follows.

Concept Connections

3. Use the figure to add the fractions.

$$\frac{1}{3} + \frac{2}{5}$$

Steps to Add or Subtract Unlike Fractions

1. Identify the LCD.
2. Write each individual fraction as an equivalent fraction with the LCD.
3. Add or subtract the resulting fractions as indicated.
4. Simplify to lowest terms, if possible.

---

example 2   Adding and Subtracting Unlike Fractions

Add or subtract as indicated.

a. $\dfrac{3}{10} + \dfrac{1}{5}$ **b.** $\dfrac{17}{18} - \dfrac{1}{6}$ **c.** $\dfrac{2}{7} + \dfrac{4}{5} - \dfrac{1}{10}$

Solution:

a. $\dfrac{3}{10} + \dfrac{1}{5}$ The LCD is 10. We must convert $\frac{1}{5}$ to an equivalent fraction with 10 as the denominator

$= \dfrac{3}{10} + \dfrac{1 \cdot 2}{5 \cdot 2}$ Multiply numerator and denominator by 2 because $5 \cdot 2 = 10$.

$= \dfrac{3}{10} + \dfrac{2}{10}$ The fractions are now like.

$= \dfrac{3 + 2}{10}$ Add the like fractions.

$= \dfrac{5}{10}$

$= \dfrac{\overset{1}{\cancel{5}}}{\underset{2}{\cancel{10}}}$ Simplify to lowest terms.

$= \dfrac{1}{2}$

Avoiding Mistakes: Do not confuse addition of fractions with multiplication of fractions. In multiplication, we multiply denominators. In addition we do not add denominators. We get a common denominator and then add only the numerators.

Skill Practice

Add or subtract as indicated. Write the answer as a fraction.

4. $\dfrac{9}{5} + \dfrac{1}{10}$

5. $\dfrac{5}{21} - \dfrac{1}{7}$

6. $\dfrac{4}{15} - \dfrac{1}{10} + \dfrac{9}{20}$

Answers

3.

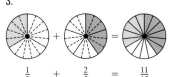

$$\begin{array}{ccccc} \frac{1}{3} & + & \frac{2}{5} & = & \frac{11}{15} \end{array}$$

4. $\dfrac{19}{10}$ 5. $\dfrac{2}{21}$ 6. $\dfrac{37}{60}$

b. $\dfrac{17}{18} - \dfrac{1}{6}$ The LCD is 18.

$= \dfrac{17}{18} - \dfrac{1 \cdot 3}{6 \cdot 3}$ Multiply numerator and denominator by 3 because $6 \cdot 3 = 18$.

$= \dfrac{17}{18} - \dfrac{3}{18}$ The fractions are now like.

$= \dfrac{14}{18}$ Subtract like fractions.

$= \dfrac{\overset{7}{14}}{\underset{9}{18}}$ Simplify to lowest terms.

$= \dfrac{7}{9}$

c. $\dfrac{2}{7} + \dfrac{4}{5} - \dfrac{1}{10}$ First find the LCD.

$\left.\begin{array}{l} 7 = 7 \\ 5 = 5 \\ 10 = 2 \cdot 5 \end{array}\right\}$ The LCD is $2 \cdot 5 \cdot 7 = 70$.

$= \dfrac{2 \cdot 10}{7 \cdot 10} + \dfrac{4 \cdot 14}{5 \cdot 14} - \dfrac{1 \cdot 7}{10 \cdot 7}$ Convert each fraction to an equivalent fraction with the LCD.

$= \dfrac{20}{70} + \dfrac{56}{70} - \dfrac{7}{70}$ The fractions are like fractions.

$= \dfrac{20 + 56 - 7}{70}$ Add and subtract as indicated.

$= \dfrac{69}{70}$ The fraction is in lowest terms.

Sometimes when denominators are large, it is helpful to write the denominators as a product of prime factors. This is demonstrated in Example 3.

Skill Practice

Add or subtract as indicated.

7. $\dfrac{9}{8} - \dfrac{3}{32} - \dfrac{1}{20}$

8. $\dfrac{7}{18} + \dfrac{4}{15} - \dfrac{17}{30}$

example 3   Adding and Subtracting Unlike Fractions

Add or subtract as indicated.

$$\dfrac{7}{12} - \dfrac{2}{15} + \dfrac{5}{48}$$

Solution:

$\dfrac{7}{12} - \dfrac{2}{15} + \dfrac{5}{48}$ To find the LCD, factor each denominator.

$= \dfrac{7}{2 \cdot 2 \cdot 3} - \dfrac{2}{3 \cdot 5} + \dfrac{5}{2 \cdot 2 \cdot 2 \cdot 2 \cdot 3}$

Answers

7. $\dfrac{157}{160}$ 8. $\dfrac{4}{45}$

$\left.\begin{array}{l} 12 = 2 \cdot 2 \cdot 3 \\ 15 = 3 \cdot 5 \\ 48 = 2 \cdot 2 \cdot 2 \cdot 2 \cdot 3 \end{array}\right\}$ The LCD is $2 \cdot 2 \cdot 2 \cdot 2 \cdot 3 \cdot 5 = 240$.

We want to convert each fraction to an equivalent fraction having a denominator of $2 \cdot 2 \cdot 2 \cdot 2 \cdot 3 \cdot 5 = 240$. Multiply numerator and denominator of each original fraction by the factors missing from the denominator.

$$= \frac{7 \cdot (2 \cdot 2 \cdot 5)}{2 \cdot 2 \cdot 3 \cdot (2 \cdot 2 \cdot 5)} - \frac{2 \cdot (2 \cdot 2 \cdot 2 \cdot 2)}{3 \cdot 5 \cdot (2 \cdot 2 \cdot 2 \cdot 2)} + \frac{5 \cdot (5)}{2 \cdot 2 \cdot 2 \cdot 2 \cdot 3 \cdot (5)}$$

$$= \frac{140}{240} - \frac{32}{240} + \frac{25}{240} \qquad \text{The fractions are now like fractions.}$$

$$= \frac{140 - 32 + 25}{240} \qquad \text{Add and subtract as indicated.}$$

$$= \frac{133}{240} \qquad \text{The fraction is in lowest terms.}$$

2. Order of Operations

In Example 4 we must apply the order of operations to simplify the expressions.

example 4   Applying the Order of Operations

Simplify:

a. $\left(\dfrac{1}{4} + \dfrac{2}{3} \right)^2$ **b.** $\dfrac{5}{12} - \dfrac{1}{4} \div \dfrac{3}{2}$

Solution:

a. $\left(\dfrac{1}{4} + \dfrac{2}{3} \right)^2$ Perform the operation within parentheses first.

$= \left(\dfrac{1 \cdot 3}{4 \cdot 3} + \dfrac{2 \cdot 4}{3 \cdot 4} \right)^2$ The common denominator is 12.

$= \left(\dfrac{3}{12} + \dfrac{8}{12} \right)^2$ The fractions within parentheses are now like fractions.

$= \left(\dfrac{11}{12} \right)^2$ Add fractions within parentheses.

$= \dfrac{11}{12} \cdot \dfrac{11}{12}$ To square a number, multiply the number by itself.

$= \dfrac{121}{144}$ The fraction is in lowest terms.

b. $\dfrac{5}{12} - \dfrac{1}{4} \div \dfrac{3}{2}$ Perform the division before the subtraction.

$= \dfrac{5}{12} - \dfrac{1}{\overset{}{\underset{2}{4}}} \cdot \dfrac{\overset{1}{2}}{3}$ To divide fractions, multiply by the reciprocal of the divisor.

Concept Connections

9. In what order would you perform the operations for this expression?

$$\left(\frac{2}{3} - \frac{1}{7} \right)^2$$

Skill Practice

Simplify.

10. $\left(\dfrac{2}{3} - \dfrac{1}{7} \right)^2$

11. $\dfrac{4}{15} \div \dfrac{2}{5} - \dfrac{1}{6}$

Answers

9. Subtract the fractions within parentheses. Then square the result.

10. $\dfrac{121}{441}$ 11. $\dfrac{1}{2}$

$$= \frac{5}{12} - \frac{1}{6} \qquad \text{The common denominator is 12.}$$

$$= \frac{5}{12} - \frac{1 \cdot 2}{6 \cdot 2} \qquad \text{Multiply numerator and denominator by 2 because } 6 \cdot 2 = 12.$$

$$= \frac{5}{12} - \frac{2}{12} \qquad \text{The fractions are now like fractions.}$$

$$= \frac{3}{12} \qquad \text{Subtract.}$$

$$= \frac{1}{4} \qquad \text{Simplify to lowest terms.}$$

3. Applications Involving Unlike Fractions

Skill Practice

12. On Monday, $\frac{2}{3}$ in. of rain fell on a certain town. On Tuesday, $\frac{1}{5}$ in. of rain fell. How much rain fell during these 2 days?

example 5   Applying Operations on Unlike Fractions

A new Kelly Safari SUV tire has $\frac{7}{16}$-in. tread. After being driven 50,000 mi, the tread depth has worn down to $\frac{7}{32}$ in. By how much has the tread depth worn away?

Tread

Solution:

In this case we are looking for the difference in the tread depth.

$$\begin{array}{l} \text{Difference in} \\ \text{tread depth} \end{array} = \left(\begin{array}{c} \text{original} \\ \text{tread depth} \end{array} \right) - \left(\begin{array}{c} \text{final} \\ \text{tread depth} \end{array} \right)$$

$$= \frac{7}{16} - \frac{7}{32} \qquad \text{The LCD is 32.}$$

$$= \frac{7 \cdot 2}{16 \cdot 2} - \frac{7}{32} \qquad \text{Multiply numerator and denominator by 2 because } 16 \cdot 2 = 32.$$

$$= \frac{14}{32} - \frac{7}{32} \qquad \text{The fractions are now like.}$$

$$= \frac{7}{32} \qquad \text{Subtract.}$$

The tire lost $\frac{7}{32}$ in. in tread depth after 50,000 mi of driving.

Skill Practice

13. Maggie mixed $\frac{3}{4}$ gal of "winter wheat" paint with $\frac{1}{3}$ gal of "forest green." Then she used $\frac{3}{4}$ of the mixture to paint a wall.

  a. How much paint did she use?

  b. How much paint is left over?

example 6   Applying Operations on Unlike Fractions

An oil tank contains 2 liters (L) of oil. A slow leak has occurred, and oil leaks out at a rate of $\frac{1}{16}$ L per day. After 7 days a mechanic notices the leak and pours $\frac{3}{8}$ L of oil back into the tank. How much oil is now in the tank?

Solution:

To find the current amount in the tank, we must account for the amount lost and the amount added.

Answers

12. The total amount of rain was $\frac{13}{15}$ in.

13. a. $\frac{13}{16}$ gal was used.

  b. $\frac{13}{48}$ gal was left over.

The amount lost is given by the amount lost per day times 7 days.

$$\left(\frac{1}{16}\right)(7) = \frac{1}{16} \cdot \frac{7}{1} = \frac{7}{16}$$ The amount lost in 7 days is $\frac{7}{16}$ L.

Therefore, the current amount in the tank is given by

$$\begin{array}{l}
\text{Current} \\
\text{amount}
\end{array} = \left(\begin{array}{c}\text{original} \\ \text{amount}\end{array}\right) - \left(\begin{array}{c}\text{amount} \\ \text{lost}\end{array}\right) + \left(\begin{array}{c}\text{amount} \\ \text{replaced}\end{array}\right)$$

$$= 2 - \frac{7}{16} + \frac{3}{8}$$

$$= \frac{2}{1} - \frac{7}{16} + \frac{3}{8}$$ Write the whole number as a fraction.

$$= \frac{2 \cdot 16}{1 \cdot 16} - \frac{7}{16} + \frac{3 \cdot 2}{8 \cdot 2}$$ The LCD is 16.

$$= \frac{32}{16} - \frac{7}{16} + \frac{6}{16}$$ The fractions are now like fractions.

$$= \frac{32 - 7 + 6}{16}$$ Add and subtract as indicated.

$$= \frac{31}{16}$$ The fraction is in lowest terms.

The tank now contains $\frac{31}{16}$ L or equivalently $1\frac{15}{16}$ L.

---

example 7   Finding Perimeter

A parcel of land has the following dimensions. Find the perimeter.

Solution:

To find the perimeter, we add the lengths of the sides.

$$\frac{1}{8} + \frac{1}{4} + \frac{5}{12} + \frac{1}{3}$$ The LCD is 24.

$$= \frac{1 \cdot 3}{8 \cdot 3} + \frac{1 \cdot 6}{4 \cdot 6} + \frac{5 \cdot 2}{12 \cdot 2} + \frac{1 \cdot 8}{3 \cdot 8}$$ Convert the fractions to like fractions.

$$= \frac{3}{24} + \frac{6}{24} + \frac{10}{24} + \frac{8}{24}$$

$$= \frac{27}{24}$$ Add the fractions.

$$= \frac{9}{8}$$ Simplify to lowest terms.

The perimeter is $\frac{9}{8}$ mi or equivalently $1\frac{1}{8}$ mi.

$\frac{1}{4}$ mi

$\frac{1}{8}$ mi

$\frac{5}{12}$ mi

$\frac{1}{3}$ mi

Skill Practice

14. Twelve members of a college hiking club hiked the perimeter of a canyon. How far did they hike?

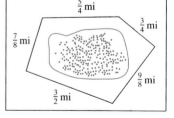

$\frac{5}{4}$ mi

$\frac{3}{4}$ mi

$\frac{7}{8}$ mi

$\frac{9}{8}$ mi

$\frac{3}{2}$ mi

Answer

14. They hiked $\frac{11}{2}$ mi. or equivalently $5\frac{1}{2}$ mi.

section 3.3   Practice Exercises

Study Skills Exercise

1. Do you need complete silence, or do you listen to music while you do your homework?

Try something different today so that you can compare and choose the best situation for you.

Review Exercises

For Exercises 2–13, rewrite the fraction with the given denominator.

2. $\dfrac{3}{5} = \dfrac{}{15}$

3. $\dfrac{6}{7} = \dfrac{}{14}$

4. $\dfrac{4}{9} = \dfrac{}{36}$

5. $\dfrac{2}{3} = \dfrac{}{21}$

6. $\dfrac{3}{1} = \dfrac{}{10}$

7. $\dfrac{5}{1} = \dfrac{}{5}$

8. $\dfrac{4}{1} = \dfrac{}{12}$

9. $\dfrac{2}{1} = \dfrac{}{4}$

10. $\dfrac{3}{4} = \dfrac{}{12}$

11. $\dfrac{4}{5} = \dfrac{}{100}$

12. $\dfrac{3}{2} = \dfrac{}{18}$

13. $\dfrac{1}{8} = \dfrac{}{40}$

Objective 1: Addition and Subtraction of Unlike Fractions

14. Explain the difference between the procedures to add fractions and to multiply fractions.

For Exercises 15–48, add or subtract. Write the answer as a fraction simplified to lowest terms. **(See Examples 1, 2, and 3.)**

15. $\dfrac{7}{8} + \dfrac{5}{16}$

16. $\dfrac{2}{9} + \dfrac{1}{18}$

17. $\dfrac{1}{10} + \dfrac{3}{20}$

18. $\dfrac{4}{15} + \dfrac{3}{5}$

19. $\dfrac{1}{4} + \dfrac{0}{3}$

20. $\dfrac{0}{5} + \dfrac{2}{3}$

21. $\dfrac{5}{6} + \dfrac{8}{7}$

22. $\dfrac{2}{11} + \dfrac{4}{5}$

23. $\dfrac{7}{8} - \dfrac{1}{2}$

24. $\dfrac{9}{10} - \dfrac{4}{5}$

25. $\dfrac{13}{12} - \dfrac{3}{4}$

26. $\dfrac{29}{30} - \dfrac{7}{10}$

27. $\dfrac{5}{2} - \dfrac{3}{5}$

28. $\dfrac{6}{5} - \dfrac{5}{6}$

29. $\dfrac{5}{8} - \dfrac{0}{11}$

30. $\dfrac{7}{12} - \dfrac{0}{5}$

31. $2 + \dfrac{9}{8}$

32. $3 + \dfrac{11}{9}$

33. $4 - \dfrac{4}{3}$

34. $2 - \dfrac{3}{8}$

35. $\dfrac{14}{3} + 1$

36. $\dfrac{12}{5} + 2$

37. $\dfrac{16}{7} - 2$

38. $\dfrac{15}{4} - 3$

39. $\dfrac{7}{10} + \dfrac{19}{100}$

40. $\dfrac{3}{10} + \dfrac{27}{100}$

41. $\dfrac{1}{10} - \dfrac{9}{100}$

42. $\dfrac{3}{100} - \dfrac{21}{1000}$

43. $\dfrac{3}{10} + \dfrac{9}{100} + \dfrac{1}{1000}$

44. $\dfrac{1}{10} + \dfrac{3}{100} + \dfrac{7}{1000}$

45. $\dfrac{5}{8} + \dfrac{3}{10} - \dfrac{1}{12}$

46. $\dfrac{7}{12} - \dfrac{2}{15} + \dfrac{5}{18}$

47. $\dfrac{1}{20} + \dfrac{5}{8} - \dfrac{7}{24}$

48. $\dfrac{5}{3} - \dfrac{7}{6} + \dfrac{5}{8}$

Objective 2: Order of Operations

For Exercises 49–62, simplify by applying the order of operations. Write the answer as a fraction. **(See Example 4.)**

49. $\dfrac{4}{5} + \dfrac{5}{8} \cdot \dfrac{16}{35}$

50. $\dfrac{1}{6} + \dfrac{3}{7} \cdot \dfrac{14}{15}$

51. $\dfrac{2}{3} \div \dfrac{1}{2} - \dfrac{3}{4}$

52. $\dfrac{3}{5} \div \dfrac{6}{7} - \dfrac{2}{5}$

53. $\left(\dfrac{11}{12} + \dfrac{1}{9}\right) \div \dfrac{7}{9}$

54. $\left(\dfrac{5}{6} - \dfrac{3}{8}\right) \div \dfrac{1}{4}$

55. $\left(\dfrac{7}{10} - \dfrac{1}{5}\right) \cdot \dfrac{8}{3}$

56. $\left(\dfrac{2}{5} + \dfrac{9}{10}\right) \cdot \dfrac{5}{6}$

57. $\left(\dfrac{1}{2} - \dfrac{1}{3}\right)^2$

58. $\left(\dfrac{2}{3} + \dfrac{1}{6}\right)^2$

59. $\left(\dfrac{2}{5}\right)^3 + \dfrac{1}{25}$

60. $\left(\dfrac{3}{2}\right)^3 - \dfrac{5}{4}$

61. $\left(\dfrac{1}{4}\right)^2 \div \left(\dfrac{5}{6} - \dfrac{2}{3}\right) + \dfrac{7}{12}$

62. $\left(\dfrac{1}{2} + \dfrac{1}{3}\right) \cdot \left(\dfrac{2}{5}\right)^2 + \dfrac{3}{10}$

Objective 3: Applications Involving Unlike Fractions

63. When doing her laundry, Inez added $\frac{3}{4}$ cup of bleach to $\frac{3}{8}$ cup of liquid detergent. How much total liquid is added to her wash?

64. What is the smallest possible length of screw needed to pass through two pieces of wood, one that is $\frac{7}{8}$ in. thick and one that is $\frac{1}{2}$ in. thick?

65. Mrs. Morgan has a bottle of eardrops that contains $\frac{2}{5}$ ounce (oz) of solution. If one dose is $\frac{1}{8}$ oz for each ear (that is, $\frac{1}{4}$ oz), is there enough solution in the bottle? If so, how much will be left over? **(See Example 5.)**

66. In one week it rained $\frac{5}{16}$ in. If a garden needs $\frac{9}{8}$ in. of water per week, how much more water does it need?

67. A contractor hired two electricians to do a job. One did $\frac{3}{5}$ of the job and the other did $\frac{3}{8}$ of the job. Did the job get completed? If not, what fraction of the job is left? **(See Example 6.)**

68. Mehule wants to take his laptop on a trip along with a manuscript that is $\frac{3}{8}$ in. thick. If the computer is $\frac{9}{4}$ in. deep, will the computer and manuscript fit into a case that is 3 in. deep? If so, what will be the clearance?

69. The information in the graph shows the distribution of a college student body by class.

    a. What fraction of the student body consists of upper classmen (juniors and seniors)?

    b. What fraction of the student body consists of freshmen and sophomores?

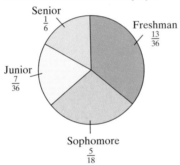

Distribution of Student Body by Class

Senior $\frac{1}{6}$

Freshman $\frac{13}{36}$

Junior $\frac{7}{36}$

Sophomore $\frac{5}{18}$

70. A group of college students took part in a survey. One of the survey questions read:

"Do you think the government should spend more money on research to produce alternative forms of fuel?"

The results of the survey are shown in the figure.

    a. What fraction of the survey participants chose to strongly agree or agree?

    b. What fraction of the survey participants chose to strongly disagree or disagree?

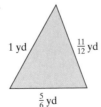

Survey Results

Strongly disagree $\frac{1}{24}$

Disagree $\frac{5}{48}$

Agree $\frac{1}{4}$

No opinion $\frac{1}{24}$

Strongly agree $\frac{27}{48}$

For Exercises 71–72, find the perimeter. **(See Example 7.)**

71.

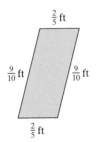

$\frac{2}{5}$ ft

$\frac{9}{10}$ ft $\frac{9}{10}$ ft

$\frac{2}{5}$ ft

72.

1 yd $\frac{11}{12}$ yd

$\frac{5}{6}$ yd

For Exercises 73–74, find the missing dimensions. Then calculate the perimeter.

73.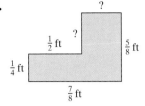

74.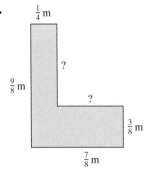

Expanding Your Skills

75. Which fraction is closest to $\frac{1}{2}$?

    a. $\frac{3}{4}$ **b.** $\frac{7}{10}$ **c.** $\frac{5}{6}$

76. Which fraction is closest to $\frac{3}{4}$?

    a. $\frac{5}{8}$ **b.** $\frac{7}{12}$ **c.** $\frac{5}{6}$

Calculator Connections

Topic: Adding and subtracting fractions

Calculator Exercises

For Exercises 77–80, the LCD for two fractions is given. Use a calculator to write each fraction as an equivalent fraction having the LCD as its denominator. Then add or subtract as indicated. Do not simplify the answer to lowest terms.

77. $\frac{37}{98} + \frac{59}{164}$; LCD = 8036

78. $\frac{11}{72} + \frac{33}{153}$; LCD = 1224

79. $\frac{89}{93} - \frac{19}{54}$; LCD = 1674

80. $\frac{21}{65} - \frac{3}{208}$; LCD = 1040

| chapter 3 | midchapter review |

1. Which operation on fractions requires that we obtain a common denominator? Select all that apply: addition, subtraction, multiplication, division.

2. Explain the procedure to subtract fractions with the same denominator.

3. Explain the procedure to add fractions with different denominators.

4. Explain the difference between the procedures to multiply and to divide fractions.

For Exercises 5–20, perform the indicated operation. Write the answer as a fraction simplified to lowest terms.

5. $\dfrac{2}{5} + \dfrac{7}{5}$ 6. $\dfrac{2}{5} \times \dfrac{7}{5}$ 7. $\dfrac{4}{3} \times \dfrac{1}{3}$

8. $\dfrac{4}{3} + \dfrac{1}{3}$ 9. $\dfrac{3}{4} - \dfrac{2}{7}$ 10. $\dfrac{3}{4} \times \dfrac{2}{7}$

11. $\dfrac{5}{3} \times \dfrac{10}{9}$ 12. $\dfrac{5}{3} - \dfrac{10}{9}$ 13. $\dfrac{5}{8} \div \dfrac{9}{8}$

14. $\dfrac{5}{8} + \dfrac{9}{8}$ 15. $\dfrac{5}{2} - \dfrac{1}{2}$ 16. $\dfrac{5}{2} \div \dfrac{1}{2}$

17. $\dfrac{13}{20} - \dfrac{9}{14}$ 18. $\dfrac{13}{20} \div \dfrac{9}{14}$ 19. $\dfrac{11}{12} \div \dfrac{5}{16}$

20. $\dfrac{11}{12} - \dfrac{5}{16}$

Objectives

1. Addition of Mixed Numbers
2. Subtraction of Mixed Numbers
3. Addition and Subtraction of Mixed Numbers by Using Improper Fractions
4. Applications of Mixed Numbers

Skill Practice

Add.

1. $1\dfrac{1}{5} + 9\dfrac{2}{5}$

2. $7\dfrac{2}{15} + 2\dfrac{1}{15}$

Answers

1. $10\dfrac{3}{5}$ 2. $9\dfrac{1}{5}$

| section 3.4 | Addition and Subtraction of Mixed Numbers |

1. Addition of Mixed Numbers

In this section we learn to add and subtract mixed numbers. To find the sum of two or more mixed numbers, add the whole-number parts and add the fractional parts.

| example 1 | Adding Mixed Numbers |

Add.

$$1\dfrac{5}{9} + 2\dfrac{1}{9}$$

Solution:

$$\begin{array}{r} 1\dfrac{5}{9} \\ +\,2\dfrac{1}{9} \\ \hline 3\dfrac{6}{9} \end{array}$$

Add the whole numbers. ⟵   ⟶ Add the fractional parts.

The sum is $3\dfrac{6}{9}$ which simplifies to $3\dfrac{2}{3}$.

Tip: To understand why mixed numbers can be added in this way, recall that $1\dfrac{5}{9} = 1 + \dfrac{5}{9}$ and $2\dfrac{1}{9} = 2 + \dfrac{1}{9}$. Therefore,

$$1\dfrac{5}{9} + 2\dfrac{1}{9} = 1 + \dfrac{5}{9} + 2 + \dfrac{1}{9}$$

$$= 3 + \dfrac{6}{9}$$

$$= 3\dfrac{6}{9}$$

$$= 3\dfrac{2}{3}$$

When we perform operations on mixed numbers, it is often desirable to estimate the answer first. When rounding a mixed number, we offer the following convention.

1. If the fractional part of a mixed number is greater than or equal to $\frac{1}{2}$ (that is, if the numerator is one-half of the denominator or more), round to the next-greater whole number.

2. If the fractional part of the mixed number is less than $\frac{1}{2}$ (that is, if the numerator is less than one-half of the denominator), the mixed number rounds down to the whole number.

example 2   **Adding Mixed Numbers**

Estimate the sum and then find the actual sum.

$$42\frac{1}{12} + 17\frac{7}{8}$$

Solution:

To estimate the sum, we first round the addends.

$$42\frac{1}{12} \quad \text{rounds to} \quad 42$$

$$+ 17\frac{7}{8} \quad \text{rounds to} \quad \frac{+ 18}{60} \quad \text{The estimated value is 60.}$$

To find the actual sum, we must first write the fractional parts as like fractions. The LCD is 24.

$$42\frac{1}{12} = 42\frac{1 \cdot 2}{12 \cdot 2} = 42\frac{2}{24}$$

$$+ 17\frac{7}{8} = + 17\frac{7 \cdot 3}{8 \cdot 3} = + 17\frac{21}{24}$$

$$\overline{\qquad\qquad\qquad\qquad\qquad\quad 59\frac{23}{24}}$$

The actual sum is $59\frac{23}{24}$. This is close to our estimate of 60.

■

Skill Practice

Estimate the sum and then find the actual sum.

5. $38\frac{2}{3} + 12\frac{1}{6}$

6. $6\frac{1}{11} + 3\frac{1}{2}$

example 3   **Adding Mixed Numbers With Carrying**

Estimate the sum and then find the actual sum.

$$7\frac{5}{6} + 3\frac{3}{5}$$

Solution:

$$7\frac{5}{6} \quad \text{rounds to} \quad 8$$

$$+ 3\frac{3}{5} \quad \text{rounds to} \quad \frac{+ 4}{12} \quad \text{The estimated value is 12.}$$

To find the actual sum, we must first write the fractional parts as like fractions. The LCD is 30.

$$7\dfrac{5}{6} = \quad 7\dfrac{5 \cdot 5}{6 \cdot 5} = \quad 7\dfrac{25}{30}$$
$$+\,3\dfrac{3}{5} = +\,3\dfrac{3 \cdot 6}{5 \cdot 6} = +\,3\dfrac{18}{30}$$
$$\overline{\phantom{+\,3\dfrac{3 \cdot 6}{5 \cdot 6}}\quad 10\dfrac{43}{30}}$$

Notice that the number $\frac{43}{30}$ is an improper fraction. By convention, a mixed number is written as a whole number and a *proper* fraction. We have $\frac{43}{30} = 1\frac{13}{30}$. Therefore,

$$10\dfrac{43}{30} = 10 + 1\dfrac{13}{30} = 11\dfrac{13}{30}$$

The sum is $11\frac{13}{30}$. This is close to our estimate of 12.

2. Subtraction of Mixed Numbers

To subtract mixed numbers, we subtract the fractional parts and subtract the whole-number parts.

example 4   Subtracting Mixed Numbers

Subtract.

$$15\dfrac{2}{3} - 4\dfrac{1}{6}.$$

Solution:

To subtract the fractional parts, we need a common denominator. The LCD is 6.

$$15\dfrac{2}{3} = \quad 15\dfrac{2 \cdot 2}{3 \cdot 2} = \quad 15\dfrac{4}{6}$$
$$-\,4\dfrac{1}{6} = -\,4\dfrac{1}{6} \quad = -\,4\dfrac{1}{6}$$
$$\overline{\phantom{-\,4\dfrac{1}{6}}\quad 11\dfrac{3}{6}}$$

Subtract the whole numbers. Subtract the fractional parts.

The difference is $11\frac{3}{6}$ which simplifies to $11\frac{1}{2}$.

Borrowing is sometimes necessary when subtracting mixed numbers. This occurs when the fractional part in the subtrahend is larger than the fractional part in the minuend.

example 5   Subtracting Mixed Numbers With Borrowing

Subtract.

$$4 - 2\dfrac{5}{8}$$

Solution:

$$\begin{array}{r} 4 \\ -\ 2\dfrac{5}{8} \\ \hline \end{array}$$ In this case, we have no fractional part from which to subtract.

$$\begin{array}{r} 4\overset{3}{\dfrac{\overset{8}{}}{8}} \\ -\ 2\dfrac{5}{8} \\ \hline 1\dfrac{3}{8} \end{array}$$ We can borrow 1 or equivalently $\frac{8}{8}$ from the whole number 4.

Tip: The borrowed 1 is written as $\frac{8}{8}$ because the common denominator is 8.

The difference is $1\frac{3}{8}$.

Tip: The subtraction problem $4 - 2\frac{5}{8} = 1\frac{3}{8}$ can be checked by adding:

$$1\dfrac{3}{8} + 2\dfrac{5}{8} = 3\dfrac{8}{8} = 3 + 1 = 4 \checkmark$$

---

example 6   **Subtracting Mixed Numbers With Borrowing**

Subtract.

a. $17\dfrac{2}{7} - 11\dfrac{5}{7}$ **b.** $14\dfrac{2}{9} - 9\dfrac{3}{5}$

Solution:

a. We cannot subtract $\frac{5}{7}$ from $\frac{2}{7}$. Therefore, borrow 1 from 17. The borrowed 1 is written as $\frac{7}{7}$ because the common denominator is 7.

$$\begin{array}{rcccr} 17\dfrac{2}{7} & = & \overset{16}{17}\dfrac{2}{7} + \dfrac{7}{7} & = & 16\dfrac{9}{7} \\ -\ 11\dfrac{5}{7} & = & -\ 11\dfrac{5}{7} & = & -\ 11\dfrac{5}{7} \\ \hline & & & & 5\dfrac{4}{7} \end{array}$$

The difference is $5\frac{4}{7}$.

b. To subtract the fractional parts, we need a common denominator. The LCD is 45.

$$\left.\begin{array}{rcccr} 14\dfrac{2}{9} & = & 14\dfrac{2 \cdot 5}{9 \cdot 5} & = & 14\dfrac{10}{45} \\ -\ 9\dfrac{3}{5} & = & -\ 9\dfrac{3 \cdot 9}{5 \cdot 9} & = & -\ 9\dfrac{27}{45} \end{array}\right\}$$ We cannot subtract $\frac{27}{45}$ from $\frac{10}{45}$. Therefore, borrow 1 (or equivalently $\frac{45}{45}$) from 14.

$$\begin{array}{rcccr} & = & \overset{13}{14}\dfrac{10}{45} + \dfrac{45}{45} & = & 13\dfrac{55}{45} \\ & = & -\ 9\dfrac{27}{45} & = & -\ 9\dfrac{27}{45} \\ \hline & & & & 4\dfrac{28}{45} \end{array}$$

The difference is $4\frac{28}{45}$.

3. Addition and Subtraction of Mixed Numbers by Using Improper Fractions

We have shown how to add and subtract mixed numbers by writing the numbers in columns. Another approach to add or subtract mixed numbers is to write the numbers first as improper fractions. Then add or subtract the fractions, as you learned in Section 3.3. To demonstrate this process, we add the mixed numbers from Example 3.

example 7   Adding Mixed Numbers by Using Improper Fractions

Add.

$$7\frac{5}{6} + 3\frac{3}{5}$$

Solution:

$$7\frac{5}{6} + 3\frac{3}{5} = \frac{47}{6} + \frac{18}{5}$$

Write each mixed number as an improper fraction.

$$= \frac{47 \cdot 5}{6 \cdot 5} + \frac{18 \cdot 6}{5 \cdot 6}$$

Convert the fractions to like fractions. The LCD is 30.

$$= \frac{235}{30} + \frac{108}{30}$$

The fractions are now like fractions.

$$= \frac{343}{30}$$

Add the like fractions.

$$= 11\frac{13}{30}$$

Convert the improper fraction to a mixed number.

$$
\begin{array}{r}
11 \\
30\overline{)343} \quad 11\frac{13}{30} \\
-30 \\
\hline
43 \\
-30 \\
\hline
13
\end{array}
$$

The mixed number $11\frac{13}{30}$ is the same as the value obtained in Example 3.

As you can see from Example 7, when we convert mixed numbers to improper fractions, the numerators of the fractions become larger numbers. Thus, we must add (or subtract) larger numerators than if we had used the method involving columns. This is one drawback. However, an advantage to converting to improper fractions first is that there is no need for carrying or borrowing.

4. Applications of Mixed Numbers

Mixed numbers come up often in real-world applications.

Answers

15. $17\frac{1}{12}$ **16.** $2\frac{13}{14}$

example 8   Subtracting Mixed Numbers in an Application

The average height of a 3-year-old girl is $38\frac{1}{3}$ in. The average height of a 4-year-old girl is $41\frac{3}{4}$ in. On average, by how much does a girl grow between the ages of 3 and 4?

Solution:

We use subtraction to find the difference in heights.

$$41\frac{3}{4} = 41\frac{3 \cdot 3}{4 \cdot 3} = 41\frac{9}{12}$$
$$- 38\frac{1}{3} = - 38\frac{1 \cdot 4}{3 \cdot 4} = - 38\frac{4}{12}$$
$$3\frac{5}{12}$$

The average amount of growth is $3\frac{5}{12}$ in.

Skill Practice

17. On December 1, the snow base at the Bear Mountain Ski Resort was $4\frac{1}{3}$ ft. By January 1, the base was $6\frac{1}{2}$ ft. By how much did the base amount of snow increase?

example 9   Adding Mixed Numbers in an Application

A cat "tree" is built from plywood and then covered in carpeting. What is the height of the model shown in Figure 3-4?

Solution:

The height is given by the sum of the heights of the individual parts. Also note that each mixed number (with the exception of $16\frac{1}{2}$) has a fractional part expressed in fourths. But $16\frac{1}{2} = 16\frac{2}{4}$. Therefore, the sum becomes

$$16\frac{2}{4}$$
$$10\frac{3}{4}$$
$$10\frac{3}{4}$$
$$1\frac{1}{4}$$
$$1\frac{1}{4}$$
$$1\frac{1}{4}$$
$$+ 1\frac{1}{4}$$
$$40\frac{12}{4}$$

Because $\frac{12}{4} = 3$, then $40\frac{12}{4} = 40 + 3 = 43$.

The total height of the cat tree is 43 in.

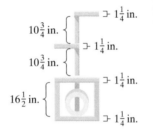

Figure 3-4

Skill Practice

18. Mr. Barter runs 6 days a week. His daily mileage for one week is given in the table. How far did he run for the week?

Day	Mileage
Monday	$2\frac{1}{4}$
Tuesday	$4\frac{1}{2}$
Wednesday	0
Thursday	5
Friday	$6\frac{1}{3}$
Saturday	$8\frac{1}{3}$
Sunday	$3\frac{1}{2}$

Answers

17. $2\frac{1}{6}$ ft   18. $29\frac{11}{12}$ mi

section 3.4   Practice Exercises

Study Skills Exercise

1. a. Do you believe that you have math anxiety?   If yes, why do you think so?

b. Of the list below, circle the activities that you think can help someone with math anxiety.

Deep breathing   Reading a book about math anxiety

Scheduling extra study time   Keeping a positive attitude

Review Exercises

For Exercises 2–8, add or subtract as indicated. Write the answer as a fraction or whole number.

2. $\dfrac{3}{16} + \dfrac{7}{12}$ **3.** $\dfrac{25}{8} - \dfrac{23}{24}$ **4.** $\dfrac{9}{5} + 3$ **5.** $4 - \dfrac{15}{7}$

6. $\dfrac{23}{6} + \dfrac{5}{6} - \dfrac{2}{3}$ **7.** $\dfrac{125}{32} - \dfrac{51}{32} - \dfrac{58}{32}$ **8.** $\dfrac{17}{10} - \dfrac{23}{100} + \dfrac{321}{1000}$

Objective 1: Addition of Mixed Numbers

For Exercises 9–16, add the mixed numbers. **(See Example 1.)**

9. $2\dfrac{1}{11}$ **10.** $5\dfrac{2}{7}$ **11.** $12\dfrac{1}{14}$ **12.** $1\dfrac{3}{20}$

$+\ 5\dfrac{3}{11}$ $+\ 4\dfrac{3}{7}$ $+\ 3\dfrac{5}{14}$ $+\ 17\dfrac{7}{20}$

13. $4\dfrac{5}{16}$ **14.** $21\dfrac{2}{9}$ **15.** $6\dfrac{2}{3}$ **16.** $7\dfrac{1}{6}$

$+\ 11\dfrac{1}{4}$ $+\ 10\dfrac{1}{3}$ $+\ 4\dfrac{1}{5}$ $+\ 3\dfrac{5}{8}$

For Exercises 17–24, round the mixed number to the nearest whole number.

17. $5\dfrac{1}{3}$ **18.** $2\dfrac{7}{8}$ **19.** $1\dfrac{3}{5}$ **20.** $6\dfrac{3}{7}$

21. $14\dfrac{15}{16}$ **22.** $7\dfrac{5}{12}$ **23.** $21\dfrac{5}{9}$ **24.** $15\dfrac{8}{11}$

For Exercises 25–32, write the mixed number in proper form (that is, as a whole number along with a proper fraction that is simplified to lowest terms).

25. $2\dfrac{6}{5}$ **26.** $4\dfrac{8}{7}$ **27.** $7\dfrac{5}{3}$ **28.** $1\dfrac{9}{5}$

29. $10\dfrac{14}{12}$ **30.** $15\dfrac{12}{8}$ **31.** $5\dfrac{28}{21}$ **32.** $8\dfrac{20}{16}$

For Exercises 33–38, round the numbers to estimate the answer. Then find the exact sum. **(See Examples 2 and 3.)**

	Estimate	Exact		Estimate	Exact		Estimate	Exact
33.	7	$6\dfrac{3}{4}$	**34.**		$8\dfrac{3}{5}$	**35.**		$14\dfrac{7}{8}$
	$+\;8$	$+\;7\dfrac{3}{4}$		$+$	$+\;13\dfrac{4}{5}$		$+$	$+\;8\dfrac{1}{4}$
	$\overline{15}$	$\overline{}$		$\overline{}$	$\overline{}$		$\overline{}$	$\overline{}$

	Estimate	Exact		Estimate	Exact		Estimate	Exact
36.		$21\dfrac{3}{5}$	**37.**		$3\dfrac{7}{16}$	**38.**		$7\dfrac{7}{9}$
	$+$	$+\;24\dfrac{9}{10}$		$+$	$+\;15\dfrac{11}{12}$		$+$	$+\;8\dfrac{5}{6}$
	$\overline{}$	$\overline{}$		$\overline{}$	$\overline{}$		$\overline{}$	$\overline{}$

For Exercises 39–42, add the mixed numbers to the whole numbers.

39. $3 + 6\dfrac{7}{8}$ **40.** $5 + 11\dfrac{1}{13}$ **41.** $32\dfrac{2}{7} + 10$ **42.** $2\dfrac{18}{37} + 16$

Objective 2: Subtraction of Mixed Numbers

For Exercises 43–50, subtract the mixed numbers. **(See Example 4.)**

43. $21\dfrac{9}{10}$ **44.** $19\dfrac{2}{3}$ **45.** $5\dfrac{9}{15}$ **46.** $33\dfrac{11}{12}$
$\;-\;10\dfrac{3}{10}$ $\;-\;4\dfrac{1}{3}$ $\;-\;3\dfrac{7}{15}$ $\;-\;14\dfrac{5}{12}$

47. $18\dfrac{5}{6}$ **48.** $21\dfrac{17}{20}$ **49.** $11\dfrac{5}{7}$ **50.** $5\dfrac{9}{11}$
$\;-\;6\dfrac{2}{3}$ $\;-\;20\dfrac{1}{10}$ $\;-\;9\dfrac{5}{14}$ $\;-\;2\dfrac{13}{22}$

51. Rewrite the number 1 as a fraction having the following denominators.

    a. 3 **b.** 5 **c.** 12 **d.** 6

52. Rewrite the number 1 as a fraction having the following denominators.

a. 20   **b.** 7   **c.** 10   **d.** 4

For Exercises 53–58, round the numbers to estimate the answer. Then find the exact difference. **(See Examples 5 and 6.)**

Estimate	Exact		Estimate	Exact		Estimate	Exact
53. 25	$25\frac{1}{4}$	**54.**		$36\frac{1}{5}$	**55.**		$17\frac{1}{6}$
$-\ 14$	$-\ 13\frac{3}{4}$			$-\ 12\frac{3}{5}$			$-\ 15\frac{5}{12}$
$\overline{11}$	$\overline{\quad}$	$-\ \underline{\quad}$		$\overline{\quad}$	$-\ \underline{\quad}$		$\overline{\quad}$

Estimate	Exact		Estimate	Exact		Estimate	Exact
56.	$22\frac{5}{18}$	**57.**		$46\frac{3}{7}$	**58.**		$23\frac{1}{2}$
	$-\ 10\frac{7}{9}$			$-\ 38\frac{1}{2}$			$-\ 18\frac{10}{13}$
$-\ \underline{\quad}$	$\overline{\quad}$	$-\ \underline{\quad}$		$\overline{\quad}$	$-\ \underline{\quad}$		$\overline{\quad}$

For Exercises 59–66, subtract the mixed numbers and whole numbers. Write the answers as mixed numbers or proper fractions.

59. $6 - 2\frac{5}{6}$

60. $9 - 4\frac{1}{2}$

61. $12 - 9\frac{2}{9}$

62. $10 - 9\frac{1}{3}$

63. $5\frac{3}{17} - 3$

64. $16\frac{4}{11} - 5$

65. $23\frac{5}{14} - 17$

66. $21\frac{3}{4} - 10$

Objective 3: Addition and Subtraction of Mixed Numbers by Using Improper Fractions

For Exercises 67–82, add or subtract the mixed numbers by using improper fractions. Write the answer as mixed numbers, if possible. **(See Example 7.)**

67. $2\frac{2}{3} + 4\frac{5}{8}$

68. $5\frac{1}{4} - 3\frac{1}{2}$

69. $1\frac{11}{15} + 4\frac{2}{5}$

70. $2\frac{10}{11} + 2\frac{1}{2}$

71. $3\frac{7}{8} - 3\frac{3}{16}$

72. $3\frac{1}{6} - 1\frac{23}{24}$

73. $4\frac{1}{12} + 5\frac{1}{9}$

74. $10\frac{2}{25} - 7\frac{13}{20}$

75. $9\frac{5}{32} - 8\frac{1}{4}$

76. $4\frac{3}{40} - 2\frac{7}{8}$

77. $6\frac{11}{14} + 4\frac{1}{6}$

78. $8\frac{3}{22} + 4\frac{1}{4}$

79. $12\frac{1}{5} - 11\frac{2}{7}$

80. $5\frac{11}{30} + 5\frac{3}{4}$

81. $10\frac{1}{8} - 2\frac{17}{18}$

82. $3\frac{8}{21} + 6\frac{8}{9}$

Objective 4: Applications of Mixed Numbers

Bird		Length
Cuban Bee Hummingbird		$2\frac{1}{4}$ inches
Sedge Wren		$3\frac{1}{2}$ inches
Great Carolina Wren		$5\frac{1}{2}$ inches
Belted Kingfisher		$11\frac{1}{4}$ inches to 15 inches

For Exercises 83–85, use the chart to answer the questions.

83. If a Belted Kingfisher measures $11\frac{1}{4}$ inches in length, how much longer is the Belted Kingfisher than the Sedge Wren?

84. How much longer is the Great Carolina Wren than the Cuban Bee Hummingbird?

85. Estimate or measure the length of your index finger. Which is longer, your index finger or a Cuban Bee Hummingbird?

86. A student has 3 part-time jobs. She tutors, delivers newspapers, and takes notes for a blind student. During a typical week she works $8\frac{2}{3}$ hr delivering newspapers, $4\frac{1}{2}$ hr tutoring, and $3\frac{3}{4}$ hr note-taking. What is the total number of hours worked in a typical week?

87. A scouting group hikes around a lake. Find the total distance.

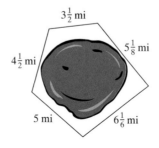

$3\frac{1}{2}$ mi

$5\frac{1}{8}$ mi

$4\frac{1}{2}$ mi

5 mi

$6\frac{1}{6}$ mi

88. Lara has a bike path on which she rides. One day she found a different path that she refers to as her shortcut. Find the perimeter of the original path and the perimeter of the shortcut. How much shorter is the shortcut?

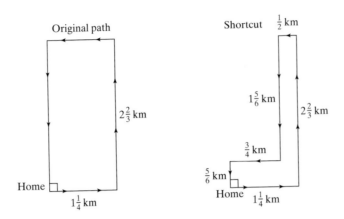

89. A water gauge in a pond measured $25\frac{7}{8}$ in. on Monday. After 2 days of rain and runoff, the gauge read $32\frac{1}{2}$ in. By how much did the water level rise? **(See Example 8.)**

90. A flight from Atlanta to San Diego takes $5\frac{1}{3}$ hr. After $2\frac{1}{2}$ hr, how much time remains?

91. In a triathlon, an athlete must swim $\frac{1}{4}$ mi, bike $10\frac{1}{2}$ mi, and run $3\frac{1}{5}$ mi. What is the total distance? **(See Example 9.)**

92. A contractor ordered three loads of gravel. The orders were for $2\frac{1}{2}$ tons, $3\frac{1}{8}$ tons, and $4\frac{1}{3}$ tons. What is the total amount of gravel ordered?

93. The number of hours worked per day for a plumber is given in the table. How many more hours did he work on Monday than on Saturday?

Monday	Tuesday	Wednesday	Thursday	Friday	Saturday	Sunday
$9\frac{1}{6}$ hr	$7\frac{3}{4}$ hr	$8\frac{1}{3}$ hr	$8\frac{1}{2}$ hr	$4\frac{1}{2}$ hr	$3\frac{3}{4}$ hr	0

94. Vertical blinds were purchased for a window that is $3\frac{5}{12}$ ft high. The blinds are $3\frac{3}{4}$ ft in length. Find the distance that the blinds will hang below the window.

Expanding Your Skills

For Exercises 95–98, fill in the blank to complete the pattern.

95. $1, 1\frac{1}{3}, 1\frac{2}{3}, 2, 2\frac{1}{3}, \square$

96. $\frac{1}{4}, 1, 1\frac{3}{4}, 2\frac{1}{2}, 3\frac{1}{4}, \square$

97. $\frac{5}{6}, 1\frac{1}{6}, 1\frac{1}{2}, 1\frac{5}{6}, \square$

98. $\frac{1}{2}, 1\frac{1}{4}, 2, 2\frac{3}{4}, 3\frac{1}{2}, \square$

section 3.5   Order of Operations and Applications of Fractions

1. Order of Operations

At this point in the text, we have learned how to add, subtract, multiply, and divide whole numbers, fractions, and mixed numbers. In this section we practice putting all these skills to use. We begin first by reviewing the order of operations.

Order of Operations

1. Perform all operations inside parentheses first.

2. Simplify expressions containing exponents or square roots.

3. Perform multiplication or division in the order that they appear from left to right.

4. Perform addition or subtraction in the order that they appear from left to right.

Objectives

1. Order of Operations
2. Applications of Fractions and Mixed Numbers
3. Applications to Geometry

Concept Connections

State the order in which you would perform the operations for the given expression.

1. $4 + \left(\dfrac{1}{3}\right)^2$

2. $2\dfrac{3}{7} + 6 \cdot \dfrac{1}{14}$

3. $\left(4 - 2\dfrac{2}{5}\right)^2 \cdot \dfrac{5}{7}$

example 1   Applying the Order of Operations

Simplify.

a. $\left(3 - \dfrac{3}{4}\right)^2$ **b.** $1\dfrac{2}{3} \div 6 \cdot \left(\dfrac{3}{10}\right)$ **c.** $\left(\dfrac{2}{5}\right)^2 + \left(2\dfrac{5}{8}\right) \cdot \dfrac{3}{7}$

Solution:

a. $\left(3 - \dfrac{3}{4}\right)^2 = \left(\dfrac{3}{1} - \dfrac{3}{4}\right)^2$

We must first subtract the numbers within parentheses. Write the whole number as an improper fraction.

$= \left(\dfrac{3 \cdot 4}{1 \cdot 4} - \dfrac{3}{4}\right)^2$

Convert the fractions to like fractions. The LCD is 4.

$= \left(\dfrac{12}{4} - \dfrac{3}{4}\right)^2$

The fractions are now like.

$= \left(\dfrac{9}{4}\right)^2$

Subtract.

$= \dfrac{9}{4} \cdot \dfrac{9}{4}$

Square the quantity $\dfrac{9}{4}$.

$= \dfrac{81}{16}$ or $5\dfrac{1}{16}$

b. $1\dfrac{2}{3} \div 6 \cdot \left(\dfrac{3}{10}\right) = \dfrac{5}{3} \div \dfrac{6}{1} \cdot \dfrac{3}{10}$

Write the mixed number and whole number as improper fractions. In this expression, we must multiply and divide in order from left to right.

$= \dfrac{5}{3} \cdot \dfrac{1}{6} \cdot \dfrac{3}{10}$

Multiply by the reciprocal of the second fraction.

$= \dfrac{\overset{1}{\cancel{5}}}{\underset{1}{\cancel{3}}} \cdot \dfrac{1}{6} \cdot \dfrac{\overset{1}{\cancel{3}}}{\underset{2}{\cancel{10}}}$

Simplify.

$= \dfrac{1}{12}$

Multiply.

Skill Practice

Simplify.

4. $4 + \left(\dfrac{1}{3}\right)^2$

5. $2\dfrac{3}{7} + 6 \cdot \dfrac{1}{14}$

6. $\left(4 - 2\dfrac{2}{5}\right)^2 \cdot \dfrac{5}{7}$

Answers

1. Square $\frac{1}{3}$ first. Then add the result to 4.
2. Multiply first. Then add the result to $2\frac{3}{7}$.
3. Subtract inside the parentheses first. Then square the result. Finally, multiply by $\frac{5}{7}$.
4. $\dfrac{37}{9}$ or $4\dfrac{1}{9}$ 5. $\dfrac{20}{7}$ or $2\dfrac{6}{7}$
6. $\dfrac{64}{35}$ or $1\dfrac{29}{35}$

c. $\left(\dfrac{2}{5}\right)^2 + \left(2\dfrac{5}{8}\right) \cdot \dfrac{3}{7}$ Perform the exponent operation first.

$= \dfrac{2}{5} \cdot \dfrac{2}{5} + \left(2\dfrac{5}{8}\right) \cdot \dfrac{3}{7}$ Square the quantity $\frac{2}{5}$.

$= \dfrac{4}{25} + \dfrac{21}{8} \cdot \dfrac{3}{7}$ Write the mixed number as an improper fraction.

$= \dfrac{4}{25} + \dfrac{\overset{3}{\cancel{21}}}{8} \cdot \dfrac{3}{\underset{1}{\cancel{7}}}$ Multiply before adding. Simplify common factors within the second two fractions. Do not try to "cancel" the 4 and the 8. The fraction $\frac{4}{25}$ is being *added*, not multiplied.

$= \dfrac{4}{25} + \dfrac{9}{8}$

$= \dfrac{4 \cdot 8}{25 \cdot 8} + \dfrac{9 \cdot 25}{8 \cdot 25}$ Add the fractions. The LCD is $25 \cdot 8 = 200$.

$= \dfrac{32}{200} + \dfrac{225}{200}$ The fractions are now like.

$= \dfrac{257}{200}$ or $1\dfrac{57}{200}$ The answer may be written as either an improper fraction or a mixed number.

Skill Practice

7. The graph gives the winning distance for men's and women's discus throw for selected Olympic games.

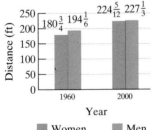

Winning Discus Throw Results for Selected Olympic Games

$224\frac{5}{12}$ $227\frac{1}{3}$

$180\frac{3}{4}$ $194\frac{1}{6}$

Distance (ft)

Year

■ Women   ■ Men

a. How much farther was the men's throw than the women's throw in 2000?

b. What was the average throw for women for these two years?

2. Applications of Fractions and Mixed Numbers

Examples 2 and 3 use operations on fractions and mixed numbers in real-world applications.

example 2 Using Mixed Numbers in a Sports Application

The graph in Figure 3-5 gives the winning height for the men's high jump for selected Olympic games.

a. What is the difference between the winning high jump in 1992 versus 1948?

b. What is the average height from these four Olympics?

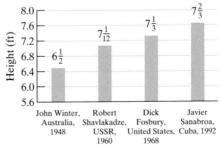

Winning High Jump Heights for Selected Olympic Games

$7\frac{2}{3}$

$7\frac{1}{3}$

$7\frac{1}{12}$

$6\frac{1}{2}$

Height (ft)

John Winter, Australia, 1948   Robert Shavlakadze, USSR, 1960   Dick Fosbury, United States, 1968   Javier Sanabroa, Cuba, 1992

Figure 3-5

Answers

7. a. $2\dfrac{11}{12}$ ft   b. $202\dfrac{7}{12}$ ft

Solution:

a. The word "difference" implies subtraction. We subtract the 1948 height from the 1992 height.

$$7\frac{2}{3} = 7\frac{2\cdot 2}{3\cdot 2} = 7\frac{4}{6}$$
$$-6\frac{1}{2} = -6\frac{1\cdot 3}{2\cdot 3} = -6\frac{3}{6}$$
$$1\frac{1}{6}$$

The difference between the winning heights in 1992 and 1948 is $1\frac{1}{6}$ ft.

b. The average height is found by taking the sum of the four heights and dividing by 4. The sum of the heights is given by

$$6\frac{1}{2} = 6\frac{6}{12}$$
$$7\frac{1}{12} = 7\frac{1}{12}$$
$$7\frac{1}{3} = 7\frac{4}{12}$$
$$+7\frac{2}{3} = +7\frac{8}{12}$$

The LCD of all four fractions is 12.

$$27\frac{19}{12} = 27 + 1\frac{7}{12} = 28\frac{7}{12}$$

Now divide by 4 to find the average:

$$28\frac{7}{12} \div 4 = \frac{343}{12} \div \frac{4}{1}$$ Write the mixed number and whole number as improper fractions.

$$= \frac{343}{12} \cdot \frac{1}{4}$$ Multiply by the reciprocal of the divisor.

$$= \frac{343}{48}$$ Multiply.

$$= 7\frac{7}{48}$$ Write the result as a mixed number.
$$\begin{array}{r}7\\48\overline{)343}\\-336\\\hline 7\end{array}$$

The average winning height for the men's high jump for the selected years is $7\frac{7}{48}$ ft.

---

example 3   Using Multiplication of Fractions in a Finance Application

Sheila wants to buy a certain stock at $5\frac{3}{4}$ per share. How much money will it cost her to buy 300 shares?

Solution:

The value $\$5\frac{3}{4}$ gives the cost for 1 share of stock. For 300 shares we multiply.

$$\text{Total cost} = \left(5\frac{3}{4}\right)(300) = \left(\frac{23}{4}\right)\left(\frac{300}{1}\right)$$

$$= \left(\frac{23}{\underset{1}{4}}\right)\left(\frac{\overset{75}{\cancel{300}}}{1}\right)$$

$$= \frac{1725}{1}$$

The total cost for 300 shares of stock is $1725.

Tip: The answer can be estimated by rounding $\$5\frac{3}{4}$ to $6. Then ($6)(300) = $1800 which is close to $1725.

3. Applications to Geometry

In Examples 4 and 5, we review the concepts of perimeter and area in applications.

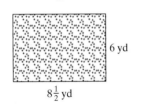
example 4   **Using Mixed Numbers in a Construction Application**

Thom has $22\frac{1}{3}$ ft of molding left over from a previous carpentry job. He needs to apply molding around the base of the room shown in Figure 3-6. How much more molding does he need?

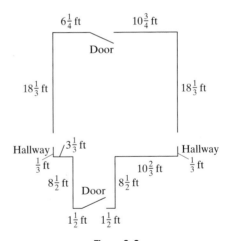

Figure 3-6

Solution:

To find the amount of molding still needed, we need to find the total required for the room and subtract $22\frac{1}{3}$ ft.

We find the total distance by adding the lengths of the segments of wall without including distances representing the hallways or doors.

Total length of wall
$$= 6\frac{1}{4} + 10\frac{3}{4} + 18\frac{1}{3} + \frac{1}{3} + 10\frac{2}{3} + 8\frac{1}{2} + 1\frac{1}{2} + 1\frac{1}{2} + 8\frac{1}{2} + 3\frac{1}{3} + \frac{1}{3} + 18\frac{1}{3}$$

Recall that mixed numbers represent addition of the whole-number part and the fractional part. Therefore, we can use the commutative and associative properties of addition to arrange the addends in an order convenient for computation.

$$= (6 + 10 + 18 + 10 + 8 + 1 + 1 + 8 + 3 + 18)$$
$$+ \underbrace{\left(\frac{1}{4} + \frac{3}{4}\right.} + \underbrace{\frac{1}{3} + \frac{1}{3} + \frac{2}{3}} + \underbrace{\frac{1}{2} + \frac{1}{2} + \frac{1}{2} + \frac{1}{2}} + \underbrace{\left.\frac{1}{3} + \frac{1}{3} + \frac{1}{3}\right)}$$

Add groups of like fractions.

$$= 83 + \left(\frac{4}{4} + \frac{4}{3} + \frac{4}{2} + \frac{3}{3}\right)$$

$$= 83 + \left(1 + 1\frac{1}{3} + 2 + 1\right)$$

$$= 88\frac{1}{3}$$

There is $88\frac{1}{3}$ ft of molding required for this room. The carpenter already has $22\frac{1}{3}$ ft. The remaining amount is found by subtracting $22\frac{1}{3}$ ft from the total.

$$88\frac{1}{3} - 22\frac{1}{3} = 66$$

The carpenter still needs 66 ft of molding.

---

example 5   Using Fractions and Mixed Numbers in a Geometry Application

Jason and Sara plan to paint a side of their house (Figure 3-7).

a. How much area will they have to paint?

b. They want to string Christmas lights around the triangular portion of the house. What length is required for the string of lights?

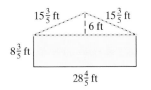

$$15\frac{3}{5}\text{ ft} \qquad 15\frac{3}{5}\text{ ft}$$
$$6\text{ ft}$$
$$8\frac{3}{5}\text{ ft}$$
$$28\frac{4}{5}\text{ ft}$$

Figure 3-7

Solution:

a. The area of the side of the house is given by the sum of the rectangular area and the triangular area.

$$\text{Area of the triangle} = \frac{1}{2}bh$$

$$= \frac{1}{2}\left(28\frac{4}{5}\right)(6)$$

$$= \frac{1}{2}\left(\frac{\overset{72}{\cancel{144}}}{5}\right)\left(\frac{6}{1}\right)$$

$$= \frac{432}{5} \text{ or } 86\frac{2}{5}$$

$$\text{Area of rectangle} = l \cdot w$$

$$= \left(28\frac{4}{5}\right)\left(8\frac{3}{5}\right)$$

$$= \frac{144}{5} \cdot \frac{43}{5}$$

$$= \frac{6192}{25} \text{ or } 247\frac{17}{25}$$

(left figure)
$$6\text{ ft}$$
$$28\frac{4}{5}\text{ ft}$$
$$+$$
$$8\frac{3}{5}\text{ ft}$$
$$28\frac{4}{5}\text{ ft}$$

Skill Practice

10. A homeowner wants to sod the yard and fence the perimeter as shown in the figure.

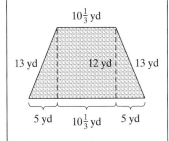

$$10\frac{1}{3}\text{ yd}$$
$$13\text{ yd} \qquad 12\text{ yd} \qquad 13\text{ yd}$$
$$5\text{ yd} \qquad 10\frac{1}{3}\text{ yd} \qquad 5\text{ yd}$$

a. How many square yards of sod are required?

b. How much fencing is required?

Answers

10. a. 184 yd² of sod is needed.
    b. $56\frac{2}{3}$ yd of fencing is needed.

The total area is given by

$$86\frac{2}{5} \text{ ft}^2 \quad \longrightarrow \quad 86\frac{10}{25} \text{ ft}^2$$

$$+ \, 247\frac{17}{25} \text{ ft}^2 \quad \longrightarrow \quad + \, 247\frac{17}{25} \text{ ft}^2$$

$$333\frac{27}{25} \text{ ft}^2 \quad \text{or} \quad 334\frac{2}{25} \text{ ft}^2$$

The total area is $334\frac{2}{25}$ ft².

b. The perimeter of the triangle is found by adding the lengths of the sides.

$$15\frac{3}{5} + 15\frac{3}{5} + 28\frac{4}{5} = 58\frac{10}{5}$$

Because $\frac{10}{5} = 2$, we have $58\frac{10}{5} = 58 + \frac{10}{5} = 58 + 2 = 60$. Jason and Sara will require a string of lights 60 ft long.

section 3.5   Practice Exercises

Study Skills Exercise

1. When you take a test, go through the test, doing all the problems that you know first. Then go back and work on the problems that were more difficult. Give yourself a time limit for how much time you spend on each problem (maybe 3 to 5 minutes the first time through). Circle the importance of each statement.

	Not important	Somewhat important	Very important
a. Read through the entire test first.	1	2	3
b. If time allows, go back and check each problem.	1	2	3
c. Write out all steps instead of doing the work in your head.	1	2	3

Review Exercises

For Exercises 2–8, perform the indicated operation.

2. $7\dfrac{3}{10} + 2\dfrac{14}{15}$

3. $16 - 3\dfrac{7}{9}$

4. $5\dfrac{5}{8} \cdot 2\dfrac{1}{9}$

5. $7\dfrac{1}{9} \div 2\dfrac{2}{3}$

6. $24\dfrac{3}{5} - 14\dfrac{3}{4}$

7. $\left(1\dfrac{5}{6}\right)^2$

8. $13\dfrac{1}{14} + 4\dfrac{5}{7}$

For Exercises 9–12, convert the mixed number to an improper fraction.

9. $5\dfrac{2}{13}$

10. $2\dfrac{7}{11}$

11. $3\dfrac{9}{10}$

12. $1\dfrac{15}{16}$

For Exercises 13–16, convert the improper fraction to a mixed number.

13. $\dfrac{29}{5}$

14. $\dfrac{50}{7}$

15. $\dfrac{30}{19}$

16. $\dfrac{25}{8}$

Objective 1: Order of Operations

For Exercises 17–32, simplify, using the order of operations. Write the answer as a mixed number, if possible. **(See Example 1.)**

17. $1\dfrac{5}{6} \cdot 2\dfrac{1}{2} \div 1\dfrac{1}{4}$

18. $2\dfrac{1}{7} \div 1\dfrac{1}{3} \cdot \dfrac{7}{10}$

19. $6\dfrac{1}{6} + 2\dfrac{1}{3} \div 1\dfrac{3}{4}$

20. $8\dfrac{7}{9} + 2\dfrac{1}{6} \cdot 3\dfrac{1}{3}$

21. $6 - 5\dfrac{1}{7} \cdot \dfrac{1}{3}$

22. $11 - 6\dfrac{1}{3} \div 1\dfrac{1}{6}$

23. $\left(3\dfrac{1}{4} + 1\dfrac{5}{8}\right) \cdot 2\dfrac{2}{3}$

24. $\left(1\dfrac{3}{5} + 2\dfrac{4}{7}\right) \cdot 5\dfrac{5}{6}$

25. $\left(1\dfrac{1}{5}\right)^2 \cdot \left(1\dfrac{7}{9} - 1\dfrac{5}{12}\right)$

26. $\left(6\dfrac{3}{4} - 2\dfrac{1}{8}\right) \div \left(1\dfrac{1}{2}\right)^3$

27. $\left(1\dfrac{1}{3}\right)^3 \div \left(2\dfrac{7}{9} + 1\dfrac{2}{3}\right)$

28. $\left(2\dfrac{1}{2} + 1\dfrac{7}{8}\right) \cdot \left(1\dfrac{1}{7}\right)^2$

29. $\left(3\dfrac{1}{4} + \dfrac{3}{5}\right) \cdot \left(3\dfrac{1}{3} + \dfrac{5}{11}\right)$

30. $\left(4\dfrac{4}{15} - 3\dfrac{1}{5}\right) \cdot \left(1\dfrac{1}{3} + \dfrac{11}{12}\right)$

31. $\left(5 - 1\dfrac{7}{8}\right) \div \left(3 - \dfrac{13}{16}\right)$

32. $\left(4 + 2\dfrac{1}{9}\right) \div \left(2 - 1\dfrac{11}{36}\right)$

Objective 2: Applications of Fractions and Mixed Numbers

33. Acceleration on cars is often compared by the time it takes to go from 0 to 60 miles per hour (mph). The graph gives the times for four cars. **(See Example 2.)**

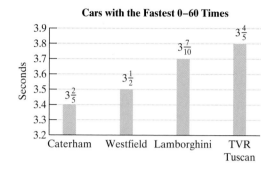

Cars with the Fastest 0–60 Times

a. What is the difference between the times for the Lamborghini and the Caterham?

b. Find the average time for these four cars.

34. Luis keeps a portfolio and tracks the number of hours he spends working on math each day.

a. How much time did Luis spend last week working on math?

b. Find the average amount of time spent per day working on math.

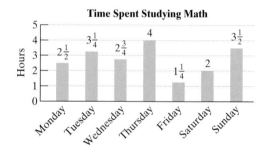

Time Spent Studying Math

35. Six women go on a weight loss program for 4 weeks. The amount of weight lost for each woman is given in the graph.

a. Find the total weight loss.

b. Find the average weight loss per person.

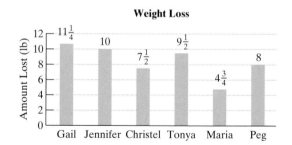

Weight Loss

c. Find the difference between the maximum weight loss and the minimum weight loss.

36. Geoff ran $4\frac{1}{4}$ mi on Monday, $2\frac{1}{2}$ mi on Tuesday, 3 mi on Wednesday, and $8\frac{3}{4}$ mi on Thursday.

a. What is the total distance he ran?

b. What is the average distance he ran per day?

37. A financial analyst followed a certain stock. On Monday, the stock was at $15\frac{5}{8}$. By Friday, it had fallen to $11\frac{3}{4}$. By how much did the stock drop?

38. On Monday a stock closed at $12\frac{3}{4}$. On Tuesday, the stock rose $1\frac{1}{2}$. What was the closing price of the stock on Tuesday?

39. George will get $\frac{1}{3}$ of an $80,250 inheritance. How much money will he receive? **(See Example 3.)**

40. Aaron pays about $\frac{7}{25}$ of his annual salary in federal income tax. How much tax does he pay if his salary is $45,000 per year?

41. A $15\frac{1}{4}$-ft cable is cut into 4 pieces of equal length. How long is each piece?

42. Twenty-seven pounds of candy is distributed in $\frac{3}{4}$-lb bags. How many bags can be filled?

43. A cheese plate advertises a total of 3 lb of assorted cheeses. At the end of a party, there was $\frac{1}{4}$ lb of Swiss cheese, $\frac{1}{3}$ lb of cheddar, and $\frac{1}{6}$ lb of Jack cheese left over. How many pounds of cheese were eaten?

44. Meade gave $\frac{1}{4}$ of a candy bar to Max and then ate $\frac{1}{3}$ of the candy bar himself. What fraction of the candy bar is left?

45. A bread recipe calls for $3\frac{1}{4}$ cups of flour. If the Daily Bread bakery has large bags of flour containing 65 cups each, how many loaves of bread can be made?

46. A carpenter worked $37\frac{1}{4}$ hr last week and earned $894. What is his hourly rate?

47. If interest rates average $6\frac{1}{2}$ points and go up $\frac{3}{4}$ point, what is the new rate?

48. The annual consumption of tea in Hong Kong is $1\frac{9}{25}$ kg per capita. The per capita tea consumption in the United Kingdom is $\frac{21}{25}$ kg more than that in Hong Kong. What is the per capita amount of tea consumed in the United Kingdom?

49. Stephanie is planning to sew her bridesmaids' dresses. The pattern calls for $2\frac{1}{2}$ yd of material for one dress with an additional $1\frac{1}{4}$ yd for the matching jacket. If she has three bridesmaids, how many yards of material will she need to buy?

50. Grace travels $1\frac{1}{4}$ hr to work each day. If she works 5 days a week, how much time is spent traveling to and from work?

51. Wilma has $6\frac{1}{2}$ lb of mixed nuts. If she gives Fred one-half of the mixture and Barney one-third of the mixture, how many pounds of nuts does she have left?

52. Jeremy mowed $\frac{2}{3}$ of his front lawn in the morning and then $\frac{1}{4}$ of the lawn in the evening. What portion of the lawn still needs to be mowed?

53. Joan waters her plants each day with $22\frac{3}{4}$ gal of water. With a new irrigation system in place, she uses only $17\frac{2}{3}$ gal of water. How many gallons of water does she save in a 30-day period with the new irrigation system?

54. A school fund-raiser began a bake sale with $36\frac{1}{2}$ lb of cookies. At the end of the day $5\frac{3}{4}$ lb remained. How many pounds of cookies were sold?

Objective 3: Applications to Geometry

55. A decorator has $14\frac{2}{3}$ ft of wallpaper border. How much more does she need to place wallpaper border around the walls of the bathroom shown in the figure? (*Note:* No border is needed on the door.) **(See Example 4.)**

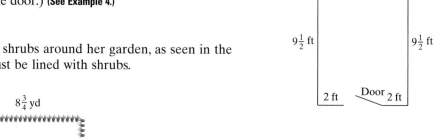

56. Leonie wants to put a border of shrubs around her garden, as seen in the figure. Find the distance that must be lined with shrubs.

57. A stop sign is in the shape of an 8-sided polygon in which each of the sides is $12\frac{1}{2}$ in. Find the perimeter.

58. Matt needs to replace gutters on his townhouse. If the front and back of the townhouse are each $20\frac{1}{2}$ ft long and the side of the house is $35\frac{1}{3}$ ft long, how much gutter should he buy to go around the three sides of the house?

59. The shutters on the front of the house need to be painted. Determine the area of the four shutters.

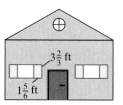

60. The cost of a new roof depends on the area of the roof. Find the area of the roof of the house in the figure.

$14\frac{1}{4}$ ft

$35\frac{7}{8}$ ft

61. Find the area of the triangular portion of the roof.

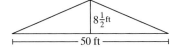

$8\frac{1}{2}$ ft

50 ft

62. Find the area of the calculator screen.

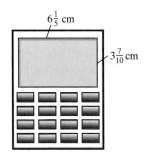

$6\frac{1}{5}$ cm

$3\frac{7}{10}$ cm

63. The Krajewskis want to improve the backyard by fertilizing the grass and putting up a decorative fence. To know how much fertilizer to use, they must know the area of the yard. **(See Example 5.)**

a. Using the figure, determine the area of the yard.

b. How many meters of fencing will they need?

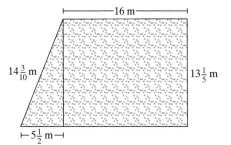

16 m

$14\frac{3}{10}$ m

$13\frac{1}{5}$ m

$5\frac{1}{2}$ m

64. A rectangular patio is $20\frac{2}{3}$ ft by $10\frac{1}{2}$ ft. Find the area and perimeter.

Expanding Your Skills

65. Richard wants to paint his garage. Determine the area that needs to be painted. (He will paint the garage door, front, back, and sides of the garage, but not the roof.)

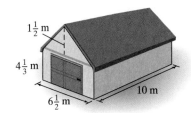

$1\frac{1}{2}$ m

$4\frac{1}{3}$ m

10 m

$6\frac{1}{2}$ m

chapter 3 | summary

section 3.1 Addition and Subtraction of Like Fractions

Key Concepts

Adding Like Fractions

1. Add the numerators.
2. Write the sum over the common denominator.
3. Simplify the fraction to lowest terms, if possible.

Subtracting Like Fractions

1. Subtract the numerators.
2. Write the difference over the common denominator.
3. Simplify the fraction to lowest terms, if possible.

When simplifying expressions with more than one operation, follow the order of operations.

Example 4 is an application involving subtraction of **like fractions**.

Examples

Example 1

$$\frac{5}{8} + \frac{7}{8} = \frac{12}{8} = \frac{\overset{1}{2} \cdot \overset{1}{2} \cdot 3}{2 \cdot 2 \cdot 2} = \frac{3}{2}$$

Example 2

$$\frac{25}{10} - \frac{7}{10} = \frac{18}{10} = \frac{2 \cdot \overset{1}{3} \cdot 3}{2 \cdot 5} = \frac{9}{5}$$

Example 3

$$\left(\frac{5}{3}\right)^2 - \left(\frac{2}{9} + \frac{5}{9}\right) = \left(\frac{5}{3}\right)^2 - \left(\frac{7}{9}\right)$$

$$= \frac{25}{9} - \frac{7}{9}$$

$$= \frac{18}{9}$$

$$= 2$$

Example 4

A nail that is $\frac{13}{8}$ in. long is driven through a board that is $\frac{11}{8}$ in. thick. How much of the nail extends beyond the board?

$$\frac{13}{8} - \frac{11}{8} = \frac{2}{8} = \frac{1}{4}$$

The nail will extend $\frac{1}{4}$ in.

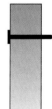

section 3.2 Least Common Multiple

Key Concepts

The numbers obtained by multiplying a number by the whole numbers 1, 2, 3, and so on are called the **multiples** of the number.

The **least common multiple (LCM)** of two given numbers is the smallest whole number that is a multiple of each given number.

Using Prime Factors to Find the LCM of Two Numbers
1. Write each number as a product of prime factors.
2. The LCM is the product of unique prime factors from both numbers. If a factor is repeated within the factorization of either number, use that factor the maximum number of times it appears in either factorization.

To determine the order of two fractions with different denominators, rewrite each fraction as an equivalent fraction with a common denominator.

The **least common denominator (LCD)** of two fractions is the LCM of their denominators.

Examples

Example 1

The numbers 5, 10, 15, 20, 25, 30, 35, and 40 are several multiples of 5.

Example 2

Find the LCM of 8 and 10.
Some multiples of 8 are 8, 16, 24, 32, 40.
Some multiples of 10 are 10, 20, 30, 40.

40 is the least common multiple.

Example 3

Find the LCM for the numbers 24 and 16.

$24 = 2 \cdot 2 \cdot 2 \cdot 3$

$16 = 2 \cdot 2 \cdot 2 \cdot 2$

$\text{LCM} = 2 \cdot 2 \cdot 2 \cdot 2 \cdot 3 = 48$

Example 4

Given $\frac{5}{6} \ \square \ \frac{7}{8}$, fill in the blank with $<$, $>$, or $=$.

First write the fractions with a common denominator.

$6 = 2 \cdot 3$

$8 = 2 \cdot 2 \cdot 2$

LCD of $\frac{5}{6}$ and $\frac{7}{8}$ is $2 \cdot 2 \cdot 2 \cdot 3 = 24$

$$\frac{5}{6} = \frac{5 \cdot 4}{6 \cdot 4} = \frac{20}{24} \qquad \frac{7}{8} = \frac{7 \cdot 3}{8 \cdot 3} = \frac{21}{24}$$

Since $\dfrac{20}{24} < \dfrac{21}{24}$, then $\dfrac{5}{6} < \dfrac{7}{8}$.

section 3.3 Addition and Subtraction of Unlike Fractions

Key Concepts

To add or subtract unlike fractions, first we must write each fraction as an equivalent fraction with a common denominator.

Steps to Add or Subtract Unlike Fractions

1. Identify the LCD.
2. Write each individual fraction as an equivalent fraction with the LCD.
3. Add or subtract the resulting fractions as indicated.
4. Simplify to lowest terms, if possible.

Examples

Example 1

Add $\dfrac{3}{10} + \dfrac{4}{15}$.

LCD = 30: $\dfrac{3}{10} = \dfrac{3 \cdot 3}{10 \cdot 3} = \dfrac{9}{30}$

$\dfrac{4}{15} = \dfrac{4 \cdot 2}{15 \cdot 2} = \dfrac{8}{30}$

$\dfrac{3}{10} + \dfrac{4}{15} = \dfrac{9}{30} + \dfrac{8}{30} = \dfrac{17}{30}$

Example 2

Subtract $\dfrac{7}{15} - \dfrac{5}{21}$.

LCD = 105: $\dfrac{7}{15} = \dfrac{7 \cdot 7}{15 \cdot 7} = \dfrac{49}{105}$

$\dfrac{5}{21} = \dfrac{5 \cdot 5}{21 \cdot 5} = \dfrac{25}{105}$

$\dfrac{7}{15} - \dfrac{5}{21} = \dfrac{49}{105} - \dfrac{25}{105} = \dfrac{24}{105} = \dfrac{8}{35}$

When simplifying expressions with more than one operation, follow the order of operations.

Example 3

$\dfrac{2}{5} \cdot \left(\dfrac{5}{2} - \dfrac{7}{3} \right) + \dfrac{13}{30} = \dfrac{2}{5} \cdot \left(\dfrac{15}{6} - \dfrac{14}{6} \right) + \dfrac{13}{30}$

$= \dfrac{2}{5} \cdot \left(\dfrac{1}{6} \right) + \dfrac{13}{30}$

$= \dfrac{2}{30} + \dfrac{13}{30}$

$= \dfrac{15}{30}$

$= \dfrac{1}{2}$

section 3.4 Addition and Subtraction of Mixed Numbers

Key Concepts

Addition of Mixed Numbers

To find the sum of two or more mixed numbers, add the whole-number parts and add the fractional parts.

Examples

Example 1

$$3\frac{5}{8} = 3\frac{10}{16}$$
$$+ 1\frac{1}{16} = 1\frac{1}{16}$$
$$\overline{\hspace{2cm}4\frac{11}{16}}$$

Example 2

$$2\frac{9}{10} = 2\frac{27}{30}$$
$$+ 6\frac{5}{6} = 6\frac{25}{30}$$
$$\overline{\hspace{1cm}8\frac{52}{30} = 8 + 1\frac{22}{30}}$$
$$= 9\frac{11}{15}$$

Subtraction of Mixed Numbers

To subtract mixed numbers, subtract the fractional parts and subtract the whole-number parts.

When the fractional part in the subtrahend is larger than the fractional part in the minuend, we borrow from the whole number.

Example 3

$$5\frac{3}{4} = 5\frac{9}{12}$$
$$- 2\frac{2}{3} = 2\frac{8}{12}$$
$$\overline{\hspace{1.5cm}3\frac{1}{12}}$$

Example 4

$$7\frac{1}{2} = \overset{6}{\cancel{7}}\frac{\overset{5+10}{5}}{10} = 6\frac{15}{10}$$
$$- 3\frac{4}{5} = 3\frac{8}{10} = 3\frac{8}{10}$$
$$\overline{\hspace{3cm}3\frac{7}{10}}$$

We can also add or subtract mixed numbers by writing the numbers as improper fractions. Then add or subtract the fractions.

Example 5

$$4\frac{7}{8} + 2\frac{1}{16} - 3\frac{1}{4} = \frac{39}{8} + \frac{33}{16} - \frac{13}{4}$$
$$= \frac{78}{16} + \frac{33}{16} - \frac{52}{16} = \frac{59}{16} = 3\frac{11}{16}$$

Example 6 illustrates an application involving addition and subtraction of mixed numbers.

Example 6

A certain stock rose $5\frac{1}{2}$ points on Monday, dropped $2\frac{1}{4}$ points on Tuesday, and rose $3\frac{3}{4}$ points on Wednesday. What is the net change in stock for the 3 days?

$$5\frac{1}{2} - 2\frac{1}{4} + 3\frac{3}{4} = \frac{11}{2} - \frac{9}{4} + \frac{15}{4}$$
$$= \frac{22}{4} - \frac{9}{4} + \frac{15}{4}$$
$$= \frac{28}{4}$$
$$= 7$$

The stock rose 7 points.

section 3.5　Order of Operations and Applications of Fractions

Key Concepts

Order of Operations

1. Perform all operations inside parentheses first.
2. Simplify expressions containing exponents or square roots.
3. Perform multiplication or division in the order that they appear from left to right.
4. Perform addition or subtraction in the order that they appear from left to right.

Example 2 is an example of an application involving mixed numbers and fractions.

Examples

Example 1

$$4\frac{2}{9} + 2\frac{1}{12} \cdot 5\frac{1}{3} = 4\frac{2}{9} + \frac{25}{\underset{3}{12}} \cdot \frac{\overset{4}{16}}{3}$$

$$= 4\frac{2}{9} + \frac{100}{9}$$

$$= \frac{38}{9} + \frac{100}{9}$$

$$= \frac{138}{9} = 15\frac{1}{3}$$

Example 2

Wallace has a budget of $750 for putting a curb around an area in his front yard. Curbing costs $3\frac{1}{2}$ per foot. To stay within his budget, how many feet of curbing can he afford?

Solution:

$$750 \div 3\frac{1}{2} = \frac{750}{1} \div \frac{7}{2}$$

$$= \frac{750}{1} \cdot \frac{2}{7}$$

$$= \frac{1500}{7} = 214\frac{2}{7}$$

Wallace can purchase up to $214\frac{2}{7}$ ft of curbing.

chapter 3 | review exercises

Section 3.1

For Exercises 1–4, add or subtract the like units.

1. 5 books + 3 books

2. 12 cm + 6 cm

3. 25 mi – 13 mi

4. 13 CDs – 2 CDs

5. Explain what is meant by the term *like fractions*.

6. Give an example of two like fractions and two unlike fractions. Answers may vary.

For Exercises 7–14, add or subtract the like fractions. Simplify the answer to lowest terms.

7. $\dfrac{5}{6} + \dfrac{4}{6}$

8. $\dfrac{4}{15} + \dfrac{6}{15}$

9. $\dfrac{5}{12} + \dfrac{1}{12}$

10. $\dfrac{2}{9} + \dfrac{7}{9}$

11. $\dfrac{15}{7} - \dfrac{6}{7}$

12. $\dfrac{14}{3} - \dfrac{10}{3}$

13. $\dfrac{21}{5} - \dfrac{6}{5}$

14. $\dfrac{12}{11} - \dfrac{9}{11}$

For Exercises 15–18, simplify the expression by using the order of operations.

15. $\dfrac{3}{8} \cdot \dfrac{3}{2} + \dfrac{3}{16}$

16. $\dfrac{4}{9} + \left(\dfrac{4}{3}\right)^2$

17. $\dfrac{21}{13} - \dfrac{5}{2} \div \dfrac{13}{4}$

18. $\left(\dfrac{7}{10} - \dfrac{2}{10}\right)^3 \cdot \dfrac{8}{7}$

19. Find the perimeter of the picture.

$\frac{13}{4}$ in.

$\frac{11}{4}$ in.

20. Refer to the table that gives the average snowfall for selected cities.

	January	February	March
Spartanburg, SC	$\dfrac{25}{10}$ in.	$\dfrac{19}{10}$ in.	$\dfrac{12}{10}$ in.
Amarillo, TX	$\dfrac{39}{10}$ in.	$\dfrac{36}{10}$ in.	$\dfrac{28}{10}$ in.
Portland, OR	$\dfrac{33}{10}$ in.	$\dfrac{10}{10}$ in.	$\dfrac{4}{10}$ in.

a. What was the total snowfall for the months of January, February, and March for Spartanburg?

b. How much more snow did Amarillo get than Portland in the month of March?

Section 3.2

21. List four multiples for each number.

a. 7   **b.** 13   **c.** 22

22. Explain the difference between a common multiple and the *least* common multiple of a pair of numbers. Use the numbers 6 and 8 in your explanation.

23. List the factors for each number.

a. 100   **b.** 65   **c.** 70

24. Find the prime factorization.

a. 100   **b.** 65   **c.** 70

For Exercises 25–28, find the LCM by using any method.

25. 30 and 25

26. 22 and 144

27. 105 and 28

28. 16, 24, and 32

29. Sharon and Tonya signed up at a gym on the same day. Sharon will be able to go to the gym every third day and Tonya will go to the gym every fourth day. In how many days will they meet again at the gym?

For Exercises 30–31, rewrite each fraction with the indicated denominator.

30. $\dfrac{5}{16} = \dfrac{}{48}$

31. $\dfrac{9}{5} = \dfrac{}{35}$

For Exercises 32–34, fill in the blanks with $<$, $>$, or $=$.

32. $\dfrac{11}{24} \, \square \, \dfrac{7}{12}$

33. $\dfrac{5}{6} \, \square \, \dfrac{7}{9}$

34. $\dfrac{5}{6} \, \square \, \dfrac{15}{18}$

35. Rank the following numbers from least to greatest: $\dfrac{7}{10}, \dfrac{72}{105}, \dfrac{8}{15}, \dfrac{27}{35}$

Section 3.3

For Exercises 36–46, add or subtract. Write the answer as a fraction simplified to lowest terms.

36. $\dfrac{1}{8} + \dfrac{7}{12}$

37. $\dfrac{9}{10} - \dfrac{61}{100}$

38. $\dfrac{11}{25} - \dfrac{2}{5}$

39. $\dfrac{3}{26} + \dfrac{5}{13}$

40. $\dfrac{25}{11} + 2$

41. $4 - \dfrac{37}{20}$

42. $\dfrac{4}{15} - \dfrac{0}{3}$

43. $\dfrac{0}{17} + \dfrac{1}{34}$

44. $\dfrac{7}{100} - \dfrac{33}{1000}$

45. $\dfrac{2}{15} + \dfrac{5}{8} - \dfrac{1}{3}$

46. $\dfrac{11}{14} - \dfrac{4}{7} + \dfrac{3}{2}$

For Exercises 47–48, simplify by applying the order of operations.

47. $\left(\dfrac{2}{5} + \dfrac{1}{40}\right) \div \dfrac{15}{8} - \dfrac{4}{25}$

48. $\dfrac{20}{7} \cdot \left(\dfrac{11}{15} - \dfrac{1}{3}\right)^2 + \dfrac{1}{7}$

For Exercises 49–50, find (a) the perimeter and (b) the area.

49.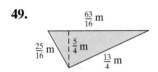

50.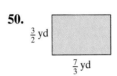

Section 3.4

For Exercises 51–62, add or subtract the mixed numbers.

51. $9\dfrac{8}{9}$
$+ 1\dfrac{2}{7}$

52. $10\dfrac{1}{2}$
$+ 3\dfrac{15}{16}$

53. $7\dfrac{5}{24}$
$- 4\dfrac{7}{12}$

54. $5\dfrac{1}{6}$
$- 3\dfrac{1}{4}$

55. $5\dfrac{3}{8}$
$- 2\dfrac{1}{3}$

56. $3\dfrac{4}{5}$
$- 1\dfrac{4}{15}$

57. $6\dfrac{4}{7}$
$+ 5\dfrac{11}{14}$

58. $3\dfrac{3}{8}$
$+ 2\dfrac{13}{16}$

59. 6
$- 2\dfrac{3}{5}$

60. 8
$- 4\dfrac{11}{14}$

61. $42\dfrac{1}{8}$
$+ 21\dfrac{13}{16}$

62. $38\dfrac{9}{10}$
$+ 11\dfrac{3}{5}$

For Exercises 63–66, round the numbers to estimate the answer. Then find the exact sum or difference.

63. $2\dfrac{1}{4} + 4\dfrac{2}{9} + 1\dfrac{29}{36}$

Estimate: _____

Exact: _____

64. $5\dfrac{2}{5} + 1\dfrac{9}{10} + 3\dfrac{19}{30}$

Estimate: _____

Exact: _____

65. $65\dfrac{1}{8} - 14\dfrac{9}{10}$

Estimate: _____

Exact: _____

66. $43\dfrac{13}{15} - 20\dfrac{23}{25}$

Estimate: _____

Exact: _____

67. Corry drove for $4\dfrac{1}{2}$ hr in the morning and $3\dfrac{2}{3}$ hr in the afternoon. Find the total number of hours he drove.

68. Denise owned $2\dfrac{1}{8}$ acres of land. If she sells $1\dfrac{1}{4}$ acres, how much will she have left?

Section 3.5

For Exercises 69–74, simplify by using the order of operations. Write the answer as a mixed number, if possible.

69. $1\dfrac{1}{5} + 4\dfrac{9}{10} \cdot 2\dfrac{2}{7}$

70. $5\dfrac{3}{4} - 23\dfrac{1}{2} \div 5\dfrac{2}{9}$

71. $\left(8\dfrac{1}{9} - 6\dfrac{2}{3}\right) \div 9\dfrac{3}{4}$

72. $\left(5\dfrac{1}{8} + 1\dfrac{1}{16}\right) \cdot 2\dfrac{10}{11}$

73. $\left(1\dfrac{1}{5}\right)^2 \cdot \left(4\dfrac{1}{2} + 3\dfrac{5}{6}\right)$

74. $\left(1\dfrac{5}{16}\right) \div \left(11\dfrac{1}{8} - 10\dfrac{3}{4}\right)^2$

75. In a certain region, the appraised value of a house is $\dfrac{9}{10}$ of its market value. If the market value of Owen's house is $160,000, what is the appraised value?

76. Nuts 'N Things makes a nut mixture from $2\dfrac{1}{4}$ lb of cashews, $7\dfrac{3}{4}$ lb of peanuts, and $2\dfrac{1}{2}$ lb of pecans. The mixture is then divided into 10 bags. How many pounds are in each bag?

chapter 3 | test

For Exercises 1–2, add or subtract the like fractions.

1. $\dfrac{4}{5} + \dfrac{3}{5}$

2. $\dfrac{23}{16} - \dfrac{15}{16}$

3. Explain the difference between evaluating these two expressions:

$$\dfrac{5}{11} - \dfrac{3}{11} \quad \text{and} \quad \dfrac{5}{11} \times \dfrac{3}{11}$$

4. a. List four multiples of 24.

    b. List all factors of 24.

    c. Write the prime factorization of 24.

5. Find the LCM for the numbers 16, 24, and 30.

For Exercises 6–8, write each fraction with the indicated denominator.

6. $\dfrac{5}{9} = \dfrac{}{63}$

7. $\dfrac{11}{21} = \dfrac{}{63}$

8. $\dfrac{4}{7} = \dfrac{}{63}$

9. Rank the fractions in Exercises 6–8 from least to greatest.

For Exercises 10–13, add or subtract as indicated. Write the answer as a fraction.

10. $\dfrac{3}{8} + \dfrac{3}{16}$

11. $\dfrac{7}{3} - \dfrac{14}{27}$

12. $\dfrac{7}{12} - \dfrac{1}{4}$

13. $\dfrac{3}{5} + \dfrac{1}{15}$

For Exercises 14–17, add or subtract the mixed numbers. Write the answer as a mixed number.

14. $6\dfrac{3}{4} + 10\dfrac{5}{8}$

15. $12\dfrac{6}{11} - 9\dfrac{10}{11}$

16. $22\dfrac{1}{4} + 35\dfrac{1}{2} + 2\dfrac{2}{3}$

17. $15\dfrac{1}{6} - 12\dfrac{3}{8} - 1\dfrac{7}{24}$

For Exercises 18–21, perform the indicated operations.

18. $4\dfrac{5}{8} \cdot 2\dfrac{2}{3} - 8\dfrac{1}{6}$

19. $3\dfrac{1}{3} \div 2\dfrac{1}{2} + 5\dfrac{2}{3}$

20. $\left(\dfrac{2}{5}\right)^2 \div \left(1\dfrac{1}{10} + 2\dfrac{5}{6}\right)$ **21.** $\left(7\dfrac{1}{4} - 5\dfrac{1}{6}\right) \cdot 1\dfrac{3}{5}$

22. A fudge recipe calls for $1\dfrac{1}{2}$ lb of chocolate. How many pounds are required for $\dfrac{2}{3}$ of the recipe?

23. The towing capacity of the 2004 Ford Expedition is $4\dfrac{19}{40}$ times that of the 2004 Buick Rendezvous. If the Rendezvous can tow 1 ton (2000 lb), what is the towing capacity of the Expedition (in pounds)?

24. Find the area and perimeter of this parking area.

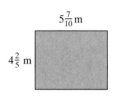

25. Justin has a budget of $14,000 to redecorate his kitchen. If he spends $\dfrac{3}{28}$ of the money on a stove and $\dfrac{1}{7}$ on a refrigerator, how much is left for new cabinets?

26. The figure gives the national records for long jump and high jump for men's and women's indoor track and field according to the International Association of Athletics Federation.

    a. What is the difference for the record long jump between men and women?

    b. What is the average height for high jump for men and women?

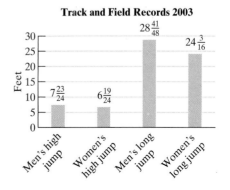

chapters 1–3 | cumulative review

1. Write the number in words: 23,400,806

2. Find the sum of 72 and 24.

3. Find the difference of 72 and 24.

4. Find the product of 72 and 24.

5. Find the quotient of 72 and 24.

6. Round the numbers to the ten-thousands place to estimate the product: $54{,}923 \times 28{,}543$.

7. Write the expression by using exponents:
$4 \cdot 4 \cdot 5 \cdot 5 \cdot 5 \cdot 5 \cdot 8 \cdot 8$

8. $72 \div (4^2 - 10) \cdot 3$

9. List all the prime numbers between 15 and 35.

10. Write the prime factorization of 70.

11. Label the numerator and denominator of the fraction $\frac{21}{17}$.

12. What fraction is represented by the figure?

13. Kevin delivered 22 pizzas one evening. Of the 22 pizzas, 17 had pepperoni. What fraction of the pizzas had pepperoni? What fraction did not have pepperoni?

14. Label the fractions as proper or improper.

a. $\frac{13}{5}$ **b.** $\frac{5}{13}$ **c.** $\frac{13}{13}$

15. Which of the numbers is divisible by 3 and 5?

a. 2390   **b.** 1245   **c.** 9321

16. Label the numbers as prime, composite, or neither.

a. 51   **b.** 52   **c.** 53

17. Find the prime factorization of 360.

18. Simplify the fraction to lowest terms: $\dfrac{180}{900}$

19. Multiply: $\dfrac{15}{16} \cdot \dfrac{2}{5}$

20. Divide: $\dfrac{20}{63} \div \dfrac{5}{9}$

21. Subtract: $\dfrac{13}{8} - \dfrac{7}{8}$

22. Add: $\dfrac{3}{16} + \dfrac{5}{16} + \dfrac{25}{16}$

23. Subtract: $4 - \dfrac{18}{5}$

24. Multiply: $6\dfrac{1}{10} \cdot 2\dfrac{3}{11}$

25. Divide: $2\dfrac{3}{5} \div 1\dfrac{7}{10}$

26. Simplify the expression.

$\left(8\dfrac{1}{4} \div 2\dfrac{3}{4}\right)^2 \cdot \dfrac{5}{18} + \dfrac{5}{6}$

27. To approximate the distance around a circle, multiply the diameter by the fraction $\frac{22}{7}$. Find the distance around a circle with diameter 28 cm.

28. Find the perimeter of the triangle.

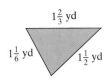

$1\frac{2}{3}$ yd

$1\frac{1}{6}$ yd $1\frac{1}{2}$ yd

29. Find the area of the triangle.

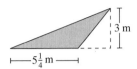

3 m

$5\frac{1}{4}$ m

30. The figure gives the earthquake intensity measured on the Richter scale for four major earthquakes in 2002 and 2003.

Major Earthquakes 2002–2003

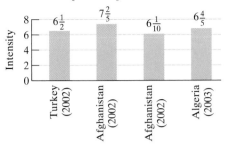

a. What was the difference in intensity between the two earthquakes that took place in Afghanistan?

b. What is the average intensity of these earthquakes?

example 4   Multiplying Decimals by Powers of 10

Multiply.

a. $14.78 \times 10{,}000$ **b.** 0.0064×100 **c.** $8.271 \times 1{,}000{,}000$

Solution:

a. $14.78 \times 10{,}000 = 147{,}800$ Move the decimal point 4 places to the right.

b. $0.0064 \times 100 = 0.64$ Move the decimal point 2 places to the right.

c. $8.271 \times 1{,}000{,}000 = 8{,}271{,}000$ Move the decimal point 6 places to the right.

Skill Practice

Multiply.

9. 81.6×1000

10. $0.0000085 \times 10{,}000$

11. $2.396 \times 10{,}000{,}000$

Multiplying a decimal by 10, 100, 1000, and so on increases its value. Therefore, it makes sense to move the decimal point to the *right*. Now suppose we multiply a decimal by 0.1, 0.01, and 0.0001. These numbers represent the decimal fractions $\frac{1}{10}$, $\frac{1}{100}$, and $\frac{1}{1000}$, respectively, and are easily recognized as powers of 0.1 (see Section 2.4). Taking one-tenth of a number or one-hundredth of a number makes the number smaller. To multiply by 0.1, 0.01, 0.001, and so on (powers of 0.1), move the decimal point to the *left*.

$$\begin{array}{ccc} 3.6 & 3.6 & 3.6 \\ \times\ 0.1 & \times\ 0.01 & \times\ 0.001 \\ \hline .36 & .036 & .0036 \end{array}$$

Multiplying a Decimal by Powers of 0.1

Move the decimal point to the left the same number of places as there are decimal places in the power of 0.1.

Note: In this case, we move the decimal point the total number of decimal places in the power of 0.1, *not* the number of zeros. For example, when we multiply by 0.01, move the decimal point 2 places to the left.

Concept Connections

12. Explain the difference between multiplying a number by 100 versus 0.01.

example 5   Multiplying by Powers of 0.1

Multiply.

a. 62.074×0.0001 **b.** 7965.3×0.1 **c.** 0.0057×0.00001

Solution:

a. $62.074 \times 0.0001 = 0.0062047$ Move the decimal point 4 places to the left. Insert extra zeros.

b. $7965.3 \times 0.1 = 796.53$ Move the decimal point 1 place to the left.

c. $0.0057 \times 0.00001 = 0.000000057$ Move the decimal point 5 places to the left.

Skill Practice

Multiply.

13. 471.034×0.01

14. $9{,}437{,}214.5 \times 0.00001$

15. 0.0004×0.001

Answers

9. 81,600 **10.** 0.085 **11.** 23,960,000
12. Multiplying a number by 100 increases its value. Therefore, we move the decimal point to the right two places. Multiplying a number by 0.01 decreases its value. Therefore, move the decimal point to the left two places.
13. 4.71034 **14.** 94.372145
15. 0.0000004

3. Naming Large Numbers

Sometimes people prefer to use number names to express very large numbers. For example, we might say that the U.S. population in 2004 was approximately 280 million. To write this in decimal form, we note that 1 million = 1,000,000. In this case, we have 280 of this quantity. Thus,

$$280 \text{ million} = 280 \times 1{,}000{,}000 \text{ or } 280{,}000{,}000$$

example 6   Naming Large Numbers

Write the decimal number representing each word name.

a. The distance between the Earth and the Sun is approximately 92.9 million mi.

b. The number of deaths in the United States due to heart disease in 2000 was approximately 7 hundred thousand.

c. The number of barrels of crude oil and natural gas reserves in the United States in 2001 was estimated to be 22.4 billion.

Solution:

a. 92.9 million = $92.9 \times 1{,}000{,}000 = 92{,}900{,}000$

b. 7 hundred thousand = $7 \times 100{,}000 = 700{,}000$

c. 22.4 billion = $22.4 \times 1{,}000{,}000{,}000 = 22{,}400{,}000{,}000$

4. Converting Dollars and Cents

The value $1.14 can be interpreted as $1 + 14¢. But since $1 = 100¢, then

$$\$1.14 = 100¢ + 14¢ = 114¢$$

From this discussion we have the following rule to convert dollars to cents.

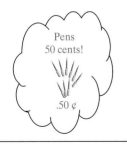
Converting Dollars to Cents

To convert dollars to cents:

1. Multiply by 100. This has the effect of moving the decimal point to the *right* two places.

2. Drop the $ symbol and attach the ¢ symbol to the result.

To convert from cents to dollars, we reverse the process. That is, 114¢ = $1.14. The decimal point is moved to the *left*.

Converting Cents to Dollars

To convert cents to dollars:

1. Multiply by 0.01. This has the effect of moving the decimal point to the *left* two places.

2. Drop the ¢ symbol and place the $ symbol in front of the result.

example 7	Converting Dollars and Cents

a. Convert \$6.82 to cents.   **b.** Convert 92¢ to dollars.

Solution:

a. \$6.82 = 682¢   Move the decimal point 2 places to the *right*.

b. 92¢ = \$0.92   Move the decimal point 2 places to the *left*.

5. Applications Involving Multiplication of Decimals

example 8	Applying Decimal Multiplication

Jane Marie bought 8 cans of tennis balls for \$1.98 each. She paid \$1.03 in tax. What was the total bill?

Solution:

The cost of the tennis balls before tax is

$$8(\$1.98) = \$15.84$$

$$\begin{array}{r} {}^{7\ 6}1.98 \\ \times\ \ \ 8 \\ \hline 15.84 \end{array}$$

Adding the tax to this value, we have

$$\begin{pmatrix} \text{Total} \\ \text{cost} \end{pmatrix} = \begin{pmatrix} \text{Cost of} \\ \text{tennis balls} \end{pmatrix} + (\text{Tax})$$

$$\begin{array}{r} = \$15.84 \\ +\ 1.03 \\ \hline \$16.87 \end{array}$$ The total cost is \$16.87.

6. Finding Area

example 9	Finding the Area of a Rectangle

The *Mona Lisa* is perhaps the most famous painting in the world. It was painted by Leonardo da Vinci somewhere between 1503 and 1506 and now hangs in the Louvre in Paris, France. The dimensions of the painting are 30 in. by 20.875 in. (Figure 4-4). What is the total area?

20.875 in.

30 in.

Figure 4-4

Solution:

Recall that the area of a rectangle is given by

$$A = \ell \cdot w$$

$$A = (30 \text{ in.})(20.875 \text{ in.})$$

$$
\begin{array}{r}
20.875 \\
\times\ 30 \\
\hline
0 \\
626250 \\
\hline
626.250 \\
\end{array}
$$

$$= 626.25 \text{ in.}^2$$

The area of the *Mona Lisa* is 626.25 in.^{2}

---

section 4.3   Practice Exercises

Study Skills Exercises

1. Look through pages 266 to 273 in your text. Write down a page number that contains

   a. Avoiding mistakes _____

   b. TIP box _____

   c. A key term (shown in bold) _____

2. Define the key term **front-end rounding**.

Review Exercises

For Exercises 3–6, expand the powers of 10 and 0.1.

   3. 10^3 **4.** 0.1^3 **5.** 0.1^2 **6.** 10^2

Objecitve 1: Multiplication of Decimals

For Exercises 7–16, round each number by using front-end rounding.

   7. 135   **8.** 481   **9.** 28   **10.** 52

   11. 6721   **12.** 8207   **13.** 0.241   **14.** 0.339

   15. 0.041   **16.** 0.056

For Exercises 17–26, multiply the decimals.

17. 0.8
     × 0.5

18. 0.6
     × 0.5

19. (0.9)(4)

20. (0.2)(9)

21. 0.4
     × 20

22. 0.9
     × 30

23. (60)(0.003)

24. (40)(0.005)

25. 22
     × 0.8

26. 31
     × 0.4

For Exercises 27–40, multiply the decimals. Then estimate the answer by using front-end rounding. **(See Examples 1–3.)**

| Exact | Estimate | | Exact | Estimate |

27. 8.3   8
     × 4.5   × 5
               ——
                40

28. 4.3
     × 9.2

29. 0.58
     × 7.2

30. 0.83
     × 6.5

31. 5.92 × 0.8

32. 9.14 × 0.6

33. (0.413)(7)

34. (0.321)(6)

35. 35.9 × 3.2

36. 41.7 × 6.1

37. 562 × 0.004

38. 984 × 0.009

39. 0.0004 × 3.6

40. 0.0008 × 6.5

Objective 2: Multiplication by a Power of 10 and by a Power of 0.1

41. If 417.43 is multiplied by 100, will the decimal point move to the left or to the right? By how many places?

42. If 2498.613 is multiplied by 10,000, will the decimal point move to the left or to the right? By how many places?

43. Multiply the numbers.
   a. 5.1 × 10   **b.** 5.1 × 100   **c.** 5.1 × 1000   **d.** 5.1 × 10,000

For Exercises 44–49, multiply the numbers by the powers of 10. **(See Example 4.)**

44. 34.9×100 **45.** 2.163×100 **46.** 96.59×1000 **47.** 18.22×1000

48. 2.001×10 **49.** 5.932×10

50. If 256.8 is multiplied by 0.001, will the decimal point move to the left or to the right? By how many places?

51. If 0.45 is multiplied by 0.1, will the decimal point move to the left or to the right? By how many places?

52. Multiply the numbers.

    a. 5.1×0.1 **b.** 5.1×0.01 **c.** 5.1×0.001 **d.** 5.1×0.0001

For Exercises 53–58, multiply the numbers by the powers of 0.1. **(See Example 5.)**

53. 93.3×0.01 **54.** 80.2×0.01 **55.** 54.03×0.001 **56.** 23.11×0.001

57. 0.5×0.0001 **58.** 0.8×0.0001

Objective 3: Naming Large Numbers

For Exercises 59–64, write the decimal number representing each word name. **(See Example 6.)**

59. The number of cattle in the United States is 96.7 million.

60. There are 42.515 million tons of yams produced in the United States.

61. About 16 thousand patents were granted in Spain during a recent year.

62. The musical *Miss Saigon* ran for about 4 thousand performances in a 10-year period.

63. The people in the United States have spent over $20.549 billion on DVDs.

64. The Bible is the highest-selling book of all time with over $6 billion in sales.

Objective 4: Converting Dollars and Cents

For Exercises 65–70, write the amount in terms of cents. **(See Example 7.)**

65. $3.24 **66.** $21.56 **67.** $61.34

68. $3.12 **69.** $0.37 **70.** $0.75

For Exercises 71–76, write the amount in terms of dollars. **(See Example 7.)**

71. 347¢

72. 512¢

73. 2041¢

74. 5712¢

75. 34¢

76. 12¢

77. a. Round $1.499 to the nearest dollar.

    b. Round $1.499 to the nearest cent.

78. a. Round $20.599 to the nearest dollar.

    b. Round $20.599 to the nearest cent.

Objective 5: Applications Involving Multiplication of Decimals

79. Corrugated boxes for shipping cost $2.27 each. How much will 10 boxes cost including tax that amounts to $1.59? **(See Example 8.)**

80. A bag of potato chips contains 11.5 oz. How many ounces are in 4 bags of chips?

81. The Athletic Department at Illinois Central College bought 20 pizzas for $10.95 each, 10 Greek salads for $3.95 each, and 60 soft drinks for $0.60 each. What was the total bill excluding tax?

82. A hotel gift shop ordered 40 T-shirts at $8.69 each, 10 hats at $3.95 each, and 20 beach towels at $4.99 each. What was the total cost of the merchandise?

83. Firestone tires cost $50.20 each. A set of four Lemans tires costs $197.99. How much can a person save by buying the set of four Lemans tires compared to four Firestone tires?

84. Certain DVDs titles are on sale for 2 for $32. If they regularly sell for $19.99, how much can a person save by buying 4 DVDs?

Objective 6: Finding Area

For Exercises 85–86, find the area. **(See Example 9.)**

85.

0.05 km

0.023 km

86.

4.5 yd

6.7 yd

87. Blake plans to build a rectangular patio that is 15 ft by 22.2 ft. What is the total area of the patio?

88. The front page of a newspaper is 56 cm by 31.5 cm. Find the area of the page.

89. Compare the quantities $(0.2)^2$ and 0.4. Are they equal?

90. Compare the quantities $(0.5)^2$ and 2.5. Are they equal?

For Exercises 91–96, simplify the expressions.

91. $(0.4)^2$ **92.** $(0.7)^2$ **93.** $(1.3)^2$ **94.** $(2.4)^2$

95. $(0.1)^3$ **96.** $(0.2)^3$

Expanding Your Skills

97. Evaluate.

    a. $(0.3)^2$ **b.** $\sqrt{0.09}$

98. Evaluate.

    a. $(0.5)^2$ **b.** $\sqrt{0.25}$

For Exercises 99–102, evaluate the square roots.

99. $\sqrt{0.01}$ **100.** $\sqrt{0.04}$ **101.** $\sqrt{0.36}$ **102.** $\sqrt{0.49}$

Calculator Connections

Topic: Multiplying decimals

Calculator Exercises

For Exercises 103–104, use a calculator to evaluate each expression.

103. $(43.75)^2$ **104.** $(9.3)^5$

105. A Hummer H2 SUV uses 1260 gal of gas to travel 12,000 mi per year. A Honda Accord uses 375 gal of gas to go the same distance. If gasoline costs $2.25 per gallon, how much is saved per year by driving a Honda Accord rather than a Hummer?

106. The actual time required for the Earth to revolve about the Sun is 365.256 days. Use this number to explain why we have a leap year every 4 years. (A leap year is a year in which February has an extra day, February 29.)

107. A homeowner pays the following average monthly expenses. What are the total expenses for the year?

Item	Monthly Charge
Mortgage payments	$678.75
Electricity	95.83
Water and sewer	47.02
House insurance	66.65
Property taxes	124.40
Internet connection	29.95
Phone	24.99
Cable TV	65.49
Association fees	50.00

chapter 4 | midchapter review

For Exercises 1–12, add, subtract, or multiply as indicated.

1. $123.04 + 100$

2. 123.04×100

3. $123.04 - 100$

4. 123.04×0.01

5. $123.04 - 0.01$

6. $123.04 + 0.01$

7. $10.82 - 0.1$

8. $10.82 + 0.1$

9. 10.82×0.1

10. $10.82 + 10$

11. 10.82×10

12. $10.82 - 10$

13. a. Add $4.8 + 2.391$.

 b. Add $2.391 + 4.8$.

 c. Are the answers to parts (a) and (b) the same?

14. What is the name of the property used in Exercise 13?

15. a. Multiply 4.8×2.391.

 b. Multiply 2.391×4.8.

 c. Are the answers to parts (a) and (b) the same?

16. What is the name of the property used in Exercise 15?

For Exercises 17–22, perform the indicated operation.

17. 0.004×6.21

18. $1.2 + 83.11$

19. $4.6 - 0.0421$

20. 5.1×0.0241

21. $65.02 + 2.012$

22. $3.012 - 1.34$

Objectives

1. Division of Decimals
2. Rounding a Quotient
3. Dividing by a Power of 10 and by a Power of 0.1
4. Applications of Decimal Division

1. Division of Decimals

Dividing decimals is much the same as dividing whole numbers. However, we must determine where to place the decimal point in the quotient. The first case we show involves dividing a decimal by a whole number.

First consider the quotient $3.5 \div 7$. We can write the numbers in fractional form and then divide.

$$3.5 \div 7 = \frac{35}{10} \div \frac{7}{1} = \frac{35}{10} \cdot \frac{1}{7} = \frac{35}{10} \cdot \frac{1}{7} = \frac{35}{70} = \frac{5}{10} = 0.5$$

Now consider the same problem by using the efficient method of long division: $7\overline{)3.5}$.

When the divisor is a whole number, we place the decimal point directly above the decimal point in the dividend. Then we divide as we would whole numbers.

decimal point placed above
the decimal point in the dividend.

$$\begin{array}{r} .5 \\ 7\overline{)3.5} \end{array}$$

Concept Connections

1. Place the decimal point in the quotient.

   $8\overline{)116.32}$

Dividing a Decimal by a Whole Number

To divide by a whole number:

1. Place the decimal point in the quotient directly above the decimal point in the dividend.
2. Divide as you would whole numbers.

Skill Practice

Divide. Check by using multiplication.

2. $153.6 \div 6$
3. $502.96 \div 8$

example 1   Dividing by a Whole Number

Divide and check the answer by multiplying.

$$30.55 \div 13$$

Solution:

Locate the decimal point in the quotient.

$$13\overline{)30.55}$$

$$\begin{array}{r} 2.35 \\ 13\overline{)30.55} \\ -26 \\ \hline 45 \\ -39 \\ \hline 65 \\ -65 \\ \hline 0 \end{array}$$

Divide as you would whole numbers.

Check by multiplying:

$$\begin{array}{r} {\scriptstyle 1\ 1} \\ 2.35 \\ \times 13 \\ \hline 705 \\ 2350 \\ \hline 30.55 \checkmark \end{array}$$

Answers

1. $8\overline{)116.32}$ (with decimal point above)
2. 25.6
3. 62.87

When dividing decimals, we do not use a remainder. Instead we insert zeros to the right of the dividend and continue dividing. This is demonstrated in Example 2.

---

example 2   Dividing by a Whole Number

Divide and check the answer by multiplying.

  a. $3.5 \div 4$ **b.** $40\overline{)5}$

Solution:

             — Locate the decimal point in the quotient.

a. $4\overline{)3.5}$ (with decimal point above)

$$
\begin{array}{r}
.8 \\
4\overline{)3.5} \\
-32 \\
\hline
3
\end{array}
$$

← Rather than using a remainder, we insert zeros in the dividend and continue dividing.

$$
\begin{array}{r}
.875 \\
4\overline{)3.500} \\
-32 \\
\hline
30 \\
-28 \\
\hline
20 \\
-20 \\
\hline
0
\end{array}
$$

Check by multiplying:

$$
\begin{array}{r}
{}^{3\;2} \\
0.875 \\
\times\; 4 \\
\hline
3.500 \checkmark
\end{array}
$$

The quotient is 0.875.

b. $40\overline{)5.}$ ← The dividend is a whole number, and the decimal point is understood to be to its right. Insert the decimal point above it in the quotient.

$$
\begin{array}{r}
.125 \\
40\overline{)5.000} \\
-40 \\
\hline
100 \\
-80 \\
\hline
200 \\
-200 \\
\hline
0
\end{array}
$$

Since 40 is greater than 5, we need to insert zeros to the right of the dividend.

Check by multiplying.

$$
\begin{array}{r}
{}^{1\;2} \\
.125 \\
\times\; 40 \\
\hline
000 \\
5000 \\
\hline
5.000 \checkmark
\end{array}
$$

The quotient is 0.125.

Sometimes when dividing decimals, the quotient follows a repeated pattern. The result is called a **repeating decimal**.

Skill Practice

Divide.

4. $6.8 \div 5$

5. $20\overline{)3}$

6. $87.5 \div 14$

Answers
4. 1.36
5. 0.15
6. 6.25

Skill Practice

Divide.

7. $2.4 \div 9$

8. $57 \div 11$

example 3   Dividing Where the Quotient Is a Repeating Decimal

Divide.

a. $1.7 \div 30$ **b.** $11\overline{)68}$

Solution:

$$.05666\ldots$$

$$
\begin{array}{r}
200 \\
-180 \\
\hline
200 \\
-180 \\
\hline
200
\end{array}
$$

Notice that as we continue to divide, we get the same values for each successive step. This causes a pattern of repeated digits in the quotient. Therefore, the quotient is a repeating decimal.

The quotient is $0.05666\ldots$. To denote the repeated pattern, we often use a bar over the first occurrence of the repeat cycle to the right of the decimal point. That is,

$$0.05666\ldots = 0.05\overline{6} \longleftarrow \text{repeat bar}$$

Avoiding Mistakes: In Example 3(a), notice that the repeat bar goes over only the 6. The 5 is not being repeated.

b.
$$
\begin{array}{r}
6.1818\ldots \\
11\overline{)68.0000} \\
-66 \\
\hline
20 \\
-11 \\
\hline
90 \\
-88 \\
\hline
20 \\
-11 \\
\hline
90 \\
-88 \\
\hline
20
\end{array}
$$

Could have stopped here

Once again, we see a repeated pattern. The quotient is a repeating decimal. Notice that we could have stopped dividing when we obtained the second value of 20.

Avoiding Mistakes: Be sure to put the repeating bar over the entire block of numbers that is being repeated. In Example 3(b), the bar extends over both the 1 and the 8. We have $6.\overline{18}$.

The quotient is $6.\overline{18}$.

Concept Connections

Identify the number as a terminating or repeating decimal.

9. 4.6666666   **10.** $4.\overline{6}$

11. $9.5\overline{37}$

12. 16.417417417

The numbers $0.05\overline{6}$ and $6.\overline{18}$ are examples of repeating decimals. A decimal that "stops" is called a **terminating decimal**. For example, 6.18 is a terminating decimal, whereas $6.\overline{18}$ is a repeating decimal.

In Examples 1–3, we performed division where the divisor was a whole number. Suppose now that we have a divisor that is *not* a whole number, for example, $0.56 \div 0.7$. Because division can also be expressed in fraction notation, we have

$$0.56 \div 0.7 = \frac{0.56}{0.7}$$

If we multiply numerator and denominator by 10, the denominator (divisor) becomes the whole number 7.

$$\frac{0.56}{0.7} = \frac{0.56 \times 10}{0.7 \times 10} = \frac{5.6}{7} \longrightarrow 7\overline{)5.6}$$

Answers

7. $0.2\overline{6}$ 8. $5.\overline{18}$
9. Terminating   10. Repeating
11. Repeating   12. Terminating

Recall that multiplying decimal numbers by 10 (or any power of 10, such as 100, 1000, etc.) has the effect of moving the decimal point to the right. We use this premise to divide decimal numbers when the divisor is not a whole number. This process is summarized as follows.

Dividing When the Divisor Is Not a Whole Number

1. Move the decimal point in the divisor to the right to make it a whole number.
2. Move the decimal point in the dividend to the right the same number of places as in step 1.
3. Place the decimal point in the quotient directly above the decimal point in the dividend.
4. Divide as you would whole numbers.

---

example 4   Dividing Decimals

Divide.

a. $0.56 \div 0.7$ **b.** $0.005\overline{)3.1}$ **c.** $50 \div 1.1$

Solution:

a. $.7\overline{).56}$ Move the decimal point in the divisor and dividend 1 place to the right.

$7\overline{)5.6}$ ← Line up the decimal point in the quotient.

$$
\begin{array}{r}
0.8 \\
7\overline{)5.6} \\
-5\,6 \\
\hline
0
\end{array}
$$

The quotient is 0.8.

b. $.005\overline{)3.100}$ Move the decimal point in the divisor and dividend 3 places to the right. Insert additional zeros in the dividend if necessary. Line up the decimal point in the quotient.

$$
\begin{array}{r}
620. \\
5\overline{)3100.} \\
-30 \\
\hline
10 \\
-10 \\
\hline
00
\end{array}
$$

The quotient is 620.

c. $1.1\overline{)50.0}$ Move the decimal point in the divisor and dividend 1 place to the right. Insert an additional zero in the dividend. Line up the decimal point in the quotient.

$$
\begin{array}{r}
45.45\ldots \\
11\overline{)500.000} \\
-44
\end{array}
$$

The quotient is a repeating decimal. Notice that the repeat cycle actually begins to the left of the decimal point. However, the repeat bar is placed on the first repeated

$$
\begin{array}{r}
-44 \\
\hline
60 \\
-55 \\
\hline
50
\end{array}
$$

The quotient is $45.\overline{45}$.

> **Avoiding Mistakes:** The repeat bar is never written over the whole-number part of a quotient.

2. Rounding a Quotient

In Example 4(c) we found that $50 \div 1.1 = 45.\overline{45}$. To check this result, we could multiply $45.\overline{45} \times 1.1$ and show that the product equals 50. However, at this point we do not have the tools to multiply repeating decimals. What we can do is round the quotient and then multiply to see if the product is *close* to 50.

example 5   Rounding a Repeating Decimal

Round $45.\overline{45}$ to the hundredths place. Then use the rounded value to estimate whether the product $45.\overline{45} \times 1.1$ is close to 50. (This will serve as a check to the division problem in Example 4(c).)

Solution:

To round the number $45.\overline{45}$, we must write out enough of the repeated pattern so that we can view the digit to the right of the rounding place. In this case, we must write out the number to the thousandths place.

$$45.\overline{45} = 45.454\cdots \approx 45.45$$

hundredths place   This digit is less than 5. Discard it and all others to its right.

Now multiply the rounded value by 1.1.

$$
\begin{array}{r}
45.45 \\
\times\ 1.1 \\
\hline
4545 \\
45450 \\
\hline
49.995
\end{array}
$$

This value is close to 50. We are reasonably sure that we divided correctly in Example 4(c).

Sometimes we may want to round a quotient to a given place value. To do so, divide until you get a digit in the quotient one place value to the right of the rounding place. At this point, you may stop dividing and round the quotient.

example 6   Rounding a Quotient

Round the quotient to the tenths place.

$$47.3 \div 5.4$$

Solution:

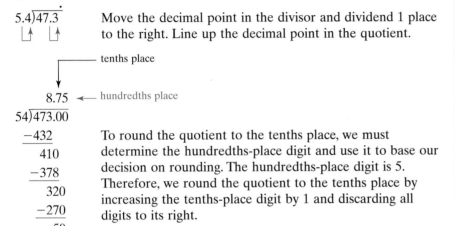

$5.4\overline{)47.3}$ Move the decimal point in the divisor and dividend 1 place to the right. Line up the decimal point in the quotient.

tenths place

8.75 ← hundredths place
$54\overline{)473.00}$
$\underline{-432}$
410
$\underline{-378}$
320
$\underline{-270}$
50

To round the quotient to the tenths place, we must determine the hundredths-place digit and use it to base our decision on rounding. The hundredths-place digit is 5. Therefore, we round the quotient to the tenths place by increasing the tenths-place digit by 1 and discarding all digits to its right.

The quotient is approximately 8.8.

Calculator Connections

Repeating decimals displayed on a calculator are rounded. This is so because the display cannot show an infinite number of digits.

On a scientific calculator, the repeating decimal $45.\overline{45}$ might appear as

$$45.45454545$$

3. Dividing by a Power of 10 and by a Power of 0.1

When we multiplied a number by 10, 100, 1000, and so on, we moved the decimal point to the right. However, dividing a number by 10, 100, or 1000 decreases its value. Therefore, we move the decimal point to the *left*.

For example, suppose 3.6 is divided by 10, 100, and 1000.

$$
\begin{array}{ccc}
.36 & .036 & .0036 \\
10\overline{)3.60} & 100\overline{)3.600} & 1000\overline{)3.6000} \\
-30 & -300 & -3000 \\
\hline
60 & 600 & 6000 \\
-60 & -600 & -6000 \\
\hline
0 & 0 & 0
\end{array}
$$

Dividing by a Power of 10

To divide a number by a power of 10, move the decimal point to the *left* the same number of places as there are zeros in the power of 10.

Answers
18. 8.37
19. 76.4

example 7   Dividing by a Power of 10

Divide.

a. $214.3 \div 10{,}000$ **b.** $0.03 \div 100$

Solution:

Insert two additional zeros.

■

To divide a number by 0.1, 0.01, 0.001, and so on, we are dividing by the fractions $\frac{1}{10}$, $\frac{1}{100}$, $\frac{1}{1000}$, etc. But dividing by these fractions is the same as multiplying by their reciprocals. Multiplying a number by 10, 100, and 1000 increases its value, and we must move the decimal point to the *right*.

$$4 \div 0.1 \quad = 4 \div \frac{1}{10} = \frac{4}{1} \cdot \frac{10}{1} = 40$$

$$4 \div 0.01 \quad = 4 \div \frac{1}{100} = \frac{4}{1} \cdot \frac{100}{1} = 400$$

$$4 \div 0.001 = 4 \div \frac{1}{1000} = \frac{4}{1} \cdot \frac{1000}{1} = 4000$$

From this discussion, we have the following rule.

Dividing by a Power of 0.1

To divide a number by a power of 0.1, move the decimal point to the *right* the same number of places as there are decimal places in the power of 0.1.

example 8   Dividing by a Power of 0.1

Divide.

a. $316.24 \div 0.01$ **b.** $0.0057 \div 0.00001$

Solution:

a. $316.24 \div 0.01 = 31{,}624$ Move the decimal point 2 places to the right.

b. $0.00570 \div 0.00001 = 570$ Move the decimal point 5 places to the right.
Insert an extra zero to the right of 0.0057.

■

4. Applications of Decimal Division

Examples 9 and 10 show how decimal division can be used in applications. Remember that division is used when we need to distribute a quantity into equal parts.

example 9   Applying Division of Decimals

A dinner costs $45.80, and the bill is to be split equally among 5 people. How much must each person pay?

Solution:

We want to distribute $45.80 equally among 5 people, so we must divide $45.80 ÷ 5.

```
      9.16
  5)45.80        Each person must pay $9.16.
   −45
    08
    −5
    30
   −30
     0
```

Division is also used in practical applications to express rates. In Example 10, we find the rate of speed in meters per second (m/sec) for the world record time in the men's 400-m run.

example 10   Using Division to Find a Rate of Speed

For a recent year, the world record time in the men's 400-m run was 43.2 sec. What is the speed in meters per second? Round to one decimal place.

Solution:

To find the rate of speed in meters per second, we must divide the distance in meters by the time in seconds.

```
43.2)400.0
```

```
                    ┌── tenths place
      9.25 ◄── hundredths place
  432)4000.00
   −3888
    1120
    −864
    2560
   −2160
     400
```

To round the quotient to the tenths place, determine the hundredths-place digit and use it to make the decision on rounding. The hundredths-place digit is 5, which is 5 or greater. Therefore, add 1 to the tenths-place digit and discard all digits to its right.

The speed is approximately 9.3 m/sec.

Skill Practice

24. A 46.5-ft cable is to be cut into 6 pieces of equal length. How long is each piece?

25. For a recent year Florence Griffith-Joyner ran a world-record time of 21.3 sec in the women's 200-m run. Find the speed in meters per second. Round to the nearest tenth.

Tip: In Example 10, we had to find speed in meters per second. The units of measurement required in the answer give a hint as to the order of the division. The word *per* implies division. So to obtain meters *per* second implies 400 m ÷ 43.2 sec.

Answers

24. Each piece is 7.75 ft.
25. The speed was 9.4 m/sec.

section 4.4   Practice Exercises

discussing the material that was covered in class. Write the names of two fellow students.

2. Define the key terms.

   a. Repeating decimal   **b. Terminating decimal**

Review Exercises

For Exercises 3–8, perform the indicated operation.

  3. 5.28×1000 **4.** $8.003 - 2.2$ **5.** 11.8×0.32

  6. $102.4 + 1.239$ **7.** $16.82 - 14.8$ **8.** 5.28×0.001

Objective 1: Division of Decimals

For Exercises 9–16, divide. Check the answer by using multiplication. **(See Example 1.)**

  9. $8.1 \div 9$ Check: _____ $\times 9 = 8.1$ **10.** $4.8 \div 6$ Check: _____ $\times 6 = 4.8$

  11. $6\overline{)1.08}$ Check: _____ $\times 6 = 1.08$ **12.** $4\overline{)2.08}$ Check: _____ $\times 4 = 2.08$

  13. $4.24 \div 8$ **14.** $5.75 \div 25$ **15.** $5\overline{)105.5}$ **16.** $7\overline{)221.2}$

For Exercises 17–40, divide. Write the quotient in decimal form. **(See Examples 2–4.)**

  17. $5\overline{)9.8}$ **18.** $30\overline{)2.07}$ **19.** $30.6 \div 12$ **20.** $16.5 \div 6$

  21. $0.28 \div 8$ **22.** $0.35 \div 4$ **23.** $5\overline{)84.2}$ **24.** $2\overline{)89.1}$

  25. $16 \div 3$ **26.** $52 \div 9$ **27.** $19 \div 6$ **28.** $9.1 \div 3$

  29. $33\overline{)71}$ **30.** $11\overline{)42}$ **31.** $11\overline{)28}$ **32.** $33\overline{)202}$

33. $57.12 \div 1.02$ **34.** $95.89 \div 2.23$ **35.** $2.38 \div 0.8$ **36.** $5.51 \div 0.2$

37. $0.3\overline{)62.5}$ **38.** $1.05\overline{)22.4}$ **39.** $6.305 \div 0.13$ **40.** $42.9 \div 0.25$

Objective 2: Rounding a Quotient

41. Round $2.\overline{4}$ to the
  a. Tenths place
  b. Hundredths place
  c. Thousandths place
  (See Example 5.)

42. Round $5.\overline{2}$ to the
  a. Tenths place
  b. Hundredths place
  c. Thousandths place

43. Round $1.\overline{8}$ to the
  a. Tenths place
  b. Hundredths place
  c. Thousandths place

44. Round $4.\overline{7}$ to the
  a. Tenths place
  b. Hundredths place
  c. Thousandths place

45. Round $3.\overline{62}$ to the
  a. Tenths place
  b. Hundredths place
  c. Thousandths place

46. Round $9.\overline{38}$ to the
  a. Tenths place
  b. Hundredths place
  c. Thousandths place

For Exercises 47–54, divide. Round the answer to the indicated place value. Use the rounded quotient to check. **(See Example 6.)**

47. $7\overline{)1.8}$ hundredths   **48.** $2.1\overline{)75.3}$ hundredths   **49.** $54.9 \div 3.7$ tenths

50. $94.3 \div 21$ tenths   **51.** $0.24\overline{)4.96}$ thousandths   **52.** $2.46\overline{)27.88}$ thousandths

53. $0.9\overline{)32.1}$ hundredths   **54.** $0.6\overline{)81.4}$ hundredths

Objective 3: Dividing by a Power of 10 and by a Power of 0.1

55. If 45.62 is divided by 100, will the decimal point move to the right or to the left? By how many places?

56. If 5689.233 is divided by 100,000, will the decimal point move to the right or to the left? By how many places?

For Exercises 57–64, divide by the powers of 10. **(See Example 7.)**

57. $3.923 \div 100$ **58.** $5.32 \div 100$ **59.** $98.02 \div 10$ **60.** $11.033 \div 10$

61. $0.027 \div 100$ **62.** $0.665 \div 100$ **63.** $1.02 \div 1000$ **64.** $8.1 \div 1000$

65. If 82.5 is divided by 0.1, will the decimal point move to the right or to the left? By how many places?

66. If 89.4201 is divided by 0.001, will the decimal point move to the right or to the left? By how many places?

For Exercises 67–74, divide by the powers of 0.1. **(See Example 8.)**

Objective 4: Applications of Decimal Division

When multiplying or dividing decimals, it is important to place the decimal point correctly. For Exercises 75–78, determine whether you think the number is reasonable or unreasonable. If the number is unreasonable, move the decimal point to a position that makes more sense.

75. Steve computed the gas mileage for his Honda Civic to be 3.2 miles per gallon.

76. The sale price of a new refrigerator is $96.0.

77. Mickey makes $8.50 per hour. He estimates his weekly paycheck to be $3400.

78. Jason works in a legal office. He computes the average annual income for the attorneys in his office to be $1400 per year.

For Exercises 79–84, solve the application. Check to see if your answers are reasonable.

79. A membership at a health club costs $560 per year. The club has a payment plan in which a member can pay $50 down and the rest in 12 equal payments. How much is each payment? **(See Example 9.)**

80. Brooke owes $39,628.68 on the mortgage for her house. If her monthly payment is $695.24, how many months does she still need to pay? How many years is this?

81. It is reported that on average 42,000 tennis balls are used and 650 matches are played at the Wimbledon tennis tournament each year. On average, how many tennis balls are used per match? Round to the nearest whole unit.

82. A package of dental floss contains 100 yd of floss. If Patty uses floss once a day and it lasts for 230 days, approximately how long is each piece that she uses? Round the answer to the nearest tenth of a yard.

83. In baseball, the batting average is found by dividing the number of hits by the number of times a batter was at bat. Babe Ruth was at bat 8399 times and had 2873 hits. What was his batting average? Round to the thousandths place. **(See Example 10.)**

84. Ty Cobb was at bat 11,434 times and had 4189 hits, giving him the all time best batting average. Find his average. Round to the thousandths place. (Refer to Exercise 83.)

Expanding Your Skills

85. What number is halfway between 47.26 and 47.27?

86. What number is halfway between 22.4 and 22.5?

87. Which numbers when divided by 8.6 will produce a quotient less than 12.4? Circle all that apply.

    a. 111.8   **b.** 103.2   **c.** 107.5   **d.** 105.78

88. Which numbers when divided by 5.3 will produce a quotient greater than 15.8? Circle all that apply.

    a. 84.8   **b.** 84.27   **c.** 83.21   **d.** 79.5

Calculator Connections

Topic: Dividing decimals

To divide numbers on a calculator, use the $\div$ key.

Expression	Keystrokes	Result
$.024\overline{).0014064}$	.0014064 $\div$ .024 Enter	0.0586
$17 \div 3$	17 $\div$ 3 Enter	5.666666667

Note that the expression $17 \div 3$ results in the repeating decimal, $5.\overline{6}$. The calculator returns the value 5.666666667. This is not the exact value.

Calculator Exercises

89. A Chevy Blazer gets 16.5 mpg and a Toyota Corolla averages 36 mpg. Suppose a driver drives 12,000 mi/yr and the cost of gasoline is $2.25 per gallon. How much money would be saved by driving the Toyota Corolla rather than the Chevy Blazer? Round to the nearest dollar.

90. The estimated national debt for 2006 is $8,726,359 million (that is, roughly 8.7 trillion dollars). How much would each person have to pay if the national debt were divided evenly among the 298 million people living in the United States? Round to the nearest dollar.

91. Population *density* is defined to be the number of people per square mile of land area. If California has 41,373,000 people with a land area of 155,959 square miles (mi^2), what is the population density? Round to the nearest whole unit.

92. If Rhode Island has 1,158,000 people with a land area of 1045 mi^2, what is the population density? Round to the nearest whole unit.

Objectives

1. Writing Fractions as Decimals

section 4.5   Fractions as Decimals

1. Writing Fractions as Decimals

Concept Connections

1. Write the fraction $\frac{2}{5}$ with a denominator of 10. Then write the equivalent decimal form.

2. Write the fraction $\frac{7}{20}$ with a denominator of 100. Then write the equivalent decimal form.

$$\frac{3}{5} = \frac{3 \cdot 2}{5 \cdot 2} = \frac{6}{10} = 0.6$$

The fraction $\frac{3}{25}$ can easily be converted to a fraction with a denominator of 100.

$$\frac{3}{25} = \frac{3 \cdot 4}{25 \cdot 4} = \frac{12}{100} = 0.12$$

This technique is useful in some cases. However, some fractions such as $\frac{1}{3}$ cannot be converted to a fraction with a denominator that is a power of 10. This is so because 3 is not a factor of any power of 10. For this reason, we recommend the following alternative method.

Recall that a fraction bar implies division of the numerator by the denominator. If we carry out that division, we convert the fraction to its decimal form.

Skill Practice

Write each fraction or mixed number as a decimal.

3. $\frac{3}{8}$

4. $\frac{43}{20}$

5. $12\frac{5}{16}$

example 1   Writing Fractions as Decimals

Write each fraction or mixed number as a decimal.

a. $\frac{3}{5}$ **b.** $\frac{68}{25}$ **c.** $3\frac{5}{8}$

Solution:

a. $\frac{3}{5}$ means $3 \div 5$.

$$\begin{array}{r} .6 \\ 5{\overline{)3.0}} \\ -30 \\ \hline 0 \end{array}$$

Divide the numerator by the denominator.

$$\frac{3}{5} = 0.6$$

b. $\frac{68}{25}$ means $68 \div 25$.

$$\begin{array}{r} 2.72 \\ 25{\overline{)68.00}} \\ -50 \\ \hline 180 \\ -175 \\ \hline 50 \\ -50 \\ \hline 0 \end{array}$$

Divide the numerator by the denominator.

$$\frac{68}{25} = 2.72$$

c. $3\frac{5}{8} = 3 + 5 \div 8$

$$\begin{array}{r} .625 \\ 8{\overline{)5.000}} \\ -48 \\ \hline 20 \\ -16 \\ \hline 40 \\ -40 \\ \hline 0 \end{array}$$

Divide the numerator by the denominator.

$$3\frac{5}{8} = 3 + 0.625$$

$$= 3.625$$

Answers

1. $\frac{4}{10}$; 0.4   2. $\frac{35}{100}$; 0.35

3. 0.375   4. 2.15   5. 12.3125

The fractions in Example 1 are represented by terminating decimals. However, many fractions convert to repeating decimals.

---

example 2   Converting Fractions to Repeating Decimals

Write each fraction as a decimal.

a. $\dfrac{4}{9}$ b. $\dfrac{5}{6}$ c. $\dfrac{4}{7}$

Solution:

a. $\dfrac{4}{9}$ means $4 \div 9$.

$$
\begin{array}{r}
.44\ldots \\
9\overline{)4.00} \\
-36 \\
\hline
40 \\
-36 \\
\hline
40
\end{array}
$$

The quotient is a repeating decimal.

$\dfrac{4}{9} = 0.\overline{4}$

b. $\dfrac{5}{6}$ means $5 \div 6$.

$$
\begin{array}{r}
.833\ldots \\
6\overline{)5.000} \\
-48 \\
\hline
20 \\
-18 \\
\hline
20 \\
-18 \\
\hline
20
\end{array}
$$

The quotient is a repeating decimal.

$\dfrac{5}{6} = 0.8\overline{3}$

c. $\dfrac{4}{7}$ means $4 \div 7$.

$$
\begin{array}{r}
.571428\ldots \\
7\overline{)4.000000} \\
-35 \\
\hline
50 \\
-49 \\
\hline
10 \\
-7 \\
\hline
30 \\
-28 \\
\hline
20 \\
-14 \\
\hline
60 \\
-56 \\
\hline
40
\end{array}
$$

The cycle will repeat.

$\dfrac{4}{7} = 0.571428571428571428571428\ldots = 0.\overline{571428}$

Several fractions are used quite often. Their decimal forms are worth memorizing and are presented in Table 4-1.

Skill Practice

Write each fraction as a decimal.

6. $\dfrac{8}{9}$

7. $\dfrac{1}{12}$

8. $\dfrac{3}{7}$

Calculator Connections

Repeating decimals displayed on a calculator must be rounded. For example, the repeating decimals from Example 2 might appear as follows.

$0.\overline{4}$	0.444444444
$0.8\overline{3}$	0.833333333
$0.\overline{571428}$	0.571428571

Answers

6. $0.\overline{8}$ 7. $0.08\overline{3}$ 8. $0.\overline{428571}$

Concept Connections

9. Describe the pattern between the fractions $\frac{1}{9}$

table 4-1

$\frac{1}{4} = 0.25$	$\frac{2}{4} = \frac{1}{2} = 0.5$	$\frac{3}{4} = 0.75$	

Skill Practice

Convert the fraction to a decimal rounded to the indicated place value.

10. $\frac{9}{7}$; tenths

11. $\frac{17}{37}$; hundredths

Example 6   Converting Fractions to Decimals with Rounding

Convert the fraction to a decimal rounded to the indicated place value.

a. $\frac{162}{7}$; tenths place   b. $\frac{21}{31}$; hundredths place

Solution:

a. $\frac{162}{7}$

tenths place
hundredths place

$$
\begin{array}{r}
23.14 \\
7)\overline{162.00} \\
-14 \\
\hline
22 \\
-21 \\
\hline
10 \\
-7 \\
\hline
30 \\
-28 \\
\hline
2
\end{array}
$$

To round to the tenths place, we must determine the hundredths-place digit and use it to base our decision on rounding. The hundredths-place digit is 4. Therefore, leave the tenths-place digit unchanged. The quotient rounds to 23.1.

The fraction $\frac{162}{7}$ is approximately 23.1.

b. $\frac{21}{31}$

hundredths place
thousandths place

$$
\begin{array}{r}
.677 \\
31)\overline{21.000} \\
-186 \\
\hline
240 \\
-217 \\
\hline
230 \\
-217 \\
\hline
13
\end{array}
$$

To round to the hundredths-place, we must determine the thousandths-place digit and use it to base our decision on rounding. The thousandths-place digit is 7. Therefore, increase the hundredths-place digit by 1. The rounded value is 0.68.

The fraction $\frac{21}{31}$ is approximately 0.68.

2. Writing Decimals as Fractions

In Section 4.1 we converted terminating decimals to fractions. We did this by writing the decimal as a decimal fraction and then reducing the fraction to lowest terms. For example,

$$
0.46 = \frac{46}{100} = \frac{\overset{23}{\cancel{46}}}{\underset{50}{\cancel{100}}} = \frac{23}{50}
$$

Answers

9. The numerator of the fraction is the repeated digit in the decimal form.

10. 1.3   11. 0.46

We do not yet have the tools to convert a repeating decimal to its equivalent fraction form. However, we can make use of our knowledge of the common fractions and their repeating decimal forms from Table 4-1.

example 4	Writing Decimals as Fractions and Fractions as Decimals

Complete the table.

	Decimal Form	Fractional Form
a.	0.475	
b.		$\frac{3}{16}$
c.		$2\frac{4}{5}$
d.	$0.\overline{6}$	
e.		$\frac{19}{11}$

Skill Practice

Complete the table.

	Decimal Form	Fractional Form
12.	0.875	
13.		$\frac{7}{20}$
14.		$2\frac{1}{3}$
15.	$0.\overline{7}$	

Solution:

a. $0.475 = \dfrac{475}{1000} = \dfrac{\cancel{5} \cdot \cancel{5} \cdot 19}{2 \cdot 2 \cdot 2 \cdot \cancel{5} \cdot \cancel{5} \cdot 5} = \dfrac{19}{40}$

b. $\dfrac{3}{16} = 3 \div 16$

$$
\begin{array}{r}
.1875 \\
16\overline{)3.0000} \\
-16 \\
\hline
140 \\
-128 \\
\hline
120 \\
-112 \\
\hline
80 \\
-80 \\
\hline
0
\end{array}
$$

Therefore, $\dfrac{3}{16} = 0.1875$

c. To convert $2\frac{4}{5}$ to decimal form, we need to convert $\frac{4}{5}$ to decimal form. This may be done by dividing. Or we can easily convert $\frac{4}{5}$ to a decimal fraction with a denominator of 10.

$$\frac{4}{5} = \frac{4 \cdot 2}{5 \cdot 2} = \frac{8}{10} = 0.8$$

Therefore, $2\dfrac{4}{5} = 2.8$

d. From Table 4-1, the decimal $0.\overline{6} = \dfrac{2}{3}$.

e. $\dfrac{19}{11}$ means $19 \div 11$.

$$
\begin{array}{r}
1.7272\ldots \\
11\overline{)19.0000} \\
-11 \\
\hline
80 \\
-77 \\
\hline
30 \\
-22 \\
\hline
80
\end{array}
$$

$\dfrac{19}{11} = 1.\overline{72}$

The cycle will repeat.

Answers

	Decimal Form	Fractional Form
12.	0.875	$\frac{7}{8}$
13.	0.35	$\frac{7}{20}$
14.	$2.\overline{3}$	$2\frac{1}{3}$
15.	$0.\overline{7}$	$\frac{7}{9}$

We can now complete the table.

	Decimal Form	Fractional Form
		$\dfrac{19}{3}$
e.	$1.\overline{72}$	$\dfrac{19}{11}$

3. Decimals and the Number Line

In Example 5, we rank the numbers from least to greatest and visualize the position of the numbers on the number line.

example 5   Ordering Decimals and Fractions

Rank the numbers from least to greatest. Then approximate the position of the points on the number line.

$$0.\overline{45}, 0.45, \frac{1}{2}$$

Solution:

First note that $\frac{1}{2} = 0.5$ and that $0.\overline{45} = 0.454545\cdots$. By writing each number in decimal form, we can compare the decimals as we did in Section 4.1.

0.454545 · · ·   0.45   0.5   0.5 is the greatest of the three numbers.

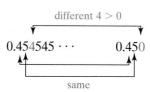

0.454545 · · ·   0.450   Notice that we inserted an extra zero to the right of 0.45 so that we could compare common place values. The number $0.\overline{45} > 0.45$.

Ranking the numbers from least to greatest, we have $0.45, 0.\overline{45}, \frac{1}{2}$.

The relative position of these numbers can be seen on the number line. First note that we have expanded the segment of the number line between 0.4 and 0.5 to see more place values to the right of the decimal point.

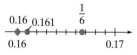
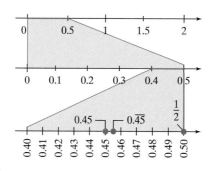

Recall that numbers that lie to the left on the number line have lesser value than numbers that lie to the right.

section 4.5 Practice Exercises

Study Skills Exercise

1. In a study group, check which activities you might try to help you learn and understand the material.

☐ Quiz one another by asking one another questions.

☐ Practice teaching one another.

☐ Share and compare class notes.

☐ Support and encourage one another.

☐ Work together on exercises and sample problems.

Review Exercises

For Exercises 2–5, write the decimal fraction in decimal form.

2. $\dfrac{9}{10}$

3. $\dfrac{39}{100}$

4. $\dfrac{141}{1000}$

5. $\dfrac{71}{10,000}$

For Exercises 6–9, write the decimals as fractions.

6. 0.6

7. 0.0016

8. 0.35

9. 0.125

Objective 1: Writing Fraction as Decimals

For Exercises 10–16, write each fraction as a decimal fraction, that is, a fraction whose denominator is a power of 10. Then write the number in decimal form.

10. $\dfrac{7}{25}$

11. $\dfrac{4}{25}$

12. $\dfrac{316}{500}$

13. $\dfrac{19}{500}$

14. $\dfrac{2}{5}$

15. $\dfrac{4}{5}$

16. $\dfrac{49}{50}$

For Exercises 17–32, write each fraction or mixed number as a decimal. **(See Example 1.)**

17. $\dfrac{7}{8}$

18. $\dfrac{16}{64}$

19. $\dfrac{5}{16}$

20. $\dfrac{31}{50}$

21. $5\dfrac{3}{12}$

22. $4\dfrac{1}{16}$

23. $1\dfrac{1}{5}$

24. $6\dfrac{5}{8}$

25. $\dfrac{18}{24}$

26. $\dfrac{24}{40}$

27. $2\dfrac{7}{20}$

28. $3\dfrac{4}{25}$

29. $7\dfrac{9}{20}$

30. $3\dfrac{11}{25}$

31. $\dfrac{22}{25}$

32. $\dfrac{11}{20}$

36   12   11   33

41. $\dfrac{14}{111}$

42. $\dfrac{58}{111}$

43. $\dfrac{41}{333}$

44. $\dfrac{68}{333}$

45. $\dfrac{1}{7}$

46. $\dfrac{2}{7}$

47. $\dfrac{1}{13}$

48. $\dfrac{9}{13}$

For Exercises 49–54, convert the fraction to a decimal and round to the indicated place value. **(See Example 3.)**

49. $\dfrac{15}{16}$; tenths

50. $\dfrac{3}{11}$; tenths

51. $\dfrac{5}{7}$; hundredths

52. $\dfrac{1}{8}$; hundredths

53. $\dfrac{25}{21}$; tenths

54. $\dfrac{18}{13}$; tenths

55. Show that $\frac{1}{4} = 0.25$, using two methods.

56. Show that $\frac{1}{2} = 0.5$, using two methods.

57. Write the fractions as decimals. Explain how to memorize the decimal form for these fractions with a denominator of 9.

   a. $\dfrac{1}{9}$ **b.** $\dfrac{2}{9}$ **c.** $\dfrac{4}{9}$ **d.** $\dfrac{5}{9}$

58. Write the fractions as decimals. Explain how to memorize the decimal forms for these fractions with a denominator of 3.

   a. $\dfrac{1}{3}$ **b.** $\dfrac{2}{3}$

59. Given that $\frac{1}{8} = 0.125$, use the method described in Exercises 57 and 58 to find the decimal form.

   a. $\dfrac{3}{8}$ **b.** $\dfrac{5}{8}$ **c.** $\dfrac{7}{8}$

60. Given that $\frac{1}{5} = 0.2$, use the method described in Exercises 57 and 58 to find the decimal form.

   a. $\dfrac{2}{5}$ **b.** $\dfrac{3}{5}$ **c.** $\dfrac{4}{5}$

Objective 2: Writing Decimals as Fractions

For Exercises 61–64, complete the table. **(See Example 4.)**

61.

	Decimal Form	Fraction Form
a.	0.45	
b.		$1\frac{5}{8}$ or $\frac{13}{8}$
c.	$0.\overline{7}$	
d.		$\frac{5}{11}$

62.

	Decimal Form	Fraction Form
a.		$\frac{2}{3}$
b.	1.6	
c.		$\frac{152}{25}$
d.	$0.\overline{2}$	

63.

	Decimal Form	Fraction Form
a.	$0.\overline{3}$	
b.	2.125	
c.		$\frac{19}{22}$
d.		$\frac{42}{25}$

64.

	Decimal Form	Fraction Form
a.	0.75	
b.		$\frac{7}{11}$
c.	$1.\overline{8}$	
d.		$\frac{74}{25}$

Historically stock prices were given as fractions or mixed numbers, but are now given as decimals. For Exercises 65–66, complete the table that gives recent stock prices taken from the *Wall Street Journal*.

65.

Stock	Symbol	Closing Price ($) (Decimal)	Closing Price ($) (Fraction)
Corning	GLW	12.38	
Walgreen	WAG	34.95	
Brookstone	BKST		$19\frac{1}{2}$
SnapOn	SNA		$33\frac{11}{25}$

66.

Stock	Symbol	Closing Price ($) (Decimal)	Closing Price ($) (Fraction)
Checkers	CTKR		$10\frac{}{20}$

Objective 3: Decimals and the Number Line

For Exercises 67–78, insert the appropriate symbol. Choose from $<$, $>$, or $=$.

67. $0.2 \;\square\; \dfrac{1}{5}$

68. $1.5 \;\square\; \dfrac{3}{2}$

69. $0.2 \;\square\; 0.\overline{2}$

70. $\dfrac{3}{5} \;\square\; 0.\overline{6}$

71. $\dfrac{1}{3} \;\square\; 0.3$

72. $\dfrac{2}{3} \;\square\; 0.66$

73. $4\dfrac{1}{4} \;\square\; 4.\overline{25}$

74. $2.12 \;\square\; 2.\overline{12}$

75. $0.\overline{5} \;\square\; \dfrac{5}{9}$

76. $\dfrac{7}{4} \;\square\; 1.75$

77. $0.27 \;\square\; \dfrac{3}{11}$

78. $6.4\overline{3} \;\square\; 6.43$

For Exercises 79–82, rank the numbers from least to greatest. Then approximate the position of the points on the number line. **(See Example 5.)**

79. $0.\overline{1}, \dfrac{1}{10}, \dfrac{1}{5}$

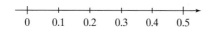

80. $3\dfrac{1}{4}, 3\dfrac{1}{3}, 3.3$

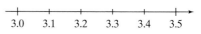

81. $1.8, 1.75, 1.\overline{7}$

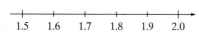

82. $5\dfrac{1}{6}, 5.\overline{6}, 5.0\overline{6}$

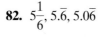

Expanding Your Skills

83. If $0.\overline{8} = \frac{8}{9}$, then what is the fraction form of $0.\overline{9}$?

For Exercises 84–86, simplify.

84. $1.\overline{9}$

85. $6.\overline{9}$

86. $15.\overline{9}$

Order of Operations and Applications of Decimals

1. Order of Operations Involving Decimals

In Example 1, we perform the order of operations with an expression involving decimal numbers.

Applying the Order of Operations by Using Decimal Numbers

Simplify.

$$16.4 - (6.7 - 3.5)^2$$

Solution:

$16.4 - (6.7 - 3.5)^2$

$= 16.4 - (3.2)^2$ Perform the subtraction within parentheses first.

$$\begin{array}{r} 6.7 \\ - 3.5 \\ \hline 3.2 \end{array}$$

$= 16.4 - 10.24$ Perform the operation involving the exponent.

$$\begin{array}{r} 3.2 \\ \times 3.2 \\ \hline 64 \\ 960 \\ \hline 10.24 \end{array}$$

$= 6.16$ Subtract.
$$\begin{array}{r} \overset{3\ 10}{1\,6.\,4\,\cancel{0}} \\ -\ 1\,0.\,2\,4 \\ \hline 6.\,1\,6 \end{array}$$

2. Calculations with Decimals and Fractions

In Sections 4.1 and 4.5 we learned how to convert between fraction notation and decimal notation. In this section we apply the order of operations on fractions and decimals combined.

Dividing a Decimal and a Mixed Number

Divide.

$$1.52 \div 1\frac{3}{5}$$

Solution:

For this example we will show two approaches. In the first approach, we convert both numbers to fractional form and then divide. In the second approach, we convert both numbers to decimal form and then divide.

Objectives

1. Order of Operations Involving Decimals
2. Calculations with Decimals and Fractions
3. Calculations with Round-off Error
4. Applications of Decimals and Fractions

Skill Practice

Simplify.

1. $34.1 - 3(1.6)^2$
2. $(5.8 - 4.3)^2 - 2$

Skill Practice

Multiply $4.2\left(\frac{3}{4}\right)$ by the following approaches.

3. Approach 1: $\frac{42}{10} \cdot \frac{3}{4}$
4. Approach 1 (modified): $\frac{4.2}{1} \cdot \frac{3}{4}$
5. Approach 2: $(4.2)(0.75)$

Answers

1. 26.42   2. 0.25
3. $\frac{63}{20}$ or 3.15   4. $\frac{63}{20}$ or 3.15
5. 3.15

Approach 1

Convert both numbers to fractional form.

$$1.52 \div 1\frac{3}{5} = \frac{152}{?} \cdot \frac{8}{?}$$ Convert the decimal and mixed number to

$$= \frac{19}{20}$$ Multiply fractions.

We can write the quotient as $\frac{19}{20}$ or in its equivalent decimal form as 0.95.

Approach 1 (Modified)

A modification to approach 1 is to write the decimal 1.52 as $\frac{1.52}{1}$. (Recall that any number divided by 1 equals the number.)

$$1.52 \div 1\frac{3}{5} = \frac{1.52}{1} \div \frac{8}{5}$$

$$= \frac{1.52}{1} \cdot \frac{5}{8}$$ Multiply by the reciprocal of the divisor.

$$= \frac{7.6}{8}$$ Multiply fractions. Note that $1.52 \times 5 = 7.6$.

$$= 0.95$$ Divide.

$$\begin{array}{r} .95 \\ 8\overline{)7.60} \\ -72 \\ \hline 40 \\ -40 \\ \hline 0 \end{array}$$

Approach 2

Convert the numbers to decimal form.

$$1.52 \div 1\frac{3}{5} = 1.52 \div 1.6$$ Convert the mixed number to a decimal.

$$= 0.95$$ Divide. $1.6\overline{)1.52}$

$$\begin{array}{r} .95 \\ 16\overline{)15.20} \\ -144 \\ \hline 80 \\ -80 \\ \hline 0 \end{array}$$

Skill Practice

6. Divide, using any approach.

$$21.7 \div \frac{7}{2}$$

Skill Practice

Simplify.

7. $5.7 \div \dfrac{1}{4} \cdot \dfrac{2}{5}$

8. $2.6 \cdot \dfrac{3}{10} \div 1\dfrac{1}{2}$

example 3   Applying the Order of Operations

Simplify.

$$6.4 \times 2\frac{5}{8} \div \left(\frac{3}{5}\right)^2$$

Answers

6. 6.2   7. 9.12   8. 0.52

Solution:

Approach 1

Convert all numbers to fractional form.

$$6.4 \times 2\frac{5}{8} \div \left(\frac{3}{5}\right)^2 = \frac{64}{10} \times \frac{21}{8} \div \left(\frac{3}{5}\right)^2 \qquad \text{Convert the decimal and mixed numbers to fractions.}$$

$$= \frac{64}{10} \times \frac{21}{8} \div \frac{9}{25} \qquad \text{Square the quantity } \tfrac{3}{5}.$$

$$= \frac{64}{10} \times \frac{21}{8} \times \frac{25}{9} \qquad \text{Multiply by the reciprocal of the divisor.}$$

$$= \frac{\overset{4}{\cancel{8}}\,\overset{}{\cancel{64}}}{\underset{\underset{1}{2}}{\cancel{10}}} \times \frac{\overset{7}{\cancel{21}}}{\underset{1}{\cancel{8}}} \times \frac{\overset{5}{\cancel{25}}}{\underset{3}{\cancel{9}}} \qquad \text{Simplify common factors.}$$

$$= \frac{140}{3} \text{ or } 46\frac{2}{3} \text{ or } 46.\overline{6} \qquad \text{Multiply.}$$

Approach 2

Convert all numbers to decimal form.

$$6.4 \times 2\frac{5}{8} \div \left(\frac{3}{5}\right)^2 = 6.4 \times 2.625 \div (0.6)^2 \qquad \text{The fraction } \tfrac{5}{8} = 0.625 \text{ and } \tfrac{3}{5} = 0.6.$$

$$= 6.4 \times 2.625 \div 0.36 \qquad \text{Square the quantity } 0.6. \text{ That is,}$$
$$(0.6)(0.6) = 0.36.$$

Multiply 6.4×2.625.

$$\begin{array}{r} 2.625 \\ \times\ 6.4 \\ \hline 10500 \\ 157500 \\ \hline 16.8000 \end{array}$$

$$= 16.8 \div 0.36 \qquad \text{Divide } 16.8 \div 0.36. \qquad .36)\overline{16.80}$$

$$= 46.\overline{6}$$

$$\begin{array}{r} 46.6\dots \\ 36)\overline{1680} \\ -144 \\ \hline 240 \\ -216 \\ \hline 240 \end{array}$$

3. Calculations with Round-off Error

| example 4 | Multiplying a Fraction and a Decimal |

Multiply.

$$2.52 \cdot \left(\frac{5}{6}\right)$$

Solution:

Approach 1
Convert 2.52 to fractional form and then multiply fractions.

0.8333 . . . and we do not know how to multiply repeating decimals. We can approximate the product by rounding the value $0.8\overline{3}$ to some desired level of accuracy. Suppose we round $0.8\overline{3}$ to the thousandths place. Then $0.8\overline{3} \approx 0.833$.

$$2.52 \cdot (0.8\overline{3}) \approx 2.52 \cdot (0.833) \qquad \text{Round } 0.8\overline{3} \approx 0.833.$$

$$= 2.09916 \qquad \text{Multiply decimals.}$$

$$
\begin{array}{r}
2.52 \\
\times\ .833 \\
\hline
756 \\
7560 \\
201600 \\
\hline
2.09916
\end{array}
$$

The approximated value 2.09916 is close to 2.1.

Notice that the second approach in Example 4 was not as accurate as the first method. This is so because we used "intermediate rounding." Intermediate rounding refers to rounding a number before it is used in a calculation. We rounded the number $0.8\overline{3}$ *before* multiplying. Keep in mind that a rounded number is not exact. Any calculation performed on a rounded number compounds the error.

To minimize the effects of round-off error, you can try to keep the fraction notation as long as possible in the expression. In this way, if you do choose to convert to decimal form, you perform the division in the last step. Any rounding is done at the end.

example 5   Dividing a Fraction and Decimal

Divide $\frac{4}{7} \div 3.6$. Round the answer to the nearest hundredth.

Solution:

If we attempt to write $\frac{4}{7}$ as a decimal, we find that it is the repeating decimal $0.\overline{571428}$. Therefore, we choose to change 3.6 to fractional form: $3.6 = \frac{36}{10}$.

$$\frac{4}{7} \div 3.6 = \frac{4}{7} \div \frac{36}{10} \qquad \text{Write 3.6 as a fraction.}$$

$$= \frac{\overset{1}{4}}{7} \cdot \frac{10}{\underset{9}{36}} \qquad \text{Multiply by the reciprocal of the divisor.}$$

$$= \frac{10}{63} \qquad \text{Multiply and reduce to lowest terms.}$$

Concept Connections

10. Why is the product 18.9×0.4 not equal to the product $18.9 \times 0.\overline{4}$?

Skill Practice

11. Divide.

$$4.17 \div \frac{3}{2}$$

12. Divide. Round the answer to the nearest hundredth.

$$4.1 \div \frac{12}{5}$$

13. Multiply. Round the answer to the nearest hundredth.

$$\frac{3}{11} \times 2.4$$

Answers

10. The numbers 0.4 and $0.\overline{4}$ are not equal. Therefore, they will form a different product when multiplied by 18.9.

11. 2.78 or $\frac{139}{50}$ or $2\frac{39}{50}$ 12. 1.71

13. 0.65

We must write the answer in decimal form, rounded to the nearest hundredth.

$$
\begin{array}{r}
.158 \\
63\overline{)10.00} \\
-63 \\
\hline
370 \\
-315 \\
\hline
550 \\
-504 \\
\hline
46
\end{array}
$$

Divide. To round to the hundredths place, divide until we find the thousandths-place digit in the quotient. Use that digit to make a decision for rounding.

≈ 0.16 Round to the nearest hundredth.

4. Applications of Decimals and Fractions

example 6   Using Decimals and Fractions in a Consumer Application

Joanne filled the gas tank in her car and noted that the odometer read 22,341.9 mi. Ten days later she filled the tank again with $11\frac{1}{2}$ gal of gas. Her odometer reading at that time was 22,622.5 mi.

a. How many miles had she driven between fill-ups?

b. How many miles per gallon did she get?

Solution:

a. To find the number of miles driven, we need to subtract the initial odometer reading from the final reading.

$$
\begin{array}{r}
\overset{5\ 12\ 1\ \ 15}{2\,2,\!6\,2\,2.\,5} \\
-\ 2\,2,\!3\,4\,1.\,9 \\
\hline
2\,8\,0.\,6
\end{array}
$$

Recall that to add or subtract decimals, line up the decimal points.

Joanne had driven 280.6 mi between fill-ups.

b. To find the number of miles per gallon (mi/gal), we divide the number of miles driven by the number of gallons.

$280.6 \div 11\frac{1}{2} = 280.6 \div 11.5$ We convert to decimal form because the fraction $11\frac{1}{2}$ is recognized as 11.5.

$= 24.4$

$$
11.5\overline{)280.6} \qquad
\begin{array}{r}
24.4 \\
115\overline{)2806.0} \\
-230 \\
\hline
506 \\
-460 \\
\hline
460 \\
-460 \\
\hline
0
\end{array}
$$

Joanne got 24.4 mi/gal.

Skill Practice

14. The odometer on a car read 46,125.9 mi. After a $13\frac{1}{4}$-hr trip, the odometer read 46,947.4 mi.

   a. Find the total distance traveled on the trip.

   b. Find the average speed in miles per hour (mph).

Answers

14. a. 821.5 mi   b. 62 mph

example 7   Using Decimals and Fractions to Compute a Lawsuit Settlement

Althea won a legal settlement for $4105.20. Her lawyer received $\frac{1}{3}$ of the

$\frac{1}{3} \cdot (4105.20)$ The fraction $\frac{1}{3}$ cannot be written as a terminating decimal.

$= \frac{1}{3} \cdot \frac{4105.20}{1}$ We can write $4105.20 as $\frac{4105.20}{1}$ and multiply fractions.

$= \frac{4105.20}{3}$ Multiply numerators. Multiply denominators.

$= 1368.4$ Divide: $4105.20 \div 3 = 1368.4$.

The lawyer got $1368.40.

b. Althea got the remaining portion of the money.

$$\begin{array}{r} \$4105.20 \\ - \quad 1368.40 \\ \hline \$2736.80 \end{array}$$

Althea received $2736.80.

Skill Practice

16. A patchwork quilt is made up of quilted squares $1\frac{1}{4}$ ft on a side. Suppose a quilt measures 4 squares by 5 squares.

   a. Find the perimeter of the quilt.

   b. Find the area of the quilt.

example 8   Applying Decimals and Fractions to Geometry

A rectangular floor is 20 m by $17\frac{1}{2}$ m. If flooring costs $12.25 per square meter (m²), how much will it cost to put down flooring in the room?

Solution:

First draw a figure representing the rectangular floor (Figure 4-5). Because the cost of the flooring is given in terms of square meters, we need to know the area of the floor. (Recall that square units such as m², ft², and in.² are units of area.)

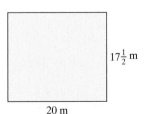

$17\frac{1}{2}$ m

20 m

Figure 4-5

For a rectangle,

$A = l \cdot w$

$= (20)\left(17\frac{1}{2}\right)$

$= (20)(17.5)$ In this case, we convert each number to decimal form because later we will have to multiply by $12.25.

$= 350$

The floor is 350 m².

$$\begin{array}{r} \overset{1\,1}{17.5} \\ \times\ 20 \\ \hline 0 \\ 3500 \\ \hline 350.0 \end{array}$$

Now multiply the cost per square meter by the number of square meters.

Cost = ($12.25)(350)

$$\begin{array}{r} 12.25 \\ \times\ 350 \\ \hline 0 \\ 61250 \\ 367500 \\ \hline 4287.50 \end{array}$$

= 4287.50

The cost of the flooring is $4287.50.

■

| example 9 | Finding an Average |

Table 4-2 represents the average snowfall for 6 winter months in Syracuse, New York. What is the mean (average) amount of snowfall per winter month? Round to the nearest tenth of an inch.

table 4-2

Month	Snowfall (in.)
November	9.3
December	26.8
January	29.6
February	26.2
March	17.3
April	4.0

Solution:

To find the average, we must add the values. Then divide by the number of values (in this case, 6).

To find the sum, line up the addends:

$$\begin{array}{r} \overset{1\,4\,2}{9.3} \\ 26.8 \\ 29.6 \\ 26.2 \\ 17.3 \\ +\ \ 4.0 \\ \hline 113.2 \end{array}$$

The total snowfall for these 6 months is 113.2 in. To find the average, divide by 6.

$$
\begin{array}{r}
18.86 \\
6\overline{)113.20} \\
-6
\end{array}
$$

To round to the tenths place, divide until we find the
hundredths-place digit. Use that digit to make a decision for

Syracuse averages about 18.9 in. of snow per month during these 6 months.

section 4.6   Practice Exercise

Study Skills Exercise

1. In addition to studying the material for a test, here are some other activities that people use when preparing for a test. Circle the importance of each statement.

	Not important	Somewhat important	Very important
a. Get a good night's sleep the night before the test.	1	2	3
b. Eat a good breakfast on the day of the test.	1	2	3
c. Wear comfortable clothes on the day of the test.	1	2	3
d. Arrive early to class on the day of the test.	1	2	3

Review Exercises

For Exercises 2–9, perform the indicated operation.

2. $\left(\dfrac{24}{7}\right)\left(\dfrac{35}{36}\right)$

3. 34.1×9.2

4. $790.9 + 23.91$

5. $\dfrac{34}{9} + \dfrac{5}{27}$

6. $56.7 \div 1.2$

7. $\dfrac{55}{16} \div \dfrac{11}{4}$

8. $\dfrac{9}{4} - \dfrac{7}{8}$

9. $13 - 6.04$

Objective 1: Order of Operations Involving Decimals

10. List the order of operations.

For Exercises 11–20, simplify by using the order of operations. **(See Example 1.)**

11. $12.46 - 3.05 - 0.8^2$ **12.** $15.06 - 1.92 - 0.4^2$ **13.** $63.75 - 9.5(4)$ **14.** $6.84 + (3.6)(9)$

15. $(3.7 - 1.2)^2$ **16.** $(6.8 - 4.7)^2$ **17.** $6.8 \div 2 \div 1.7$ **18.** $8.4 \div 2 \div 2.1$

19. $2.2 + [9.34 + (1.2)^2]$ **20.** $(3.1)^2 - (4.2 \div 2.1)$

Objective 2: Calculations with Decimals and Fractions

For Exercises 21–26, simplify by using the order of operations. Express the answer in decimal form. **(See Examples 2–3.)**

21. $\dfrac{3}{4} \times 89.8$ **22.** $30.12 \times \dfrac{5}{8}$ **23.** $20.04 \div \dfrac{4}{5}$

24. $(78.2 - 60.2) \div \dfrac{9}{13}$ **25.** $14.4 \times \left(\dfrac{7}{4} - \dfrac{1}{8}\right)$ **26.** $6.5 + \dfrac{1}{8} \times 0.24$

Objective 3: Calculations with Round-off Error

For Exercises 27–32, perform the indicated operations. Round the answer to the nearest hundredth when necessary. **(See Examples 4–5.)**

27. $2.3 \times \dfrac{5}{9}$ **28.** $4.6 \times \dfrac{1}{6}$ **29.** $6.5 \div \dfrac{3}{5}$

30. $\dfrac{1}{12} \times 6.24 \div 2.1$ **31.** $(42.81 - 30.01) \div \dfrac{9}{2}$ **32.** $\dfrac{2}{7} \times 5.1 \times \dfrac{1}{10}$

For Exercises 33–36, perform the indicated operation. Write the answer as a repeating decimal.

33. $\dfrac{2}{9} \times 4.21$ **34.** $6.02 \div \dfrac{22}{23}$ **35.** $5.32 \div \dfrac{6}{5}$ **36.** $\dfrac{34}{11} \times 2.5$

Objective 4: Applications of Decimals and Fractions

37. Professor McGonagal earns $14.50 per hour for the first 40 hr worked each week. For hours worked over 40 hr, she earns time and a half. **(See Example 6.)**

a. What is Professor McGonagal's hourly overtime wage?

b. How much does she earn in a week in which she works 50 hr?

38. Jennifer earns $18.00 per hour. Alex's hourly wage is $\frac{3}{4}$ of what Jennifer makes per hour.

  a. How much does Alex make per hour?

40. A night at a hotel in Dallas costs $129.95 with a nightly room tax of $20.75. The hotel also charges $1.10 per phone call made from the phone in the room. If Radcliff stays for 5 nights and makes 3 phone calls, how much is his total bill?

41. Susan's diet allows her 60 grams (g) of fat per day. If she has $\frac{1}{4}$ of her total fat grams for breakfast and a McDonald's Quarter Pounder (20.7 g of fat) for lunch, how many grams does she have left for dinner? **(See Example 7.)**

42. Todd is establishing his beneficiaries for his life insurance policy. The policy is for $150,000.00 and $\frac{1}{2}$ will go to his daughter, $\frac{3}{8}$ will go to his stepson, and the rest will go to his grandson. What dollar amount will go to the grandson?

43. Caren bought three packages of printer paper for $4.79 each. The sales tax for the merchandise was $0.86. If Caren paid with a $20 bill, how much change should she receive?

44. Mr. Timpson bought dinner for $28.42. He left a tip of $6.00. He paid the bill with two $20 bills. How much change should he receive?

45. Duncan earned test grades of 92, 84, 77, and 62. What is his test average?

46. Owen earned quiz grades of 19, 14, 16, and 20. What is his quiz average?

47. The average snowfall amounts for 5 winter months in Burlington, Vermont, are given in the table. Find the average snowfall per month. **(See Example 9.)**

Month	Snowfall (in.)
November	6.6
December	18.1
January	18.8
February	16.8
March	12.4

48. The average rainfall for 4 summer months for Houston, Texas, is given in the table. Find the average rainfall per month.

Month	Rainfall (in.)
June	5.6
July	5.2
August	3.3
September	3.7

49. The price of one share of stock of Microsoft for a 3-month period is given in the graph. Melanie bought stock on March 15 and sold it on April 30.

   a. By how much had the stock increased in value per share?

   b. If Melanie purchased 200 shares, how much money did she make?

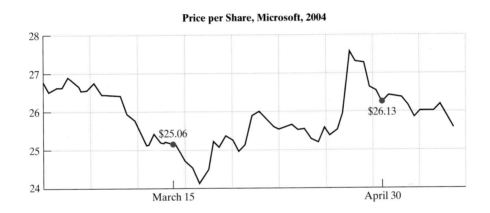

50. The price of one share of stock of Hershey Foods for a 3-month period is given in the graph. Taylor bought stock on March 1 and sold it on May 3.

   a. By how much had the stock increased in value per share?

   b. If Taylor purchased 250 shares, how much money did he make?

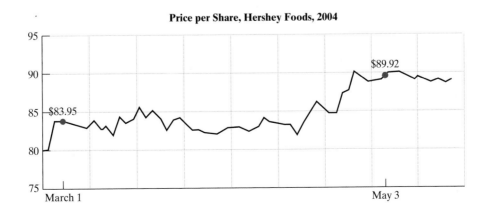

Use the following formula and table for Exercises 51–54. Round values to the tenths place if necessary.

In the spring of 1998, the National Institutes of Health (NIH) issued new guidelines for determining ~~~~

BMI	Weight Status
18.5–24.9	Considered ideal
25.0–29.9	Considered overweight
30.0 or above	Considered obese

51. Find your own body mass index.

52. a. Find the body mass index for a 150-lb person who is 5 ft 10 in. (70 in.) tall.

   b. Is this person considered ideal, overweight, or obese?

53. a. Find the body mass index for a 220-lb person who is 6 ft 0 in. (72 in.) tall.

   b. Is this person considered ideal, overweight, or obese?

54. a. Find the body mass index for a 141-lb person who is 5 ft 3 in. (63 in.) tall.

   b. Is this person considered ideal, overweight, or obese?

Expanding Your Skills

For Exercises 55–58, perform the indicated operation.

55. $0.\overline{3} \times 0.3 + 3.375$ **56.** $0.\overline{5} \div 0.\overline{2} - 0.75$ **57.** $(0.\overline{8} + 0.\overline{4}) \times 0.39$ **58.** $(0.\overline{7} - 0.\overline{6}) \times 5.4$

Calculator Connections

Topic: Applications using the order of operations with decimals

Calculator Exercises

59. Marty bought a home for $145,000. He paid $25,000 as a down payment and then financed the rest with a 30-yr mortgage. His monthly payments are $798.36 each and go toward paying off the loan and interest on the loan.

    a. How much money does Marty have to finance?

    b. How many months are in a 30-yr period?

    c. How much money will Marty pay over a 30-yr period to pay off the loan?

    d. How much money did Marty pay in interest over the 30-yr period?

60. Gwen bought a home for $109,000. She paid $15,000 as a down payment and then financed the rest with a 15-yr mortgage. Her monthly payments are $849.00 each and go toward paying off the loan and toward interest on the loan.

    a. How much money does Gwen have to finance?

    b. How many months are in a 15-yr period?

    c. How much money will Gwen pay over a 15-yr period to pay off the loan?

    d. How much money did Gwen pay in interest over the 15-yr period?

61. An inheritance for $80,460.60 is to be divided equally among four heirs. However, before the money can be distributed, approximately one-third of the money must go to the government for taxes. How much does each person get after the taxes have been subtracted?

62. For the fall semester, Sylvia bought 4 textbooks for $80.25, $42.50, $77.05, and $32.20. What is the average price per textbook?

chapter 4 | summary

Identify the place values of a decimal number.

$$1\ 2\ 3\ 4\ .\ 5\ 6\ 7\ 8$$

thousands
hundreds
tens
ones
decimal point
tenths
hundredths
thousandths
ten-thousandths

Reading a Decimal Number

1. The part of the number to the left of the decimal point is read as a whole number. *Note*: If there is not a whole-number part, skip to step 3.
2. The decimal point is read "and."
3. The part of the number to the right of the decimal point is read as a whole number but is followed by the name of the place position of the digit farthest to the right.

Converting a Decimal to a Mixed Number or Proper Fraction

1. The digits to the right of the decimal point are written as the numerator of the fraction.
2. The place value of the digit farthest to the right of the decimal point determines the denominator.
3. The whole-number part of the number is left unchanged.
4. Once the number is converted to a fraction or mixed number, simplify the fraction to lowest terms, if possible.

Writing a Decimal Number Greater Than 1 as an Improper Fraction

1. The denominator is determined by the place position of the rightmost digit to the right of the decimal point.
2. The numerator is obtained by removing the decimal point of the original number. The resulting whole number is then written over the denominator.
3. Simplify the improper fraction to lowest terms, if possible.

Example 2

In the number 34.914, the 1 is in the hundredths place.

Example 3

23.089 reads "twenty-three and eighty-nine thousandths."

Example 4

$$4.2 = 4\frac{\overset{1}{\cancel{2}}}{\underset{5}{\cancel{10}}} = 4\frac{1}{5}$$

Example 5

$$5.24 = \frac{\overset{131}{\cancel{524}}}{\underset{25}{\cancel{100}}} = \frac{131}{25}$$

Comparing Two Decimal Numbers

1. Starting at the left (and moving toward the right), compare the digits in each corresponding place position.
2. As we move from left to right, the first instance in which the digits differ determines the order of the numbers. The number having the greater digit is greater overall.

Rounding Decimals to a Place Value to the Right of the Decimal Point

1. Identify the digit one position to the right of the given place value.
2. If the digit in step 1 is 5 or greater, add 1 to the digit in the given place value. Then discard the digits to its right.
3. If the digit in step 1 is less than 5, discard it and any digits to its right.

In the U.S. system of currency, one dollar ($1) equals one hundred cents (100¢). That is, 1 cent is equivalent to $\frac{1}{100}$ of a dollar.

Example 6

3.024 > 3.019 because

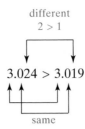

Example 7

Round 4.8935 to the nearest hundredth.

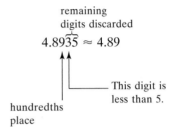

Example 8

$50.14 represents fifty and fourteen hundredths dollars, which is equivalent to fifty dollars and fourteen cents.

section 4.2   Addition and Subtraction of Decimals

number of digits to the right of the decimal point.)

2. Add the digits in columns from right to left as you would whole numbers. The decimal point in the answer should be lined up with the decimal points from the addends.

Subtracting Decimals

1. Write the numbers in a column with the decimal point and corresponding place values lined up. (You may insert additional zeros after the last digit to the right of the decimal point. These will act as placeholders so that each number has the same number of digits to the right of the decimal point.)
2. Subtract the digits in columns from right to left as you would whole numbers. The decimal point in the answer should be lined up with the other decimal points.

Example 3 illustrates an application involving addition and subtraction of decimals.

18.921

Check by rounding:

6.92 rounds to 7 and 0.001 rounds to 0.

$7 + 12 + 0 = 19$, which is close to 18.921.

Example 2

Subtract $41.03 - 32.4$.

$$
\begin{array}{r}
\overset{\overset{10}{3\ \cancel{\emptyset}\ \ 10}}{\cancel{4}\ \cancel{1}.\cancel{\emptyset}\ 3} \\
-\ 3\ 2\ .\ 4\ 0 \\
\hline
8\ .\ 6\ 3
\end{array}
$$

Check by rounding:

41.03 rounds to 41 and 32.40 rounds to 32.

$41 - 32 = 9$, which is close to 8.63.

Example 3

Toni has $181.50 in her bank account. If she deposits $250 and then writes a check for $389.99, will she have enough left to withdraw $80 for concert tickets?

$$181.50 + 250 - 389.99 = 431.50 - 389.99$$

$$= 41.51$$

Toni has only $41.51 in her account which is not enough for the tickets.

▰▰▰▰ section 4.3 Multiplication of Decimals

Key Concepts	Examples

Key Concepts

Multiplying Two Decimals

1. Ignore the decimal point and multiply as you would whole numbers.
2. Place the decimal point in the product so that the number of decimal places equals the combined number of decimal places of both factors.

Multiplying a Decimal by Powers of 10

Move the decimal point to the right the same number of decimal places as the number of zeros in the power of 10.

Multiplying a Decimal by Powers of 0.1

Move the decimal point to the left the same number of places as there are decimal places in the power of 0.1.

Large numbers are often expressed using number names, for example, 34.2 million.

Converting Dollars to Cents

1. Multiply by 100. This has the effect of moving the decimal point to the *right* two places.
2. Drop the $ symbol and attach the ¢ symbol to the result.

Converting Cents to Dollars

1. Multiply by 0.01. This has the effect of moving the decimal point to the *left* 2 places.
2. Drop the ¢ symbol and place the $ symbol in front of the result.

Examples 7 and 8 illustrate multiplication of decimals.

Example 7

A group of 5 college students attend a movie. The cost is discounted to $6.25 for students. What is the total cost of the tickets?

$6.25 \times 5 = 31.25$

The total cost is $31.25.

Examples

Example 1

Multiply 5.02×2.8.

$$\begin{array}{r} \overset{1}{5.02} \\ \times\ 2.8 \\ \hline 4016 \\ \underline{10040} \\ 14.056 \end{array}$$

Example 2

$83.251 \times 100 = 8325.1$

Move 2 places to the right.

Example 3

$149.02 \times 0.001 = 0.14902$

Move 3 places to the left.

Example 4

$34.2 \text{ million} = 34.2 \times 1{,}000{,}000$

$$= 34{,}200{,}000$$

Example 5

Convert $5.12 to cents.

$5.12 = 512¢$

Example 6

Convert 2399¢ to dollars.

$2399¢ = 23.99

Example 8

Find the area of the TV remote control.

$16.7 \times 5.8 = 96.86$

The area is 96.86 cm^2.

16.7 cm

5.8 cm

section 4.4 Division of Decimals

$$\begin{array}{r} -20 \\ \hline 26 \\ -24 \\ \hline 20 \\ -20 \\ \hline 0 \end{array}$$

Dividing When the Divisor Is Not a Whole Number

1. Move the decimal point in the divisor to the right to make it a whole number.
2. Move the decimal point in the dividend to the right the same number of places as in step 1.
3. Place the decimal point in the quotient directly above the decimal point in the dividend.
4. Divide as you would whole numbers.

Example 2

$81.1 \div 0.9 \qquad .9\overline{)81.1}$

$$\begin{array}{r} 90.11\ldots \\ 9\overline{)811.00} \\ -81 \\ \hline 01 \\ 00 \\ \hline 10 \\ -9 \\ \hline 10 \end{array}$$ The pattern repeats.

The answer is the repeating decimal $90.\overline{1}$.

Example 3

Round $6.\overline{56}$ to the thousandths place.

6.5656

thousandths place

The digit $6 > 5$ so increase the thousandths-place digit by 1.

$6.\overline{56} \approx 6.566$

Dividing by a Power of 10

To divide a number by a power of 10, move the decimal point to the *left* the same number of places as there are zeros in the power of 10.

Example 4

$302.9 \div 100 = 3.029$

Move 2 places to the left.

Dividing by a Power of 0.1

To divide a number by a power of 0.1, move the decimal point to the *right* the same number of places as there are decimal places in the power of 0.1.

Example 5

$78.114 \div 0.001 = 78{,}114$ Move 3 places to the right.

To round a repeating decimal, be sure to expand the repeating digits to one digit beyond the indicated rounding place.

section 4.5 **Fractions as Decimals**

Key Concepts

To write a fraction as a decimal, divide the numerator by the denominator. See Examples 1 and 2.

These are some common fractions represented by decimals.

$$\frac{1}{4} = 0.25 \qquad \frac{1}{2} = 0.5 \qquad \frac{3}{4} = 0.75$$

$$\frac{1}{9} = 0.\overline{1} \qquad \frac{2}{9} = 0.\overline{2} \qquad \frac{1}{3} = 0.\overline{3}$$

$$\frac{4}{9} = 0.\overline{4} \qquad \frac{5}{9} = 0.\overline{5} \qquad \frac{2}{3} = 0.\overline{6}$$

$$\frac{7}{9} = 0.\overline{7} \qquad \frac{8}{9} = 0.\overline{8}$$

To write a decimal as a fraction, first write the number as a decimal fraction and reduce. See Examples 3 and 4.

To rank decimals from least to greatest, compare corresponding digits from left to right.

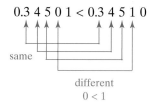

$$0.3\,4\,5\,0\,1 < 0.3\,4\,5\,1\,0$$

same

different
$0 < 1$

Examples

Example 1

$$\frac{17}{20} = 0.85 \qquad 20)\overline{17.00} {\scriptstyle .85}$$

$$\begin{array}{r} .85 \\ 20)\overline{17.00} \\ -160 \\ \hline 100 \\ -100 \\ \hline 0 \end{array}$$

Example 2

$$\frac{14}{3} = 4.\overline{6} \qquad 3)\overline{14.00}$$

$$\begin{array}{r} 4.66\ldots \\ 3)\overline{14.00} \\ -12 \\ \hline 20 \\ -18 \\ \hline 20 \end{array}$$

The pattern repeats.

Example 3

$$6.84 = \frac{\overset{171}{\cancel{684}}}{\underset{25}{\cancel{100}}} = \frac{171}{25} \quad \text{or} \quad 6\frac{21}{25}$$

Example 4

$$4.\overline{8} = 4\frac{8}{9} \quad \text{or} \quad \frac{44}{9}$$

Example 5

Plot the decimals 2.6, $2.\overline{6}$, and 2.58 on a number line.

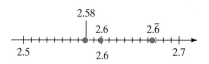

section 4.6 Order of Operations and Applications of Decimals

Example 2

$$\frac{2}{3}\left(2.2 + \frac{7}{5}\right) = \frac{2}{3}\left(\frac{22}{10} + \frac{7}{5}\right)$$

$$= \frac{2}{3}\left(\frac{11}{5} + \frac{7}{5}\right)$$

$$= \frac{2}{\overset{}{3}}\left(\frac{\overset{6}{18}}{5}\right) = \frac{12}{5} = 2.4$$

Example 3 illustrates an application of the order of operations involving decimals.

Example 3

For one month, Dan brought home paychecks worth $824.25, $840.05, $915.21, and $880.89. What was his average weekly pay?

$(824.25 + 840.05 + 915.21 + 880.89) \div 4$

$= (3460.40) \div 4 = 865.1$

Dan brings home an average of $865.10 a week.

---

chapter 4 | review exercises

Section 4.1

1. Identify the place values for each of the digits in the number 32.16.

2. Identify the place values for each of the digits in the number 2.079.

For Exercises 3–6, write the word name for the decimal.

3. 5.7

4. 10.21

5. 51.008

6. 109.01

For Exercises 7–8, write the decimal as a proper fraction or mixed number.

7. 4.8

8. 0.025

For Exercises 9–10, write the decimal as an improper fraction.

9. 1.3

10. 6.75

For Exercises 11–12, fill in the blank with either < or >.

11. 15.032 ☐ 15.03

12. 7.209 ☐ 7.22

13. The midseason earned run average (ERA) for five members of the National Baseball League for a recent year is given in the table. Rank the averages from least to greatest.

Player	ERA
G. Maddux	4.41
B. Laurence	4.40
B. Webb	4.48
V. Padilla	4.07
B. Meyers	4.24

For Exercises 14–15, round the decimal to the indicated place value.

14. 89.9245; hundredths

15. 34.8895; thousandths

16. A quality control manager tests the amount of cereal in several brands of breakfast cereal against the amount advertised on the box. She selects one box at random. She measures the contents of one 12.5-oz box and finds that the box has 12.46 oz.

   a. Is the amount in the box less than or greater than the advertised amount?

   b. If the quality control manager rounds the measured value to the tenths place, what is the value?

17. Which number is equivalent to 571.24? Circle all that apply.

   a. 571.240   **b.** 571.2400

   c. 571.024   **d.** 571.0024

18. Which number is equivalent to 3.709? Circle all that apply.

   a. 3.7   **b.** 3.7090

   c. 3.709000   **d.** 3.907

Section 4.2

For Exercises 19–26, add or subtract as indicated.

19. $45.03 + 4.713$ **20.** $239.3 + 33.92$

21. $34.89 - 29.44$ **22.** $5.002 - 3.1$

23. $221 - 23.04$ **24.** $34 + 4.993$

25. $17.3 + 3.109 - 12.6$

26. $189.22 + 13.1 - 120.055$

27. Find the values of x and y. Then find the perimeter of the figure.

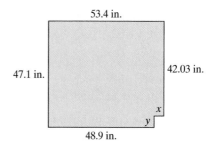

28. Gas prices for one month are shown in the table.

   a. Determine the difference in price between the consecutive weeks.

   b. Between which two weeks did the price increase the most?

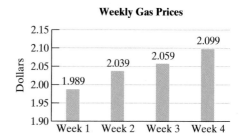

Section 4.3

For Exercises 29–36, multiply the decimals.

29. 3.9×2.1 **30.** 57.01×1.3

31. 60.1×4.4 **32.** 7.7×45

33. 85.49×1000 **34.** 1.0034×100

Population Density for Texas

38. The population of Guadeloupe is approximately 4.32 hundred-thousand.

39. Write the amount in terms of dollars.

   a. 234¢   **b.** 55¢

40. Write the amount in terms of cents.

   a. $5.25   **b.** $0.12

41. A store advertises a package of two 9-volt batteries for sale at $1.99.

   a. What is the cost of buying 8 batteries?

   b. If another store has an 8-pack for the regular price of $9.99, how much can one save by buying batteries at the sale price?

42. If long-distance phone calls cost $0.07 per minute, how much will a 23-min long-distance call cost?

43. Find the area and perimeter of the rectangle.

23.5 ft

40 ft

44. Population density gives the approximate number of people per square mile. The population density for Texas is given in the graph for selected years.

   a. Approximately how many people would have been located in a 200-mi² area in 1960?

   b. Approximately how many people would have been located in a 200-mi² area in 2000?

Section 4.4

For Exercises 45–50, divide. Write the answer in decimal form.

45. $8.55 \div 0.5$ **46.** $64.2 \div 1.5$

47. $0.06\overline{)0.248}$ **48.** $0.3\overline{)2.63}$

49. $18.9 \div 0.7$ **50.** $0.036 \div 1.2$

51. For each number, round to the indicated place.

	$8.\overline{6}$	$52.\overline{52}$	$0.\overline{409}$
Tenths			
Hundredths			
Thousandths			
Ten-thousandths			

For Exercises 52–53, divide and round the answer to the nearest hundredth.

52. $104.6 \div 9$ **53.** $71.8 \div 6$

For Exercises 54–57, divide by powers of 10 and 0.1.

54. $493.93 \div 100$ **55.** $90.234 \div 10$

56. $553.8 \div 0.001$ **57.** $2.6 \div 0.01$

58. a. A package of 5 rolls of 35-mm film costs $9.99. What is the cost per roll? (Round the answer to the nearest cent, that is, the nearest hundredth of a dollar.)

   b. Another package of 4 rolls of 35-mm film costs $8.99. What is the cost per roll?

   c. Which of the two packages offers the better buy?

Section 4.5

For Exercises 59–61, write the fraction as a decimal fraction. Then write the number in decimal form.

59. $\dfrac{3}{5}$ **60.** $\dfrac{7}{20}$ **61.** $\dfrac{27}{500}$

For Exercises 62–65, write the fraction or mixed number as a decimal.

62. $2\dfrac{2}{5}$ **63.** $3\dfrac{13}{25}$

64. $\dfrac{24}{125}$ **65.** $\dfrac{7}{16}$

For Exercises 66–69, write the fraction as a repeating decimal.

66. $\dfrac{7}{12}$ **67.** $\dfrac{55}{36}$

68. $4\dfrac{7}{22}$ **69.** $\dfrac{2}{13}$

For Exercises 70–73, write the fraction as a decimal rounded to the nearest hundredth.

70. $\dfrac{5}{17}$ **71.** $\dfrac{20}{23}$

72. $\dfrac{11}{3}$ **73.** $\dfrac{17}{6}$

For Exercises 74–77, write the fraction or mixed number for the repeating decimal.

74. $0.\overline{2}$ **75.** $1.\overline{6}$

76. $3.\overline{3}$ **77.** $5.\overline{7}$

78. Complete the table, giving the closing value of small-cap stocks as reported in the *Wall Street Journal*.

Stock	Symbol	Closing Price ($) (Decimal)	Closing Price ($) (Fraction)
Isonics	ISON	1.66	
EnPointe	ENPT		$2\frac{1}{20}$
LucilleFarm	LUCY	1.75	
Workstream	WSTM		$2\frac{4}{5}$

For Exercises 79–81, insert the appropriate symbol. Choose from <, >, or =.

79. $1\dfrac{1}{3}$ ☐ 1.33   **80.** 2.25 ☐ $\dfrac{9}{4}$

81. 0.14 ☐ $\dfrac{1}{7}$

For Exercises 82–83, determine what decimal number is represented by the point on the number line.

82.
0.25   0.30

83.
0.71   0.72

Section 4.6

For Exercises 84–87, perform the indicated operations. Write the answer in decimal form.

84. $7.5 \div \dfrac{3}{2}$ **85.** $2(3.14)(20)$

86. $3.14(5)^2$ **87.** $\dfrac{1}{3}(3.14)(2)^2(6)$

88. The Pimsleur Spanish course is available online at one website for the following prices. How much money is saved by buying the combo package versus the three levels individually?

Level	Price
Spanish I	$189.95
Spanish II	199.95
Spanish III	219.95
Combo (Spanish I, II, III combined)	519.95

89. Marvin drives the route shown in the figure each day, making deliveries. He completes one-third of the route before lunch. How many more miles does he still have to drive after lunch?

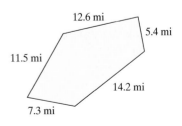

chapter 4 | test

4. The field goal percentages for four members of the San Antonio Spurs in the 2004 playoffs are given in the table. Rank the averages from least to greatest.

Player	Average
Tim Duncan	0.522
Jason Hart	0.550
Robert Horry	0.465
Devin Brown	0.486

5. Which statement is correct?

a. $0.043 > 0.430$ **b.** $0.692 < 0.926$

c. $0.078 < 0.0780$

For Exercises 6–13, perform the indicated operation.

6. $49.002 + 3.83$ **7.** $34.09 - 12.8$

8. 28.1×4.5 **9.** $25.4 \div 5$

10. $4 - 2.78$ **11.** $12.03 + 0.1943$

12. $39.82 \div 0.33$ **13.** 42.7×10.3

14. The temperature of a cake is recorded in 10-min intervals after it comes out of the oven. See the graph.

a. What was the difference in temperature between 10 and 20 min?

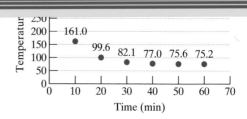

15. In the 2000 U.S. Presidential election, George Bush received approximately 50.5 million votes. In the same election, Al Gore received approximately 51.0 million votes.

a. Write a decimal number representing the number of votes received by George Bush.

b. Write a decimal number representing the number of votes received by Al Gore.

c. What is the approximate difference between the number of votes received by Al Gore and the number of votes received by George Bush?

16. Explain the difference between dividing a number by 10 and multiplying a number by 10.

17. Explain the difference between dividing a number by 0.01 and multiplying a number by 0.01.

For Exercises 18–21, multiply or divide by the powers of 10 and 0.1.

18. 45.92×0.1 **19.** 579.23×100

20. $80.12 \div 0.01$ **21.** $2.931 \div 1000$

22. A picture is framed and matted as shown in the figure.

   a. Find the area of the picture itself.

   b. Find the area of the matting *only*.

   c. Find the area of the frame *only*.

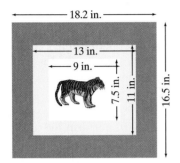

23. What is mathematically incorrect about the advertisement shown in the figure?

Note Cards 75 cents

.75¢

24. The table shows the winning times in seconds for women's speed skating for several years. Complete the table.

Year	Decimal	Fraction
1984		$41\frac{1}{50}$ sec
1988	39.10	
1992	40.33	
1994		$39\frac{1}{4}$

25. Rank the numbers and plot them on a number line.

$$3\frac{1}{2}, \ 3.\overline{5}, \ 3.2$$

For Exercises 26–27, simplify by using the order of operations.

26. $(8.7)\left(1.6 - \frac{1}{2}\right)$ **27.** $\frac{7}{3}\left(5.1 + \frac{3}{4}\right)$

28. Faulkner walked every day one week, and the distances are recorded in the table.

   a. Find the total distance walked.

   b. Find the average distance walked per day. Round to the nearest tenth of a mile.

Day	Distance
Monday	2.4 mi
Tuesday	1.6 mi
Wednesday	3.6 mi
Thursday	2.2 mi
Friday	2.8 mi
Saturday	2.9 mi
Sunday	4.3 mi

chapters 1–4 | cumulative review

1. Simplify: $(17 + 12) - (8 - 3) \cdot 3$

2. Convert the number to standard form: 4 thousands + 3 tens + 9 ones

3. Add: $3902 + 34 + 904$

4. Subtract: $4990 - 1118$

5. Multiply and round the answer to the thousands place: $23{,}444 \times 103$

6. Divide 4530 by 225. Then identify the dividend, divisor, whole-number part of the quotient, and

21. Find the area and perimeter.

Retail Sales

For Exercises 9–14, multiply or divide as indicated. Write the answer as a fraction.

9. $\dfrac{1}{5} \cdot \dfrac{6}{11}$

10. $\left(\dfrac{6}{15}\right)\left(\dfrac{10}{7}\right)$

11. $\left(\dfrac{7}{10}\right)^2$

12. $\left(\dfrac{32}{22}\right) \div \left(\dfrac{8}{11}\right)$

13. $\dfrac{8}{3} \div 4$

14. $\left(\dfrac{0}{5}\right) \div \left(\dfrac{3}{5}\right)$

15. A settlement for a lawsuit is made for $15,000. The attorney gets $\frac{2}{5}$ of the settlement. How much is left?

16. Simplify by using the order of operations:

$$\dfrac{8}{25} + \dfrac{1}{5} \div \dfrac{5}{6} - \left(\dfrac{2}{5}\right)^2$$

For Exercises 17–20, add or subtract as indicated. Write the answer as a fraction.

17. $\dfrac{7}{10} + \dfrac{27}{100}$

18. $\dfrac{5}{11} + 3$

19. $5 - \dfrac{2}{7}$

20. $\dfrac{12}{5} - \dfrac{9}{10}$

22. Cliff walks in the mornings for exercise. For the last 4 days he has walked for $\frac{9}{10}$, $1\frac{2}{5}$, $1\frac{1}{4}$, and $1\frac{1}{5}$ km. What is the average distance?

For Exercises 23–27, perform the indicated operations.

23. $50.9 + 123.23$

24. $700.8 - 32.01$

25. 301.1×0.25

26. $51.2 \div 3.2$

27. $\dfrac{4}{3}(3.14)(9)^2$

28. Divide $79.02 \div 1.7$ and round the answer to the nearest hundredth.

29. a. Multiply 0.004×938.12.

   b. Multiply 938.12×0.004.

   c. Identify the property that has been demonstrated in parts (a) and (b).

30. The table gives the average length of several bones in the human body. Complete the table by writing the mixed numbers as decimals and the decimals as mixed numbers.

Bone	Length (in.) (Decimal)	Length (in.) (Mixed Number)
Femur	19.875	
Fibula		$15\frac{15}{16}$
Humerus		$14\frac{3}{8}$
Innominate bone (hip)	7.5	

STUDENT ANSWER APPENDIX

Chapter 1

Chapter 1 Preview, p. 2

1. Ten-thousands place **3.** One hundred thirty is less than two hundred forty-four. **5.** 262 **7.** 766 **9.** 930 **11.** 248 **13.** 105 R2 **15.** 0 **17.** 140 m^2 **19.** 6 **21.** 187 mi

Section 1.1 Practice Exercises, pp. 7–10

3. 7: ones; 5: tens; 4: hundreds; 3: thousands; 1: ten-thousands; 2: hundred-thousands; 8: millions **5.** Tens **7.** Ones **9.** Hundreds **11.** Thousands **13.** Hundred-thousands **15.** Billions **17.** Ten-thousands **19.** Millions **21.** Ten-millions **23.** Billions **25.** 5 tens + 8 ones **27.** 5 hundreds + 3 tens + 9 ones **29.** 5 hundreds + 3 ones **31.** 1 ten-thousand + 2 hundreds + 4 tens + 1 one **33.** 2 millions + 6 thousands + 4 ones **35.** 524 **37.** 150 **39.** 1,906 **41.** 85,007 **43.** Answers will vary. **45.** Ones, thousands, millions, billions **47.** Two hundred forty-one **49.** Six hundred three **51.** Nine thousand, five hundred thirty-five **53.** Thirty-one thousand, five hundred thirty **55.** One hundred thousand, two hundred thirty-four **57.** Twenty thousand, three hundred twenty **59.** One thousand, three hundred seventy-seven **61.** 6,005 **63.** 672,000 **65.** 1,484,250
67.

69. 10 **71.** 4 **73.** 8 is greater than 2, or 2 is less than 8 **75.** 3 is less than 7, or 7 is greater than 3 **77.** < **79.** > **81.** < **83.** > **85.** < **87.** < **89.** False **91.** 99 **93.** There is no greatest whole number. **95.** 7 **97.** 964

Section 1.2 Practice Exercises, pp. 18–23

3. 3 hundreds + 5 tens + 1 one **5.** 1 hundred + 7 ones **7.** 4012
9.

+	0	1	2	3	4	5	6	7	8	9
0	0	1	2	3	4	5	6	7	8	9
1	1	2	3	4	5	6	7	8	9	10
2	2	3	4	5	6	7	8	9	10	11
3	3	4	5	6	7	8	9	10	11	12
4	4	5	6	7	8	9	10	11	12	13
5	5	6	7	8	9	10	11	12	13	14
6	6	7	8	9	10	11	12	13	14	15
7	7	8	9	10	11	12	13	14	15	16
8	8	9	10	11	12	13	14	15	16	17
9	9	10	11	12	13	14	15	16	17	18

11. Addends: 2, 8; sum: 10 **13.** Addends: 11, 10; sum: 21 **15.** Addends: 5, 8, 2; sum: 15 **17.** 74 **19.** 58 **21.** 48 **23.** 19 **25.** 588 **27.** 798 **29.** 237 **31.** 198 **33.** 84 **35.** 115 **37.** 937 **39.** 850 **41.** 41 **43.** 29 **45.** 1003 **47.** 836 **49.** 24,004 **51.** 13,121 **53.** 21 + 30 **55.** 13 + 8 **57.** 23 + (9 + 10) **59.** (41 + 3) + 22 **61.** The sum of any number and 0 is that number. **a.** 423 **b.** 25 **c.** 67 **63.** 100 + 42; 142 **65.** 23 + 81; 104 **67.** 76 + 2; 78 **69.** 1320 + 448; 1768 **71.** 78 + 12 + 22; 112 **73.** For example: The sum of 33 and 15 **75.** For example: 15 added to 70 **77.** For example: The total of 11, 41, and 53 **79.** 521 deliveries **81.** 423 mi **83.** 1,206,655 athletes **85.** $245 **87.** 821,024 nonteachers **89.** 13,538 participants **91.** 60 in. **93.** 35 m **95.** 26 ft **97.** 360 ft

Calculator Connections 1.2, p. 23

99. 908,788 **101.** 21,491,394 **103.** 121,480,019 votes

Section 1.3 Practice Exercises, pp. 29–33

3. 1151 **5.** 899 **7.** 0 < 10 **9.** Minuend: 12; subtrahend: 8; difference: 4 **11.** Minuend: 21; subtrahend: 12; difference: 9 **13.** Minuend: 9; subtrahend: 6; difference: 3 **15.** 18 + 9 = 27 **17.** 27 + 75 = 102 **19.** 5 **21.** 3 **23.** 6 **25.** 45 **27.** 61 **29.** 1126 **31.** 321 **33.** 10,004 **35.** 1103 **37.** 34,331 **39.** 17 **41.** 49 **43.** 104 **45.** 521 **47.** 23 **49.** 4764 **51.** 1303 **53.** 2217 **55.** 378 **57.** 722 **59.** 30,941 **61.** 5,662,119 **63.** 78 − 23; 55 **65.** 78 − 6; 72 **67.** 422 − 100; 322 **69.** 1090 − 72; 1018 **71.** 50 − 13; 37 **73.** For example: Subtract 85 from 165. **75.** For example: The expression 7 − 4 means 7 minus 4, yielding a difference of 3. The expression 4 − 7 means 4 minus 7 which results in a difference of −3. (This is a mathematical skill we have not yet learned.) **79.** $33 **81.** 55 more hits **83.** 8 plants **85.** 9190 yd **87.** 13 m **89.** 10 yd **91.** 7748 **93.** 107,489

Calculator Connections 1.3, p. 33

95. 4,447,302 **97.** 49,408 mi^2 **99.** The difference in land area between Colorado and Rhode Island is 102,673 mi^2.

Section 1.4 Practice Exercises, pp. 38–41

45. 6 **47.** 10 **49.** 0 **51.** No, addition and subtraction should be performed in the order in which they appear from left to right.

Midchapter Review, p. 41

1. 1033 **2.** 3381 **3.** 101 **4.** 9542 **5.** Thousands **6.** Hundreds
7. Hundred-thousands **8.** Millions **9.** 15,000 **10.** 4,100,000
11. 268 **12.** 222 **13.** 21 **14.** 123

Section 1.5 Practice Exercises, pp. 50–55

3. 1,010,000 **5.** 5400 **7.** $6 \times 5; 30$ **9.** $3 \times 9; 27$
11. Factors: 6, 4; product: 24 **13.** Factors: 13, 42; product: 546
15. Factors: 3, 5, 2; product: 30 **17.** For example:
$5 \times 12; 5 \cdot 12; 5(12)$ **19.** d **21.** e **23.** c **25.** 8×14
27. $(6 \times 2) \times 10$ **29.** $(5 \times 7) + (5 \times 4)$ **31.** 144 **33.** 52 **35.** 655
37. 1376 **39.** 11,280 **41.** 23,184 **43.** 378,126 **45.** 448 **47.** 1632
49. 864 **51.** 2431 **53.** 6631 **55.** 19,177 **57.** 186,702
59. 21,241,448 **61.** 24,000 **63.** 2,100,000 **65.** 72,000,000
67. 36,000,000 **69.** 60,000,000 **71.** 2,400,000,000 **73.** $1000
75. $780,000 **77.** 375 lb **79.** $1665 **81.** 287,500 sheets
83. 372 miles **85.** 276 ft^2 **87.** 5329 cm^2 **89.** 128 ft^2
91. a. 2552 in.^{2} **b.** 42 windows **c.** 107,184 in.^{2}

Calculator Connections 1.5, p. 55

93. 7,665,000,000 bbl **95.** $215,644,000

Section 1.6 Practice Exercises, pp. 63–66

3. 4944 **5.** 1253 **7.** 664,210 **9.** 902 **11.** 9; the dividend is 72; the divisor is 8; the quotient is 9 **13.** 8; the dividend is 64; the divisor is 8; the quotient is 8 **15.** 5; the dividend is 45; the divisor is 9; the quotient is 5 **17.** You cannot divide a number by zero (the quotient is undefined). If you divide zero by a number (other than zero), the quotient is always zero. **19.** 15 **21.** 0 **23.** Undefined
25. 1 **27.** Undefined **29.** 0 **31.** $2 \times 3 = 6, 2 \times 6 \neq 3$
33. Multiply the quotient and the divisor to get the dividend.
35. 13 **37.** 41 **39.** 486 **41.** 409 **43.** 952 **45.** 822
47. Correct **49.** Correct **51.** Correct **53.** Incorrect; 25 R3
55. 7 R5 **57.** 10 R2 **59.** 27 R1 **61.** 197 R2 **63.** 42 R4
65. 1557 R1 **67.** 751 R6 **69.** 835 R2 **71.** 479 R9 **73.** 43 R19
75. 308 **77.** 1259 R26 **79.** 229 R96 **81.** 302 **83.** 497 ÷ 71; 7
85. 877 ÷ 14; 62 R9 **87.** 42 ÷ 6; 7 **89.** 14 classrooms
91. 5 cases; 8 cans left over **93.** 52 mph **95.** 22 lb **97.** Yes, they can all attend if they sit in the second balcony.
99. 1200 ÷ 20 = 60; approximately 60 words per minute

Calculator Connections 1.6, p. 66

101. 234 **103.** $180 billion

Section 1.7 Practice Exercises, pp. 71–74

3. True **5.** False **7.** True **9.** 9^4 **11.** 2^7 **13.** 3^6 **15.** $4^4 \cdot 2^3$
17. $8 \cdot 8 \cdot 8 \cdot 8$ **19.** $4 \cdot 4 \cdot 4 \cdot 4 \cdot 4 \cdot 4 \cdot 4 \cdot 4$ **21.** 8 **23.** 9
25. 27 **27.** 125 **29.** 32 **31.** 81 **33.** 1 **35.** 1 **37.** The number 1 raised to any power equals 1. **39.** 1000 **41.** 100,000 **43.** 2

11. 24 ÷ 6; 4 **13.** For example: sum, added to, increased by, more than, plus, total of **15.** For example: difference, minus, decreased by, less, subtract **17.** The whole screen has 12,096 pixels. **19.** There will be 9 gal used. **21.** Denali is 6074 ft higher than White Mountain Peak. **23.** Jeannette will pay $29,560 for one year.
25. The Insight can go 1320 mi. **27.** There will be 120 classes of Beginning Algebra. **29.** The maximum capacity is 3150 seats.
31. There will be $36 left in Gina's account. **33.** The total bill was $154,032. **35. a.** Latayne will receive $48. **b.** She can buy 6 CDs.
37. Michael Jordan scored 33,454 points with the Bulls. **39. a.** The difference was 8,410,500 passengers. **b.** There was a total of 143,306,500 passengers. **41. a.** The distance is 360 mi. **b.** 14 in. represents 840 mi. **43.** 104 boxes will be filled completely with 2 books left over. **45. a.** Marc needs five $20 bills. **b.** He will receive $16 in change. **47.** Jackson's monthly payment was $390.
49. Each trip will take 2 hr. **51.** Perimeter **53.** It will cost $1650.
55. The cost is $1020. **57.** He earned $520.

Chapter 1 Review Exercises, pp. 92–96

1. Ten-thousands **3.** 92,046
5. 3 millions + 4 hundred-thousands + 8 hundreds + 2 tens
7. Two hundred forty-five **9.** 3602

11.

```
  |---|---|---|---|---|---|---|---|---|---|---|---|--->
  1   2   3   4   5   6   7   8   9   10  11  12  13
```

13. True **15.** Addends: 105, 119; sum: 224 **17.** 71 **19.** 17,410
21. a. Commutative property **b.** Associative property
c. Commutative property **23.** 44 + 92; 136 **25.** 23 + 6; 29
27. 45,797 thousand seniors **29.** Minuend: 14; subtrahend: 8; difference: 6 **31.** 26 **33.** 121 **35.** 31,019 **37.** 38 − 31; 7
39. 251 − 42; 209 **41.** 71,892,438 tons **43.** 2336 thousand visitors
45. 9,330,000 **47.** 1500 **49.** 163,000 m^3 **51.** Factors: 33, 40; product: 1320 **53.** c **55.** d **57.** b **59.** 52,224 **61.** $429 **63.** 7; divisor: 6, dividend: 42, quotient: 7 **65.** 3 **67.** Undefined
69. Multiply the quotient and the divisor to get the dividend.
71. 58 **73.** 52 R3 **75.** $9)\overline{108}$ (12) **77. a.** 4 T-shirts **b.** 5 hats
79. $2^4 \cdot 5^3$ **81.** 256 **83.** 1,000,000 **85.** 12 **87.** 15 **89.** 55
91. $89 **93. a.** The Cincinnati Zoo has 13,000 more animals than the San Diego Zoo. **b.** The San Diego Zoo has 50 more species than the Cincinnati Zoo. **95.** He will receive $19,600,000 per year.

Chapter 1 Test, pp. 97–98

1. a. Hundreds **b.** Thousands **c.** Millions **d.** Ten-thousands
2. a. 4,065,000 **b.** Twenty-one million, three hundred twenty-five thousand **c.** Twelve million, two hundred eighty-seven thousand
d. 729,000 **e.** Eleven million, four hundred ten thousand
3. a. 14 > 6 **b.** 72 < 81 **4.** 129 **5.** 328 **6.** 113 **7.** 227
8. 2842 **9.** 447 **10.** 21 R9 **11.** 546 **12.** 8103 **13.** 20
14. 1,500,000,000 **15.** 336 **16.** 0 **17.** Undefined **18. a.** The associative property of multiplication; the expression shows a change in grouping. **b.** The commutative property of

multiplication; the expression shows a change in the order of the factors.   **19. a.** 4900 **b.** 12,000 **c.** 8,000,000 **20.** There were approximately 1,430,000 people. **21.** 4 **22.** 24 **23.** 48 **24.** Jennifer has a higher average of 29. Brittany has an average of 28. **25.** There were 20,099 foreign adoptions in 2002. **26. a.** 12,392 subscribers **b.** The largest increase was between the years 1999 and 2000. **27.** The North Side Fire Department is the busiest with an average of 5 calls per week. **28.** 156 mm **29.** Perimeter: 350 ft; area: 6016 ft^2 **30.** 4,560,000 m^2

Chapter 2

Chapter 2 Preview, p. 100

1. a. Proper **b.** Improper **c.** Improper **3.** $5\frac{4}{7}$ **5.** $\frac{3}{8}$
7. 1, 3, 5, 9, 15, 45 **9.** a **11.** $\frac{1}{10}$ **13.** 5 cm^2 **15.** $\frac{9}{16}$ **17.** 120 ft^2
19. 17 **21.** $6\frac{1}{2}$

Section 2.1 Practice Exercises, pp. 107–111

3. $\frac{3}{4}$ **5.** $\frac{5}{9}$ **7.** $\frac{1}{6}$ **9.** $\frac{3}{8}$ **11.** $\frac{3}{4}$ **13.** Numerator: 2; denominator: 3
15. Numerator: 12; denominator: 11 **17.** 6 ÷ 1; 6 **19.** 2 ÷ 2; 1
21. 0 ÷ 3; 0 **23.** 2 ÷ 0; undefined **25.** $\frac{2}{5}$ **27.** $\frac{10}{21}$ **29.** Proper
31. Improper **33.** Improper **35.** $\frac{5}{2}$ **37.** $\frac{12}{4}$ **39.** $\frac{7}{4}$; $1\frac{3}{4}$
41. $\frac{13}{8}$; $1\frac{5}{8}$ **43.** $\frac{7}{4}$ **45.** $\frac{38}{9}$ **47.** $\frac{24}{7}$ **49.** $\frac{29}{4}$ **51.** $\frac{137}{12}$ **53.** $\frac{171}{8}$
55. $\frac{133}{16}$ **57.** $\frac{269}{20}$ **59.** 19 **61.** 7 **63.** $4\frac{5}{8}$ **65.** $7\frac{4}{5}$ **67.** $2\frac{7}{10}$
69. $5\frac{7}{9}$ **71.** $12\frac{1}{11}$ **73.** $3\frac{5}{6}$ **75.** $7\frac{5}{9}$ **77.** $8\frac{1}{8}$ **79.** $44\frac{1}{7}$ **81.** $1056\frac{1}{5}$
83. $810\frac{3}{11}$
85.

$\frac{3}{4}$

0   1

87.

$\frac{1}{3}$

0   1

89.

$\frac{2}{3}$

0   1

91.

$1\frac{1}{6}$

0   1   2

93.

$1\frac{2}{3}$

0   1   2

95. False **97.** True

Calculator Connections 2.1, p. 111

99. $\frac{8586}{407}$ **101.** $\frac{5399}{112}$

Section 2.2 Practice Exercises, pp. 116–119

3. $\frac{8}{12}$; $\frac{4}{12}$ **5.** $\frac{5}{4}$; $\frac{3}{4}$ **7.** $\frac{7}{12}$; proper **9.** $4\frac{3}{5}$ **11.** For example, 2 · 4
and 1 · 8 **13.** For example, 4 · 6 and 2 · 2 · 2 · 3 **15.** For example,
8 · 4 and 2 · 2 · 2 · 2 · 2

17.

Product	36	42	30	15	81
Factor	12	7	30	15	27
Factor	3	6	1	1	3
Sum	15	13	31	16	30

19. A whole number is divisible by 2 if it is an even number.
21. A whole number is divisible by 3 if the sum of its digits is divisible by 3. **23. a.** No **b.** Yes **c.** Yes **d.** No **25. a.** Yes **b.** Yes
c. No **d.** No **27. a.** Yes **b.** Yes **c.** No **d.** No **29. a.** Yes **b.** No
c. Yes **d.** Yes **31. a.** No **b.** No **c.** No **d.** No **33.** Yes
35. There are two whole numbers that are neither prime nor composite, 0 and 1. **37.** False **39.** 2, 3, 5, 7, 11, 13, 17, 19, 23, 29, 31, 37, 41, 43, 47 **41.** Prime **43.** Composite **45.** Composite
47. Prime **49.** Neither **51.** Composite **53.** Prime **55.** Composite
57. No, 9 is not a prime number. **59.** Yes **61.** 2 · 5 · 7
63. 2 · 2 · 5 · 13 or 2^2 · 5 · 13 **65.** 3 · 7 · 7 or 3 · 7^2
67. 2 · 3 · 23 **69.** 2 · 2 · 2 · 7 · 11 or 2^3 · 7 · 11
71. Prime **73.** 1, 2, 3, 4, 6, 12 **75.** 1, 2, 4, 8, 16, 32
77. 1, 3, 9, 27, 81 **79.** 1, 2, 3, 4, 6, 8, 12, 16, 24, 48 **81.** No
83. Yes **85.** Yes **87.** No **89.** Yes **91.** No **93.** Yes **95.** No

Section 2.3 Practice Exercises, pp. 124–127

3. 5 · 29 **5.** 2 · 2 · 23 or 2^2 · 23 **7.** 5 · 17 **9.** 3 · 5 · 13
11.  **13.** **15.** False **17.** ≠ **19.** =
21. = **23.** ≠ **25.** $\frac{1}{2}$ **27.** $\frac{1}{3}$ **29.** $\frac{9}{5}$ **31.** $\frac{5}{4}$ **33.** $\frac{4}{5}$ **35.** 1
37. 2 **39.** 1 **41.** $\frac{3}{4}$ **43.** 3 **45.** $\frac{7}{10}$ **47.** $\frac{13}{15}$ **49.** $\frac{77}{39}$ **51.** $\frac{2}{5}$
53. $\frac{5}{2}$ **55.** $\frac{3}{4}$ **57.** $\frac{5}{3}$ **59.** $\frac{21}{11}$ **61.** $\frac{17}{100}$ **63.** Heads: $\frac{5}{12}$; tails: $\frac{7}{12}$
65. a. $\frac{3}{22}$ **b.** $\frac{9}{22}$ **67. a.** Jonathan: $\frac{5}{7}$; Jared: $\frac{6}{7}$ **b.** Jared sold the
greater fractional part. **69. a.** Raymond: $\frac{10}{11}$; Travis: $\frac{9}{11}$
b. Raymond read the greater fractional part.
71. For example, $\frac{6}{8}, \frac{9}{12}, \frac{12}{16}$ **73.** For example, $\frac{6}{9}, \frac{4}{6}, \frac{2}{3}$

Midchapter Review, p. 127

1. A fraction in which the numerator is greater than or equal to the denominator is an improper fraction. **2.** A fraction in which the numerator is less than the denominator is a proper fraction.
3. $\frac{2}{3}$ is a proper fraction and $\frac{3}{2}$ is an improper fraction.
4. **5.** **6. a.** 1, 2, 4, 8, 16
b. 1, 3, 7, 9, 21, 63 **c.** 1, 2, 4, 5, 8, 10, 20, 40 **d.** 1, 2, 3, 5, 6, 10, 15, 30
7. a. 2 · 2 · 2 · 2 or 2^4 **b.** 3 · 3 · 7 or 3^2 · 7 **c.** 2 · 2 · 2 · 5 or 2^3 · 5
d. 2 · 3 · 5 **8.** $\frac{8}{15}$ **9.** $\frac{2}{3}$ **10.** $\frac{5}{4}$ **11.** $\frac{5}{4}$ **12.** $\frac{3}{2}$ **13.** $\frac{5}{6}$ **14.** $2\frac{1}{2}$
15. $2\frac{3}{4}$ **16.** $1\frac{1}{3}$

Section 2.4 Practice Exercises, pp. 135–139

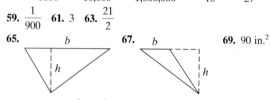

21. $\frac{8}{11}$ **23.** $\frac{24}{5}$ **25.** $\frac{65}{36}$ **27.** $\frac{2}{15}$ **29.** $\frac{5}{8}$ **31.** $\frac{35}{4}$ **33.** $\frac{8}{3}$ **35.** $\frac{4}{5}$

37. 8   **39.** 12   **41.** $\frac{30}{7}$ **43.** 10   **45.** $\frac{5}{3}$ **47.** $\frac{3}{8}$ **49.** 24

51. a. $\frac{1}{1000}$ **b.** $\frac{1}{10,000}$ **c.** $\frac{1}{1,000,000}$ **53.** $\frac{1}{16}$ **55.** $\frac{64}{27}$ **57.** 8

59. $\frac{1}{900}$ **61.** 3   **63.** $\frac{21}{2}$

65.   **67.**   **69.** 90 in.²

71. 4 yd²   **73.** $\frac{8}{3}$ or $2\frac{2}{3}$ mm²   **75.** 8 m²   **77.** $\frac{23}{32}$ ft²   **79.** 36 m²

81. 24 m²   **83.** The cost is \$13,750.   **85.** $\frac{1}{10}$ of the sample has

O negative blood.   **87.** Nancy spends $\frac{9}{4}$ or $2\frac{1}{4}$ hr a day.

89. Frankie mowed 960 yd². He has 480 yd² left to mow.

91. a. $\frac{4}{49}$ **b.** $\frac{2}{7}$ **93.** $\frac{1}{10}$ **95.** $\frac{3}{2}$ **97.** $\frac{2}{81}$ **99.** They are the same.

Calculator Connections 2.4, p. 139

101. $\frac{555}{5356}$ **103.** $\frac{275,152}{225}$

Section 2.5 Practice Exercises, pp. 145–149

3. $\frac{18}{5}$ **5.** 2   **7.** $\frac{5}{3}$ **9.** 1   **11.** 1   **13.** $\frac{8}{7}$ **15.** $\frac{9}{10}$ **17.** $\frac{1}{4}$

19. No reciprocal exists.   **21.** $\frac{1}{3}$ **23.** Multiplying   **25.** $\frac{8}{25}$ **27.** $\frac{35}{26}$

29. $\frac{35}{9}$ **31.** 5   **33.** 1   **35.** $\frac{21}{2}$ **37.** 20   **39.** 16   **41.** $\frac{3}{5}$ **43.** $\frac{1}{4}$

45. $\frac{90}{13}$ **47.** 20   **49.** $\frac{154}{3}$ **51.** $\frac{7}{2}$ **53.** $\frac{5}{36}$ **55.** 8   **57.** $\frac{2}{5}$ **59.** $\frac{40}{3}$

61. 2   **63.** $\frac{55}{56}$ **65.** $\frac{3}{2}$ **67.** $\frac{2}{3} \cdot 6$ multiplies $\frac{2}{3}$ by $\frac{6}{1}$, and $\frac{2}{3} \div 6$

multiplies $\frac{2}{3}$ by $\frac{1}{6}$. So $\frac{2}{3} \cdot 6 = 4$ and $\frac{2}{3} \div 6 = \frac{1}{9}$.   **69.** 3   **71.** $\frac{7}{6}$

73. $\frac{7}{32}$ **75.** $\frac{9}{400}$ **77.** 49   **79.** 18   **81.** 24 cups of juice

83. Li wrapped 54 packages.   **85.** The stack will be 12 in. high.

87. a. 27 commercials in 1 hr   **b.** 648 commercials in 1 day

89. a. She plans to sell $\frac{3}{4}$ acre.   **b.** She will keep $\frac{3}{2}$ or $1\frac{1}{2}$ acres.

91. She can prepare 14 samples.   **93. a.** Ricardo's mother will

pay \$16,000.   **b.** Ricardo will have to pay \$8000.   **c.** He will have

to finance \$216,000.   **95.** 12 ft, because $\frac{5}{2} \cdot 12 = 30$.

Calculator Connections 2.5, p. 149

... $\frac{3}{4}$ ... $\frac{1}{8}$ ... Tabitha earned \$56.   **57. a.** 7 weeks

old   **b.** $8\frac{1}{2}$ weeks old   **59. a.** Lucy earned \$72 more than Ricky.

b. Together they earned \$922.   **61.** 2   **63.** $5\frac{1}{3}$ **65.** 0   **67.** $1\frac{1}{6}$

69. 0   **71.** $1\frac{1}{2}$ **73.** Undefined   **75.** The total cost is \$168.

Chapter 2 Review Exercises, pp. 162–165

1. $\frac{1}{2}$ **3. a.** $\frac{5}{3}$ **b.** Improper   **5.** $\frac{7}{15}$ **7.** $\frac{7}{6}$ or $1\frac{1}{6}$ **9.** $\frac{57}{5}$ **11.** $5\frac{2}{9}$

13., 15.

17. $60\frac{11}{13}$ **19.** 55, 140, 260, 1200   **21.** Prime   **23.** Neither

25. $2 \cdot 2 \cdot 2 \cdot 2 \cdot 2 \cdot 2$ or 2^6 **27.** $2 \cdot 2 \cdot 3 \cdot 3 \cdot 5 \cdot 5$ or $2^2 \cdot 3^2 \cdot 5^2$

29. 1, 2, 4, 5, 8, 10, 16, 20, 40, 80   **31.** =   **33.** $\frac{2}{7}$ **35.** $\frac{7}{3}$ **37.** 2

39. $\frac{7}{10}$ **41. a.** $\frac{3}{5}$ **b.** $\frac{2}{5}$ **43.** $\frac{32}{9}$ **45.** 15   **47.** $\frac{12}{7}$ **49.** $\frac{1}{625}$

51. $\frac{1}{17}$ **53.** $A = lw$ **55.** $\frac{10}{3}$ or $3\frac{1}{3}$ m²   **57.** Maximus requires $\frac{7}{2}$

or $3\frac{1}{2}$ yd of lumber.   **59.** There are 300 Asian American students.

61. There are 750 Caucasian male students.   **63.** 1   **65.** $\frac{1}{7}$ **67.** 6

69. Multiplying   **71.** $\frac{7}{5}$ **73.** $\frac{1}{6}$ **75.** 14   **77.** $\frac{4}{5}$ **79.** $\frac{1}{52}$

81. $18 \div \frac{2}{3}; 27$ **83.** Amelia earned \$576.   **85.** Yes. $9 \div \frac{3}{8} = 24$ so

he will have 24 pieces, which is more than enough for his class.

87. $23\frac{2}{3}$ **89.** $22\frac{1}{2}$ **91.** $1\frac{1}{2}$ **93.** $4\frac{1}{2}$ **95.** $\frac{3}{5}$ **97.** It will take $3\frac{1}{8}$ gal.

Chapter 2 Test, pp. 166–167

1. a. $\frac{5}{8}$ **b.** Proper   **2. a.** $\frac{7}{3}$ **b.** Improper   **3.** $\frac{11}{2}$; $5\frac{1}{2}$ **4.** $\frac{7}{7}$ is an

improper fraction because the numerator is greater than or equal to

the denominator.   **5. a.** $3\frac{2}{3}$ **b.** $\frac{34}{9}$

6.   **7.**

8.

9.

10. a. Composite **b.** Neither **c.** Prime **d.** Neither **e.** Prime
f. Composite **11. a.** 1, 2, 4, 5, 8, 10, 16, 20, 40, 80
b. $2 \cdot 2 \cdot 2 \cdot 2 \cdot 5$ or $2^4 \cdot 5$ **12. a.** Add the digits of the number. If
the sum is divisible by 3, then the original number is divisible by 3.
b. Yes. **13. a.** No **b.** Yes **c.** Yes **d.** No **14.** = **15.** ≠
16. $\frac{10}{7}$ or $1\frac{3}{7}$ **17.** $\frac{6}{7}$ **18. a.** Christine; $\frac{3}{5}$; Brad: $\frac{4}{5}$ **b.** Brad has the

greater fractional part completed. **19.** $\frac{19}{69}$ **20.** $\frac{25}{2}$ or $12\frac{1}{2}$ **21.** $\frac{4}{9}$

22. $\frac{1}{2}$ **23.** $\frac{4}{15}$ **24.** $\frac{3}{4}$ **25.** $\frac{4}{35}$ **26.** $9\frac{3}{5}$ **27.** $\frac{13}{12}$ **28.** $\frac{44}{3}$ or $14\frac{2}{3}$ cm^2

29. $20 \div \frac{1}{4}$ **30.** 48 quarter-pounders **31.** 5 dogs are female pure

breeds. **32.** They can build on a maximum of $\frac{2}{5}$ acre.

Chapters 1 and 2 Cumulative Review, pp. 167–168

1.

Mountain	Standard Form	Height (ft) Words
Mt. Foraker (Alaska)	17,400	Seventeen thousand, four hundred
Mt. Kilimanjaro (Tanzania)	19,340	Nineteen thousand, three hundred forty
El Libertador (Argentina)	22,047	Twenty-two thousand, forty-seven
Mont Blanc (France-Italy)	15,771	Fifteen thousand, seven hundred seventy-one

2. 1430 **3.** 139 **4.** 214,344 **5.** 24 **6.** 1863 **7.** 18 R2
8. 120,000,000,000 **9.** 184 **10.** 6 **11.** 22 **12.** 16 **13.** 4 **14.** d
15. c **16.** b **17.** e **18.** a **19. a.** $\frac{4}{7}$ **b.** $\frac{7}{3}$ or $2\frac{1}{3}$ **20. a.** Proper

b. Improper **c.** Improper **21. a.** 1, 2, 3, 5, 6, 10, 15, 30
b. $2 \cdot 3 \cdot 5$ **22. a.** $\frac{12}{7}$ or $1\frac{5}{7}$ **b.** $\frac{2}{5}$ **23.** $\frac{119}{171}$ **24.** $\frac{5}{6}$

25. Yes. $\frac{8}{13} \cdot \frac{5}{16} = \frac{5}{26}$ and $\frac{5}{16} \cdot \frac{8}{13} = \frac{5}{26}$

26. Yes. $\left(\frac{1}{2} \cdot \frac{2}{9}\right) \cdot \frac{5}{3} = \frac{1}{9} \cdot \frac{5}{3} = \frac{5}{27}$ and $\frac{1}{2} \cdot \left(\frac{2}{9} \cdot \frac{5}{3}\right) = \frac{1}{2} \cdot \left(\frac{10}{27}\right) = \frac{5}{27}$

27. $\frac{6}{25}$ **28.** $\frac{11}{9}$ or $1\frac{2}{9}$ m^2 **29.** 50 ft^2 **30.** $\frac{3}{40}$ of the students are

males from out of state.

Chapter 3

Chapter 3 Preview, p. 170

1. $\frac{13}{2}$ **3.** $\frac{7}{4}$ **5.** 72 **7.** $\frac{8}{15}, \frac{11}{20}, \frac{7}{12}, \frac{3}{5}$ **9.** $\frac{11}{16}$ **11.** $\frac{3}{2}$ **13.** $2\frac{1}{14}$

15. $\frac{7}{9}$ **17.** Area: 201 ft^2

Section 3.1 Practice Exercises, pp. 175–178

3. 8 ft **5.** 20 m **7.** 7 fourths

9. 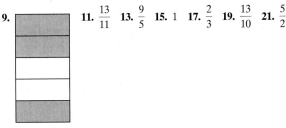 **11.** $\frac{13}{11}$ **13.** $\frac{9}{5}$ **15.** 1 **17.** $\frac{2}{3}$ **19.** $\frac{13}{10}$ **21.** $\frac{5}{2}$

23. Bethany has $\frac{5}{2}$ or $2\frac{1}{2}$ cups of bleach and water mixture.

25. 11 baskets **27.** 6 fifths

29. **31.** $\frac{3}{8}$ **33.** $\frac{3}{2}$ **35.** 2 **37.** $\frac{2}{3}$ **39.** $\frac{2}{5}$ **41.** $\frac{1}{4}$

43. $\frac{1}{4}$ g is left. **45.** $\frac{3}{2}$ **47.** $\frac{12}{5}$ **49.** 1 **51.** $\frac{4}{5}$ **53.** $\frac{5}{2}$ **55.** $\frac{9}{5}$

57. $\frac{5}{3}$ **59.** $\frac{16}{7}$ **61.** $\frac{8}{27}$ **63.** $\frac{13}{3}$ **65.** There was $\frac{1}{2}$ gal left over.

67. He used $\frac{3}{8}$ L. **69.** $\frac{12}{7}$ or $1\frac{5}{7}$ m **71.** $\frac{7}{2}$ or $3\frac{1}{2}$ in.

73. a. Thilan walked $5\frac{1}{2}$ mi total. **b.** He walked an average of $\frac{11}{12}$ mi

per day. **75.** Perimeter: 2 ft; area: $\frac{15}{64}$ ft^2 **77.** Perimeter: $\frac{70}{3}$ or

$23\frac{1}{3}$ yd; area: $\frac{286}{9}$ or $31\frac{7}{9}$ yd^2 **79.** $\frac{3}{5} + \frac{2}{5}$; 1 **81.** $\frac{11}{15} - \frac{8}{15}$; $\frac{1}{5}$

Section 3.2 Practice Exercises, pp. 184–188

3. $\frac{1}{2}$ **5.** $\frac{5}{3}$ **7.** 6 **9. a.** 48, 72, 240 **b.** 4, 8, 12 **11. a.** 72, 360,

108 **b.** 6, 12, 9 **13.** 5, 10, 15, 20, 25 **15.** 14, 28, 42, 56, 70
17. 16, 32, 48, 64, 80 **19.** 50 **21.** 48 **23.** 120 **25.** $2 \cdot 2 \cdot 2 \cdot 3$
27. $2 \cdot 2 \cdot 2 \cdot 5$ **29.** $2 \cdot 2 \cdot 3 \cdot 3$ **31.** 72 **33.** 60 **35.** 75 **37.** 540
39. 60 **41.** 120 **43.** 210 **45.** 240 **47.** 180 **49.** 32 **51.** 120
53. 180 **55.** 80 **57.** 72 **59.** 84 **61.** 360 **63.** 120 **65.** 180
67. The shortest length of floor space is 60 in. **69.** It will take 84

months (7 years) for the planets to be aligned again. **71.** $\frac{14}{21}$

73. $\frac{10}{16}$ **75.** $\frac{12}{16}$ **77.** > **79.** < **81.** = **83.** $\frac{7}{8}$ **85.** $\frac{2}{3}, \frac{3}{4}, \frac{7}{8}$

87. $\frac{1}{4}, \frac{5}{16}, \frac{3}{8}$ **89.** $\frac{13}{12}, \frac{17}{15}, \frac{4}{3}$ **91.** The greatest amount is $\frac{2}{3}$ lb of

turkey. The least amount is $\frac{3}{5}$ lb of ham. **93.** a and b

Section 3.3 Practice Exercises, pp. 194–197

3. $\frac{12}{14}$ **5.** $\frac{14}{21}$ **7.** $\frac{25}{5}$ **9.** $\frac{8}{4}$ **11.** $\frac{80}{100}$ **13.** $\frac{5}{40}$ **15.** $\frac{19}{16}$ **17.** $\frac{1}{4}$

19. $\frac{1}{4}$ **21.** $\frac{83}{42}$ **23.** $\frac{3}{8}$ **25.** $\frac{1}{3}$ **27.** $\frac{19}{10}$ **29.** $\frac{5}{8}$ **31.** $\frac{25}{8}$ **33.** $\frac{8}{3}$

35. $\frac{17}{3}$ **37.** $\frac{2}{7}$ **39.** $\frac{89}{100}$ **41.** $\frac{1}{100}$ **43.** $\frac{391}{1000}$ **45.** $\frac{101}{120}$ **47.** $\frac{23}{60}$

49. $\frac{38}{35}$ **51.** $\frac{7}{12}$ **53.** $\frac{37}{28}$ **55.** $\frac{4}{3}$ **57.** $\frac{1}{36}$ **59.** $\frac{13}{125}$ **61.** $\frac{23}{24}$

63. Inez added $\frac{9}{8}$ or $1\frac{1}{8}$ cup. **65.** Yes. There will be $\frac{3}{20}$ oz left.

67. The job did not get completed. There is still $\frac{1}{40}$ of the job left.

69. a. $\frac{13}{36}$ **b.** $\frac{23}{36}$ **71.** $\frac{13}{5}$ or $2\frac{3}{5}$ ft **73.** Perimeter: 3 ft **75.** b

Calculator Connections 3.3, p. 197

59. The total area of the four shutters is $26\frac{8}{?}$ ft^2 **61.** The area is

Simplify the product to lowest terms, if possible. To divide fractions, multiply the first fraction by the reciprocal of the second fraction.

Simplify to lowest terms, if possible.   **5.** $\frac{9}{5}$ **6.** $\frac{14}{25}$ **7.** $\frac{4}{9}$ **8.** $\frac{5}{3}$

9. $\frac{13}{28}$ **10.** $\frac{3}{14}$ **11.** $\frac{50}{27}$ **12.** $\frac{5}{9}$ **13.** $\frac{5}{9}$ **14.** $\frac{7}{4}$ **15.** 2   **16.** 5

17. $\frac{1}{140}$ **18.** $\frac{91}{90}$ **19.** $\frac{44}{15}$ **20.** $\frac{29}{48}$

Section 3.4 Practice Exercises, pp. 204–208

3. $\frac{13}{6}$ **5.** $\frac{13}{7}$ **7.** $\frac{1}{2}$ **9.** $7\frac{4}{11}$ **11.** $15\frac{3}{7}$ **13.** $15\frac{9}{16}$ **15.** $10\frac{13}{15}$

17. 5   **19.** 2   **21.** 15   **23.** 22   **25.** $3\frac{1}{5}$ **27.** $8\frac{2}{3}$ **29.** $11\frac{1}{6}$ **31.** $6\frac{1}{3}$

33. $14\frac{1}{2}$ **35.** $23\frac{1}{8}$ **37.** $19\frac{17}{48}$ **39.** $9\frac{7}{8}$ **41.** $42\frac{2}{7}$ **43.** $11\frac{3}{5}$ **45.** $2\frac{2}{15}$

47. $12\frac{1}{6}$ **49.** $2\frac{5}{14}$ **51. a.** $\frac{3}{3}$ **b.** $\frac{5}{5}$ **c.** $\frac{12}{12}$ **d.** $\frac{6}{6}$ **53.** $11\frac{1}{2}$ **55.** $1\frac{3}{4}$

57. $7\frac{13}{14}$ **59.** $3\frac{1}{6}$ **61.** $2\frac{7}{9}$ **63.** $2\frac{3}{17}$ **65.** $6\frac{5}{14}$ **67.** $7\frac{7}{24}$ **69.** $6\frac{2}{15}$

71. $\frac{11}{16}$ **73.** $9\frac{7}{36}$ **75.** $\frac{29}{32}$ **77.** $10\frac{20}{21}$ **79.** $\frac{32}{35}$ **81.** $7\frac{13}{72}$ **83.** $7\frac{3}{4}$ in.

85. The index finger is longer.   **87.** The total distance is $24\frac{7}{24}$ mi.

89. The water rose $6\frac{5}{8}$ in.   **91.** The total distance is $13\frac{19}{20}$ mi.

93. He worked $5\frac{5}{12}$ hr more on Monday.   **95.** $2\frac{2}{3}$ **97.** $2\frac{1}{6}$

Section 3.5 Practice Exercises, pp. 214–219

3. $12\frac{2}{9}$ **5.** $2\frac{2}{3}$ **7.** $3\frac{13}{36}$ **9.** $\frac{67}{13}$ **11.** $\frac{39}{10}$ **13.** $5\frac{4}{5}$ **15.** $1\frac{11}{19}$ **17.** $3\frac{2}{3}$

19. $7\frac{1}{2}$ **21.** $4\frac{2}{7}$ **23.** 13   **25.** $\frac{13}{25}$ **27.** $\frac{8}{15}$ **29.** $14\frac{7}{12}$ **31.** $1\frac{3}{7}$

33. a. The difference is $\frac{3}{10}$ sec.   **b.** The average is $3\frac{3}{5}$ sec.

35. a. The total weight loss is 51 lb.   **b.** The average is $8\frac{1}{2}$ lb.

c. The difference is $6\frac{1}{2}$ lb.   **37.** The stock dropped $$3\frac{7}{8}$.

39. George will receive $26,750.   **41.** Each piece is $3\frac{13}{16}$ ft.

43. $2\frac{1}{4}$ lb of cheese was eaten.   **45.** 20 loaves can be made.

47. The new rate is $7\frac{1}{4}$ points.   **49.** Stephanie will need $11\frac{1}{4}$ yd for

the dresses.   **51.** Wilma has $1\frac{1}{12}$ lb left.   **53.** Joan saves $152\frac{1}{2}$ gal.

55. She needs $15\frac{1}{3}$ ft more.   **57.** The perimeter is 100 in.

c. 22, 44, 66, 88   **23. a.** 1, 2, 4, 5, 10, 20, 25, 50, 100   **b.** 1, 5, 13, 65
c. 1, 2, 5, 7, 10, 14, 35, 70   **25.** 150   **27.** 420   **29.** They will meet on
the 12th day.   **31.** $\frac{63}{35}$ **33.** >   **35.** $\frac{8}{15}, \frac{72}{105}, \frac{7}{10}, \frac{27}{35}$ **37.** $\frac{29}{100}$ **39.** $\frac{1}{2}$

41. $\frac{43}{20}$ **43.** $\frac{1}{34}$ **45.** $\frac{17}{40}$ **47.** $\frac{1}{15}$ **49. a.** $\frac{35}{4}$ or $8\frac{3}{4}$ m

b. $\frac{315}{128}$ or $2\frac{59}{128}$ m^2 **51.** $11\frac{11}{63}$ **53.** $2\frac{5}{8}$ **55.** $3\frac{1}{24}$ **57.** $12\frac{5}{14}$ **59.** $3\frac{2}{5}$

61. $63\frac{15}{16}$ **63.** Estimate: 8   Exact: $8\frac{5}{18}$ **65.** Estimate: 50

Exact: $50\frac{9}{40}$ **67.** Corry drove a total of $8\frac{1}{6}$ hr.   **69.** $12\frac{2}{5}$ **71.** $\frac{4}{27}$

73. 12   **75.** The appraised value is $144,000.

Chapter 3 Test, p. 227

1. $\frac{7}{5}$ **2.** $\frac{1}{2}$ **3.** When subtracting like fractions, keep the same

denominator and subtract the numerators. When multiplying
fractions, multiply the denominators as well as the numerators.
4. a. 24, 48, 72, 96   **b.** 1, 2, 3, 4, 6, 8, 12, 24   **c.** $2 \cdot 2 \cdot 2 \cdot 3$ or $2^3 \cdot 3$

5. 240   **6.** $\frac{35}{63}$ **7.** $\frac{33}{63}$ **8.** $\frac{36}{63}$ **9.** $\frac{11}{21}, \frac{5}{9}, \frac{4}{7}$ **10.** $\frac{9}{16}$ **11.** $\frac{49}{27}$ **12.** $\frac{1}{3}$

13. $\frac{2}{3}$ **14.** $17\frac{3}{8}$ **15.** $2\frac{7}{11}$ **16.** $60\frac{5}{12}$ **17.** $1\frac{1}{2}$ **18.** $\frac{25}{6}$ or $4\frac{1}{6}$

19. 7   **20.** $\frac{12}{295}$ **21.** $\frac{10}{3}$ or $3\frac{1}{3}$ **22.** 1 lb is needed.   **23.** The Ford

Expedition can tow 8950 lb.   **24.** Area: $25\frac{2}{25}$ m^2; perimeter: $20\frac{1}{5}$ m

25. Justin has $10,500 for cabinets.   **26. a.** The difference is $4\frac{2}{3}$ ft.

b. The average is $7\frac{3}{8}$ ft.

Chapters 1–3 Cumulative Review, pp. 228–229

1. Twenty-three million, four hundred thousand, eight hundred six
2. 96   **3.** 48   **4.** 1728   **5.** 3   **6.** 1,500,000,000   **7.** $4^2 \cdot 5^4 \cdot 8^2$
8. 36   **9.** 17, 19, 23, 29, 31   **10.** $2 \cdot 5 \cdot 7$ **11.** Numerator: 21;
denominator: 17   **12.** $\frac{5}{8}$ **13.** $\frac{17}{22}$ had pepperoni and $\frac{5}{22}$ did not have
pepperoni.   **14. a.** Improper   **b.** Proper   **c.** Improper   **15.** b
16. a. Composite   **b.** Composite   **c.** Prime

17. $2 \cdot 2 \cdot 2 \cdot 3 \cdot 3 \cdot 5$ or $2^3 \cdot 3^2 \cdot 5$ **18.** $\frac{1}{5}$ **19.** $\frac{3}{8}$ **20.** $\frac{4}{7}$ **21.** $\frac{3}{4}$

22. $\frac{33}{16}$ **23.** $\frac{2}{5}$ **24.** $\frac{305}{22}$ or $13\frac{19}{22}$ **25.** $\frac{26}{17}$ or $1\frac{9}{17}$ **26.** $\frac{10}{3}$ or $3\frac{1}{3}$

27. The distance around is approximately 88 cm.   **28.** $4\frac{1}{3}$ yd

29. $\frac{63}{8}$ or $7\frac{7}{8}$ m^2 **30. a.** The difference in the intensity is $1\frac{3}{10}$.

b. The average intensity is $6\frac{7}{10}$.

Chapter 4

Chapter 4 Preview, p. 232

1. Forty-five and three hundredths **3. a.** < **b.** > **5.** 74.001
7. $1296.37 **9.** 23,889 **11.** 63.48 cm^2 **13.** 124.$\overline{6}$
15.

	Decimal form	Fraction form
a.	0.55	$\frac{11}{20}$
b.	1.8	$1\frac{8}{9}$
c.	2.$\overline{3}$	$2\frac{1}{3}$ or $\frac{7}{3}$
d.	4.35	$4\frac{7}{20}$
e.	0.$\overline{27}$	$\frac{3}{11}$

17. 3.31

Section 4.1 Practice Exercises, pp. 239–243

3. 100 **5.** 10,000 **7.** $\frac{1}{100}$ **9.** $\frac{1}{10,000}$ **11.** Tenths **13.** Hundredths
15. Tens **17.** Ten-thousandths **19.** Thousandths **21.** Ones
23. Seven-tenths **25.** Nineteen hundredths **27.** Fifty-one
thousandths **29.** Four and twenty-six hundredths **31.** Three and
four-tenths **33.** Twenty-one and five-tenths **35.** Seven and three
hundred thirty-eight thousandths **37.** One and two hundred one
ten-thousandths **39.** $1\frac{9}{10}$ **41.** $4\frac{1}{5}$ **43.** $\frac{3}{4}$ **45.** $\frac{9}{20}$ **47.** $32\frac{181}{200}$
49. $\frac{5}{2}$ **51.** $\frac{113}{20}$ **53.** $\frac{73}{5}$ **55.** $\frac{2133}{100}$ **57.** < **59.** > **61.** > **63.** <
65. a, c, d **67.** 12.4, 12.46, 12.49, 12.5 **69.** 0.0499, 0.04999, 0.05001,
0.4999, $\frac{5}{10}$ **71.** 148.124, 148.148, 148.295, 148.466 **73.** 49.9
75. 33.42 **77.** 9.096 **79.** 21.0 **81.** 16.80 **83.** 7.1 **85.** a

	Number	Hundreds	Tens	Tenths	Hundredths	Thousandths
87.	349.2395	300	350	349.2	349.24	349.240
89.	79.0046	100	80	79.0	79.00	79.005

91. Five and twenty-three hundredths dollars **93.** Fifteen and
three-hundredths dollars **95.** Twenty-one and thirteen hundredths
dollars **97.** 0.279

Section 4.2 Practice Exercises, pp. 248–253

3. b, c **5.** a, d **7.** 42.31 **9.** 1.0 **11.** 63.2 **13.** 8.951 **15.** 15.991
17. 79.8005 **19.** 31.0148 **21.** 62.6032 **23.** 100.414 **25.** 128.44
27. 82.063 **29.** 14.24 **31.** 3.68 **33.** 12.32 **35.** 5.677 **37.** 1.877
39. 57.368 **41.** 21.6646 **43.** 14.765 **45.** 159.558 **47.** 15.347
49. 6.581 **51.** 19.912 **53.** 10.3327 **55. a.** 321.724 days
b. 156.73 days **57. a.** The water is rising 1.7 in./hr. **b.** At 1:00 P.M.
the level will be 11 in. **c.** At 3:00 P.M. the level will be 14.4 in.
59.

Check No.	Description	Credit	Debit	Balance
				$ 245.62
2409	Electric bill		$ 52.48	193.14
2410	Groceries		72.44	120.70
2411	Department store		108.34	12.36
	Payroll	$1084.90		1097.26
2412	Restaurant		23.87	1073.39
	Transfer from savings	200		1273.39

61. The new price is $2.158. **63.** The pile containing the two
nickels and two pennies is higher. **65.** $x = 8.9$ in.; $y = 15.4$ in.;

the perimeter is 98.8 in. **67.** $x = 2.075$ ft; $y = 2.59$ ft; the perimeter
is 22.17 ft. **69.** 27.2 mi **71.** 7 mm

Calculator Connections 4.2, pp. 253–254

73. 26.6 million **75.** 1831.6 million

Section 4.3 Practice Exercises, pp. 260–264

3. 1000 **5.** 0.01 **7.** 100 **9.** 30 **11.** 7000 **13.** 0.2 **15.** 0.04
17. 0.4 **19.** 3.6 **21.** 8 **23.** 0.18 **25.** 17.6 **27.** 37.35 **29.** 4.176
31. 4.736 **33.** 2.891 **35.** 114.88 **37.** 2.248 **39.** 0.00144
41. The decimal point will move to the right 2 places. **43. a.** 51
b. 510 **c.** 5100 **d.** 51,000 **45.** 216.3 **47.** 18,220 **49.** 59.32
51. The decimal point will move to the left 1 place. **53.** 0.933
55. 0.05403 **57.** 0.00005 **59.** 96,700,000 **61.** 16,000
63. $20,549,000,000 **65.** 324¢ **67.** 6134¢ **69.** 37¢ **71.** $3.47
73. $20.41 **75.** $0.34 **77. a.** $1 **b.** $1.50 **79.** The total cost is
$24.29. **81.** The bill was $294.50. **83.** $2.81 can be saved.
85. 0.00115 km^2 **87.** The area is 333 ft^2. **89.** $(0.2)^2 = 0.04$, which
is not equal to 0.4. **91.** 0.16 **93.** 1.69 **95.** 0.001 **97. a.** 0.09
b. 0.3 **99.** 0.1 **101.** 0.6

Calculator Connections 4.3, pp. 264–265

103. 1914.0625 **105.** $1991.25 is saved. **107.** The yearly total is
$1183.08.

Midchapter Review, p. 265

1. 223.04 **2.** 12,304 **3.** 23.04 **4.** 1.2304 **5.** 123.03 **6.** 123.05
7. 10.72 **8.** 10.92 **9.** 1.082 **10.** 20.82 **11.** 108.2 **12.** 0.82
13. a. 7.191 **b.** 7.191 **c.** Yes **14.** The commutative property of
addition **15. a.** 11.4768 **b.** 11.4768 **c.** Yes **16.** The
commutative property of multiplication **17.** 0.02484 **18.** 84.31
19. 4.5579 **20.** 0.12291 **21.** 67.032 **22.** 1.672

Section 4.4 Practice Exercises, pp. 274–277

3. 5280 **5.** 3.776 **7.** 2.02 **9.** 0.9 **11.** 0.18 **13.** 0.53 **15.** 21.1
17. 1.96 **19.** 2.55 **21.** 0.035 **23.** 16.84 **25.** 5.$\overline{3}$ **27.** 3.1$\overline{6}$
29. 2.$\overline{15}$ **31.** 2.$\overline{54}$ **33.** 56 **35.** 2.975 **37.** 208.$\overline{3}$ **39.** 48.5
41. a. 2.4 **b.** 2.44 **c.** 2.444 **43. a.** 1.9 **b.** 1.89 **c.** 1.889
45. a. 3.6 **b.** 3.63 **c.** 3.626 **47.** 0.26 **49.** 14.8 **51.** 20.667
53. 35.67 **55.** The decimal point will move to the left 2 places.
57. 0.03923 **59.** 9.802 **61.** 0.00027 **63.** 0.00102 **65.** The
decimal point will move to the right 1 place. **67.** 503 **69.** 9.92
71. 3200 **73.** 12,340 **75.** Unreasonable; 32 miles per gallon
77. Unreasonable; $340.00 **79.** The monthly payment is $42.50.
81. 65 balls per match. **83.** Babe Ruth's batting average was 0.342.
85. 47.265 **87.** b, d

Calculator Connections 4.4, p. 277

89. $886 **91.** 265 people per square mile

Section 4.5 Practice Exercises, pp. 283–286

3. 0.39 **5.** 0.0071 **7.** $\frac{1}{625}$ **9.** $\frac{1}{8}$ **11.** $\frac{16}{100}$; 0.16 **13.** $\frac{38}{1000}$; 0.038
15. $\frac{8}{10}$; 0.8 **17.** 0.875 **19.** 0.3125 **21.** 5.25 **23.** 1.2 **25.** 0.75
27. 2.35 **29.** 7.45 **31.** 0.88 **33.** 3.$\overline{8}$ **35.** 0.4$\overline{6}$ **37.** 0.52$\overline{7}$
39. 0.5$\overline{4}$ **41.** 0.1$\overline{26}$ **43.** 0.$\overline{123}$ **45.** 0.$\overline{142857}$ **47.** 0.$\overline{076923}$
49. 0.9 **51.** 0.71 **53.** 1.2 **55.** Multiply the numerator and
denominator by 25 to make the denominator a power of 10.
$\frac{1 \cdot 25}{4 \cdot 25} = \frac{25}{100} = 0.25$; or divide $4\overline{)1.00}^{\,0.25}$ **57. a.** 0.$\overline{1}$ **b.** 0.$\overline{2}$ **c.** 0.$\overline{4}$

		9			22	
d.	$0.\overline{45}$	$\dfrac{5}{11}$	**d.**	1.68	$\dfrac{42}{25}$	

65.

Stock	Symbol	Closing Price ($) (Decimal)	Closing Price ($) (Fraction)
Corning	GLW	12.38	$12\dfrac{19}{50}$
Walgreen	WAG	34.95	$34\dfrac{19}{20}$
Brookstone	BKST	19.50	$19\dfrac{1}{2}$
SnapOn	SNA	33.44	$33\dfrac{11}{25}$

67. =   **69.** <   **71.** >   **73.** <   **75.** =   **77.** <

79. $\dfrac{1}{10}, 0.\overline{1}, \dfrac{1}{5}$

81. $1.75, 1.\overline{7}, 1.8$

83. $\dfrac{9}{9} = 1$ **85.** 7

Section 4.6 Practice Exercises, pp. 294–298

3. 313.72   **5.** $\dfrac{107}{27}$ **7.** $\dfrac{5}{4}$ **9.** 6.96   **11.** 8.77   **13.** 25.75   **15.** 6.25
17. 2   **19.** 12.98   **21.** 67.35   **23.** 25.05   **25.** 23.4   **27.** 1.28
29. 10.83   **31.** 2.84   **33.** $0.93\overline{5}$ **35.** $4.4\overline{3}$ **37. a.** Professor McGonagal makes $21.75 per hour overtime.   **b.** She earns $797.50.   **39.** Jorge will be charged $98.75.   **41.** She has 24.3 g left for dinner.   **43.** Caren should get $4.77 in change.   **45.** Duncan's average is 78.75.   **47.** The average snowfall per month is 14.54 in.
49. a. The stock increased by $1.07.   **b.** Melanie made $214.00.
51. Answers will vary.   **53. a.** 29.8   **b.** Overweight   **55.** 3.475
57. 0.52

Calculator Connections 4.6, p. 299

59. a. Marty will have to finance $120,000.   **b.** There are 360 months in 30 years.   **c.** He will pay $287,409.60   **d.** He will pay $167,409.60 in interest.   **61.** Each person will get approximately $13,410.10.

	Tenths	8.7	52.5	0.4
	Hundredths	8.67	52.53	0.41
	Thousandths	8.667	52.525	0.409
	Ten-thousandths	8.6667	52.5253	0.4094

53. 11.97   **55.** 9.0234   **57.** 260   **59.** $\dfrac{6}{10}; 0.6$ **61.** $\dfrac{54}{1000}; 0.054$
63. 3.52   **65.** 0.4375   **67.** $1.52\overline{7}$ **69.** $0.\overline{153846}$ **71.** 0.87   **73.** 2.83
75. $1\dfrac{2}{3}$ **77.** $5\dfrac{7}{9}$ **79.** >   **81.** <   **83.** 0.713   **85.** 125.6   **87.** 25.12
89. Marvin must drive 34 mi more.

Chapter 4 Test, pp. 310–311

1. a. Tens place   **b.** Hundredths place   **2.** Five hundred nine and twenty-four thousandths   **3.** $1\dfrac{13}{50}; \dfrac{63}{50}$ **4.** 0.465, 0.486, 0.522, 0.550
5. b is correct.   **6.** 52.832   **7.** 21.29   **8.** 126.45   **9.** 5.08   **10.** 1.22
11. 12.2243   **12.** $120.\overline{6}$ **13.** 439.81   **14. a.** 61.4°F   **b.** 1.4°F
15. a. 50,500,000 votes   **b.** 51,000,000 votes   **c.** The difference is approximately 500,000 in favor of Al Gore.   **16.** When dividing by 10, move the decimal point 1 place to the left. When multiplying by 10, move the decimal point 1 place to the right.   **17.** When dividing by 0.01, move the decimal point 2 places to the right. When multiplying by 0.01, move the decimal point 2 places to the left.
18. 4.592   **19.** 57,923   **20.** 8012   **21.** 0.002931   **22. a.** 67.5 in.^{2}
b. 75.5 in.^{2} **c.** 157.3 in.^{2} **23.** 75 cents equals 75¢ which is the same as $0.75. The number .75¢ means seventy-five hundredths of a cent.
24.

Year	Decimal	Fraction
1984	41.02 sec	$41\frac{1}{50}$ sec
1988	39.10	$39\frac{1}{10}$
1992	40.33	$40\frac{33}{100}$
1994	39.25	$39\frac{1}{4}$

25. $3.2, 3\dfrac{1}{2}, 3.\overline{5}$

26. 9.57   **27.** 13.65

28. a. Faulkner walked 19.8 mi.   **b.** The average is 2.8 mi.

Chapters 1–4 Cumulative Review Exercises, pp. 311–312

1. 14   **2.** 4039   **3.** 4840   **4.** 3872   **5.** 2,415,000   **6.** Dividend: 4530; divisor: 225; whole-number part of the quotient: 20; remainder: 30   **7.** To check a division problem, multiply the whole-number part of the quotient and the divisor. Then add the remainder to get the dividend. That is, 20 × 225 + 30 = 4530.
8. The difference between sales for Wal-Mart and Sears is

$181,956 million. **9.** $\frac{6}{55}$ **10.** $\frac{4}{7}$ **11.** $\frac{49}{100}$ **12.** 2 **13.** $\frac{2}{3}$ **14.** 0

15. There is $9000 left. **16.** $\frac{2}{5}$ **17.** $\frac{97}{100}$ **18.** $\frac{38}{11}$ **19.** $\frac{33}{7}$ **20.** $\frac{3}{2}$

21. Area: $\frac{15}{64}$ ft^2; perimeter: 2 ft **22.** The average is $1\frac{3}{16}$ km.

23. 174.13 **24.** 668.79 **25.** 75.275 **26.** 16 **27.** 339.12 **28.** 46.48
29. a. 3.75248 **b.** 3.75248 **c.** Commutative property of multiplication
30.

Bone	Length (in.) (Decimal)	Length (in.) (Mixed Number)
Femur	19.875	$19\frac{7}{8}$
Fibula	15.9375	$15\frac{15}{16}$
Humerus	14.375	$14\frac{3}{8}$
Innominate bone (hip)	7.5	$7\frac{1}{2}$

Chapter 5

Chapter 5 Preview, p. 314

1. 3 : 11, $\frac{3}{11}$ **3.** $\frac{13}{20}$ **5.** $\frac{26}{1}$ **7.** 492.5 mi/hr or mph **9.** $1.05 per
pound for the 8-lb bag, $1.25 per pound for the 4-lb bag, and $0.65
per pound for the 40-lb bag. The best buy is the 40-lb bag.
11. a. $2.05 **b.** $0.1025/yr **13.** $\frac{22}{14} = \frac{33}{21}$ **15.** $x = 0.5$ **17.** There
are approximately 96,900 births. **19.** The tree is 14.4 ft tall.

Section 5.1 Practice Exercises, pp. 319–322

3. 5 : 6 and $\frac{5}{6}$ **5.** 11 to 4 and $\frac{11}{4}$ **7.** 1 : 2 and 1 to 2 **9. a.** $\frac{3}{2}$

b. $\frac{2}{3}$ **c.** $\frac{3}{5}$ **11. a.** $\frac{21}{52}$ **b.** $\frac{21}{31}$ **13.** $\frac{2}{3}$ **15.** $\frac{1}{5}$ **17.** $\frac{4}{1}$ **19.** $\frac{11}{5}$

21. $\frac{6}{5}$ **23.** $\frac{1}{2}$ **25.** $\frac{3}{2}$ **27.** $\frac{6}{7}$ **29.** $\frac{8}{9}$ **31.** $\frac{7}{1}$ **33.** $\frac{1}{8}$ **35.** $\frac{4}{3}$ **37.** $\frac{1}{15}$

39. a. $\frac{6}{16} = \frac{3}{8}$ **b.** $\frac{\frac{1}{2}}{1\frac{1}{3}} = \frac{3}{8}$ **41.** $\frac{41}{5}$ **43.** $\frac{1}{12}$ **45.** $\frac{15}{32}$ **47.** $\frac{20}{61}$

49. $\frac{2}{3}$ **51.** $\frac{1}{4}$

Section 5.2 Practice Exercises, pp. 327–330

3. 3:5 and $\frac{3}{5}$ **5.** $\frac{4}{3}$ **7.** $\frac{9}{17}$ **9.** $\frac{33}{37}$ **11.** $\frac{44 \text{ ft}}{5 \text{ sec}}$ **13.** $\frac{7 \text{ blooms}}{3 \text{ plants}}$

15. $\frac{112 \text{ words}}{5 \text{ min}}$ **17.** $\frac{1 \text{ in.}}{3 \text{ hr}}$ **19.** $\frac{7 \text{ plants}}{11 \text{ ft}}$ **21.** $\frac{25 \text{ students}}{2 \text{ advisers}}$

23. 113 mi/day **25.** 96 km/hr **27.** $55 per payment **29.** $0.38/lb
31. $256,000 per person **33.** 0.069 sec/m **35.** $0.050 per oz
37. $0.995 per liter **39.** $52.50 per tire **41.** $5.417 per bodysuit
43. 305,000 vehicles/year **45. a.** $415/year **b.** $135/year
c. Private colleges **47.** Cheetah: 29 m/sec; antelope: 24 m/sec. The
cheetah is faster. **49.** The larger can is $0.041 per ounce, and the
smaller can is $0.051 per ounce. The larger can is the better buy.

Calculator Connections 5.2, pp. 331–332

51. a. 9.9 wins/yr **b.** 8.6 wins/yr **c.** Shula **53. a.** $0.18
b. $0.14 **c.** $0.08; The best buy is Irish Spring. **55. a.** $0.299 per
ounce **b.** $0.208 per ounce; The best buy is the 4-pack of 6-oz cans
for $4.99. **c.** $0.332 per ounce

Midchapter Review, p. 3?

1. A ratio is a comparison of tw
rate is a comparison of two quar

2. A rate needs to have the un

5. $\frac{13}{24}$ **6.** $\frac{9 \text{ bushels}}{2 \text{ trees}}$ **7.** $\frac{36 \text{ pla}}{5 \text{ y}}$

11. $\frac{1}{4}$ **12.** $\frac{4 \text{ m}}{3 \text{ sec}}$ **13.** $\frac{25 \text{ tiles}}{2 \text{ ft}^2}$

Section 5.3 Practice E

3. $\frac{1}{15}$ **5.** $\frac{3 \text{ apples}}{1 \text{ pie}}$ **7.** $\frac{22 \text{ m}}{3 \text{ ga}}$

13. $\frac{2}{3} = \frac{4}{6}$ **15.** $\frac{30}{25} = \frac{12}{10}$ **17**
21. No **23.** Yes **25.** Yes
35. 2 **37.** 5 **39.** 8 **41.** 0.(
49. $x = 3$ **51.** $p = 75$ **53.**

59. $x = 12$ **61.** $m = \frac{15}{2}$ or

Section 5.4 Practice Exercises, pp. 346–349

3. = **5.** ≠ **7.** $n = \frac{20}{3}$ or $6\frac{2}{3}$ or $6.\overline{6}$ **9.** $k = 6$ **11.** $y = 4.9$

13. Pam can drive 610 mi on 10 gal of gas. **15.** 78 kg of crushed
rock will be required. **17.** The actual distance is about 80 mi.
19. There were 55 Republicans. **21.** Heads would come up about
315 times. **23.** There would be approximately 3 for a 9-inning
game. **25.** Pierre can buy 743.4 €. **27. a.** 340 women would be
expected. **b.** 160 men would be expected. **29.** There are
approximately 357 bass in the lake. **31.** There are approximately
4000 bison in the park. **33.** $x = 24$ cm, $y = 36$ cm **35.** $x = 1$ yd,
$y = 10.5$ yd **37.** The flagpole is 12 ft high. **39.** The platform is
2.4 m tall. **41.** $x = 17.5$ in. **43.** $x = 6$ ft, $y = 8$ ft **45.** $x = 21$ ft;
$y = 21$ ft; $z = 53.2$ ft

Calculator Connections 5.4, p. 350

47. There were approximately 166,005 crimes committed.
49. Approximately 15,400 women would be expected to have
breast cancer.

Chapter 5 Review Exercises, pp. 354–357

1. 5 to 4 and $\frac{5}{4}$ **3.** 8 : 7 and 8 to 7 **5. a.** $\frac{4}{5}$ **b.** $\frac{5}{4}$ **c.** $\frac{5}{9}$ **7.** $\frac{4}{1}$

9. $\frac{2}{5}$ **11.** $\frac{9}{2}$ **13.** $\frac{4}{3}$ **15. a.** This year's enrollment is 1520 students.

b. $\frac{4}{19}$ **17.** $\frac{1}{5}$ **19.** $\frac{4 \text{ hot dogs}}{9 \text{ min}}$ **21.** $\frac{650 \text{ tons}}{9 \text{ ft}}$ **23.** All unit rates

have a denominator of 1, and reduced rates may not. **25.** 33 mi/hr
or mph **27.** 90 times/sec **29.** $0.599 per ounce **31.** $0.050 per
bag **33.** The difference is about 12¢ per roll or $0.12 per roll.

35. $0.057/yr **37.** $\frac{16}{14} = \frac{12}{10\frac{1}{2}}$ **39.** $\frac{5}{3} = \frac{10}{6}$ **41.** $\frac{\$11}{1 \text{ hr}} = \frac{\$88}{8 \text{ hr}}$

43. No **45.** Yes **47.** Yes **49.** No **51.** $x = 4$ **53.** $b = 3$
55. $h = 13.6$ **57.** The human equivalent is 84 years. **59.** Alabama
has approximately 4,500,000 people. **61.** $x = 10$ in.,
$y = 62.1$ in. **63.** $x = 1.6$ yd, $y = 1.8$ yd

Chapter 5 Test, pp. 357–358

1. 25 to 521, 25 : 521, $\frac{25}{521}$ **2. a.** $\frac{17}{23}$ **b.** $\frac{17}{6}$ **3.** $\frac{9}{7}$ **4.** $\frac{3}{1}$ **5.** $\frac{5}{8}$

6. a. $\frac{21}{125}$ **b.** $\frac{9}{125}$ **c.** The poverty ratio was greater in New Mexico.

7. a. $\dfrac{\frac{1}{2}}{1\frac{1}{2}} = \dfrac{1}{3}$ **b.** $\dfrac{30}{90} = \dfrac{1}{3}$ **8.** $\dfrac{85 \text{ mi}}{2 \text{ hr}}$ **9.** $\dfrac{10 \text{ lb}}{3 \text{ weeks}}$ **10.** $\dfrac{1 \text{ g}}{2 \text{ cookies}}$
11. 21.45 g/cm³ **12.** 2.3 oz/lb **13.** $0.22 per ounce **14.** $0.50 per
ring **15.** Generic: $0.05/tablet; Aleve: $0.08/capsule. The generic
pain reliever is the better buy. **16.** They form equal ratios or rates.
17. $\dfrac{42}{15} = \dfrac{28}{10}$ **18.** $\dfrac{20 \text{ pages}}{12 \text{ min}} = \dfrac{30 \text{ pages}}{18 \text{ min}}$ **19.** $\dfrac{\$15}{1 \text{ hr}} = \dfrac{\$75}{5 \text{ hr}}$ **20.** No
21. $p = 35$ **22.** $x = 12.5$ **23.** $n = 5$ **24.** $y = 6$ **25.** It will take
7.5 min. **26.** There are 80 Republicans. **27.** There are approximately
27 fish in her pond. **28.** $x = 1\frac{1}{2}$ mi, $y = 8$ mi **29.** $x = 21$ cm

Chapters 1–5 Cumulative Review, pp. 359–360

1. Five hundred three thousand, forty-two **2.** Approximately
1400 **3.** 22,600,000 **4.** 22 R 3 **5.** Multiply the divisor and the
whole-number part of the quotient. Then add the remainder to get
the dividend. $16(22) + 3 = 355$ **6.** 6

7. 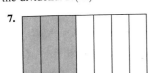   **8.** $\dfrac{7}{5}$ **9.** $\dfrac{39}{14}$ **10.** $\dfrac{9}{25}$

11. Bruce has $4\frac{1}{2}$ in. of sandwich left. **12.** 2 **13.** $\dfrac{35}{9}$ **14.** $\dfrac{9}{13}$

15. Emil needs $13\frac{1}{12}$ ft of wallpaper border. **16.** It sold $61\frac{11}{16}$ acres,
and $20\frac{9}{16}$ acres is left. **17.** There are 59 ninths. **18.** One thousand
four and seven hundred one thousandths. **19.** 28.057 **20.** $\dfrac{109}{25}$

21. 4392.3 **22.** 2.379 **23.** 130.9 cm **24.** $\dfrac{212}{221}$ or 212 : 221

25. $\dfrac{13}{1}$ **26.** 5.525 in./month **27.** 125 people/mi² **28. a.** Yes
b. No **29.** $x = 4.5$ **30.** Jim can drive 100 mi on 4 gal.

Chapter 6

Chapter 6 Preview, p. 362

1. 43% **3.** 50% **5.** $0.7; \dfrac{7}{10}$ **7.** $0.004; \dfrac{1}{250}$ **9.** $33.\overline{3}\%$ or $33\frac{1}{3}\%$
11. 150% **13.** 45% **15.** 0.25% **17.** 200 **19.** 155.6%
21. $27,686 **23.** $2800 in interest is earned in 4 years.

Section 6.1 Practice Exercises, pp. 368–371

3. 48% **5.** 50% **7.** 25% **9.**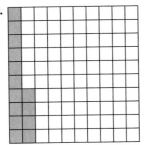

11. 5% **13.** 26% **15.** $\dfrac{13}{100}$ **17.** $\dfrac{21}{25}$ **19.** $\dfrac{1}{4}$ **21.** $\dfrac{7}{20}$ **23.** $\dfrac{23}{20}$ or
$1\frac{3}{20}$ **25.** $\dfrac{7}{4}$ or $1\frac{3}{4}$ **27.** $\dfrac{1}{200}$ **29.** $\dfrac{1}{400}$ **31.** $\dfrac{2}{3}$ **33.** $\dfrac{49}{200}$
35. Replace the % symbol by $\times 0.01$ (or $\div 100$). **37.** 0.72
39. 0.66 **41.** 0.129 **43.** 0.4105 **45.** 2.01 **47.** 1.265 **49.** 0.1625
51. 0.622 **53.** 25% **55.** 100% **57.** 150% **59.** d **61.** b **63.** a

65. d **67.** b **69.** c **71.** $0.138; \dfrac{69}{500}$ **73.** $0.043; \dfrac{43}{1000}$ **75.** $0.2; \dfrac{1}{5}$
77. $0.35; \dfrac{7}{20}$ **79.** $40\% = 0.4$ or $\dfrac{2}{5}$; $42\% = 0.42$ or $\dfrac{21}{50}$; $59\% = 0.59$
or $\dfrac{59}{100}$; $73\% = 0.73$ or $\dfrac{73}{100}$

Section 6.2 Practice Exercises, pp. 377–380

3. $\dfrac{13}{10}$ or $1\frac{3}{10}$ **5.** $\dfrac{1}{200}$ **7.** $0.06\overline{3}$ **9.** 0.003 **11.** 162% **13.** 26%
15. 125% **17.** 77% **19.** Write the whole number as a fraction by
writing the number over 1. Then multiply the numerators and
multiply the denominators. Simplify the fraction to lowest terms.
21. a. 0.17 **b.** 17% **23. a.** $\dfrac{37}{100}$ **b.** 37% **25.** 27% **27.** 19%
29. 175% **31.** 12.4% **33.** 0.6% **35.** 101.4% **37.** 71%
39. 95% **41.** 87.5% or $87\frac{1}{2}\%$ **43.** 81.25% or $81\frac{1}{4}\%$ **45.** $83.\overline{3}\%$
or $83\frac{1}{3}\%$ **47.** $44.\overline{4}\%$ or $44\frac{4}{9}\%$ **49.** 25% **51.** 10% **53.** $66.\overline{6}\%$
or $66\frac{2}{3}\%$ **55.** 175% **57.** 135% **59.** $122.\overline{2}\%$ or $122\frac{2}{9}\%$
61. $166.\overline{6}\%$ or $166\frac{2}{3}\%$ **63.** 42.9% **65.** 7.7% **67.** 45.5%
69. 86.7% **71.** The fraction $\frac{1}{2} = 0.5$ and $\frac{1}{2}\% = 0.5\% = 0.005$.
73. $25\% = 0.25$ and $0.25\% = 0.0025$ **75.** a, c **77.** a, c
79.

	Fraction	Decimal	Percent
a.	$\dfrac{1}{4}$	0.25	25%
b.	$\dfrac{23}{25}$	0.92	92%
c.	$\dfrac{3}{20}$	0.15	15%
d.	$\dfrac{8}{5}$ or $1\frac{3}{5}$	1.6	160%
e.	$\dfrac{1}{100}$	0.01	1%
f.	$\dfrac{1}{200}$	0.005	0.5%

81.

	Fraction	Decimal	Percent
a.	$\dfrac{7}{50}$	0.14	14%
b.	$\dfrac{87}{100}$	0.87	87%
c.	1	1	100%
d.	$\dfrac{1}{3}$	$0.\overline{3}$	$33.\overline{3}\%$ or $33\frac{1}{3}\%$
e.	$\dfrac{1}{500}$	0.002	0.2%
f.	$\dfrac{19}{20}$	0.95	95%

83. $1.4 > 100\%$ **85.** $0.052 < 50\%$

Section 6.3 Practice Exercises, pp. 387–392

3. 55% **5.** 0.06% **7.** 250% **9.** $\dfrac{5}{8}$ **11.** $\dfrac{77}{100}$ **13.** 0.003 **15.** Yes
17. No **19.** Yes **21.** 45 **23.** 48 **25.** Amount: 12; base: 20;
$p = 60$ **27.** Amount: 99; base: 200; $p = 49.5$ **29.** Amount: 50;
base: 40; $p = 125$ **31.** $\dfrac{10}{100} = \dfrac{12}{120}$ **33.** $\dfrac{80}{100} = \dfrac{72}{90}$
35. $\dfrac{104}{100} = \dfrac{21,684}{20,850}$ **37.** 0.2 **39.** 108 employees **41.** 560
43. Pedro pays $20,160 in taxes. **45.** Jesse Ventura received
approximately 762,200 votes. **47.** 36 **49.** 230 lb **51.** 1350
53. Albert makes $1600 per month. **55.** Amiee has a total of
35 e-mails. **57.** 35% **59.** 120% **61.** 87.5% **63.** She answered
72.5% correctly. **65.** 20% **67.** 26.7% **69.** 70 mm of rain fell in
August. **71.** Approximately 1900 freshmen were admitted.
73. Smith had approximately 47.2% completion of three-point
shots. **75. a.** 106 five-person households own a dog. **b.** 23 three-
person households own a dog. **77.** 73 were Chevys. **79.** There
were 180 total vehicles. **81.** $331.20 **83.** $11.60 **85.** $6.30

Section 6.4 Practice Exercises, pp. 397–401

3. Divided both sides of the equation by 26 to get $x = 2.5$.
5. $x = 4$ **7.** $x = 187.5$ **9.** $x = (0.35)(700); x = 245$
11. $(0.55)(900) = x; x = 495$ **13.** $x = (0.33)(600); x = 198$
15. 50% equals one-half of the number. So divide the number by 2.
17. $2 \times 14 = 28$ **19.** $\frac{1}{2} \times 40 = 20$ **21.** There is 3.84 oz of sodium
hypochlorite in household bleach. **23.** Marino completed
approximately 5015 passes. **25.** $18 = 0.4x; x = 45$
27. $0.92x = 41.4; x = 45$ **29.** $3.09 = 1.03x; x = 3$ **31.** There were
1175 subjects tested. **33.** At that time, the population was about
280 million. **35.** 13% **37.** 108% **39.** 0.5% **41.** 17%
43. $x \cdot 480 = 120; x = 25\%$ **45.** $666 = x \cdot 740; x = 90\%$
47. $x \cdot 300 = 375; x = 125\%$ **49.** 70% of the hot dogs were sold.
51. a. There are 80 total employees. **b.** 12.5% missed 3 days of
work. **c.** 75% missed 1 to 5 days of work. **d.** 62.5% missed at
least 4 days of work. **53.** There were 35 million total hospital stays
that year. **55.** Approximately 12.6% of Florida's panthers live in
Everglades National Park. **57.** 416 parents would be expected to
have started saving for their children's education. **59.** 15.6 min of
commercials would be expected. **61.** 6,350,000 people ages 25–34
made over $10/hr. **63.** There are a total of 16,000,000 workers in
the 16–24 age group. **65. a.** 200 beats per minute. **b.** Between
120 and 170 beats per minute. **67. a.** Answers will vary.
b. Answers will vary.

Midchapter Review, p. 401

1. 41% **2.** 75% **3.** $33\frac{1}{3}\%$ **4.** 100% **5.** c **6.** b **7.** Greater
than **8.** Less than **9.** Greater than **10.** Greater than
11. 3000 **12.** 24% **13.** 4.8 **14.** 15% **15.** 70 **16.** 36

Section 6.5 Practice Exercises, pp. 409–413

3. 12 **5.** 28 **7.** 81 **9.** 24 **11.** 115%

	Cost of Merchandise	Sales Tax Rate	Amount of Tax	Total Cost
13.	$ 56.00	6%	$ 3.36	$ 59.36
15.	$212.00	7%	$14.84	$ 226.84
17.	$ 55.00	6%	$ 3.30	$ 58.30

19. The total bill is $71.66. **21.** The tax rate is 7%. **23.** The price
is $44.50.

	Total Sales	Commission Rate	Amount of Commission
25.	$ 20,000.00	5%	$ 1000.00
27.	$125,000.00	8%	$ 10,000.00
29.	$ 5400.00	10%	$ 540.00

31. Zach made $3360 in commission. **33.** Rodney's commission
rate is 15%. **35.** Her sales were $1,400,000.
37. Jeff's commission totaled $5810.00.

	Original Price	Discount Rate	Amount of Discount	Sale Price
39.	$175.00	15%	$ 26.25	$ 148.75
41.	$900.00	30%	$270.00	$630.00
43.	$ 110.00	30%	$ 33.00	$ 77.00
45.	$ 58.40	40%	$ 23.36	$ 35.04

47. a. The discount is $55. **b.** The discounted yearly membership
will cost $495. **49.** The discount rate is 20%. **51.** The set of
dishes is not free. After the first discount, the price was 50% or
one-half of $112, which is $56. Then the second discount is 50% or
one-half of $56, which is $28. **53.** The discount is $47.00, and the
discount rate is 20%.

	Original Price	Markup Rate	Amount of Markup	Retail Price
55.	$ 92.00	5%	$ 4.60	$ 96.60
57.	$110.00	8%	$ 8.80	$118.80
59.	$ 325.00	30%	$ 97.50	$422.50
61.	$ 45.00	20%	$ 9.00	$ 54.00

63. a. The markup is $27.00. **b.** The retail price is $177.00.
c. The total price is $189.39. **65.** The markup rate is 25%.
67. The markup rate is 54%.

Section 6.6 Practice Exercises, pp. 416–418

3. a. The total price will be $68.25. **b.** The total price with the 20%
discount would be $54.60. **c.** Chris will save $13.65. **5.** Katie's
commission is $31.50. **7.** Multiply the decimal by 100% by moving
the decimal point 2 places to the right and attaching the % sign.
9. 5% **11.** 12% **13. a.** Increase **b.** 11 **15. a.** Decrease
b. 10 **17. a.** Decrease **b.** 9 **19. a.** Increase **b.** 12 **21.** c
23. 75% **25.** 75% **27.** a **29.** 5% **31.** 15%

Calculator Connections 6.6, pp. 418–420

33. 97% **35.** 4% **37.** 10% **39.** 37.5%

	Country	Population in 2000 (Millions)	Population in 2005 (Millions)	Change (Millions)	Percent Increase or Decrease
41.	Mexico	100.3	110.8	10.5	10.5% increase
43.	Bulgaria	8.15	8.11	0.04	0.5% decrease

	Item	Value in 1995	Value in 2000	Change	Percent Increase or Decrease
45.	Number of unemployed people in the U.S.	7.4 million	5.6 million	1.8 million	24.3% decrease
47.	U.S. federal debt	$4.9 trillion	$5.7 trillion	$0.8 trillion	16.3% increase

Section 6.7 Practice Exercises, pp. 426–430

	U.S. National Parks	Visitors in 2000 (Thousands)	Visitors in 2002 (Thousands)	Change	Percent Increase or Decrease
3.	Bryce Canyon, UT	1099	886	213	19% decrease
5.	Great Basin, NV	81	86	5	6% increase
7.	Dry Tortugas, FL	84	80	4	5% decrease

9. Interest: $240; Total Amount: $4240   **11.** Interest: $576; Total Amount: $5376   **13.** Interest: $2761.97; Total Amount: $8991.97
15. a. $350   **b.** $2850   **17. a.** $48   **b.** $448   **19.** $12,360
21. $5625

23.

Year	Interest	Total
1	$20.00	$520.00
2	20.80	540.80
3	21.63	562.43

25. There are 6 total compound periods.   **27.** There are 24 total compound periods.   **29.** $6365.40; $365.40   **31. a.** $8960
b. $8998.91   **c.** $38.91   **33.** A = total amount in the account; P = principal; r = annual interest rate; n = number of compounding periods per year; t = time in years

Calculator Connections 6.7, p. 430

35. Total Amount: $6230.91   **37.** Total Amount: $6622.88
39. Total Amount: $10,934.43   **41.** Total Amount: $16,019.47

Chapter 6 Review Exercises, pp. 437–441

1. 75%   **3.** 125%   **5.** b, c   **7.** f   **9.** a   **11.** c   **13.** e   **15.** f
17. d   **19.** $\frac{21}{50}$; 0.42   **21.** 0.0615   **23.** $\frac{183}{2000}$ **25.** 17%   **27.** 80%
29. 12%   **31.** 0.5%   **33.** 87.5%   **35.** 20%

	Fraction	Decimal	Percent
37.	$\frac{9}{20}$	0.45	45%
39.	$\frac{3}{50}$	0.06	6%
41.	$\frac{9}{1000}$	0.009	0.9%

43. Amount: 67.50; base: 150; p = 45   **45.** Amount: 30.24; base: 144; p = 21   **47.** $\frac{6}{8} = \frac{75}{100}$ **49.** $\frac{840}{420} = \frac{200}{100}$ **51.** 6
53. 12.5%   **55.** 39   **57.** Approximately 11 people would be no-shows.   **59.** Victoria spends 40% on rent.
61. $0.18 \cdot 900 = x$; $x = 162$ **63.** $18.90 = x \cdot 63$; $x = 30\%$
65. $30 = 0.25 \cdot x$; $x = 120$ **67.** The original price is $68.00.
69. Elaine can consume 720 fat calories.   **71.** The sales tax is $14.28.
73. a. The tax is $0.54.   **b.** The tax rate is 8%.   **75.** The commission rate was approximately 10.6%.   **77.** Sela will earn $75 that day.   **79.** The discount is $8.69. The sale price is $20.26.
81. The markup rate is 30%.   **83. a.** Increase   **b.** 25%   **85.** 47.5%
87. 700%   **89.** Interest: 12,224; Total Amount: $11,424
91. Jean-Luc will have to pay $2687.50.

93.

Year	Interest	Total
1	$240.00	$6240.00
2	249.60	6489.60
3	259.58	6749.18

95. Total Amount: $995.91   **97.** Total Amount: $16,976.32

Chapter 6 Test, pp. 441–443

1. 22%   **2.**

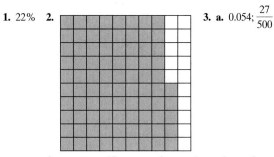

3. a. 0.054; $\frac{27}{500}$
b. 0.009; $\frac{9}{1000}$ **c.** 1.70; $\frac{17}{10}$ **4. a.** $\frac{1}{100}$ **b.** $\frac{1}{4}$ **c.** $\frac{1}{3}$ **d.** $\frac{1}{2}$ **e.** $\frac{2}{3}$
f. $\frac{3}{4}$ **g.** 1   **h.** $\frac{3}{2}$ **5.** 0.006; $\frac{3}{500}$ **6.** 0.099; $\frac{99}{1000}$ **7.** Multiply the fraction by 100%.   **8.** 60%   **9.** 0.4%   **10.** 175%   **11.** 71.4%
12. Multiply the decimal by 100%.   **13.** 32%   **14.** 5.2%   **15.** 130%
16. 0.6%   **17.** 36   **18.** 19.2   **19.** 350   **20.** 200   **21.** 90%
22. 50%   **23. a.** 730 mg   **b.** 98.6%   **24.** 390 m³   **25.** 420 m³
26. a. The amount of sales tax is $2.10.   **b.** The sales tax rate is 7%.   **27.** Charles will earn $610.   **28.** The discount rate of this product is 60%.   **29.** 37.5%   **30. a.** $1200   **b.** $6200
31. $23,397.17   **32.** $31,268.76

Chapters 1–6 Cumulative Review, pp. 443–444

1. Millions place   **2. a.** 3,539,245   **b.** Eight hundred thirty thousand   **c.** Four thousand, seven hundred   **d.** 401,044
3. 3,488,200   **4.** 87   **5.** 3185   **6.** 11   **7. a.** Improper
b. Improper   **c.** Proper   **d.** Proper   **8.** $\frac{4}{3}$ or $1\frac{1}{3}$ **9.** 24
10. $\frac{3}{2}$ or $1\frac{1}{2}$ **11.** $\frac{2}{3}$ **12.** $\frac{15}{32}$ yd²   **13.** 9 km   **14.** $\frac{473}{1000}$ **15.** $24\frac{3}{10}$
16. $\frac{459}{2}$ or $229\frac{1}{2}$ in.²   **17. a.** 18, 36, 54, 72   **b.** 1, 2, 3, 6, 9, 18
c. $2 \cdot 3^2$ **18. a.** $\frac{5}{2}$ **b.** $\frac{5}{6}$ **19.** 0.375   **20.** $1.\overline{3}$ **21.** $0.\overline{7}$ **22.** 0.75
23. 65.3%   **24.** 42.1%   **25.** 0.085   **26.** 8500   **27.** 8.5   **28.** 850,000
29. p = 20   **30.** p = 3.75   **31.** $p = 6\frac{1}{4}$ **32.** p = 27   **33.** It will take $2\frac{1}{2}$ hr.   **34.** The unit price is $0.25 per ounce.   **35.** It will take about 7.2 min.   **36.** The DC-10 flew 514 mph.   **37.** The increase will be about 370%.   **38. a.** 4.6 million   **b.** 0.046 million people per year or 46,000 people per year   **39.** Kevin will have $15,080.   **40.** There is $91,473.02 paid in interest.

Chapter 7

Chapter 7 Preview, p. 446

1. 18 ft   **3.** $3\frac{1}{3}$ min   **5.** 5 qt   **7.** 9 ft   **9.** 5903 g   **11.** 5600 cL
13. 250 dm   **15.** 42.6 ft   **17.** 6.3 qt   **19.** 22.2 lb   **21.** 77°F
23. 5000 ft·lb   **25.** 583,500 ft·lb   **27.** 5500 $\frac{\text{ft·lb}}{\text{sec}}$

Section 7.1 Practice Exercises, pp. 452–456

3. 1 mi **5.** = 3 ft **7.** $\frac{1}{3}$ yd **9.** 6 ft **11.** 72 in. **13.** 10,560 ft

15. 8 yd **17.** $\frac{3}{4}$ ft **19.** $\frac{1}{3}$ mi **21. b** **23. a** **25.** $\frac{3}{8}$ ft **27.** 42 in.

29. $2\frac{1}{4}$ mi **31.** 18 ft **33.** $4\frac{2}{3}$ yd **35.** 563,200 yd **37.** $4\frac{3}{4}$ yd

39. 72 in. **41.** 50,688 in. **43.** $\frac{1}{10}$ mi **45. a.** 76 in. **b.** $6\frac{1}{3}$ ft

47. a. 8 ft **b.** $2\frac{2}{3}$ yd **49.** 7′7″ **51.** 6 ft **53.** 11′2″ **55.** 3 ft 4 in.

57. 4′4″ **59.** 8 ft 10 in. **61.** 28 ft **63.** 3′2″ **65.** 6 ft 1 in.

67. $5\frac{1}{2}$ ft **69.** 18 pieces of border are needed. **71.** The plumber
used 7′2″ of pipe. **73.** 7 ft is left over. **75.** The cable is $0.50 per
foot. **77.** The total length is 46′. **79.** 6 yd^2 **81.** 720 in.^{2}

Section 7.2 Practice Exercises, pp. 461–463

	Object	in.	ft	yd	mi
3.	Length of a hallway	144 in.	12 ft	4 yd	
5.	Height of a tree	216 in.	18 ft	6 yd	
7.	Perimeter of a backyard	1,800 in.	150 ft	50 yd	

9. 2 pt **11.** 16 oz **13.** 365 days **15.** 4 qt **17.** 1 hr **19.** 730 days

21. $1\frac{1}{2}$ hr **23.** 3 min **25.** 3 days **27.** 1 hr **29.** 80.5 min

31. 175.25 min **33.** Gil ran for 5 hr 35 min. **35.** The total time is
1 hr 34 min. **37.** 2 lb **39.** 4000 lb **41.** 64 oz

43. $1\frac{1}{2}$ tons or 1.5 tons **45.** 10 lb 8 oz **47.** 8 lb 2 oz **49.** 6 lb 8 oz

51. The total weight is 312 lb 8 oz. **53.** The truck will have to
make 2 trips. **55.** 2 c **57.** 24 qt **59.** 16 c **61.** $\frac{1}{2}$ gal **63.** 16 fl oz

65. 6 tsp **67.** Yes, 3 c is 24 oz, so the 48-oz jar will suffice.
69. The unit price for the 24-fl-oz jar is about $0.112 per ounce, and
the unit price for the 1-qt jar is about $0.103 per ounce; therefore
the 1-qt jar is the better buy.

	Object	fl oz	c	pt	qt	gal
71.	Bottle of canola oil	32 fl oz	4 c	2 pt	1 qt	0.25 gal
73.	Laundry detergent	128 fl oz	16 c	8 pt	4 qt	1 gal
75.	Bottle of Gatorade	16 fl oz	2 c	1 pt	0.5 qt	0.125 gal
77.	Bottle of spring water	8 fl oz	1 c	0.5 pt	0.25 qt	0.0625 gal
79.	Jug of maple syrup	64 fl oz	8 c	4 pt	2 qt	0.5 gal

Section 7.3 Practice Exercises, pp. 469–473

3. 1.25 mi **5.** 3 lb **7.** 1440 min **9.** 56 oz **11. b, f, g** **13.** 3.2 cm
or 32 mm **15.** 2.1 cm or 21 mm **17. a.** 5 cm **b.** 2 cm **c.** 14 cm
d. 10 cm^2 **19. a.** 4 cm **b.** 4 cm **c.** 16 cm **d.** 16 cm^2 **21. a**

23. d **25. d** **27.** $\frac{1 \text{ km}}{1000 \text{ m}}$ **29.** $\frac{1 \text{ m}}{100 \text{ cm}}$ **31.** $\frac{1 \text{ m}}{10 \text{ dm}}$ **33.** 2.43 km

35. 10.3 m **37.** 5 dam **39.** 4000 m **41.** 431 dam **43.** 0.3328 km
45. 3.45 dam **47.** 250 m **49.** 4.003 dam **51.** 700 cm **53.** 2091 cm
55. 2.538 km **57.** 0.269 km **59.** No, she needs 1.04 m of molding.
61. It will take 13 tiles. **63.** 150 cm or 1.5 m **65.** 3 dm^2
67. 41,000 cm^2

Section 7.4 Practice Exercises, pp. 478–483

	Object	mm	cm	m	km
3.	Distance between Orlando and Miami	670,000,000	67,000,000	670,000	670
5.	Length of a screw	25	2.5	0.025	0.000025
7.	Thickness of a dime	1.35	0.135	0.00135	0.00000135
9.	World record in men's long jump as of the year 2000	2,450	245	2.45	0.00245

11. Centigram **13.** Kilogram **15.** Dekagram **17.** 0.1 g **19.** 0.01 g
21. 0.001 g **23.** 0.539 kg **25.** 2500 g **27.** 33.4 mg **29.** 0.09 hg
31. 0.45 kg

	Object	mg	cg	g	kg
33.	Bag of cat food	1,580,000	158,000	1580	1.58
35.	Can of tuna	170,000	17,000	170	0.17
37.	Box of raisins	425,000	42,500	425	0.425
39.	Dose of acetaminophen	325	32.5	0.325	0.000325

41. < **43.** > **45.** = **47.** < **49.** Cubic centimeter **51.** 3.2 L
53. 700 cL **55.** 0.42 dL **57.** 64 mL **59.** 40 cc

	Object	mL	cL	L	kL
61.	1 Tablespoon	15	1.5	0.015	0.000015
63.	Bottle of vinegar	355	35.5	0.355	0.000355
65.	Bottle of soda pop	2,000	200	2	0.002
67.	Capacity of a cooler	37,700	3,770	37.7	0.0377

69. c **71. b** **73. c, d** **75.** 11.2014 dm **77.** 0.6 g **79.** 0.019 kL
81. Stacy gets 9.45 g per week. **83.** The price is $0.50 per liter.
85. A 6-pack contains 4.26 L. **87.** 5.25 g of the drug would be
given in 1 wk. **89.** 520 mg of sodium per 1-qt bottle **91.** 2 mL
93. 3.3 metric tons **95.** 10,900 kg **97.** 20 μg **99.** 50 μg

Midchapter Review, p. 483

1. 9 qt **2.** 2.2 m **3.** 12 oz **4.** 300 mL **5.** 4 yd **6.** 6030 g
7. 4.5 m **8.** $\frac{3}{4}$ ft **9.** 2640 ft **10.** 3 tons **11.** 4 qt **12.** $\frac{1}{2}$ T
13. 0.021 km **14.** 6.8 cg **15.** 36 cc **16.** 4 lb **17.** 4.322 kg
18. 5000 mm **19.** 2.5 c **20.** 8.5 min

Section 7.5 Practice Exercises, pp. 489–492

3. d, f **5. b, e** **7. c, f** **9. b, g** **11. a.** Numerator
b. Denominator **13. d** **15. c** **17. b** **19.** 5.1 cm **21.** 8.8 yd
23. 122 m **25.** 1.6 mi **27.** 168 g **29.** 8.9 lb **31.** 0.5 oz
33. 0.135 kg ≈ 0.1 kg **35.** 5.7 L **37.** 4 fl oz **39.** 32 fl oz
41. 18 mi is about 28.98 km. Therefore the 30-km race is longer
than 18 mi. **43.** The box of sugar costs $0.100 per ounce, and the
packets cost $0.118 per ounce. The 2-lb box is the better buy.
45. 97 lb is approximately 43.65 kg. **47.** The price is approximately
$6.08 per gallon. **49.** A hockey puck is 1 in. thick. **51.** Mario
weighs about 222 lb. **53.** 45 cc is 1.5 fl oz. **55.** 77°F **57.** 20°C
59. 86°F **61.** 7232°F **63.** It is a hot day. The temperature is 95°F.

65. $F = \frac{9}{5}C + 32 = \frac{9}{5} \cdot 100 + 32 = 9(20) + 32 = 180 + 32 = 212$

67. The Navigator weighs approximately 2.565 metric tons.
69. The average weight of the blue whale is approximately 240,000 lb.

Section 7.6 Practice Exercises, pp. 495–499

	Description	°F	°C
3.	Heat of oven for baking cookies	350°F	176.7°C
5.	Temperature of a typical winter day in Modesto, California	41°F	5°C

7. 22,800 ft·lb   **9.** 1200 ft·lb   **11.** 15,000 ft·lb   **13.** 31,120,000 ft·lb
15. 10,892,000 ft·lb   **17.** 5 Btu   **19.** 41 Btu   **21.** 96,472,000 ft·lb
23. 70,020,000 ft·lb   **25.** $\frac{2}{3}$ hr or 0.67 hr   **27.** $\frac{5}{4}$ hr or 1.25 hr
29. $\frac{12}{5}$ hr or 2.4 hr   **31.** 933 Cal   **33.** 770 Cal   **35.** 304 Cal
37. 295 Cal   **39.** 25 $\frac{\text{ft·lb}}{\text{sec}}$ **41.** 100 $\frac{\text{ft·lb}}{\text{sec}}$ **43.** 400 $\frac{\text{ft·lb}}{\text{sec}}$ **45.** 1 hp
47. 9 hp   **49.** 2.8 hp   **51.** 220,000 $\frac{\text{ft·lb}}{\text{sec}}$ **53.** 302,500 $\frac{\text{ft·lb}}{\text{sec}}$
55. 167,750 $\frac{\text{ft·lb}}{\text{sec}}$ **57. a.** 22,500 Wh   **b.** 22.5 kWh   **c.** $2.48
59. $6.39

Chapter 7 Review Exercises, pp. 507–510

1. 4 ft   **3.** 3520 yd   **5.** $1\frac{1}{3}$ mi   **7.** 72 in.   **9.** 9 ft 3 in.   **11.** 2′10″
13. 21′   **15.** 2 ft 1 in.   **17.** $7\frac{1}{2}$ ft   **19.** 3 days   **21.** 80 oz   **23.** $1\frac{1}{2}$ c
25. $1\frac{3}{4}$ tons   **27.** 0.5 hr   **29.** $\frac{3}{4}$ lb   **31.** 144.5 min   **33.** 375 lb will
go to each location.   **35.** 5.5 cm by 3.5 cm   **37. b**   **39. c**
41. 520 mm   **43.** 2338 m   **45.** 3.4 m   **47.** 0.004 dam   **49.** 1200 dm
51. The difference is 3688 m.   **53.** 610 cg   **55.** 3.212 g   **57.** 50 mg
59. 0.3 L   **61.** 8.3 L   **63.** 22.5 cL   **65.** Perimeter: 6.5 m; area:
2.5 m^2 **67.** The difference is 64.8 kg.   **69.** There is 1.2 cc or 1.2 mL
of fluid left.   **71.** 15.75 cm   **73.** 5 oz   **75.** 1.04 m   **77.** 74.53 mi
79. 45 cc   **81.** The difference in height is 38.2 cm.   **83.** The total
amount of cough syrup is approximately 0.42 L.
85. $C = \frac{5}{9}(F - 32)$ **87.** $F = \frac{9}{5}C + 32$ **89.** 15,400 ft·lb
91. 11,670,000 to 23,340,000 ft·lb   **93.** 16,000 Btu   **95.** She will
burn 200 Cal more by walking briskly.   **97.** 100 $\frac{\text{ft·lb}}{\text{sec}}$ **99.** 0.5 hp

		hp	ft·lb/sec
101.	Dodge Viper	450	247,500
103.	Chevrolet	345	189,750
	Corvette		

Chapter 7 Test, pp. 510–511

1. c, d, g, j   **2.** f, h, i   **3.** a, b, e   **4.** $8\frac{1}{3}$ yd   **5.** 5.5 tons   **6.** 10 mi
7. 10 oz of liquid   **8.** 20 min   **9.** 9′   **10.** 4′2″   **11.** He lost 7 oz.
12. 19 ft 7 in.   **13.** 75.25 min   **14.** 2.4 cm or 24 mm   **15. c**
16. 1.158 km   **17.** 15 mL   **18. a.** Cubic centimeters
b. 235 cc   **c.** 1000 cc   **19.** 41,100 cg   **20.** 7 servings   **21.** 2.1 qt
22. 109 yd   **23.** 2.8 mi   **24.** 2929 m   **25.** 50.8 cm tall and 96.52-cm
wingspan   **26.** 11 lb   **27.** 190.6°C   **28.** 35.6°F   **29.** 1100 Cal
30. 270 ft·lb   **31.** 77,800,000 ft·lb   **32.** 2475 $\frac{\text{ft·lb}}{\text{sec}}$

Chapters 1–7 Cumulative Review, pp. 512–513

1. a. 2000   **b.** 42,100   **2.** 56 cm   **3.** 180 cm^2 **4.** 4   **5. a.** Ford
Motor Company spends the most. That amount is $7400 million or
$7,400,000,000.   **b.** The difference between IBM and Motorola is
$302 million or $302,000,000.   **c.** The total amount spent is $26,917
million or $26,917,000,000.   **6.** $\frac{6}{39}$ **7.** The number 32,542 is not
divisible by 3 because the sum of the digits (16) is not divisible by
3.   **8.** $2 \cdot 2 \cdot 3 \cdot 3 \cdot 3$ **9.** 540 in.^{2} **10.** $\frac{1}{4}$ of the recipe would call
for $\frac{3}{4}$ c of oatmeal. This is less than 1 c so Keesha does have enough.
11. 10   **12.** $\frac{7}{5}$ **13.** $9\frac{1}{2}$ **14.** $18\frac{8}{9}$ **15.** $2\frac{6}{17}$ **16.** $3\frac{5}{6}$

	Fraction	Decimal
17.	$\frac{1}{3}$	$0.\overline{3}$
18.	$\frac{9}{20}$	0.45
19.	$\frac{5}{4}$	1.25
20.	$\frac{7}{2}$	3.5
21.	$\frac{3}{8}$	0.375
22.	$\frac{1}{25}$	0.04

23. a. $\frac{6}{5}$ **b.** $\frac{6}{11}$ **24. a.** $6100   **b.** $610 per year   **c.** $4700
d. $470 per year   **e.** Men   **25.** 90 cars   **26.** 6.7 beds per nurse
27. No, because $\frac{6}{8} \neq \frac{2}{3}$.   **28.** 80%   **29.** $x = \frac{16}{3}$ yd   **30.** 2290 trees
31. 27 people   **32.** 6%   **33.** $15,000 in sales   **34.** $1020 in interest
35. 5.8 kg   **36.** 12.9 lb   **37.** 182.9 cm   **38.** 6 ft   **39.** 7 pt   **40.** 3.3 L

Chapter 8

Chapter 8 Preview, p. 516

1. The complement is 68° and the supplement is 158°.   **3.** False
5. True   **7.** 30 mm   **9.** 0.48 mi^2 **11.** 119 m^2 **13. c**   **15. a**

Section 8.1 Practice Exercises, pp. 522–527

3. A line extends forever in both directions. A line segment
is a portion of a line between two endpoints.
5. Ray   **7.** Point   **9.** Line   **11.** For example:

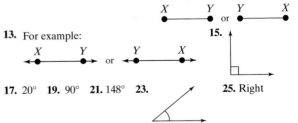

13. For example:

15.

17. 20°   **19.** 90°   **21.** 148°   **23.**   **25.** Right

27. Obtuse   **29.** Acute   **31.** Straight   **33.** 10°   **35.** 63°   **37.** 60.5°
39. 1°   **41.** 100°   **43.** 53°   **45.** 142.6°   **47.** 1°   **49.** No   **51.** Yes

53. A 90° angle   **55.**

57.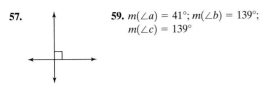

59. $m(\angle a) = 41°$; $m(\angle b) = 139°$; $m(\angle c) = 139°$

61. $m(\angle a) = 26°$; $m(\angle b) = 112°$; $m(\angle c) = 26°$; $m(\angle d) = 42°$
63. The two lines are perpendicular.   **65.** a, c or b, h or e, g or f, d
67. a, e or f, b **69.** $m(\angle a) = 55°$; $m(\angle b) = 125°$;
$m(\angle c) = 55°$; $m(\angle d) = 55°$; $m(\angle e) = 125°$; $m(\angle f) = 55°$;
$m(\angle g) = 125°$ **71.** True   **73.** True   **75.** False   **77.** True
79. True   **81.** 70°   **83.** 90°   **85. a.** 48°   **b.** 48°   **c.** 132°
87. 180°   **89.** 120°

Section 8.2 Practice Exercises, pp. 533–538

3. Yes   **5.** No   **7.** No   **9.** $m(\angle a) = 54°$ **11.** $m(\angle b) = 78°$
13. $m(\angle a) = 60°$, $m(\angle b) = 80°$ **15.** $m(\angle a) = 40°$, $m(\angle b) = 72°$
17. c, f, g   **19.** b, d   **21.** b, c, e, g   **23.** 7   **25.** 49   **27.** 16   **29.** 4
31. 6   **33.** 36   **35.** 81   **37.** 9

Square Root	Estimate	Calculator Approximation (Round to 3 Decimal Places)
$\sqrt{50}$	is between 7 and 8	7.071
39. $\sqrt{10}$	is between __3__ and __4__	3.162
41. $\sqrt{116}$	is between __10__ and __11__	10.770
43. $\sqrt{5}$	is between __2__ and __3__	2.236

45. 20.682   **47.** 1116.244   **49.** 0.7   **51.** 0.748   **53.** $c = 5$ m
55. $b = 12$ yd   **57.** Leg = 10 ft   **59.** Hypotenuse = 40 in.   **61.** The
brace is 20 in. long.   **63.** The height is 9 km.   **65.** The car is 25 mi
from the starting point.   **67.** 24 m   **69.** 30 km   **71.** $c = 5$ in.;
perimeter = 28 in.   **73.** Perimeter = 72 ft

Calculator Connections 8.2, p. 538

75. $b = 21$ ft   **77.** Hypotenuse = 11.180 mi   **79.** Leg = 18.439 in.
81. The diagonal length is 1.41 ft.

Section 8.3 Practice Exercises, pp. 546–552

3. An isosceles triangle has two sides of equal length.   **5.** An
acute triangle has all acute angles.   **7.** An obtuse triangle has an
obtuse angle.   **9.** A quadrilateral is a polygon with four sides.
11. A trapezoid has one pair of opposite sides that are parallel.
13. A rectangle has four right angles.   **15.** True   **17.** False
19. 80 cm   **21.** 260 mm   **23.** 10.7 m   **25.** 10 ft 6 in.   **27.** 5 ft
29. $x = 550$ mm; $y = 3$ dm; perimeter = 26 dm or 2600 mm
31. 280 ft of rain gutters is needed.   **33.** 576 yd²   **35.** 54 m²
37. 656 in.²   **39.** 18.4 ft²   **41.** 12.375 ft²   **43.** 217.54 ft²
45. 280 mm²   **47.** 60 in.²   **49.** The area to be carpeted is 382.5 ft².
The area to be tiled is 13.5 ft².   **51.** The area is 276 m².   **53.** The
area is 1.625 ft².   **55.** The area is increased by 9 times.

Midchapter Review, p. 552

1. Perimeter   **2.** Perimeter   **3.** Area   **4.** Area   **5.** Area = 25 ft²;
perimeter = 20 ft   **6.** Area = 12 m² or 120,000 cm²;
perimeter = 14 m or 1400 cm   **7.** Area = 0.473 km² or 473,000 m²;
perimeter = 3.24 km or 3240 m   **8.** Area = 6 yd²;
perimeter = 12 yd   **9.** Area = 88 in.²; perimeter = 40 in.

Section 8.4 Practice Exercises, pp. 557–561

3. 1260 cm²   **5.** 630 cm²   **7.** Yes. Since a rectangle is a special
type of parallelogram (one that contains four right angles), the area
formula for a parallelogram applies to a rectangle.   **9.** 12 in.
11. 3 m   **13.** 5.6 km   **15.** 4 in.   **17.** 7.5 km   **19.** 8.3 m   **21.** c
23. π is the circumference divided by the diameter. That is, $\pi = \frac{C}{d}$.
25. 12.56 m   **27.** 62.8 cm   **29.** 13.188 cm   **31.** 15.7 km
33. 18.84 cm   **35.** 14.13 in.   **37.** 6.908 cm   **39.** 154 m²
41. 346.5 cm²   **43.** 491 mm²   **45.** 121 ft²   **47.** 2.72 ft²   **49.** 55.04 in.²
51. 18.28 in.²   **53.** 113.04 mm²   **55. a.** \$1051.75   **b.** \$9377.28
57. 2826 ft²   **59. a.** 81.64 in.   **b.** 147 times   **61.** 69,080 in. or 5757 ft
63.

Diameter	Cost	Area	Cost per in.²
8 in.	\$ 6.50	50.24 in.²	\$ 0.129
12 in.	12.40	113.04 in.²	0.110

The 12-in. is the better buy.

Section 8.5 Practice Exercises, pp. 566–570

3. $C = 25.12$ in; $A = 50.24$ in.²   **5.** $C = 18.84$ m; $A = 28.26$ m²
7. b, d   **9.** Area = 1 ft²; volume = 1 ft³   **11.** Area = 1 km²;
volume = 1 km³   **13.** 2.744 cm³   **15.** 48 ft³   **17.** 12.56 mm³
19. 235.5 cm³   **21.** 113.04 yd³   **23.** 452.16 ft³   **25.** 289 in.³
27. 314 ft³   **29.** 10 ft³   **31.** 32 ft³   **33.** 39.8 in.³   **35.** $\frac{11}{36}$ ft³ or
0.306 ft³ or 528 in.³   **37.** 109.3 in.³   **39.** 450 ft³
41. 267,946,666,667 mi³   **43.** 84.78 in.³

Chapter 8 Review Exercises, pp. 576–580

1. d   **3.** c   **5.** $\overrightarrow{SR}$ or $\overrightarrow{SQ}$ **7.** S   **9.** The measure of an acute angle
is between 0° and 90°.   **11.** The measure of a straight angle is 180°.
13. a. 58°   **b.** 148°   **15.** 60°   **17.** 175°   **19.** b   **21.** True   **23.** False
25. True   **27.** $m(\angle x) = 40°$ **29.** An obtuse triangle has one
obtuse angle.   **31.** A right triangle has a right (90°) angle.   **33.** An
isosceles triangle has two sides of equal length and two angles of
equal measure.   **35.** 5   **37.** 10   **39.** 3.742   **41.** 2.236   **43.** The
sum of the squares of the legs of a right triangle equals the square
of the hypotenuse.   **45.** $c = 20$ ft   **47.** They both have sides of
equal length, but a square also has four right angles.   **49.** A square
is a rectangle with four sides of equal length.   **51.** 90 cm   **53.** 56 mi
55. 42 ft   **57.** 20 in.²   **59.** 7056 ft²   **61.** 90 mm   **63.** 22.5 mm
65. $C = 50.24$ m; $A = 200.96$ m²   **67.** $C = 440$ in.; $A = 15,400$ in.²
69. 134.88 in.²   **71.** 5.57 yd²   **73.** 226.08 ft³   **75.** 37.68 km³
77. 113 in.³   **79.** 28,500 in.³

Chapter 8 Test, pp. 580–582

1. Yes   **2.** Yes   **3.** Yes   **4.** No   **5.** Yes   **6.** No   **7.** No
8. Yes   **9.** No   **10.** No   **11.** Obtuse   **12.** Acute   **13.** Acute
14. Obtuse   **15.** Right   **16.** Acute   **17.** Straight   **18.** Acute
19. $m(\angle x) = 125°$, $m(\angle y) = 55°$ **20.** They are each 45°.   **21.** 49°
22. 180°   **23.** $m(\angle A) = 80°$ **24.** 12 ft   **25.** 100 m   **26.** d   **27.** c
28. f   **29.** b   **30.** a   **31.** e   **32.** 96 in.   **33.** 3 rolls are needed.
34. The area is 72 in.².   **35.** The area of the rectangular pizza is
96 in.² The area of the round pizza is approximately 113.04 in.² The
round pizza is larger by about 17 in.²   **36.** The volume is about
151 ft³.   **37.** The volume is 1260 in.³   **38.** The volume is 2002 cm³.

Chapters 1–8 Cumulative Review, pp. 582–583

1. 3835   **2.** 0   **3.** Undefined   **4.** 666,000   **5.** 2,511,000
6. $\frac{1}{3}$ $\frac{3}{5}$ $\frac{5}{6}$ **7.** There is $10\frac{1}{2}$ oz left.   **8.** 18

0 ─────── 1

9. $\frac{1}{18}$ **10.** $\frac{6}{5}$ **11.** 60 **12.** $\frac{67}{60}$ **13.** $\frac{67}{60}$ **14.** $16\frac{1}{2}$ **15.** $\frac{46}{9}$

16. Four glasses cost $47.96. **17.** Geraldo will save the cost of one shirt which is $13.49.

	Fraction	Decimal
18.	$\frac{3}{8}$	0.375
19.	$\frac{2}{9}$	$0.\overline{2}$
20.	$\frac{1}{50}$	0.02

21. $\frac{2}{3}$ **22.** $n = 37.35$

23. 17 pizzas **24. a.** 0.58 **b.** 0.52 **c.** O'Neal **25.** $3436 per hour **26.** 52.8 **27.** 72 **28.** 130% **29.** 20% markup **30.** 16% discount **31.** 10 ft **32.** Yes, $4\frac{1}{2}$ ft is 54 in. **33.** There is a total of $1\frac{1}{4}$ c or 10 fl oz of liquid. **34.** 100 kph $\approx$ 62 mph

35. 165,000 $\frac{\text{ft·lb}}{\text{sec}}$ **36.** 13.3 m **37.** 11 ft **38.** 1256 cm^2 **39.** 3 yd^2 or 27 ft^2 **40.** 452 in.^{3}

Chapter 9

Chapter 9 Preview, p. 586

1. a. New York **b.** California **3. a.** 398 Hispanic students **b.** 94 Asian/Pacific Islander students **5.** $\frac{13}{20}$

Section 9.1 Practice Exercises, pp. 592–599

3. Mt. Everest **5.** Mt. Kosciusko; Australia **7.** 11,200 ft **9.** 2.5 yr **11.** 1.7 yr **13.** Women

15.

	Attends Church	Does Not Attend Church
With children	7	4
Without children	4	3

17.

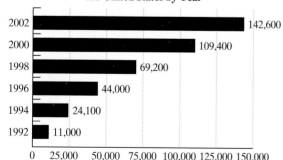

Number of Cellular Phone Subscriptions in the United States by Year

19. a. The health care industry has 219,400 new jobs, which is the greatest number.

b.

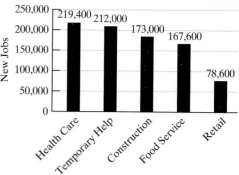

Number of New Jobs for Selected Industries

21. a. Each computer icon represents 10% of adults who access the Internet. **b.** About 60% **c.** International news **23. a.** About 2.25 million **b.** About 2 million **25.** 8.6% **27.** The trend for men over 65 in the labor force shows a significant decrease until 1980 and then levels off. **29.** For example: 10.5% **31.** In the year 1990 the least number of SUVs was sold. There were 98 million sold. **33.** 2 million **35.** 2000–2002

37.

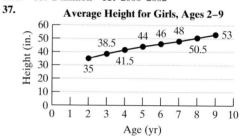

Average Height for Girls, Ages 2–9

39. There is 630 mg of sodium in one container. **41.** The daily value of cholesterol is about 294 mg.

Section 9.2 Practice Exercises, pp. 602–608

3. There are 72 data. **5.** 9–12 **7. a.** The class of 65–67 has the most values. **b.** There are 20 values represented in the table. **c.** Of the professors, 25% retire when they are 68 to 70 years old.

Class Intervals (Age Group)	Tally	Frequency (Number of Professors)
56–58	II	2
59–61	I	1
62–64	I	1
65–67	IIII II	7
68–70	IIII	5
71–73	IIII	4

9. a. The 12.0–13.9 class has the highest frequency. **b.** There are 16 data values represented in the table. **c.** Of the customers, 12.5% purchase 18 to 19.9 gal of gas.

Class Intervals (Amount Purchased)	Tally	Frequency (Number of Customers)
8.0–9.9	IIII	4
10.0–11.9	I	1
12.0–13.9	IIII	5
14.0–15.9	IIII	4
16.0–17.9		0
18.0–19.9	II	2

11. 1. Whenever possible, make the classes the same width. 2. The classes should not overlap. That is, a data value should

belong to one and only one class.   **3.** In general, we usually create a frequency distribution with between 5 and 15 classes.
13. The class widths are not the same.   **15.** There are too few classes.   **17.** The class intervals overlap. For example, it is unclear whether the data value 5 should be placed in the first class or the second class.

19.

Class Interval (Weight, lb)	Frequency (Number of Females)
115–124	6
125–134	2
135–144	5
145–154	3
155–164	3
165–174	0
175–184	1

21.

Class Interval (Amount, $)	Frequency (Number of Customers)
0–49	3
50–99	4
100–149	7
150–199	1
200–249	5

23.

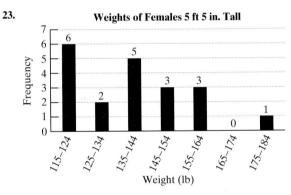

25.

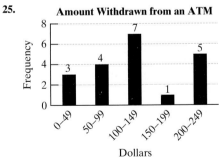

27.

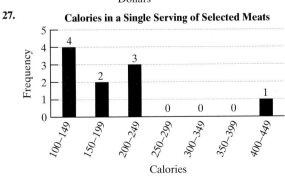

29.

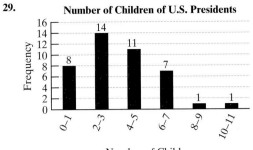

Section 9.3 Practice Exercises, pp. 613–616

3. 20,400 troops   **5.** 300 more troops   **7.** Approximately 11.3%
9. There are 5.5 times more troops from the United Kingdom than from Ukraine.   **11.** There are 20 million viewers represented.
13. There are 1.8 times as many viewers who watch *The Young and the Restless* as *Guiding Light*.   **15.** Of the viewers, 18% watch *General Hospital.*   **17.** There are 960 Latina CDs.   **19.** There are 640 CDs that are either classical or jazz.   **21.** There were 9 Super Bowls played in Louisiana.   **23.** There were 2 Super Bowls played in Georgia.   **25.**   **27.**

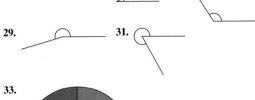

29.   **31.**

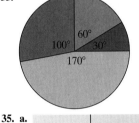

33.

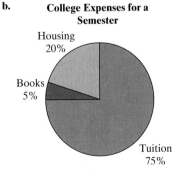

35. a.

	Expenses	Percent	Number of Degrees
Tuition	$9000	75%	270°
Books	600	5%	18°
Housing	2400	20%	72°

b.

College Expenses for a Semester

Housing 20%
Books 5%
Tuition 75%

37.

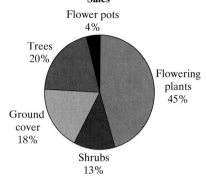

Sunshine Nursery Distribution of Sales

Flower pots 4%
Trees 20%
Flowering plants 45%
Ground cover 18%
Shrubs 13%

Midchapter Review, pp. 616–617

1.

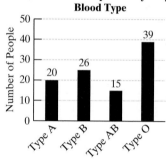

Number of People Surveyed by Blood Type

2.

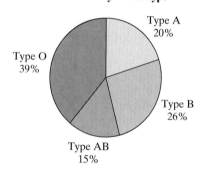

Percent by Blood Type

Type A 20%
Type O 39%
Type B 26%
Type AB 15%

3.

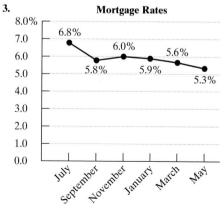

Mortgage Rates

6.8%
5.8%
6.0%
5.9%
5.6%
5.3%

4.

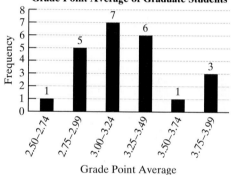

Mortgage Rates

6.8%   5.8%   6.0%   5.9%   5.6%   5.3%

July   September   November   January   March   May

5.

Grade Point Average	Frequency
2.50–2.74	1
2.75–2.99	5
3.00–3.24	7
3.25–3.49	6
3.50–3.74	1
3.75–3.99	3

6.

Grade Point Average of Graduate Students

1   5   7   6   1   3

2.50–2.74   2.75–2.99   3.00–3.24   3.25–3.49   3.50–3.74   3.75–3.99

Grade Point Average

Section 9.4 Practice Exercises, pp. 623–628

3. 6 **5.** 4 **7.** 15.2 **9.** 8.76 in. **11.** 5.8 hr **13. a.** 397 Cal
b. 386 Cal **c.** There is only an 11-Cal difference in the means.
15. a. 86.5% **b.** 81% **c.** The low score of 59% decreased Zach's
average by 5.5%. **17.** 17 **19.** 110.5 **21.** 52.5 **23.** 3.93 deaths
per 1000 **25.** 58 years old **27.** 3.1 million albums **29.** 4
31. No mode **33.** 21, 24 **35.** 39 **37.** 5.2% **39.** These data are
bimodal: $2.49 and $2.51.

41.

Age (yr)	Number of Students	Product
16	2	32
17	9	153
18	6	108
19	3	57
Total:	20	350

The mean age is approximately 17.5 years.
43. The weighted mean is about 26 students initially enrolled in
each class. **45.** 2.38 **47.** 2.77

Section 9.5 Practice Exercises, pp. 632–637

3. Mean: 17.2; median: 16; no mode **5.** Mean: 8.875; median: 8.5;
mode: 8 **7.** Mean: 82%; median: 88.5%; mode: 88%
9. {1, 2, 3, 4, 5, 6, 7, 8, 9, 10} **11.** {2, 3, 4, 5, 6, 7, 8, 9, 10, 11, 12}

13. For example: {2} That is, a 2 comes up when the die is rolled.
15. c, d, g, h   **17.** $\frac{2}{6} = \frac{1}{3}$ **19.** $\frac{3}{6} = \frac{1}{2}$ **21.** $\frac{2}{8} = \frac{1}{4}$ **23.** 0
25. An impossible event is one in which the probability is 0.
27. 1   **29.** $\frac{12}{52} = \frac{3}{13}$ **31.** $\frac{12}{16} = \frac{3}{4}$ **33. a.** $\frac{3}{20}$ **b.** $\frac{9}{40}$ **c.** 30%
35. a. $\frac{21}{60} = \frac{7}{20}$ **b.** 50%   **37. a.** $\frac{7}{29}$ **b.** $\frac{11}{29}$ **c.** 62%   **39.** $1 - \frac{2}{7} = \frac{5}{7}$
41. $100\% - 1.2\% = 98.8\%$ **43. a.** $\frac{312}{530} = \frac{156}{265}$ **b.** $\frac{14}{206} = \frac{7}{103}$

Chapter 9 Review Exercises, pp. 643–645

1. Godiva   **3.** Blue Bell has 2 times more sodium than Edy's Grand.   **5.** 374 acres   **7.** The difference is 4 acres.   **9.** 1 house represents 10,000 detached single-family houses.   **11.** About 6.0 ten-thousands or 60,000 houses.   **13.** 1999   **15.** Decreasing
17.

Class Intervals (Age)	Frequency
18–21	4
22–25	5
26–29	4
30–33	3
34–37	1
38–41	1
42–45	2

19. There are 24 types of subs.   **21.** $\frac{1}{3}$ of the subs do not contain beef.   **23.** Mean: 17.5; median: 18; mode: 20   **25.** The median is 20,562 seats.   **27.** {blue, green, brown, black, gray, white}
29. a, c, d, e, g   **31.** 0

Chapter 9 Test, pp. 646–648

1.

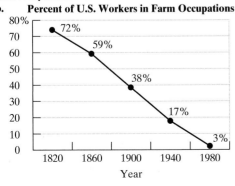

World's Major Producer's of Primary Energy (Quadrillions of Btu)

United States 72, Russia 43, China 35, Saudi Arabia 43, Canada 18, United Kingdom 11, Iran 10

2. a. The year 1820 had the greatest percent of workers employed in farm occupations. This was 72%.
b.

Percent of U.S. Workers in Farm Occupations

72% (1820), 59% (1860), 38% (1900), 17% (1940), 3% (1980)

c. It appears that 10% of U.S. workers were employed in farm occupations in the year 1960.   **3. a.** $1000   **b.** $4500   **c.** February
4.

Number of Days Late	Tally	Number of Employees
0	III	3
1	II	2
2	IIII I	5
3	IIII I	6
4	IIII	5
5	III	3
6	I	1
7	III	3
8	II	2

5.

Number of Minutes Used Monthly	Tally	Frequency
51–100	IIII I	6
101–150	II	2
151–200	III	3
201–250	II	2
251–300	IIII	4
301–350	III	3

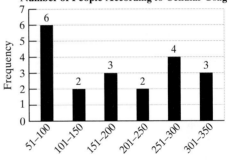

Number of People According to Cellular Usage

51–100: 6, 101–150: 2, 151–200: 3, 201–250: 2, 251–300: 4, 301–350: 3

6. a. 66 people would have carpet.   **b.** 40 people would have tile.
c. 270 people would have something other than linoleum.
7. a. 19,173 ft   **b.** 19,340 ft   **c.** There is no mode.   **8.** Mean: $14.60; median: $15   **9.** The mode is $14.97.   **10. a.** {1, 2, 3, 4, 5, 6, 7, 8}
b. $\frac{1}{8}$ **c.** $\frac{4}{8} = \frac{1}{2}$ **d.** $\frac{2}{8} = \frac{1}{4}$ **11. a.** $\frac{4}{14} = \frac{2}{7}$ **b.** $1 - \frac{2}{7} = \frac{5}{7}$
12. 3.09

Chapters 1–9 Cumulative Review, pp. 648–651

1. a. Millions   **b.** Ten-thousands   **c.** Hundreds   **2.** 12,645
3. $700 \times 1200 = 840,000$ **4.** Divisor: 23; dividend: 651; quotient:
28; remainder: 7   **5.** $\frac{3}{8}$ **6.** $\frac{2}{3}$ **7.** $\frac{5}{2}$ **8.** $\frac{3}{2}$ **9.** $\frac{1}{3}$ **10.** $\frac{37}{100}$ **11.** 2
12. $\frac{1}{6}$ **13.**

Stock	Yesterday's Closing Price ($)	Increase/ Decrease	Today's Closing Price ($)
RylGold	13.28	0.27	13.55
NetSolve	9.51	−0.17	9.34
Metals USA	14.35	0.10	14.45
PAM Transpt	18.09	0.09	18.18
Steel Tch	21.63	−0.37	21.26

14. 6841.2 **15.** 6.8412 **16.** 68,412 **17. a.** 1,900,000 **b.** 95,000 people per year **18.** Quick Cut Lawn Company's rate is 0.55 hr per customer. Speedy Lawn Company's rate is 0.5 hr per customer. Speedy Lawn Company is faster. **19.** 125 min or 2 hr 5 min
20. $x = 5$ m, $y = 22.4$ m **21.** 122 people **22.** 17.02 million
23. 65% **24.** $1404 **25.** 29 in. **26.** 18 qt **27.** 9 yd 1 ft
28. 9.64 km or 9640 m **29.** 2 lb 11 oz **30.** Obtuse **31.** Right
32. Acute **33.** Area: 8 ft² **34.** 66 m³
35.

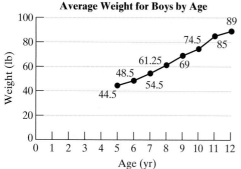

Average Weight for Boys by Age

36. a. 0.5% **b.** 31.9% **c.** 59.0%
37.

Number of Videos	Tally	Number of Customers
0	Ⅲ	5
1	Ⅲ Ⅲ	10
2	Ⅲ Ⅱ	7
3	‖‖	4
4	‖	3
5		0
6			1

38. {yellow, blue, red, green} **39.** $\frac{1}{4}$ **40.** $\frac{3}{4}$

Chapter 10

Chapter 10 Preview, p. 654

1. a. 3,740,000 **b.** −2,446,000 **3. a.** $\frac{4}{3}$ **b.** 4.2 **5.** −8 **7.** 0
9. −2.3 + 8; 5.7 **11.** −34 + 6; −28 **13.** −16.2 **15.** 23
17. −2 − 16; −18 **19.** 19 **21.** 0 **23.** 81 **25.** 2
27. a. 4.502×10^9 **b.** 2.2301×10^{-4}

Section 10.1 Practice Exercises, pp. 659–662

3. −86 m **5.** $3800 **7.** −$500 **9.** −14 lb **11.** 140,000
13. [number line: point at 4]
15. [number line: points at −4 and 2]
17. [number line: points at −3 and 4]
19. [number line: points at −1 and 2]
21. [number line: point at 3]
23. [number line: points at −3 and 1]
25. Rational **27.** Rational **29.** Rational **31.** Irrational
33. Irrational **35.** Rational **37.** > **39.** > **41.** < **43.** <
45. > **47.** > **49.** < **51.** < **53.** 2 **55.** 4.5 **57.** $\frac{5}{2}$

59. 0 **61.** 3.2 **63.** 21 **65. a.** −8 **b.** |−12| **67. a.** 7.8 **b.** |7.8|
69. |−5| **71.** Neither, they are equal. **73.** −5 **75.** 12 **77.** $\frac{1}{6}$
79. $-\frac{2}{11}$ **81.** −8.1 **83.** 1.14 **85.** −6 **87.** −(−2) **89.** |7|
91. |−3| **93.** −|14| **95.** −2 **97.** −5.3 **99.** 15 **101.** 4.7
103. $-\frac{12}{17}$ **105.** $\frac{3}{8}$

Section 10.2 Practice Exercises, pp. 669–672

3. > **5.** = **7.** < **9.** −2 **11.** 2 **13.** −8 **15.** 6 **17.** −7
19. −4 **21.** To add two numbers with the same sign, add their absolute values and apply the common sign. **23.** 15 **25.** −73
27. −124 **29.** 89 **31.** 52 **33.** −22 **35.** −24 **37.** 45 **39.** 0
41. 0 **43.** 9 **45.** −26 **47.** −41 **49.** −150 **51.** −17 **53.** −41
55. 2 **57.** −30 **59.** 10 **61.** −8 **63.** −23 **65.** 24 **67.** 17.2
69. −20.6 **71.** $-\frac{1}{2}$ **73.** $-\frac{13}{12}$ **75.** 77.7 **77.** −1.3 **79.** $-\frac{4}{9}$
81. $-\frac{9}{20}$ **83.** −23 + 49; 26 **85.** 3 + (−10) + 5; −2
87. −2.2 + (−4.2); −6.4 **89.** $-\frac{1}{4} + 8; \frac{31}{4}$ **91.** $-\frac{3}{4} + 6; \frac{21}{4}$
93. 8°F **95.** $333.29 **97.** −$170.50 **99.** For example: −12 + 2
101. For example: −1 + (−1)

Calculator Connections 10.2, p. 672

103. −120 **105.** −68.221 **107.** 711

Section 10.3 Practice Exercises, pp. 677–680

3. −47 **5.** $\frac{1}{36}$ **7.** $-\frac{41}{36}$ **9.** −4 **11.** 2 + (−9); −7 **13.** 4 + 3; 7
15. −3 + (−15); −18 **17.** −11 + 13; 2 **19.** 52 **21.** −33
23. −12 **25.** 8 **27.** 0 **29.** 161 **31.** −34 **33.** −22 **35.** −26
37. −1 **39.** 32 **41.** −15 **43.** *Minus, difference, decreased, less than, subtract from* **45.** 14 − 23; −9 **47.** 5 − 12; −7
49. 105 − 110; −5 **51.** 320 − (−20); 340 **53.** −35 − 24; −59
55. −34 − 21; −55 **57.** −8.3 **59.** −4.2 **61.** 5.5 **63.** 8.3
65. $\frac{5}{6}$ **67.** $\frac{2}{5}$ **69.** $-\frac{3}{2}$ **71.** $-\frac{7}{4}$ **73.** 0 **75.** −1 **77.** 16 **79.** 1
81. 52 **83.** 5.2 **85.** 398°C **87.** The contestant won $400.
89. The difference is 0.18 point. **91.** His new balance is −$375.
93. The range is 3° − (−8°) = 11°. **95.** For example, 4 − 10
97. −11, −15, −19 **99.** −1, $-\frac{4}{3}$, $-\frac{5}{3}$ **101.** Positive **103.** Positive
105. Negative **107.** Negative

Calculator Connections 10.3, p. 680–681

109. −413 **111.** 66.77 **113.** 112.8

Midchapter Review, p. 681

1. −7 **2.** 5 **3.** −14 **4.** −15 **5.** 17 **6.** 18 **7.** 7 **8.** −5
9. −9 **10.** −3 **11.** 6 **12.** 11 **13.** −3 + (−9) **14.** −2 + (−3)
15. 5 + (6) **16.** 8 + (11) **17.** −7 **18.** 5 **19.** −14 **20.** −15
21. 17 **22.** 18 **23.** 7 **24.** −5 **25.** −1.98 **26.** 4.6 **27.** $\frac{11}{8}$
28. $-\frac{17}{18}$

Section 10.4 Practice Exercises, pp. 687–690

3. 19 **5.** −44 **7.** 17 **9.** −15 **11.** −48 **13.** −45 **15.** −72
17. 3.84 **19.** −2.4 **21.** −7.7 **23.** 0 **25.** $\frac{4}{7}$ **27.** $-\frac{1}{7}$

29. $-\dfrac{5}{2}$ or $-2\dfrac{1}{2}$ **31.** $\dfrac{13}{3}$ or $4\dfrac{1}{3}$ **33.** 0 **35.** $-3(-1)$; 3
37. $-5 \cdot 3$; -15 **39.** $1.3(-3)$; -3.9 **41.** 400 **43.** -88 **45.** 0
47. 1 **49.** -1 **51.** -100 **53.** 100 **55.** -27 **57.** -27
59. -0.008 **61.** $-\dfrac{8}{27}$ **63.** -3 **65.** -7 **67.** $\dfrac{5}{3}$ **69.** $\dfrac{2}{3}$

71. Undefined **73.** 0 **75.** 4 **77.** 1.3 **79.** $\dfrac{10}{7}$ **81.** Undefined

83. $-\dfrac{3}{8}$ **85.** -34 **87.** $-100 \div 20$; -5 **89.** $-32 \div (-64)$; $\dfrac{1}{2}$

91. $-52 \div 13$; -4 **93.** 2 **95.** -48 **97.** 3 **99.** 3 **101.** 20

103. -15 **105.** $-\dfrac{2}{5}$ **107.** $\dfrac{7}{6}$ **109.** $(-2)^{50}$ **111.** $(5)^{41}$

113. Negative **115.** Negative **117.** Positive

Calculator Connections 10.4, p. 690

119. $-359{,}723$ **121.** 54

Section 10.5 Practice Exercises, pp. 694–696

3. 25 **5.** -6 **7.** -11 **9. a.** 7 **b.** -7 **11.** 16 **13.** -20
15. -16 **17.** 11 **19.** 2 **21.** -5 **23.** -8 **25.** 8 **27.** -96
29. -2 **31.** $-\dfrac{3}{2}$ **33.** $\dfrac{1}{3}$ **35.** $\dfrac{11}{2}$ **37.** $-2°$ **39.** -2.9 **41.** 10^4
43. 10^3 **45.** 10^{-3} **47.** 10^{-4} **49.** No **51.** Yes **53.** Yes **55.** No
57. $\$7.455 \times 10^{12}$ **59.** 2×10^{-7} mm **61.** 2×10^7 **63.** 8.1×10^6
65. 3×10^{-3} **67.** 2.5×10^{-2} **69.** 1.42×10^5 **71.** 4.91×10^{-5}
73. 8.2×10^{-2} **75.** 4.92×10^3 **77.** 6000 **79.** 0.08 **81.** 0.44
83. 37,000 **85.** 326 **87.** 0.0129 **89.** 0.000002003 **91.** 900,100,000
93. 3 **95.** -1

Chapter 10 Review Exercises, pp. 701–703

1. $-76{,}704$ **3.** 15° **5. & 7.**

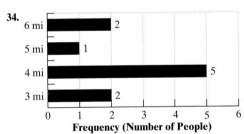

9. 4, 4 **11.** $-3.5, 3.5$ **13. a.** 9 **b.** -9 **15.** $>$ **17.** $>$
19. $<$ **21.** 4 **23.** -5 **25.** To add two numbers with the same sign, add their absolute values and apply the common sign. **27.** 13
29. -70 **31.** -10.66 **33.** $-\dfrac{9}{10}$ **35.** $23 + (-35)$; -12
37. $-5 + (-13) + 20$; 2 **39.** $-12 + 3$; -9 **41.** 3 **43.** 1. Leave the first number (the minuend) unchanged. 2. Change the subtraction sign to an addition sign. 3. Add the opposite of the second number (the subtrahend). **45.** -25 **47.** -419 **49.** -0.7
51. $\dfrac{20}{21}$ **53.** For example: 23 minus negative 6 **55.** For example: Subtract -7 from -25. **57.** Sam's balance is now \$92. **59.** -18
61. 15 **63.** -70 **65.** $\dfrac{7}{4}$ **67.** Undefined **69.** -32 **71.** -36
73. $-\dfrac{27}{64}$ **75.** -1 **77.** Positive **79.** $-4 \cdot 19$; -76
81. $-136 \div (-8)$; 17 **83.** -2 **85.** 4 **87.** -1 **89.** $-1°$
91. 1.0302×10^7 **93.** 9.042×10^{-3} **95.** 8,700,000,000
97. 0.0000602 **99.** In the number 9.11, move the decimal point 31 places to the left (inserting 30 zeros).

Chapter 10 Test, pp. 703–704

1. a. $-\$220$ **b.** 26 **2.** $-3, 0, 4, -1$ **3.** $-3, -\dfrac{3}{5}, 0, 4, -1, \dfrac{4}{7}$

4. $\sqrt{7}, -\pi$ **5.** $<$ **6.** $>$ **7.** $>$ **8.** $>$ **9.** $<$ **10.** $<$
11. -5 **12.** -28 **13.** 9 **14.** -41 **15.** 6 **16.** -23 **17.** -72
18. 88 **19.** 2 **20.** -18 **21.** Undefined **22.** 0 **23. a.** Positive
b. Negative **24. a.** 64 **b.** -64 **c.** -64 **d.** -64 **25.** $-3(-7)$; 21

26. $-13 + 8$; -5 **27.** $18 - (-4)$; 22 **28.** $6 \div \left(-\dfrac{2}{3}\right)$; -9

29. $-8.1 + 5$; -3.1 **30.** $-3 + 15 + (-6) + (-1)$; 5 **31.** 3

32. -60 **33.** -19 **34.** -55 **35.** $-\dfrac{22}{15}$ **36.** $\dfrac{2}{13}$ **37.** 1°

38. 1×10^{-9} m **39.** 5.8078×10^8 **40. a.** 30,501,000,000
b. 0.0004009

Chapters 1–10 Cumulative Review, pp. 704–706

1. 3613 **2.** 2569 **3.** 177 **4.** 18,960 **5.** $2 \cdot 2 \cdot 2 \cdot 2 \cdot 3 \cdot 3 \cdot 5$ or $2^4 \cdot 3^2 \cdot 5$ **6.** $\dfrac{5}{8}$ **7.** Harold got $\dfrac{11}{14}$ of the quiz correct. **8.** Amy will have 8 packages. **9.** 80 **10.** $\dfrac{5}{16}$ **11.** $6\dfrac{7}{15}$ **12.** $3\dfrac{4}{7}$

13. a. 34.230 **b.** 9.0 **14.** \$2.0999 **15.** 490.92 **16.** 115 **17.** $\dfrac{2}{5}$

18. The aircraft used 2491 gal/hr. **19.** 21 mi **20.** $x = 2.7$ cm; $y = 7$ cm **21.** 192 **22.** 112% **23.** 250 **24.** The sale price is $68.80. **25.** 28 in. **26.** 5 gal **27.** 0.06 L **28.** $1\dfrac{7}{8}$ lb **29.** The distance is 10 mi. **30.** 16.5 yd^2 **31.** $5\dfrac{1}{16}$ m^2 **32.** $A = 7.065$ km^2; $C = 9.42$ km

33.

Number of Miles	Tally	Frequency (Number of Walkers)
3	II	2
4	IIII I	5
5	I	1
6	II	2

34.

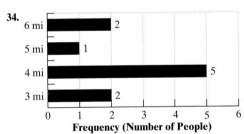

Frequency (Number of People)

35. 4.3 mi **36.** $216 **37.** 55 **38.** -12 **39.** -20 **40.** $\dfrac{1}{6}$

Chapter 11

Chapter 11 Preview, p. 708

1. $\$17.95x$ **3.** -25 **5.** $6r + 11s$ **7.** -5 is not a solution
9. $q = -10$ **11.** $w = -\dfrac{5}{2}$ **13.** $c = 36$ **15.** $b = -8$

17. $n + 10 = 6n$; the number is 2 **19.** Garnett made $25.2 million and O'Neal made $24 million.
21., 23.

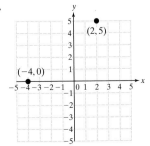

Section 11.1 Practice Exercises, pp. 714–716

3. $8p$ **5.** $l + \dfrac{1}{2}$ **7.** $\dfrac{4}{n}$ **9. a.** -12 **b.** 30 **11. a.** 5 **b.** -15

13. a. -49 **b.** -49 **15. a.** -16 **b.** -64 **17.** 3 **19.** 5 **21.** -4

23. 24 **25.** -4 **27.** $\dfrac{1}{2}$ **29.** 6 **31.** 5 **33.** $P = 16.6$ in.

35. $A = \dfrac{77}{2}\,\text{m}^2$ **37.** $V = 1256\,\text{cm}^3$ **39.** $w + 5$ **41.** $b + (-\frac{1}{3})$ or

$b - \frac{1}{3}$ **43.** $2r$ **45.** $-st$ **47.** $-9 + a$ **49.** $-p + 7$

51. $(-2 \cdot 6)b; \ -12b$ **53.** $(3 + 8) + t; \ 11 + t$

55. $(-4.2 + 2.5) + r; \ -1.7 + r$ **57.** $(3 \cdot 6)x; \ 18x$

59. $\left(-\dfrac{4}{7} \cdot -\dfrac{7}{4}\right)d; \ d$ **61.** $(-9 + (-12)) + h; \ -21 + h$ **63.** $4x + 32$

65. $-2p - 8$ **67.** $4a + 16b - 4c$ **69.** $\dfrac{8}{3} + 4g$ **71.** $-3 + n$

73. $a + 8$ **75.** $-3x - 9 + 5y$ **77.** $5q + 2s + 3t$ **79.** $12x$

81. $12 + 6x$ **83.** $-4 - p$ **85.** $-32 + 8p$ **87.** $5 + \dfrac{5}{9}y$ **89.** $5y$

Section 11.2 Practice Exercises, pp. 720–722

3. $6p + 18$ **5.** $-24q$ **7.** $9 - h$ **9.** $2a$: variable term; $5b^2$:
variable term; 6: constant term **11.** 8: constant term; $9a$: variable term
13. $4pq$: variable term; $-9p$: variable term **15.** $10h^2$: variable term;
-15: constant term; $-4h$: variable term **17.** $6, -4$ **19.** $-14, 12$
21. $1, -1$ **23.** $5, -8, -3$ **25.** *Like* terms **27.** Unlike terms
29. *Like* terms **31.** Unlike terms **33.** Unlike terms **35.** *Like*
terms **37.** $14rs$ **39.** $8h$ **41.** $3x^2 + 9$ **43.** $6x - 15y$ **45.** $-3k$
47. $4uv + 6u$ **49.** $-16m - 9$ **51.** $-9a + 5b + 20$

53. $-6p^2 - 2p + 7$ **55.** $2y - \dfrac{5}{6}$ **57.** $\dfrac{5}{8}a + 9$ **59.** $-3x^2 - 1.9x$

61. $-0.9a + 7.6$ **63.** $5t - 28$ **65.** $-6x - 16$ **67.** $6y - 14$
69. $7q$ **71.** $-2n - 4$ **73.** $-6a - b$ **75.** $4x + 23$ **77.** $2z - 11$
79. $-w - 4y + 9$ **81.** $8a - 9b$ **83.** $-5m + 6n - 10$ **85.** $12z + 7$
87. $-7x - 7$ **89.** $-21y + 28$ **91.** $-2q + 20$ **93.** $107a - 213b$

Section 11.3 Practice Exercises, pp. 727–729

3. $-13a + 16b$ **5.** $8h - 2k + 13$ **7.** $-3z + 4$ **9.** -1 is a solution.
11. 26 is a solution. **13.** 12 is not a solution.

15. $-\dfrac{1}{2}$ is a solution. **17.** 0 is a solution. **19.** 4 is not a solution.

21. 0 **23.** 7 **25.** -3.2 **27.** $\dfrac{3}{8}$ **29.** $g = 37$ **31.** $k = 16$

33. $n = -15$ **35.** $p = \dfrac{7}{6}$ **37.** $k = 3.1$ **39.** 52 **41.** 0 **43.** 100

45. $x = -28$ **47.** $b = 3$ **49.** $t = -46$ **51.** $m = -13.6$

53. $a = -\dfrac{13}{10}$ **55.** $p = -1$ **57.** $t = -6$ **59.** $y = \dfrac{13}{12}$

61. $m = -1.4$ **63.** $w = 12$ **65.** $x = -5$ **67.** $a = 13$

69. $p = -0.79$ **71.** $t = 1\dfrac{5}{8}$ **73.** $z = 49$ **75.** $h = -1$

77. $t = 3$ **79.** $r = 10$

Section 11.4 Practice Exercises, pp. 734–736

3. $p = 45$ **5.** $h = 21$ **7.** $p = -13$ **9.** $n = -\dfrac{7}{6}$ **11.** $\dfrac{1}{3}$ **13.** $-\dfrac{7}{4}$

15. -7 **17.** 5.1 **19.** $b = -3$ **21.** $k = -7$ **23.** $t = 13$

25. $m = 21$ **27.** $b = -21$ **29.** $t = 4$ **31.** $u = 30$ **33.** $w = -\dfrac{1}{3}$

35. $x = 4.1$ **37.** $k = -\dfrac{2}{5}$ **39.** $m = 0$ **41.** $x = \dfrac{4}{15}$ **43.** $k = 20$

45. $p = -31$ **47.** $p = \dfrac{5}{6}$ **49.** $a = 0$ **51.** If the operation between

a number and a variable is subtraction, use the addition property to
isolate the variable. **53.** If the operation between a number and a
variable is multiplication, use the division property to isolate the
variable. **55.** $x = -16$ **57.** $y = -3$

59. $q = -8$ **61.** $h = -48$ **63.** $t = \dfrac{1}{3}$ **65.** $a = \dfrac{4}{3}$ **67.** $r = 30$

69. $y = -15$ **71.** $p = \dfrac{5}{12}$ **73.** $x = -\dfrac{21}{10}$ **75.** $t = 27.9$

77. $u = -1.8$ **79.** $x = -5$ **81.** $p = 3$ **83.** $a = -1$

Section 11.5 Practice Exercises, pp. 741–743

3. $b = -12$ **5.** $w = -\dfrac{5}{8}$ **7.** $h = 0$ **9.** $m = 4$ **11.** $c = -6$

13. $z = 5$ **15.** $x = \dfrac{4}{3}$ **17.** $d = -2.4$ **19.** $h = -1.12$ **21.** $b = 9$

23. $w = -12$ **25.** $x = \dfrac{1}{4}$ **27.** $b = -3$ **29.** $t = \dfrac{9}{8}$ **31.** $d = 1$

33. $p = \dfrac{7}{3}$ **35.** $z = 2$ **37.** $p = 6$ **39.** $a = -3$ **41.** $w = -4$

43. $y = \dfrac{4}{5}$ **45.** $n = -12$ **47.** $q = 15$ **49.** $m = 3$ **51.** $k = 6$

53. $z = -\dfrac{1}{2}$ **55.** $w = \dfrac{15}{11}$ **57.** $u = 5$

Midchapter Review, pp. 743–744

1. a. $7x - 15$ **b.** $-3x - 9$ **c.** $x = \dfrac{3}{5}$ **2. a.** $6y + 2$

b. $-6y + 6$ **c.** $y = \dfrac{1}{3}$ **3.** Expression; $8x - 12$ **4.** Equation; $t = 3$

5. Equation; $h = 1$ **6.** Expression; $10k$ **7.** Equation; $w = 0$

8. Expression; 2 **9.** Expression; $m + \dfrac{1}{8}$ **10.** Equation; $m = -\dfrac{1}{8}$

11. Expression; $-3y - 1$ **12.** Equation; $y = -\dfrac{5}{3}$

13. Equation; $t = 3$ **14.** Expression; $t + 5$ **15.** Equation; $x = -\dfrac{1}{6}$

16. Expression; $6x + 1$ **17.** Expression; $3p + 3$
18. Equation; $p = -1$

Section 11.6 Practice Exercises, pp. 750–753

3. $b = -45$ **5.** $r = \dfrac{14}{5}$ **7.** $p = -0.75$ **9. a.** $\dfrac{x}{3} = -8$ **b.** The

number is -24. **11. a.** $-30 - x = 42$ **b.** The number is -72.

13. a. $30 + x = 13$ **b.** The number is -17. **15. a.** $\dfrac{x}{4} - 5 = -12$

b. The number is -28. **17. a.** $\dfrac{1}{2} + x = 4$ **b.** The number is $\dfrac{7}{2}$ or

$3\dfrac{1}{2}$. **19. a.** $-12x = x + 26$ **b.** The number is -2.

21. a. $10(x + 5.1) = 56$ **b.** The number is 0.5.
23. a. $3x = 2x - 10$ **b.** The number is -10. **25.** The pieces are

$1\dfrac{1}{3}$ ft and $2\dfrac{2}{3}$ ft long. **27.** Metallica had 10 hits while Boyz II Men

had 16 hits. **29.** The soccer field is 100 yd by 130 yd. **31.** Jim
used 50 min over the 500 min. **33.** Tampa Bay had 48 points and
Oakland had 21 points. **35.** Charlene's rent is $650 a month with a
security deposit of $300. **37.** Stefan worked 6 hr of overtime.
39. Raul took 12 hr in fall and signed up for 16 hr in spring.
41. Local calls are $0.20 per minute, and long-distance calls are
$0.25 per minute. **43.** London is connected to 61 countries on the
Internet.

Section 11.7 Practice Exercises, pp. 757–762

3. $9 - x = 2x$; The number is 3.   **5.** $\dfrac{a}{-6} = 13$; the number is -78

7., 9., 11., 13.

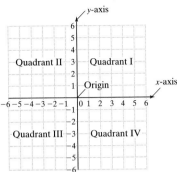

15., 17.

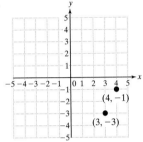

19. First move to the left 1.8 units from the origin. Then go up 3.1 units. Place a dot at the final location. The point is in Quadrant II.

21., 23., 25.

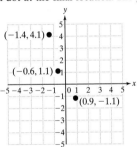

27., 29., 31

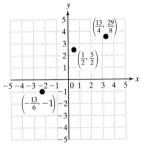

33., 35., 37.

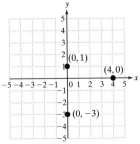

39. Quadrant IV   **41.** Quadrant III   **43.** x-axis   **45.** y-axis
47. Quadrant II   **49.** Quadrant I   **51.** $(0, 3)$ **53.** $(2, 3)$

55. $(-5, -2)$ **57.** $(4, -2)$ **59.** $(1, -7), (2, -3), (3, 1), (4, 6), (5, 12),$
$(6, 17), (7, 18), (8, 18), (9, 14), (10, 6), (11, -1), (12, -7)$

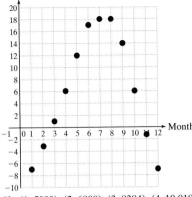

61. $(1, 5000), (2, 6800), (3, 8384), (4, 10{,}010), (5, 11{,}509), (6, 12{,}782)$

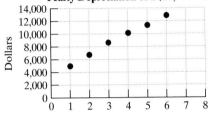

63. $(1997, 1736), (1998, 1789), (1999, 1896), (2000, 1104), (2001, 2268),$
$(2002, 2393)$

65. $(1, 26.8), (2, 19.6), (3, 14.4), (4, 2.8), (5, 0), (6, 0), (7, 0), (8, 0),$
$(9, 0), (10, 1.1), (11, 11.7), (12, 21.8)$

Chapter 11 Review Exercises, pp. 769–771

1. a. $a + 8$ **b.** 43 years old   **3.** -18 **5. a.** $-5 + t$ **b.** $3h$
7. $6b + 15$ **9.** $3a^2$ is a variable term with coefficient 3; $-5a$ is a
variable term with coefficient -5; 12 is a constant term with
coefficient 12   **11.** Unlike terms   **13.** *Like* terms

15. $6x + 4y + 10$ **17.** $-u - 11v$ **19.** -3 is a solution. **21.** If a constant is being added to the variable term, use the subtraction property. If a constant is be subtracted from a variable term, use the addition property. **23.** $k = -12$ **25.** $q = 24$ **27.** $n = 5$

29. $b = -\dfrac{11}{10}$ **31.** $d = -7$ **33.** $t = -26$ **35.** $y = 20$

37. $m = -2$ **39.** $w = \dfrac{9}{7}$ **41.** $p = 6$ **43.** $x = -1$

45. $m = 8$ **47.** $m = 10$ **49.** $x = -28$ **51.** $w = \dfrac{4}{3}$

53. $a = -3$ **55.** $-6x = x + 2; \ x = -\dfrac{2}{7}$

57. $\dfrac{1}{3} - x = 2; \ x = -\dfrac{5}{3}$ **59.** Tom Hanks starred in 35 films, and Tom Cruise starred in 30 films. **61.** The width is 40 in. and the length is 72 in. **63.** $(2, 0)$ **65.** $(-4, -2)$ **67.** $(-1, 2)$

69. $\left(-3, -3\dfrac{1}{3}\right)$ **71., 73., 75.**

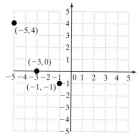

Chapter 11 Test, pp. 772–773

1. $19.95m$ **2.** -15 **3.** $A = 34.25 \ \text{ft}^2$ **4.** Associative property of multiplication **5.** Commutative property of addition **6.** Associative property of addition **7.** Distributive property of multiplication over addition **8.** Commutative property of multiplication **9.** $4a + 24$ **10.** $-13b + 8$ **11.** $16y + 3$ **12.** $7 - 7w$ **13.** An expression is a collection of terms. An equation has an equal sign that indicates that two expressions are equal. **14. a.** Expression **b.** Equation **c.** Expression **d.** Equation **e.** Expression **f.** Expression **15.** $x = -2$

16. $x = 18$ **17.** $x = -72$ **18.** $x = -\dfrac{1}{2}$ **19.** $p = -1$ **20.** $m = 0.2$

21. $p = -\dfrac{13}{16}$ **22.** $n = \dfrac{1}{2}$ **23.** $h = 3$ **24.** $x = -84$ **25.** $q = 0$

26. $k = 2$ **27.** The number is -5. **28.** The U.S. has 16 million antennas, and the United Kingdom has 5.2 million antennas. **29.** Sela used 620 kWh.
30.–35.

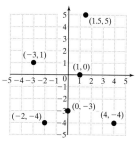

36. Quadrant IV **37.** Quadrant I **38.** Quadrant III **39.** Quadrant II

40. $(30, 33), (40, 35), (50, 40), (60, 37), (70, 30)$

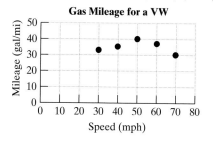

Chapters 1–11 Cumulative Review, pp. 773–775

1. a. Hundreds **b.** Ten-thousands **c.** Hundred-thousands **2.** 46,000 **3.** 1,290,000 **4.** 25,400 **5.** Dividend is 39,190; divisor is 46; quotient is 851; remainder is 44. **6. a.** Prime **b.** Composite **c.** Composite **7.** $\dfrac{23}{8}$ **8.** $\dfrac{6}{5}$ **9.** $\dfrac{28}{125}$ **10.** $\dfrac{13}{100}$

11. $\dfrac{79}{150}$ **12.** $7 \ \text{ft}^2$ **13.** $\dfrac{31}{8}$ **14.** $5\dfrac{3}{5}$ **15.** $8\dfrac{2}{3}$ **16.** 13.95 **17.** 0.5 **18.** 31.221 **19.** 43.752 **20.** 3.56 **21.** Sarah makes $20 per room.

22. $p = 8.1$ **23.** $n = \dfrac{4}{5}$ **24.** $m = 56$ **25.** Kitty Treats costs $0.92 per ounce. Cat Goodies costs $0.90 per ounce. Cat Goodies is the better buy.

	Decimal	Fraction	Percent
26.	0.15	$\dfrac{3}{20}$	15%
27.	0.125	$\dfrac{1}{8}$	12.5%
28.	1.1	$\dfrac{11}{10}$	110%
29.	$0.\overline{2}$	$\dfrac{2}{9}$	$22.\overline{2}\%$
30.	0.002	$\dfrac{1}{500}$	0.2

31. 21 cups can be filled. **32.** 101.75 min **33.** 0.68 L **34.** 3200 m **35.** 4500 cg **36.** 12.56 in.^{2} **37.** The area is 67.5 in.^{2}. **38.** 995 in.^{3} **39.** $C = 18.84$ yd **40.** 24 mm **41.** 10 **42.** 9.5 **43.** 12
44.

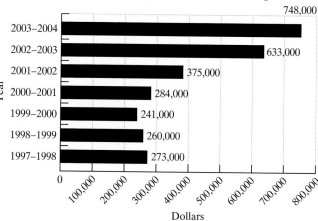

45. a. Approximately 166 students   **b.** 130 students   **46.** 3
47. -12 **48.** -25 **49.** -9 **50. a.** 3.001×10^6 **b.** 0.00004
51. $-5x - 13$ **52.** $-2y - 18$ **53.** $p = -4$ **54.** $t = -8$
55.

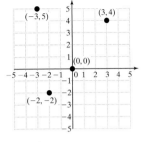

Applications Index

CONSTRUCTION AND DESIGN

CONSUMER APPLICATIONS

ENTERTAINMENT AND LEISURE ACTIVITIES

ENVIRONMENT/EARTH SCIENCE/GEOGRAPHY

GARDENING AND LANDSCAPING

INVESTMENT

POLITICS AND GOVERNMENT

Index